SERVICES MARKETING
TEXT AND READINGS

Edited by
David Carson and Audrey Gilmore

MERCURY
PUBLICATIONS

Mercury Publications Limited, Dublin

in association with

The Marketing Institute, Dublin

Mercury Publications Limited
37 Main Street
Donnybrook
Dublin 4

British Library Cataloguing in Publication Data

A catalogue record for this book is available from the British Library.

ISBN 0-9523597-0-7

Typesetting by Verbatim Typesetting & Design Ltd., Dublin
Printed in Ireland by Colour Books Ltd.

CONTENTS

Part III

Part IV

Part V

Preface

PREFACE

There has been a significant growth in the services sector of most developed economies world-wide. This growth has resulted in an ever-expanding interest in services marketing. The evolving mass of research and publications in this area has been influenced by the changing nature of economies and the needs of management to be more efficient and effective.

This management need is manifested most strikingly in the services sector of small and developing countries and in regional areas of larger developed countries. Countries such as Ireland, Bahrain and Finland and other Scandinavian countries are typical examples of smaller economies, and areas such as the northern regions of Scotland, Wales and Spain reflect typical regional economy dimensions. Whilst these areas all strive to expand their economies through an industrial and manufacturing base, it is increasingly being recognised that the services sector can offer significant growth at substantially less capital investment. Small countries recognise the benefits of creating financial centres for international trade and many have created these with startling success, for example, Bahrain and Ireland. Of course, such success does not come automatically. Whilst the key stimulus for growth in financial industries is likely to be political and government support, much will also depend on the ability of the firms in this industry to market effectively.

A similar example of the growth in services in such economies is presented by the tourism sector, a service industry that has marketing as its primary focus. Such services marketing is also inherently international, another important dimension of services marketing. The issue is expanded in the context of isolated or island economies where travel is an essential ingredient. Travel, while closely linked with tourism, covers a much wider domain of transportation of goods as well as travel for business purposes. All these segments require substantial services marketing.

Accordingly, this book of text and readings recognises that first-rate services marketing is crucial to the growth of large developed economies *and* to the fortunes of smaller countries and more peripherally located economies. It is established that large developed economies have significant services sectors to support the sophisticated nature of these economies. However, it is less often acknowledged that small economies/countries, and remoter regional economies, have fast-growing services sectors and that these sectors require appropriate marketing theories drawn from the research literature. The literature on services marketing is entirely appropriate, we argue, for all economic frameworks.

The distinguishing competitive position of this book is that it positions the literature in a chronology. It traces the literature from its early origins and tentative formulations through its establishing tracks and trends. In doing so it expands and covers the key topical areas within the domain and extends these topic considerations into a speculation on the future areas of development. In taking this approach this book can be deemed to be the first collection of seminal articles organised in this way. It offers the reader and student of services marketing the unique opportunity to observe the historical development of the services domain, particularly in terms of the expansion of its scope of influence and its increasing complexity and sophistication.

The early services marketing literature focused on defining and refining the specific characteristics of services, and on the different classifications of the service product which have an impact on the nature of marketing.

However, by the end of the 1970s the focus was more widely upon the managerial issues for services managers. An international study, commissioned by the Marketing Science Institute of Cambridge, Massachusetts and authored by Langeard et al. (1981), represented the most comprehensive analysis and description of services marketing at this time. The study focused on marketing issues that were considered to be central to the management of consumer service business. The findings, based on evidence from several large services companies and surveys of both consumers and managers, linked three separate themes: consumer participation in service production and delivery; management's ability to understand customers' needs; and the relationship between operations, marketing and personnel functions in a service organisation. The report's main recommendations largely reflected the principal areas of research interest by scholars in the field at that time. Specifically, it was recommended that future research should focus on the following: new ways to measure and evaluate consumer's propensity to participate as a segmentation variable; transnational studies to determine the impact of customer traits on consumers' propensity to participate in service delivery; and an exploration of the customer's role as both a producer and a consumer of services.

In addition it was recommended that research should also be carried out on:

▷ how best to control and motivate customer-contact personnel;

▷ the role of marketing specialists in managing change, especially product innovation within a service organisation;

▷ how best to conceptualise the different elements of the service marketing mix;

▷ how to assign management responsibility for each element and how to diffuse marketing skills throughout a service organisation.

Whilst the services marketing literature has answered many of the issues raised as important research areas in the early 1980s, it has evolved and progressed into new and more integrated services marketing approaches and concepts. It was at this time that the most meaningful and comprehensive empirical confirmation of the main concepts and frameworks occurred. Indeed, in many instances empirical studies helped both to reinforce concepts and to create new concepts and theories towards more effective and efficient services marketing.

Recently some authors have carried out reviews of the scope and focus of the services marketing literature since its origins. Notable examples of such reviews are Lapierre and Filiatrault (1994), who identify 'three waves of research' in the domain of service quality. They describe the conceptual works of Grönroos (1984) and Parasuraman et al. (1985), who kindled the concern for service

TABLE 1:   SUMMARY OF RESEARCH ON SERVICES AND PROFESSIONAL SERVICES QUALITY

PROCESS AND RESULTS DIMENSIONS		SERVICE DIMENSIONS	
Lovelock and Young (1979)	**Si	Sarkar and Saleh (1974)	*PSi
Czepiel (1980)	**Si	Albert and Pearson (1983)	**PSi
Booms and Nyquist (1981)	**S/PSi	Hull and Burns (1984)	**PSii
Gummesson (1981b)	**PSii		
Quelch and Ash (1981)	*PSi	Parasuraman et al. (1985, 1986,	
Zeithaml (1981)	**S/PSi	1988, 1991, 1993, 1994)	*Si
Lewis and Booms (1983)	**Si		
		Cravens et al. (1985)	*PSii
Grönroos (1984)	*S/PSi	Jackson et al. (1985)	*Psi
		Knoll and Hoffman (1986)	**Si
Becker (1985)	**PSi	Andrews et al. (1987)	**Si
Watson (1986)	**PSii	Baumgarten and Hensel (1987)	PSi
Crosby and Stephens (1987)	*Si	Lindquist (1987)	*Si
Grönroos (1987)	**Si	Little and Myers (1987)	*PSi
Judd (1987)	**Sii	Day et al. (1988)	*PSi/ii
Kelley (1987)	**Si	Teas (1988)	*Sii
King (1987)	**Si	Hedvall and Paltschik (1989)	PSi
Wheatley (1987)	**PSii	Carman (1988, 1990)	*S/PSi
Lindquist (1987)	*Si	Bojanic (1991)	*PSi
Edvardsson (1988)	*PSii	Bolton and Drew (1991a, b)	*Si
Teas (1988)	*Sii	Consulting Engineers Ass. (1991)	**PSi/ii
Lehtinen and Lehtinen (1991)	*Si	Nha (1991)	*Si
Lapierre (1993)	*PSii	Babakus and Boller (1992)	*Si
		Cronin and Taylor (1992, 1994)	Si
		Boulding et al. (1993)	*Si
		Freeman and Dart (1993)	*PSii
		Lapierre (1993)	*PSii
		Teas (1993a, b, 1994)	*Si
		Brown, Churchill and Peter (1993)	*Si

Key:
* = Empirical study; ** = Theoretical study; S = Services generally; PS = Professional services; i = Consumers;
ii = Organisations.

Source: Lapierre, J. and P. Filiatrault (1994), 'An Analysis of the Foundations of Research on the Quality of Professional Services to Organisations', Proceedings, Quality Management in Services IV, European Institute for Advanced Studies in Management (EIASM), Paris, May.

quality; the generic dimensions of service quality – technical and functional (Grönroos, 1984), leading to Parasuraman et al.'s (1985) identification of the dimensions of service quality; and a third wave, the careful scrutiny and criticism of the conceptual and methodological domains of service quality research. Lapierre and Filiatrault summarise much of the work of these schools in Table 1 above.

Brown et al. (1995) offer their personal interpretations as participant-observers together with a data-based analysis of the evolution of the services marketing literature. Using an evolutionary metaphor as the framework, the authors trace the literature through three stages: 'crawling out', 'scurrying about' and 'walking erect'. They use the three stages to illustrate how the literature has evolved from the early 'services marketing is different' debate to the maturation of specific topics, such as service quality and service encounters, and the legitimisation of the services marketing literature by major marketing journals.

Furthermore the large contribution by Parasuraman, Zeithaml and Berry (1985–94) in relation to the measurement of services quality has also provided the seed-corn for many critiques, reviews and replications of their work. One of the more recent examples of this is Buttle's (1996) review and critique of the theoretical and operational concerns which have been raised concerning SERVQUAL. However, in spite of these concerns, it is important to recognise that SERVQUAL has been widely used and applied to a variety of industrial, commercial and not-for-profit settings.

In the early 1990s many academics in the services marketing arena, particularly those from a European background, considered it was time to move beyond SERVQUAL and the previous overall focus on the service product dimensions and look to broader horizons (Gilmore and Carson, 1992).

While accepting that the future is always uncertain, the way forward for services marketing might be founded upon the following: looking for a more holistic understanding of service quality dimensions and more contextual considerations of definitions of service quality; different ways of evaluating service quality beyond SERVQUAL; and the development of more industry/situation-specific studies.

As a reflection of these comments so far, this book of text and readings is structured in five parts, each incorporating several articles. Part I deals with the origins of services marketing, and early discussions about the suitability of traditional marketing tools for services situations and the identification of the characteristics of services. Part II builds on the issues identified in Part I and develops the discussion in terms of the establishment of the services marketing domain within the literature. The main conceptual developments identified in the services marketing literature include descriptions of the service product, identifying services marketing dimensions, marketing in a services-specific situation and measuring service quality.

Part III focuses on the consolidation and management of service quality by considering the implications of the nature and characteristics of services for managers. The key aspects identified in the literature include designing systems for services management, managing marketing functional tasks, and managing human performance and the use of internal marketing.

Part IV addresses the functional aspects of services marketing such as product, pricing, communication, place and customer service.

Finally, Part V considers the future issues in relation to services marketing and management. Initially, readings in this part consider some of the literature surrounding services in specific contexts, such as in financial retailing, and it concludes with considerations of the more recent developments pertaining to the services literature which focus on implications for managers operating in services contexts in the 1990s.

It is intended that the book can be used as a useful reference for seminal articles in this area and therefore will be attractive to the students of services marketing. It will also be of interest to the services marketing manager as a 'one-stop' text that will allow him/her to explore the history and development of the academic domain. S/he will be able to set this development in the context of his/her own services marketing situation.

REFERENCES

Brown, S.W. , R.P. Fisk and M.J. Bitner (1995), 'The Development and Emergence of Services Marketing Thought' in W.J. Glynn and J. Barnes (eds.), *Understanding Services Management: Integrating Marketing, Organisational Behaviour, Operations and Human Resource Management*, Oak Tree Press, Dublin.

Buttle, F. (1996), 'SERVQUAL: Review, Critique, Research Agenda', *European Journal of Marketing*, vol. 30, no. 1.

Gilmore, A. and D. Carson (1992), 'Research in Service Quality: Have the Horizons Become too Narrow?', *Marketing Intelligence and Planning*, vol. 10. no. 7, pp. 5–7.

Grönroos, C. (1984), "A Service Quality Model and its Marketing Implications', *European Journal of Marketing*, vol. 18, no. 4, pp. 36–44.

Langeard, Eric, John Bateson, E.G. Lovelock, H. Christopher and Pierre Eiglier (1981), 'Services Marketing: New Insights from Consumers and Managers', Marketing Science Institute, Cambridge, Massachusetts, August, Report No. 81-104.

Lapierre, J. and P. Filiatrault (1994), 'An Analysis of the Foundations of Research on the Quality of Professional Services to Organisations', Proceedings, Quality Management in Services IV, European Institute for Advanced Studies in Management (EIASM), Paris, May.

Parasuraman, A., Valarie A. Zeithaml and Leonard L. Berry (1985), 'A Conceptual Model of Service Quality and its Implications for Future Research', *Journal of Marketing*, vol. 49, Fall, pp. 41–50.

Parasuraman, A., Valarie A. Zeithaml and Leonard L. Berry (1988), 'SERVQUAL: A Multiple-item Scale for Measuring Consumer Perceptions of Service Quality', *Journal of Retailing*, vol. 64, no. 1, Spring, pp. 12–35.

Parasuraman, A., Valarie A. Zeithaml and Leonard L. Berry (1991), 'Refinement and Reassessment of the SERVQUAL Scale', *Journal of Retailing*, vol. 67, no. 4, pp. 420–50.

Parasuraman, A., Valarie A. Zeithaml and Leonard L. Berry (1991), 'Understanding Customer Expectations of Service', *Sloan Management Review*, Spring, pp. 39–48.

Parasuraman, A., Valarie A. Zeithaml and Leonard L. Berry (1994), 'Reassessment of Expectations as a Comparison Standard in Measuring Service Quality: Implications for Future Research', *Journal of Marketing*, 58, January, pp. 111–24.

THE EDITORS

David Carson is professor of marketing at the University of Ulster, Northern Ireland. His research interests lie in marketing for SMEs and marketing in service industries, particularly in travel and tourism. He has published widely in both of these areas. He has extensive business experience both in consultancy and directorship roles. He is also the editor of the *European Journal of Marketing*.

Audrey Gilmore is a lecturer in marketing at the University of Ulster, Northern Ireland. Her teaching and research interests are in quality in marketing and marketing in service industries, particularly in travel and tourism. She is especially interested in developing a holistic approach to quality in services marketing within specific contexts. Audrey has published widely in the area of quality in services marketing and management. Prior to her academic career, she has had considerable experience in a variety of managerial roles in the service and retail sectors.

PART I

The Origins of
Services Marketing

THE ORIGINS OF SERVICES MARKETING

Part I of this book focuses on the origins and foundations of the services marketing literature and features some of the earlier research and subsequent debates surrounding the characteristics and nature of services which make marketing in this context different from marketing physical goods.

Marketing can be considered broadly as having a fundamental philosophy which is based around the customer/consumer; this philosophy is indeed the essence of marketing. In meeting the requirements of the customer the management of marketing activity must be organised in such a way that it is customer-oriented as well as organisationally efficient. On the basis of these two concepts, a customer-oriented philosophy and efficient management organisation, marketing activity itself will be performed.

Services marketing has its foundations in the fundamental concepts of marketing. The evolution of the philosophy of customer orientation can be traced over many years and is well documented as beginning with a production-oriented era, which gave way to a sales-oriented era, which in turn led to the marketing-oriented era of more recent times.

This marketing orientation puts the customer at the core of thinking and activity. In many organisations the philosophy is manifested in terms such as, 'everything an organisation does is with the customer in mind', 'the customer is the focus of everything we do', 'what the customer wants is paramount', and numerous other such phrases. In striving to achieve this philosophy, marketing practitioners seek to satisfy every whim of their customers. Indeed, some writers suggest that many companies have developed a 'marketing mania' whereby they have become obsessively responsible to such customer whims. Today, more enlightened companies encompass the philosophy of marketing orientation by concentrating on 'looking after' their customers and 'maximising' their satisfaction.

This philosophy of reaching the customer more precisely, it can be argued, has dictated marketing activity in some form or other throughout its history. Thus, the origins of services marketing can be linked to such customer orientation. In the early part of the twentieth century trading in 'commodity services' was in essence a form of services marketing. Indeed, this notion is recognised by Regan (1963) as the origins of services marketing in his article about the 'service revolution'. In reinforcing that such a revolution was taking place in the early 1960s, Regan and others, such as Judd (1964) and Rathmell (1966), set about trying to define services in their perceived widening domain. Such debate recognised, and in some cases anticipated, the emergence of more formal and autonomous services marketing in areas such as transportation, communication, education and retailing. Attempts were made at this time to redefine services and divisions of service activities in a way that would allow descriptions of services in a wider context. This provided the groundwork for further research and discussion.

SCOPE AND COMPLEXITY OF MARKETING AND SERVICES

During the 1960s and 1970s the marketing domain expanded and competition increased in line with a significant increase in consumer disposable income, together with ever more discerning decision-making and choice. This in turn led to significantly increased consumer sophistication, and marketing activity in general became substantially more complex. This complexity was most manifest in the widening and broadening of the marketing domain. There were many areas of marketing activity which began to merit their own distinctive literature, techniques and concepts. The debate surrounding the differences between industrial and consumer marketing and the progression of this debate to goods versus services marketing provides just such an example.

From the early 1960s the services marketing literature became a significant and growing entity within the broader, more complex domain of marketing. At the same time it was still generally recognised that services, whilst a growing area, was still an integral part of marketing in terms of concepts and description. Scholars focusing on services at this time were increasingly turning their attention to determining the distinguishing 'characteristics' of services and services marketing. Rathmell (1966), building on some of the classifications of Regan (1963), which included intangibility, perishability, heterogeneity and ubiquity, presented a continuum of personal expenditures and identified and described thirteen marketing characteristics of services. These are:

▷ The monetary value of a service is more likely to be expressed as a rate, fee, admission, charges, tuition, contributions or interest than as a 'price'.

▷ The buyer is a 'client' rather than a 'customer', thus the client literally puts himself 'in the hands' of the seller.

▷ The variety of marketing systems in the services category take on highly differentiated characteristics. For example, the marketing of recreation bears little resemblance to the marketing of medical services.

▷ Services are acts or processes which are produced as they are consumed, therefore they cannot be inventoried.

▷ The economic nature of some services may create ambiguous goals for the marketer, for example, payments to charitable and religious bodies and non-profit educational institutions.

▷ In some instances there are more formal or professional approaches to the marketing of many services, for example, financial, medical, legal and educational services.

▷ As services cannot be mass-produced, standards cannot be precise.

▷ 'Price-making' practices may vary greatly within the services category.

▷ Economic concepts of supply and demand and costs are difficult to apply to a service because of its intangible nature.

▷ Most fringe benefits take the form of services, for example, pensions, insurance, unemployment benefits, eye and dental care.

▷ There appears to be limited concentration, in the form of 'services chains', in the services sector of the economy.

▷ Some service firms fail to differentiate between the production and the marketing of services where performance is perceived to be equivalent to marketing the service.

▷ In the case of services, symbolism derives from performance rather than possession.

Throughout the 1970s and into the early 1980s, scholars further defined and refined the definitions and characteristics of services marketing. Much of the early conceptual thinking became recognised as acceptable aspects of marketing activity and was presented in textbooks for student learning. One of the first texts in the area was written by Rathmell (1974). This text generally reflected the groundwork established by this author and his contemporaries over the previous ten years and more. Much of this early conceptual thought was taken up and built upon by a growing new generation of 'specialist' scholars in the area who, it can be argued, truly established services marketing as a new paradigm. Writers such as Shostack (1977) refined the notion of services and customer perceptions of services as existing along a continuum of both concept and activity. Others, led by the Scandinavians Grönroos and Gummesson, in recognising such frameworks focused on the importance of consumers as integral players in the services marketing context and argued that the 'satisfaction' of the services consumer was paramount to the success and effectiveness of services marketing. The 'measurement' of services marketing performance became the dominant preoccupation of scholars in the field. The establishment and progression of these key conceptual developments in services marketing are discussed further in Part II of this book.

Although there were still some scholars who argued that many marketing concepts in relation to product marketing were entirely appropriate to service products, a notion typified by the arguments of Middleton (1983), the services marketing paradigm had established most of its main conceptual frameworks by this time.

The articles in Part I can be viewed as a summary of the origins of the services marketing literature. The papers chosen to reflect this evolutionary period of services marketing include the key contributions at this stage of development. These are:

Regan, William J. (1963), 'The Service Revolution', *Journal of Marketing*, 27, July, pp. 57–62.
Judd, Robert C. (1968), 'Similarities or Differences in Product and Service Retailing', *Journal of Retailing*, vol. 43, no. 4, Winter, pp. 1–9.
Middleton, Victor T.C. (1983), 'Product Marketing – Goods and Services Compared', *The Quarterly Review of Marketing*, Summer, pp. 1–10.
Shostack, G. Lynn (1977), 'Breaking Free from Product Marketing', *Journal of Marketing*, vol. 41, April, pp. 73–80.

We consider that these papers note the key conceptual shifts in the progression of the services paradigm. Regan's article in 1963 highlights that a large and growing market for commodities exists in the development of service systems. In this article he considers some definitions of services and their characteristics. He argues that the potential development of the service revolution depends upon the recognition of markets for business expansion, the development of service technologies, consideration of limits and impersonalisation of services, the 'massification of taste' and the proliferation of services.

Judd (1968) takes account of the characteristics of services marketing in the context of retailing. In particular he examines the similarities or differences in product and service retailing by focusing on the differences in the marketing required in terms of product and service development, sales effort, and pricing.

Middleton (1983) rejects the idea of contrasting products and services marketing by contending that service characteristics could be applied to both services and goods depending upon their specific characteristics. He outlines the similarities between goods and services marketing by emphasising that the mass production of products has similarities with the mass production of services (FMCGs and FMCSs). He contends that there are more differences in marketing various types of physical goods, by relating to the differences recognised in marketing shopping goods and convenience goods, than there are between goods and services marketing.

Shostack's (1977) article on 'Breaking Free from Product Marketing' begins the development and discussion of concepts and strategies relevant to services. This article focuses upon the predominantly intangible nature of services by using a continuum to illustrate the differences between goods and service products. Finally she discusses some of the implications for marketing managers.

KEY LEARNING QUESTIONS

1. What characteristics differentiate service products from physical good products?
2. Describe some of the similarities between goods and services marketing in the context of fast-moving consumer goods and fast-moving consumer services.
3. How does the intangible nature of services impact upon the effectiveness of traditional marketing techniques?

REFERENCES

Judd, Robert C. (1964), 'The Case for Redefining Services', *Journal of Marketing*, 28, January, pp. 58–9.

Judd, R.C. (1968), 'Similarities or Differences in Product and Service Retailing', *Journal of Retailing*, vol. 43, no. 4, Winter, pp. 1–9.

Middleton, V.T.C. (1983), 'Product Marketing – Goods and Services Compared', *The Quarterly Review of Marketing*, Summer, July, pp. 1–10.

Rathmell, John M. (1966), 'What Is Meant by Services?' *Journal of Marketing*, 30, October, pp. 32–6.

Rathmell, J.M. (1974), *Marketing in the Service Sector*, Winthrop Publishers Inc., Cambridge, Mass.

Regan, William J. (1963), "The Service Revolution', *Journal of Marketing*, 27, July, pp. 57–62.

Shostack, G.L. (1977), "Breaking Free from Product Marketing', *Journal of Marketing*, vol. 41, April, pp. 73–80.

The Service Revolution

William J. Regan

Although critics lament the apparent thing-mindedness of the 'consumption carousel',[1] business managements, workers, consumers, financiers, promoters and government groups unconsciously have combined to turn the wheel of consumption in a new direction. The thesis of this article is that the United States is well advanced into a *service revolution* that may in time bring to its beneficiaries wholly new quantitative and qualitative patterns of service consumption.

The growth of services is a logical result of several converging forces. As the marginal attraction of services increases faster than that of more goods, entrepreneurial capital and business managements are turning more to the development of service markets. Because the expansion of these markets requires business organisation, managements borrow applicable techniques that were successful in the mass production of goods.

In the short run, the emerging service systems both limit the range and impersonalise the nature of services. In the long run it is possible that a desirable proliferation of services will develop paralleling that for commodities.

WHAT ARE SERVICES?

Services are 'activities, benefits or satisfactions which are offered for sale, or are provided in connection with the sale of goods'.[2] More specifically, they represent either intangibles yielding satisfactions directly (insurance), tangibles yielding satisfactions directly (transportation, housing), or intangibles yielding satisfactions jointly when purchased either with commodities or with other services (credit, delivery).

The time, place and possession utilities delivered by a marketing system yield satisfactions jointly (and often indirectly), either through accompanying the form utility of the purchased commodity or through accompanying the nonform utility of a purchased service.

Such commodity-associated services make separate classification and reporting of service expenditure difficult. The Office of Business Economics of the Department of Commerce must distinguish between such joint commodity service groups as purchased meals (classified as a nondurable commodity) and shoe repair (classified as a service). But how much service is involved in dining at a restaurant or a snack bar? How much commodity goes into shoe repair?

The fifty-five service items for which consumer expenditure is tabulated 'are comprised of several hundred separate series of estimates; and these represent the incorporation of numerous types of data from many government and private sources, processed by procedures virtually running the gamut of those used in national income estimation'.[3] Clearly the data on consumer service expenditures need careful interpretation.

TABLE 1: PERSONAL SERVICE EXPENDITURES AS PERCENTAGES OF GROSS NATIONAL PRODUCT
AND TOTAL PERSONAL CONSUMPTION EXPENDITURES (1929 THROUGH 1960)*

In billions (of current dollars)

Year	Gross national product	Personal consumption expenditures	Services	% services of gross national product	% services of personal consumption expenditures
1929	104.4	79.0	32.1	30.7	40.6
1932	58.5	49.3	22.9	39.1	46.5
1933	56.0	46.4	20.7	37.0	44.6
1939	91.1	67.6	25.8	28.3	38.2
1940	100.6	71.9	26.9	26.7	37.4
1941	125.8	81.9	29.0	23.1	35.4
1945	213.6	121.7	40.4	18.9	33.2
1946	210.7	147.1	46.4	22.0	31.5
1947	234.3	165.4	51.4	21.9	31.1
1948	259.4	178.3	56.9	21.9	31.9
1950	284.6	195.0	64.9	22.8	33.3
1952	347.0	219.8	75.6	21.8	34.4
1954	363.1	238.0	86.3	23.8	36.3
1955	397.5	256.9	92.5	23.3	36.0
1956	419.2	269.9	100.0	23.9	37.1
1957	442.8	285.2	107.1	24.2	37.6
1958	444.2	293.5	114.2	25.7	38.9
1959	482.1	313.8	122.8	25.5	39.1
1960	504.4	328.9	132.2	26.2	40.2

* *Sources:* Data for 1929–59 adapted from Table C-1, "Gross National Product or Expenditure, 1929–60," and Table C-7, "Personal Consumption Expenditures, 1929–60", *Economic Report of the President*, 18 January 1961, pp. 127, 136; Data for 1960 from *Survey of Current Business*, United States Department of Commerce, July 1961.

The intangibility, perishability, heterogeneity and ubiquity make total comprehension of services difficult. In addition, the phrase takes on variable meanings depending upon whether its usage is directed to employment, national income accounting, or marketing activities. The tabulations in this article are based on the US Department of Commerce's definition of service expenditures. This consists of the market value of purchases of services by individuals and non-profit institutions, and include the imputed rental value of owner-occupied houses.[4]

Table 1 summarises personal service expenditures from 1929 through 1960. Table 2 presents the changes in services in each of the twelve classification headings used by the Department of Commerce to record aggregate personal consumption expenditures in the years 1929, 1941 and

1960. They indicate that service expenditures rose steadily from 1947 to 1960 but had not yet quite reached the relative level experienced in 1929. Although the 1929 level probably will be exceeded within the next year or two, the 46.5 per cent figure of 1932 remains well above current ratios.

Service expenditures proved less elastic than commodity expenditures during the depression of the 1930s. Also, the carry-over effects of price controls, rationing and service stringencies from World War II caused service expenditures to sink to a low point of 31.1 per cent of personal consumption expenditures in 1947, before beginning a steady rise to pre-war, pre-depression levels.

Between 1929 and 1960, four groups of services increased their relative shares, and seven decreased for a net decline over the entire period. Although a sizeable increase in consumer service

TABLE 2: CURRENT DOLLAR SERVICE EXPENDITURES AND THEIR PERCENTAGES OF PERSONAL
CONSUMPTION EXPENDITURES (1929, 1941, 1960)*

	1929		1941		1960		
	In millions of dollars	% of personal consumption expenditures	In millions of dollars	% of personal consumption expenditures	In millions of dollars	% of personal consumption expenditures	Change 1929 to 1960 (%)
Food and Tobacco (No service classifications)							
Clothing, accessories and jewellery	1,264	1.60	1,162	1.42	3,673	1.12	−.48
Personal care	525	.66	555	.68	2,358	.72	+.06
Housing	11,446	14.50	10,046	12.27	42,209	12.83	−1.67
Household operation	4,037	5.11	4,251	5.19	19,608	5.96	+.85
Medical care and death expenses	2,809	3.55	2,900	3.54	16,177	4.92	+1.37
Personal business	5,086	6.44	3,894	4.75	20,602	6.26	−.18
Transportation	2,562	3.24	2,410	2.94	10,470	3.18	−.06
Recreation	1,696	2.14	1,836	2.24	6,390	1.94	−.20
Private education and research	664	.84	702	.86	4,467	1.36	+.52
Religious and welfare	1,196	1.51	1,060	1.29	4,687	1.42	−.09
Foreign travel and remittances – net	778	.99	192	.23	1,583	.48	−.51
Total durable commodities	9,212	11.67	9,659	11.80	44,312	13.47	+1.80
Total non-durable commodities	37,677	47.72	43,208	52.77	152,390	46.33	−1.39
Total services	32,063	40.61	29,008	35.43	132,224	40.20	−.41
Total personal consumption expenditures	78,952		81,875		328,926		

Sources: *Statistical Abstract of the United States*, 1960, and *Survey of Current Business*, United States Department of Commerce, July 1961.

expenditures was recorded between 1941 and 1960, a case can be made supporting either the growth or the decline in service expenditures, depending upon the base year selected for comparison. Most commentaries in recent years have used the post-World War II growth in service expenditures to predict continuing service growth. Over a longer time span, consumer purchases of services at current prices increased more than fourteen times between the decades of 1869–78 and 1919–28, while total consumer expenditures were increasing less than twelve times.[5]

The constitution of many services has changed markedly since 1929 accompanied by differ-

ential rates of income growth between service workers and commodity workers. Together, these changes mean that the same relative dollar expenditure today for ostensibly the same services and commodities will buy a different physical mix of the two as compared with earlier periods.

Thus, there is no way of readily measuring the actual level of services delivered today as compared with any earlier period. All that is measured are aggregate dollar expenditures for classification items identified as services.

STAGES OF ECONOMIC GROWTH
The well-known Clark-Fisher hypothesis states

generally that agriculture, forestry, hunting and fishing receive major attention in primary or low-level economies, and that secondary-stage emphasis turns to manufacturing, 'defined as a process, not using the resources of nature directly, producing, on a large scale, and by a continuous process, transportable goods'.[6] Tertiary-level activities, it is hypothesised, emphasise trade and transport; finance and communication; building and construction; and professional, personal and governmental activities. Since these activities are mostly services, a tertiary-level economy should experience a rising share of expenditures in the service sector.

The lesser-known 'Foote-Hatt hypothesis' limits the tertiary group to 'domestic and quasi-domestic services: restaurants and hotels, barber and beauty shops, laundry and dry cleaning, repairing and maintenance, and the sprinkling of handcrafts, once performed at home'.[7] Transport, commerce, communication, finance and administration are identified as quaternary industries, while a quinary group is conceptualised as refining and extending human capacities through medical care, education, research and recreation, including the arts.

These patterns of growth serve to enunciate more specifically the essence of Ernst Engel's 'law' set forth in 1857– one part of which stated that as income increases, the percentage spent for sundries increases rapidly.

FIVE PROPOSITIONS

With continuity in data only from 1929 and with ambiguous conclusions possible, new interpretations of service growth are needed. Five basic propositions supporting the service revolution hypothesis are:

1. Market potentials for business expansions today are greater in the area of human wants than in what are classified as services by the Department of Commerce.

2. Mass production techniques used in manufacturing commodities are being adapted to develop service technologies.

3. Use of service systems leads to the arbitrary administration of standard services and the impersonalisation of services.

4. Substitution of manufactured equipment for personalised attention encourages a reduction in the extrinsic quality of service in the short run and a general 'massification of taste'.

5. A desirable proliferation of services will emerge in the long run that is adaptable to a wide variety of tastes in much the same manner that mass production of goods led to diversity in commodity choice today.

Each of these propositions will be discussed briefly in the following sections.

MARKETS FOR BUSINESS EXPANSION

In meeting human wants, the most obvious and attractive markets to businessmen are those requiring tangible commodities to satisfy physiological wants. Less obvious and less attractive markets are those requiring commodity-associated services or 'pure' services to answer psychological wants or complex combinations of physiological-psychological wants.

Having exhausted most of the visible growth potential in domestic markets of *physical goods and physiological wants,* large-scale manufacturing enterprises increasingly have turned to other markets that are more difficult to serve but have higher potential rates of return. These are markets where commodity-associated services or 'productified' services render utilitarian satisfactions to business consumers and functional satisfactions to household consumers.[8]

Market demand for yet undeveloped services beyond these utilitarian service benefits lies largely hidden in high-risk obscurity. The Clark-Fisher, Foote-Hatt and Engel theories suggest that higher-level consumption will make service groups such as education, medicine and research increasingly important.

Controlling the potentials of technological applications, business today is competing vigorously in applying technology to services. Thus, data-processing, automation, self-service, automatic vending and materials-handling equipment and systems are examples where business has complemented or replaced office clerks, secretaries, sales clerks, and labourers with equipment or commodities.

Small, single-unit firms physically dominate the service community. However, the 3.5 per cent of consumer service establishments reporting total receipts above $100,000 received almost half of total receipts shown in the 1954 Census of Business.[9] Leadership in the development of service systems clearly rests with the integrated, successful and aggressive business firms. Co-operation between large manufacturing corporations making service system components and progressive marketing organisations using these components provides the main thrust in this service revolution.

DEVELOPMENT OF SERVICE TECHNOLOGIES

In the Clark-Fisher hypothesis, attention in the secondary level of economic development centres upon mass production and the attempts to minimise unit costs. In the tertiary period, more consideration is allocated to the expansion of service technologies and the discovery of optimum scales for delivering such services. Standardisation of work procedures, specialisation of talents, the use of equipment and machinery, and administrative control procedures are all increasingly common. These elements are co-ordinated into systems which have been defined as assemblages or combinations of things or parts forming complex or unitary wholes. The purpose of these systems is to routinise servicing operations so that services can be provided faster, more conveniently and at lower unit costs for mass markets.

Technical and equipment-directed systems have been successfully developed for communications, through data processing, radio and television; for transportation, through mass-transit systems; and for education, through television courses and testing systems. Technological applications for individual instruction based on teaching machines have been identified as '1.

individual reading pacers; 2. individual viewing and listening equipment for existing slides, film-strips, motion pictures and recordings; 3. language laboratories; 4. specifically programmed printed materials such as scrambled textbooks; 5. actual teaching machines containing carefully worked out programs with various ingenious mechanical or electronic arrangements to test student reaction, and inform him of his progress'.[10] Some organisational aspects of systems have been applied to insurance through group insurance and comprehensive coverage plans, to medicine through group health plans, and to travel through group tours.

Self-service technology for retail trade has become a commonplace. Systems of layout, display, communication and control have been co-ordinated to facilitate self-service buying. Automatic vending equipment represents a further technological development in retail trade that is being more widely applied.

LIMITS AND IMPERSONALISATION OF SERVICES

In the beginning of its life cycle, a new consumer service usually is offered to and is sought by higher socio-economic levels. If sufficiently desired, it tends to become a symbol of status and will be sought by the next lower socio-economic group. Obviously each lower group has less income to support this service than the group immediately above it. Social pressure and legal means are then invoked to help realise this service for a wider market.

The opportunity profitably to service larger numbers of people creates a business challenge. Hence the component elements in a service are identified, segmented, analysed and structured. Economic feasibility often limits the application of technology to the central core of essential elements in the service. Personalised service attention is supposed to take care of the remaining 'non-productified' and non-systematised portions of the service.

If cost were no consideration, most people would prefer a full quota of personalised attention in their purchases of services. However, personal service seems to retain its qualitative features better when rendered to a relatively small percentage of the population. Delivery of personalised service to large numbers necessarily results in some loss of the deferential aspects which are the very essence of its attraction. When service becomes partly dehumanised, it loses some of its ego-satisfying properties.

Perhaps a subhypothesis is: The quantity and quality of the personalised attention in a service varies inversely with the percentage of the population effectively desiring it. Implicit assumptions are that service gates or facilities will not expand proportionally with the demand for the service and that special influences are irrelevant.

'MASSIFICATION OF TASTE'[11]

The changing character of services caused by increasing technology (science) and decreasing personalisation (art) seems to apply generally to medicine and education. The delivery of these services to more and more people has required greater reliance upon systems and less upon the personal ministrations of doctor or teacher. Certainly medical care and education have become increasingly impersonal. This is not to say that their intrinsic value consisting of the essential design and function is necessarily less, although it may be.

For a service such as medical care, the intrinsic essentials might consist of accurate diagnosis and proper remedy. Extrinsically added elements might be abundant personal 'loving care', luxurious and spacious facilities, the reputations of doctor or hospital. The intrinsic essentials of the college education might include only the bare opportunity to learn or to be exposed to a prescribed series of courses. Extrinsically, it has come to include all of the extracurricular activity and colour associated with campus life.

The intrinsic value of these increasingly impersonalised services may also remain the same or even increase. Most decreases are induced by dissatisfactions associated with reductions in the extrinsic values added. Equating the value of the entire service with the extrinsic element only has

led many to condemn the entire systematisation of services.

These extrinsic dissatisfactions include increases in waiting and queuing time, the use of standardised forms, the ordering of procedural steps and double-checking to maintain the integrity of the system. Increasingly less servile attendants also reduce the extrinsic values.

The total impact of systems in codifying and standardising services encourages a general 'massification of taste'. Service systems contribute to this conformity in tastes by organising and structuring the range of service expectations. They do this by limiting the service channels to profitable ones and by minimising exceptional treatment cases.

PROLIFERATION OF SERVICES

The application of technology to the delivery of mass services may do for services what technology did for mass production. Applied to mass production, it resulted in the presentation of better-quality goods of far wider varieties at lower unit prices. With few exceptions, customers no longer expect the maker of goods to custom-produce items to individual order.

There is now the challenge of a similar revolution for services. The tools are now available and the beginning is well launched. Specialists with greater sophistication in quantitative data-handling techniques and supported by computer ability are assisting business in the development of efficient service patterns in transportation, communication and inventory control systems. Governmental agencies use these practitioners in solving large logistics problems. It is possible that some of the new service system techniques will be applied to other service areas such as in education and medicine.

The assumption that today's or yesterday's qualitative standards of service will be the ones delivered tomorrow to twice as many recipients is not valid. Intrinsically the service may be better or the same, but extrinsically it will probably be poorer until acceptable substitutes are developed for loss of personalisation. Even if the supply of qualified physicians, teachers and other service specialists were more responsive to the demand for them, it is questionable that society could or would support the traditional cost structure. Greater per capita consumption of these services will be facilitated by a lowering of their average unit costs. Since the supply of such specialists is not readily expandable in the short run, an accompanying impersonalisation and systematisation of services appear reasonable expectations.

The longer-run picture for services is considerably brighter. The intrinsic value of services will increase as knowledge from all investigative areas and advancing technology are combined in effective service systems. The extrinsic value of services may also increase through developing more comprehensive and flexible systems to deliver service satisfactions. Delivery of satisfactory intrinsic and extrinsic elements of services to wider segments of the population can be accomplished only through expanding the structure of commodity-associated and systematised services.

NOTES

1. William Gomberg (1961), 'Problems of Economic Growth and Automation', *California Management Review*, vol. 3, Summer, pp. 4–17 at p. 13.

2. Committee on Definitions of the American Marketing Association (1960), *Marketing Definitions: A Glossary of Marketing Terms*, American Marketing Association, Chicago, p. 21.

3. US Department of Commerce, Office of Business Economics (1954), *National Income Supplement to Survey of Current Business*, p. 117.

4. *National Income Supplement*, p. 59.

5. Simon Kuznets (1946), *Gross National Product since 1869*, National Bureau of Economic Research, Part III, p. 144.

6. Colin Clark (1957), *The Conditions of Economic Progress*, 3rd edition, Macmillan & Company Ltd, London, p. 491.

7. Nelson N. Foote and Paul K. Hatt (1953), 'Social Mobility and Economic Advancement', *American Economic Review*, vol. 43, May, pp. 364–78 at p. 365.

8. William J. Regan and Cornelis Visser (1962), 'The Elusive Service Market' in Eugene J. Kelley and William Lazer (eds), *Managerial Marketing: Perspectives and Viewpoints*, revised edition, Richard D. Irwin Inc, Homewood, Illinois, pp. 151–8.

9. Donald D. Parker (1960), *The Marketing of Consumer Services*, University of Washington, Bureau of Business Research, p. 17.

10. James D. Finn (1960), 'Automation and Education: III. Technology and the Educational Process', *Audio-visual Communication Review*, vol. 8, Winter, pp. 5–26 at p. 17.

11. Foote and Hatt, 'Social Mobility and Economic Advancement' at p. 366.

Similarities or Differences in Product and Service Retailing

Robert C. Judd

With the growth of both expenditures for and the range of personal and business services it seems timely that service retailing be examined. Review of the literature suggests there has been an implicit assumption that there is a similarity of service marketing to product marketing.[1] This assumption of similarity may explain the comparative neglect of services in marketing texts, let alone retailing texts, where even less on retailing of services is to be found.

If services are defined as transactions where the object of the transaction is other than the transfer of ownership of a tangible commodity, then services will require retailing just as products require retailing. The question is, 'Are product retailing and service retailing substantially identical, and if not, what are the similarities and what are the differences?'

To answer this question, product and service retailing can be examined in at least three aspects:

1. Product and service development;
2. Sales effort;
3. Pricing.

PRODUCT AND SERVICE DEVELOPMENT

Now the product or service producer's concern with product or service development is the result of changing consumer preferences and of competitive pressures. But the retailer must be just as alert to product or service development opportunities and follow each step in the process to gain a maximum market advantage. This means studying opportunities for greater marketing efficiency, enlarging a product or service line, and careful choice of timing in new product or service introduction.

INCENTIVES

An important factor in both product and service development is the desire to utilise capacity. This is of concern to the retailer of a *product* particularly, as it may permit the spreading of overhead costs over a greater number of units and thus favourably affect the costs to be recovered in price. The same factor influences the service retailer to plan or develop companion services to those now offered. In service retailing the matter of capacity takes on added urgency since services cannot usually be stored. Because services are highly perishable, it is all the more important that the labour and the capital costs, implicit in service availability, be recaptured as regularly and completely as possible. The leased but half-filled beauty salon, the floor waxer that is not rented today, and the interior decorator who has only one appointment in eight hours, exhibit unused capacity. They may or may not be able to reverse this underutilisation of capacity through a service equivalent to product development.

SOURCES OF IDEAS

The most important place in which social and competitive pressures are translated into product or service development is in the market. Wholesalers, retailers and other sales agencies can and do make valuable suggestions for product change based on user reactions to existing products or services. To the extent that ideas for product change are transmitted back through the complex channels of trade to the source of the product, the market-place acts as an important source for product planning ideas. In the service industry, suggestions for change come from service personnel. Often these service people are employees or agents of the service retailer. Thus, in services, the communication channel is typically shorter. From the standpoint of retailing, there is a clear advantage on the service side.

STAGES OF DEVELOPMENT
SIMILARITIES
Adopting a sales and marketing programme by a small product or service retailer is a simple, informal operation. But the marketing programme of a large retailer takes on a more complex and formal pattern. In other words, in creating a marketing programme there are very real differences in the actions taken, but the differences are more the result of size and organisation form than in the fact of product versus service output.

DIFFERENCES
A significant difference between product and service retailing is the lack of legal protection for service ideas. While this spares the service enterprise the expense of legal investigation into the so-called 'patentability' of a new idea, it means the service retailer must do without the legal protection that a patent affords a manufacturer. The consequences of this for 'competition through imitation' are evident in the ease of entry into a great many service retailing fields and the existence of the many small service retailers.

BRANDING
In the product planning area of branding, the passage of the Lanham Act in 1946 meant that, from its effective date in 1947, services shared in the legal counterpart, the trade-mark, to the business term 'brand'. This enactment gave

specific recognition to the 'service mark'. It went even further and provided for a 'certification mark' and a 'collective mark'. These are categories that could become important in the promotion of services. Because of the wide usage of 'brand' to denote a physical commodity, it is understandable that services have not adopted this business term. But relatively few service retailers have used service marks and thereby gained the advantages of branding. The use of a service mark does not seem to have conferred as much market control nor as much pricing independence to service retailers as has the use of brands by the same retailers. Greater use of the service mark and greater competitive advantages to service mark users seem likely in the future.

PACKAGING AND LABELLING
Except for the wrapping in which a shirt is returned from the laundry or the bag that envelops a dress returned from the cleaner, or the jacket that encloses a new insurance policy, packaging is not a service function. It seems fair to record it as a difference between product retailing and service retailing. While the absence of packaging or labelling avoids the creative and legal problems, it deprives services of the promotional possibilities that packaging and labelling make possible for product retailers. On the other hand, service retailers can only infrequently be perfectly duplicated even though effective duplication by competitive retailers is likely.

WARRANTY AND SERVICE POLICY
There does not seem to be any application of the Uniform Sales Act with respect to warranties as related to services. All references to warranties in the Act refer to goods. This represents a difference in the situation because the product retailer must consider the implications of implied, if not express, warranties.

SALES EFFORT
To the buying public, sales effort is understandably the most conspicuous aspect of product retailing but there are other factors to be considered.

ADVERTISING

The objectives of advertising are the same whether employed on behalf of a service or a product. Basically, service advertising is as concerned with conveying information as is the product retailer. In some cases the method of persuasion employed in advertising a service will be different from that employed by a product because it is more difficult or even impossible to illustrate a service form and its benefits in use. Services depend on image appeals. But image appeals are also found in product advertising. Here they represent an advantage to the retailer as a product advertiser since he can employ either image or form.

The advertising institutions and media employed are similar. Large retailers use advertising agencies to effect product or service advertising while small firms tend to do without the aid of an agency. There are no media that do not carry some advertising for services. But there is a difference in the degree to which some media will be employed. Thus the very small service retailers may content themselves with listings in the classified directory while the very small product retailers such as 'mama & papa' stores may limit themselves to a local advertising programme. These differences are caused more by size than by product versus service characteristics.

SALES PROMOTION

Similarities. The first similarity in sales promotion between products and services is that both employ printed promotion material to get sales. The most obvious device used by each is direct mail. While many services lack any way of using such devices as the counter card or window banner, their means of marking their location and reminding the public of it are effective equivalents.

The second similarity is the use of coupons in the promotion of both products and services. While service retailers have infrequently used coupons, it seems reasonable to expect that as the size of a service operation increases, the use of coupons will grow.

The third similarity is the use of contests and prizes. Service retailers have used contests and prizes although thus far the practice has been limited because of the small and local scale of the enterprise. Once the size of a service retailer gets larger the possibilities for the use of contests and prizes seems at least as good as the prospects for increased use of coupons.

Differences. The first difference between the retail sales promotion of services and products is that services infrequently have anything tangible to display. Physical products that are part of a service are presumably in use. Thus services are prevented from using mass counter and aisle displays.

Services differ from products because they lack the samples that form an important part of product promotion. The only alternative for the service retailer is to offer some kind of get-acquainted special, but this is not a sample.

Similar reasoning applies to the use of demonstrations. Services are not able to demonstrate their service without offering the service they seek to sell. While a washing machine can be demonstrated at a woman's club by a retailer, the alternative-laundry service of another retailer can not.

SALES MANAGEMENT AND SELLING

In terms of selling, the similarities seem basic. Both products and services use selling to achieve their volume goals. The selling process for either category involves gaining attention, interest, desire and action. The product retailer places heavy reliance on form in advertising and selling. This reliance is not present in the selling of the service retailer. Instead of product benefits in use he must turn to images that communicate the benefits to the purchaser. Thus service selling may be for some sales personnel a more difficult and demanding task than selling tangible products.

PRODUCT DIFFERENTIATION

Product differentiation is the final aspect of sales effort to be considered. By product differentiation is usually meant: 1. creation of real differences in a product over its competitors; 2. the addition of services to accompany the product that make it distinctive; 3. the acceptance in the customer's mind of a real or fancied difference. The creation of a fancied difference may be a conscious effort on the part of the product retailer zin his advertising, sales promotion and selling techniques. But it may be only a by-product of those efforts without the product retailer's conscious intent.

The literature on service marketing is silent about any service equivalent to product differentiation. This seems strange because, lacking the definite comparative qualities of many products, service differentiation should be an easier goal to achieve. Comparison between competitive services is less exact than between two competing products. This is true because of the greater intangibility of services and should make the development and promotion of service differentiation all the more important. The absence of demonstrable real differences and the ease of fostering fancied differences gives the service retailer a substantial advantage over his product retailing counterpart. But for this advantage to be realised, the service retailer must know about service differentiation and put it to use in his advertising and sales efforts.

PRICING

On a topic as extensive as retail pricing, it is difficult to touch on other than the most obvious likenesses and differences between selling products and services.

The usefulness or utility of a product or service is the measure of its value. It is translatable, though inexactly, into dollars as the basis of price. But in service retailing the extreme perishability of services, together with the varying mental state of the customer, in a very short unit of elapsed time, makes appraisal of value less accurate than in product retailing. Nevertheless, both service and product retailing depend on value approximations as a basis for price.

Much the same line of reasoning places the cost aspect of a price basis in the 'similar' category. The problem of cost as a basis for price in service retailing arises because in many service areas a large portion of the cost basis for price is represented by implicit costs of the services enterpriser. These implicit costs take the form of wages to the enterpriser or a return on his time and investment in education or training in terms of the alternate

uses of his time. Some very small product enterprises face this implicit cost problem. In 'mama & papa' stores, for example, implicit costs exist but there are also explicit fixed and variable costs to guide them in making price decisions. On the premise that service retailers are likely to become more aware of the implicit cost factor, and that the scale of service enterprises probably will increase and bring with it explicit costs, it has seemed wise to list the cost factor as a similarity.

PRICE MANAGEMENT
SIMILARITIES
Price variation is a factor in price management and gets similar treatment from both service and product retailers. Generally, local service retailers, like product retailers, use a single price policy. The means used to effect these policies in service retailing parallel the short-run price variation practices of product retailing.

Another similarity between product marketing and service marketing is price law. The Federal Trade Commission Act and the Robinson-Patman Act, though limited, are the principal factors here. The Robinson-Patman Act has had limited application to the service field because services tend not to use functional discounts and cumulative discounts. The Federal Trade Commission, under its powers to prohibit 'unfair methods of competition', has only occasionally turned its attention to services. Probably the smallness of many service retailers has kept them from governmental action with respect to their pricing practices. As services increase in scale of enterprise, their essential equality before the law will become more evident.

DIFFERENCES
In the area of price management, service retailing differs from product retailing in the absence of trade discounts, quantity discounts and geographical pricing methods. This is a natural consequence of shorter and less complex channels of trade. As the scale of service enterprises increases, there is a possibility that one or more of these devices will find a counterpart function in the service retailing field. Lacking this development, it is only logical to record this area of price practice as a difference

TABLE 1

	Similarities	Differences
1. PRODUCT (SERVICE) DEVELOPMENT		
a. Product or service development: incentives	1. Utilisation of capacity problem	—
b. Product or service development: sources of ideas	1. The market-place as a source	—
c. Product or service stages	1. Marketing programme	1. Patent unavailability for services
d. Branding	1. Trade and service marks	—
e. Packaging and labelling	—	1. Services lack use for packaging
f. Warranty and service policy	—	1. Law of warranty appears inapplicable
2. SALES EFFORT		
a. Advertising	1. Objectives	—
	2. Institutions and media used	—
b. Sales promotion	1. Use of printed promotion material	1. Lack of physical display in services
	2. Use of coupons	2. No samples possible in services
	3. Use of contests and prizes	3. No demonstrations possible in services
c. Sales management and selling	1. Selling techniques	—
d. Product differentiation	1. Service differentiation urged to parallel product differentiation	—
3. PRICING		
a. Price basis	1. Value	—
	2. Cost	—
b. Price management	1. Price variation principles	1. Services do not use discount structure generally

between product and service retailing.

SUMMARY

From the foregoing, it is possible to summarise the similarities and differences in service and product retailing as in Table 1 above.

From this summary it is clear that the extent of differences between product and service retailing is greater than can be dismissed as incidental. But the extent of similarities is substantial. If services do have the similarities and differences that appear to exist and are delineated above, then service retailing merits further study within the retailing field.

NOTE

1. For exceptions to this compare Percival White and Walter S. Hayward (1924), *Marketing Practice,* Doubleday, Page & Co., Garden City, NY, ch. XIX; John F. Pyle (1936), *Marketing Principles,* McGraw-Hill Book Company Inc., New York, ch. XIV; Paul D. Converse, Harvey W. Huegy and Robert V. Mitchell (1965), *Elements of Marketing,* 7th edition, Prentice-Hall Inc., Englewood Cliffs, NJ, ch. 22 with other marketing and retailing texts.

Product Marketing – Goods and Services Compared

Victor T.C. Middleton

This article aims to clarify and develop some of the main marketing concepts about goods and services which have been advanced in recent years. The semantics involved in the continuing debate about the characteristics of goods and services are not only sterile or 'debilitating' as Baker put it in 1981,[1] but thoroughly confusing for practitioners and especially students whose vocational direction is towards service industries.

The typical contrasting of *product marketing* and *service marketing* (Stanton, 1981),[2] or *products* and *services* (Baker, 1981),[3] or even *tangibles* and *intangibles* (Levitt, 1981)[4] is rejected as unhelpful. The by now traditional notions of heterogeneity, perishability, intangibility and inseparability of services, are reviewed in the light of discussion of large-scale nationally distributed services operating with mass-production methods. A new taxonomy of *products*, whether based on goods or services, is proposed, which simply adapts the classification of physical goods, developed over several decades. Organisation structures for marketing management, adapting product/brand management systems, are shown to be as relevant to service operations as they are to manufacturers marketing physical goods. The concept of fast-moving consumer services (f.m.c.s.) is introduced.

Throughout, the unifying and simplifying notion of the *product* as a basis for effective marketing management is stressed.

SOME DEFINITIONS OF SERVICES

Seeking guidance in the confusion of concepts already noted and further discussed below, the student may for example turn to Kotler (1980)[5] to discover that services 'have the characteristics of being intangible, perishable, variable and personal'. In Baker (1979)[6] he will discover, under 'Classification of Products', the AMA definitions for consumer and industrial goods but services are not discussed. Stanton (1981)[7] has it that 'in a very narrow sense, a product is a set of tangible, physical attributes assembled in an identifiable form' and reinforces this by claiming that 'since services are essentially intangible, it is impossible for customers to sample – to taste, feel, see, hear or smell – services before they buy them'. The Stanton view of marketing services has been much quoted in many contributions in this field and it is, to say the least, influential in the present climate of thinking about services. In the judgement of this writer, the Stanton view is, in practice, largely irrelevant to many service industries and tends to distort the understanding of an effective marketing approach.

Seeking clarification in articles, the student may turn to Wyckham et al. (1975)[8] for a broad rejection of the Stanton view and find that 'services are not different from products' (*sic*). An alternative view from Grönroos (1978)[9] argues that 'services do differ from goods as objects of

Reprinted with permission from *The Quarterly Review of Marketing*, Summer, pp. 1–10.

marketing ... A new service marketing mix concept is needed.' Shostack (1982),[10] whose molecular analogies and systems view of services has contributed much to understanding product planning issues, especially where goods and services are offered in complex combinations, continues to draw distinctions between *products* and *services*. Unusually in the literature on this subject, Christopher et al. (1980)[11] draw distinctions between *service products* and the *product service*, with the former representing predominantly service offerings. But they also note that service products involve an 'intangible series of benefits'.

It appears that the only safe ground in the distinction between goods and services lies in the generally accepted, if broad, proposition which Rathmell (1974)[12] summarised as, 'Goods are produced. Services are performed.' Of course there are also many products which are combinations of goods and services, but in dealing with services this article adopts the Shostack (1982)[13] notion of 'service-dominant entities'. The essence of the Rathmell view is that the buyer of goods concludes an exchange transaction which confers ownership of a physical item to consume as and when he will. By contrast the buyer of services concludes an exchange transaction which permits the use of particular services for a relatively brief and specified time period only and does not result in ownership of a physical item. Whilst even this broad proposition permits of exceptions, it is adopted as a suitable common-ground starting-point for this article.

PRODUCTS: THE BROAD VIEW
A route to a better understanding of the so-called *services* vs. *products* debate may emerge if three approaches, outlined in this article, are adopted. The first is to insist that, whenever comparisons between services and physical goods are made, the comparisons are appropriate, comparing like with like. In practice this will mean classifying services using the same broad criteria which have been applied to manufactured physical goods for nearly sixty years. The second approach is to broaden the product concept along the lines propounded

by Kotler (1975)[14] and generally accepted in principle, that *product* covers 'anything that can be offered to a market for attention, acquisition or consumption: physical objects, services, persons, places, organisations or ideas'. Interestingly in an earlier article (1969) Kotler and Levy[15] actually used the term *intangible goods* (*sic*) to define services. The third approach is to focus not on the characteristics of services compared with physical goods but upon the characteristics of the customer-purchasing behaviour involved in the exchange process.

Thus in the body of this article we aim to speak only of *products* as a basis for marketing strategy and tactics whether or not these products are based on physical, manufactured goods, or on services. With the three approaches outlined above we are attempting to develop the Baker view (1981)[16] that 'we must look for similarities between products and services rather than differences'. We seek also to pursue the direction suggested by Wyckham et al. in proposing a more effective taxonomy of market offerings. By focusing on the characteristics of buyer behaviour we seek to avoid the sterilities of over-precise product definitions and to remain firmly consumer-oriented.

In this article we deal only with commercial products aimed at the final consumer. The underlying thought processes are believed to be equally relevant to many non-commercial service sectors and also to the important sector of industrial services.

PRODUCTS AND BENEFITS
The well-accepted view that products are best understood and defined in terms of customer benefits is central to this article. Two quotes from leading marketing authorities summarise the point succinctly. 'People do not buy products, they buy the expectation of benefits' (Levitt, 1969),[17] 'Customers are looking for particular utilities. Existing products are only a current way of packaging these utilities' (Kotler, 1976).[18] It follows from these views and related notions such as products as 'bundles of goods and/or services'

(Sasser et al., 1978)[19] or the 'sum of the physical and psychological satisfactions the buyer receives' (Miracle, 1965)[20] that all *products*, goods or services, may be defined in terms of benefits or utilities to be obtained through purchase.

It is surprising that, although the benefit concept of products is so widely accepted, it has not been rigorously applied to services in the academic literature in this field.

SERVICES AND MANUFACTURED GOODS – COMPARING LIKE WITH LIKE

If any writer of marketing theory were to lump together washing powders and matches with fridges and carpets or houses and grand pianos and seek to evolve a unified set of marketing principles, such writer would be ridiculed. If the same author threw into this 'broad category' of goods, bespoke suits, handmade pottery or leather saddles, the results would be absurd. Yet in the treatment of services this is exactly what has been done in recent years. Cobbling and dentistry, haircuts and transportation, restaurant service and fast-food outlets, accountancy and tour operating are juxtaposed with little or no qualification or differentiation. For example, no differentiation as a basis for marketing strategy will be found in Rathmell (1974), Stanton (1981) or in any of the contributions already referred to. Even Shostack (1982) finds it appropriate to use a 'corner shoeshine' to illustrate a systems-blueprinting process for service products.

As a contribution to a useful taxonomy of services, we propose simply to adopt the 1923 distinctions of Copeland[21] which, modified for example by Miracle and others, are accepted and used internationally. The classification of convenience, shopping and speciality goods based on customers' buying behaviour is probably best summarised in McCarthy (1978)[22] and is familiar territory to all involved in marketing. For reasons developed later, it is essential to distinguish between services of the 'convenience' variety, which are standardised, frequent-purchase, low-cost items, and others which are shopping or speciality services characterised by infrequent purchase, high cost and a high level of personal commitment. Products, whether based on goods or services, may then be placed on the *same* spectrum.

Miracle (1965)[23] explains the reason for product classification succinctly. 'An observable relationship exists between the characteristics of a product and the approximate marketing mix for that product.' Applying that statement unequivocally to manufactured goods or to services creates no theoretical problem provided always that we continue to compare like with like. Manufactured goods implicitly are usually taken to be mass-produced in volume sufficient to secure national shares of their market sector. No writer pretends that baked beans and handmade lampshades are in the same spectrum of marketing choice. In the same terms why should one expect to make sense of marketing airline seats or commuter rail services by reference to corner shoeshines or haircuts? The view is developed below that mass-produced services and mass-produced physical goods co-exist on the same spectrum of exchange transactions, which is defined by the characteristics of customer buying behaviour. Both types of product can then be seen to have common characteristics which will tend to determine the appropriate marketing mix strategy and tactics.

MASS PRODUCTION OF PRODUCTS

Baker (1979),[24] in reviewing recent contributions on industrial structure and market conduct, demonstrates convincingly that much of the modern rationale for marketing stems from the mass production of manufactured physical goods. Middleton (1975)[25] commented on mass production and mass consumption in the hotel and catering industry, drawing implications for marketing. Mass production based on technological development not only creates a need for consumer orientation in achieving continuous consumption but tends to generate excess capacity competing heavily for the available demand. Interestingly Baker makes no direct reference to mass-produced services, yet the market circumstances and rationale are often identical.

Apart from military services in which the

methods of mass production are arguably centuries old, one may look for the origin of modern mass-production techniques in services rather than in manufacturing. It is commonly supposed that production-line manufacturing methods using steam technology originated the standardised mass-produced physical items with which most marketing texts deal. In fact it is probably in nineteenth-century transport systems that one may trace the earliest really large-scale commercial operations. The expansion and operation of railway systems for example was possible only on the basis of highly systematic production scheduling, timetabling, logistics and quality-control procedures. Such multi-site operations involved standardised products, quality-controlled production and delivery systems and forced attention upon the management of consumption to match the output potential and secure profit. All of these are thoroughly modern concerns for marketing management.

The essence of mass production lies in effective product design and quality control. Once the technical problems of production are solved, the ability to mass-produce forces management attention on the systematic organisation of *continuous* consumption. If demand cannot be so organised, the prospects for financial loss are apparent, be it services such as airline seats since 1979 or manufactured items such as British Leyland cars.

The drives for mass production and economies of scale are, of course, justified by a potential reduction in unit costs with consequent implications for market growth through price reductions or greater profitability. The arguments are well covered in Pickering (1974)[26] for example whilst the profit implications of increasing market shares are noted by Day (1975).[27] Both these contributions focus on manufactured goods rather than services but the emphasis is more on economies of scale in operations than on the techniques of factory production.

At the present time there are no readily accessible data to demonstrate the realities of national and international concentration in service industries output over the last twenty-five years and

especially in the 1970s. Observers, however, can have no doubt that in commercial sectors such as hotels, fast food, industrial catering, transportation, holidays, entertainment, banks, building societies, car rental or telecommunications, the trend to fewer larger companies, noted in manufacturing sectors, has been paralleled in services. As a judgement one may suggest that in each of the sectors noted above, the largest six producers now dominate their respective market sectors. That is to say they are leaders in product design and formulation, research and development, pricing, quality control, distribution and communication techniques.

It is the reality of large-scale mass production of many service products which provides the essential like with like comparison with physical manufactured products. Of course this characteristic has little if anything to do with lawyers, undertakers, cobblers or beauticians. But then neither has it any relevance to basket-weavers, jobbing potters, saddlemakers or gunsmiths. A dentist and a corner shoeshiner have more in common (in marketing terms) with each other and with bakers and candlestick-makers than any of them has in common with mass-produced goods or services.

Academic contributions to practitioners in service sectors tends to reinforce the mass-production concepts discussed here. In a far-sighted article Regan (1963)[28] noted that 'mass production techniques used in manufacturing commodities are being adapted to develop service technologies'. Levitt is more often identified with the proposition in an article on the industrialisation of service production systems (1981).[29] Shostack (1982)[30] pushes the argument one stage further with the notion of 'service blueprinting' as a route to production engineering and quality control in service operations. It bears repeating that large-scale mass production is possible only with standardised, quality-controlled items, the design (or product formulation) of which involves decisions which influence the whole operation. In this we cannot distinguish between the needs and approaches in principle of managers involved –

goods or services – in the key functions of product planning, production operations, distribution, sales or advertising. We must of course stress that mass production is based on overall economies of scale for organisations and in no sense is it implied here that production is restricted to only one or two undifferentiated products. All the complexities of segmentation and product or brand differentiation are as relevant to large producers of services as they are to the manufacturers of physical goods.

MARKETING CAPACITY OR MARKETING PRODUCTS?

If the concept of mass production is wholly applicable to service producers, from an overall standpoint, one can conceive of large-scale producers generating an enormous daily *potential* capacity for service operations. The increasing importance of large multi-site (or multi-outlet) corporations such as hotels, banks, travel agents, car rental firms and so on reinforces the significance of this notion of potential volume capacity.

But the marketing task, with the exception of corporate image campaigns, cannot be handled effectively on an overall capacity basis. Accordingly, large-scale producers of services are obliged to split up their operations into cohesive sub-systems which can be treated as cost/profit centres. This process of subdivision is increasingly just another part of the rationale for product or market management types of organisation, along lines familiar to producers of physical goods. The evidence suggests at least that large service producers are currently reorganising their product/market portfolios in order to manage and market their businesses more effectively.

Thus a hotel chain organises itself to market weekend breaks, conferences, banquets, special events, business accounts, holidays and so on. Airlines, within regional constraints, create marketing campaigns for shuttle services, business class travellers, youth travellers, advance purchase fares, and different types of freight. Banks create campaigns for credit cards, special loan plans, investment services, foreign credit facilities and so

on. The product management implications are obvious.

Large-scale national and international service organisations are now common throughout the Western world. Such firms see themselves as completely involved in product marketing, as their literature and trade press illustrate. They would not recognise any sterile distinctions between *services* and *products* and have already organised themselves for marketing through product management systems. Since many service marketers commenced their careers with manufacturers and subsequently switched to services, it is not surprising that they simply adapted and applied the marketing thought process. It is instructive to see that practitioners of services marketing have already achieved considerable success and business growth in the areas of product design and formulation and product augmentation. (See, for example, Middleton, 1979.)[31] Of course the product management system also has the obvious advantage of securing the economies of large-scale operations and mass production whilst at the same time designing specific products or product variants to meet the identified needs of market segments.

A COMMON CLASSIFICATION OF PRODUCTS – GOODS OR SERVICES

Drawing together the threads of the discussion so far, we can now propose a classification of products (goods or services) on a common basis. Subsequently we may review the characteristics normally associated with services and challenge their relevance. There are three strands in the development of the classification proposed below. The first, already discussed, is the inclusion of mass-produced items only. The second strand draws on the distinctions between physical goods originated by Copeland (1923), and developed by Aspinwall (1961)[32] and Miracle (1965). The only known contribution to this issue in services is from Enis and Roering (1981),[33] who outlined a model for differentiating the marketing mix having regard to the amount of effort buyers put into purchasing products and the amount of 'risk'

TABLE 1:   SPECTRUM OF BUYER BEHAVIOUR CHARACTERISTICS – GOODS OR SERVICES

CONVENIENCE PRODUCTS	SHOPPING PRODUCTS
Mainly low unit value/price	Mainly high unit value/price
Mainly perceived necessities	

<———>

Low problem-solving	High problem-solving
Low information search	High information search
Low customer commitment	High customer commitment
High purchase frequency	Low purchase frequency
High brand loyalty	Low brand loyalty
High-speed decision process	Low decision process speed
High rapidity of consumption	Low rapidity of consumption
Extensive distribution expected	Limited distribution expected

---

perceived by the buyer in his purchase decision. The third strand draws on the concepts of problem-solving by buyers which were developed by Howard and Sheth (1967).[34]

In Table 1, the purchase characteristics are for the most part self-explanatory in the terms used by contributors already noted. It is perhaps worth stressing that low problem-solving implies 'routinised response behavior' as defined by Howard and Sheth. Commitment implies psychological involvement, peer group influences and self-image in so far as these are associated with product purchases. High brand loyalty is used more to denote predisposition towards repeat purchase than any concern for a particular brand, although such concern may well exist.

It is suggested that most, if not all, mass-produced consumer goods and services may be located on the spectrum of buyer behaviour characteristics noted in Table 1. No obvious exceptions have been identified and some typical examples are noted in Table 2.

The examples are chosen and placed at the ends of the spectrum for the purposes of illustration. All products can be located somewhere along the spectrum.

It bears repeating that the spectrum of buyer behaviour is based upon market segments. An airline flight for a senior manager may well be perceived as a convenience product but for a first-time flying pensioner the same flight may be at the furthest end of shopping products. Of course the same is true for manufactured goods since one buyer may select a car as a family workhorse/run-about whilst another sees the same mass-produced model as the fulfilment of his self-image fantasies.

At the convenience end of the products spectrum are located physical goods which are commonly classified as fast-moving consumer goods (f.m.c.g.). The spectrum serves to indicate that there are also services with similar characteristics which it would be appropriate to classify as fast moving consumer services (f.m.c.s.). There would appear to be an obvious route from determining the place of a product (goods or services based) on the spectrum to theorising about market mix implications. Present attempts to produce generally valid models do not appear notably successful and the temptation to propose another model is resisted pending further research.

THE MARKETING CHARACTERISTICS OF SERVICE PRODUCTS

In the light of the preceding discussion of the spectrum of products, it is now possible to review the four characteristics of services which Stanton and others hold to be differences in principle between goods and services. The characteristics are important since, if true, they determine marketing

TABLE 2:   SPECTRUM OF PRODUCTS ASSOCIATED WITH THE SPECTRUM OF BUYER BEHAVIOUR

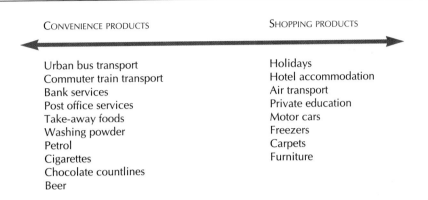

CONVENIENCE PRODUCTS	SHOPPING PRODUCTS
Urban bus transport	Holidays
Commuter train transport	Hotel accommodation
Bank services	Air transport
Post office services	Private education
Take-away foods	Motor cars
Washing powder	Freezers
Petrol	Carpets
Cigarettes	Furniture
Chocolate countlines	
Beer	

mix responses. As noted earlier they are *heterogeneity, intangibility, perishability* and *inseparability*. Heterogeneity means that every service is literally unique and therefore that rigorous product quality control methods are impossible to achieve. From the earlier discussion of mass production for service operations it will be clear that successful marketing of service-based convenience products is in fact a function of efficient production quality controls and that homogeneity in products is as much a matter for concern for producers of fast-moving consumer services as it is for producers of fast-moving consumer goods. Heterogeneity cannot be therefore a distinguishing characteristic of all services. It may be a feature of craft industries and of haircutting and dentistry, but they are not our concern in this article.

Intangibility means that service products cannot be felt, touched, measured, seen or sampled prior to consumption. Yet the very frequency of repeat consumption at banks, industrial canteens or urban transport implies a buyer familiarity with products which effectively nullifies any notion of intangibility in relation to fast-moving consumer services. Certainly some service products such as holidays are predominantly intangible but so too, as several authors have pointed out, are cars, many consumer durables and in the final analysis virtually all products. With sophisticated items such as cars, TV sets, video recorders

or home computers, customers have to place trust in the producers' ability to deliver the sought benefits, and in this we cannot see any difference in principle with the case of 'shopping' type service products.

Perishability of service products means that producers are unable to store or stockpile their output in response to fluctuations in demand. It is of course apparent that service producers operate a capacity for production by the hour or the day which, if not sold at those times, cannot be stocked and subsequently sold. This characteristic places special emphasis on demand management, as Sasser et al. (1978)[35] and others have noted. But in market conditions of fierce competition, financial stringency and cash flow problems, *any* mass-produced physical product also has a strictly limited capacity for stock-building. The impact on profit of unsold stocks of manufactured convenience goods (f.m.c.g.) is immediate and we cannot see that a focus on demand management is an important distinguishing characteristic of service products (f.m.c.s.).

Inseparability means that service products are produced and consumed at the same time, usually on the producers' premises. By contrast most physical goods are manufactured in factory premises in conditions and places and at times which are not directly linked with the act of consumption or use. Inseparability, sometimes referred to as the simultaneity of production and consumption, is the only one of Stanton's four characteristics which can be justified as distinguishing in principle between goods and services.

As the main distinguishing characteristic, the fact of inseparability is typically held to be a disadvantage in the marketing of products which are service-based. In comparison with the clinical conditions and automation of processes which apply in most modern factories, producers of convenience services have a much more difficult task in achieving product quality control. Employees' behaviour and attitudes are involved in, and in some cases are the main basis of, customers' satisfaction with a product. Somewhat akin to a 'live' as contrasted with a pre-recorded broadcast, the consistent delivery of the designed product cannot be engineered precisely. Even where in Levitt's phrase 'industrialisation' of service components has occurred, the scope for faulty performance is still considerable. Having customers on the premises may also create problems if different segments of buyers for the same products are not mutually sympathetic. The attitudes of a segment of young people may drive older customers from a pub. A football special train may alienate regular rail travellers. Social class differences or racial antagonisms may generate dissonance between market segments with damaging effects upon total demand. With so many behavioural variables at work with and between groups of employees and consumers it is not a matter for surprise that product consistency in services is often an elusive goal. Nevertheless the management attempt to achieve consistency does not appear to be different in kind between goods and services although, of course, the methods applied are vastly different.

Less obviously, inseparability also conveys advantages to marketers of service products. It means that producer and consumer are in constant and immediate communication. It is, for example, possible to design and control precisely the environment in which consumption or use of the product occurs. Having customers on the premises opens low-cost routes for obtaining market feedback and research information which manufacturers of physical goods must envy. The active participation of the customer in the product delivery process allows scope for product differentiation and augmentation which gives flexibility in product design. Contrary to the common view that test marketing is difficult to achieve in services, the opposite appears true for multi-site operators who seek to test customer responses to innovation. Above all, the fact of inseparability permits of techniques of on-site sales promotion and merchandising at the point of consumption under fully controlled conditions and without the competitive 'noise' which surrounds the point of purchase of most manufactured goods. One may speculate that it has been the practical advantage of inseparability of consumer and producer more than any other product characteristic which has made it less necessary historically for service producers to engage in many of the orthodox marketing techniques designed for producers of goods. Interestingly, much of this advantage is lost where large-scale multi-site operations are controlled by headquarters remote from the service delivery process. Perhaps it is not so surprising that some of Levitt's illustrations of 'marketing myopia' were early, multi-site, service producers who over time lost touch with their vital natural asset of inseparability.

Although not specifically discussed by Stanton, the concept of inseparability has important implications for the distribution process for service products, which has frequently been held to distinguish services from goods. Thus Lovelock (1981)[36] noted that 'the marketer's task in manufacturing firms includes developing strategies for physically moving the product from the factory to the customer. Because services delivered to the person or the consumer are consumed as they are produced, the service factory, retail outlet and consumption point are often one and the same …' Lovelock also states that, 'Because a service is a deed or performance, rather than a tangible item, it cannot be inventoried.' Writing specifically in the context of the American hospitality industry in 1981, Reneghan[37] made the same point, 'service cannot be inventoried'. In view of the vast international reservations systems operated by airlines, hotels, car rental and tour operators, this distribution fallacy is astonishing. It appears to arise from confusing inseparability of production and consumption with inseparability of consumption and purchase. In practice, much of the thrust and emphasis of services marketing is specifically designed to separate consumption and purchase by selling services in advance of the date of consumption. A successful hotel is one which is fully booked in July by the end of May. A successful tour operator will be able to predict occupancy rates for August by the end of February. Both organisations have effectively inventoried their monthly capacity, packaged it in product form and sold it weeks in advance of actual service delivery.

In considering the distribution of service products the Grönroos (1978)[38] notion of accessibility is helpful. Instead of managing the physical movement or flow of goods from producer to consumer, service producers create access to their inventory whereby consumers can reserve and purchase the future performance of service products. For example, retail travel agents perform an access function for travel products which is in many ways precisely analogous to the distribution function which other retailers perform for physical goods. Thus by substituting access channels for physical distribution channels we can overcome any theoretical difficulties about inventories and seek to apply distribution theories to service products. Channels have been discussed by several people including Kaven (in Rathmell, 1974),[39] Donelly (1976),[40] Middleton (1980),[41] and Bitner and Booms (1981).[42] Modern information technology and the use of computers in controlling reservation systems are providing new tools for service marketers and whilst the logistics of moving physical products to consumers are not relevant in services, the significance of distribution strategies in marketing services is certainly well recognised.

SUMMARY

This article has sought to align the marketing of goods and services alike through the unifying concept of the product. A necessary proviso is that any realistic comparison of goods and services rests firmly on the characteristics of large-scale, mass-production operations generating products which are mostly in national distribution. The exclusion of craft-based goods and services is an essential aspect of the discussion.

The by now traditional and perhaps hackneyed characteristics attributed to services are firmly rejected as sterile and distorting. A consumer-oriented analysis of buyer behaviour is used to provide the dimensions of a marketing spectrum of products which accommodates both goods and services.

The characteristics of purchases of fast-moving consumer goods (f.m.c.g.) are seen to be equally applicable to many services and we therefore coin the phrase fast-moving consumer services (f.m.c.s.) in order to draw the parallels rather than the distinctions between goods and services. So far as is known the notion of f.m.c.s. has not been used elsewhere.

Applying the unifying concept of the product, we find that attempting to differentiate between the marketing of goods and services is unhelpful. A more productive approach focuses on common characteristics of product types, whether they are based on goods or services, and the marketing mix implications which these product types have in common.

NOTES

1. M.J. Baker (1981), 'Services: Salvation or Servitude?', *Quarterly Review of Marketing*, vol. 6, no. 3, Spring.

2. W.J. Stanton (1981), *Fundamentals of Marketing*, 6th edition, McGraw-Hill, NY.

3. Baker, 'Services: Salvation or Servitude?'

4. T. Levitt (1981), 'Marketing Intangible Products and Product Intangibles', *Harvard Business Review*, May–June.

5. P. Kotler (1980), *Marketing Management, Analysis, Planning and Control*, 4th edition, Prentice-Hall Int., London.

6. M.J. Baker (1979), *Marketing, an Introductory Text*, 3rd edition, Macmillan, London.

7. Stanton, *Fundamentals of Marketing*.

8. R.G. Wyckham, T. Fitzroy and G.D. Mandry (1975), "Marketing Services', *European Journal of Marketing*, vol. 9, no. 1.

9. C. Grönroos (1978), 'A Service-oriented Approach to Marketing of Services', *European Journal of Marketing*, vol. 12, no. 8.

10. G.L. Shostack (1982), 'How to Design a Service', *European Journal of Marketing*, vol. 16, no. 1.

11. M. Christopher, S.H. Kennedy, M. McDonald and G. Wills (1980), *Effective Marketing Management*, Farnborough, Gower.

12. J.M. Rathmell (1974), *Marketing in the Services Sector*, Winthrop, Cambridge, Mass.

13. Shostack, 'How to Design a Service'.

14. P. Kotler (1975), *Marketing for Non Profit Organisations*, Prentice Hall, NY.

15. P. Kotler and S.J. Levy (1969), 'Broadcasting the Concept of Marketing', *Journal of Marketing*, vol. 33, no. 1.

16. Baker, *Marketing, an Introductory Text*.

17. T. Levitt (1969), *European Business*.

18. P. Kotler (1976), *Marketing Management, Analysis, Planning and Control*, 3rd edition, Prentice-Hall Int., London.

19. W.E. Sasser, R.P. Olsen and D.D. Wyckoff (1978), *Management of Service Operations*, Allyn and Bacon, Boston, Mass.

20. G.E. Miracle (1965), 'Product Characteristics and Marketing Strategy', *Journal of Marketing*, vol. 29, no. 1, January.

21. M.T. Copeland (1923), 'Relation of Consumers' Buying Habits to Marketing Methods', *Harvard Business Review*, vol. 1, April.

22. E.J. McCarthy (1978), *Basic Marketing: A Managerial Approach*, 6th edition, Irwin, Ill.

23. Miracle, 'Product Characteristics'.

24. Baker, *Marketing, an Introductory Text*.

25. V.T.C. Middleton (1975), 'The Marketing of Accommodation' in R. Kotas, *Marketing Orientation in the Hotel and Catering Industry*, University Press, Surrey, London.

26. J.F. Pickering (1974), *Industrial Structure and Market Conduct*, Martin Robertson, London.

27. G.S. Day (1975), 'A Strategic Perspective on Product Planning', *Journal of Contemporary Business*, vol. 4, no. 2, Spring.

28. William J. Regan (1963), 'The Service Revolution', *Journal of Marketing*, vol. 27, no. 1, July.

29. T. Levitt (1981), 'Production Line Approach to Service', *Harvard Business Review*, May–June.

30. Shostack, 'How to Design a Service'.

31. V.T.C. Middleton (1979), 'Tourism Marketing – Product Implications', *International Tourism Quarterly*, no. 3.

32. L.V. Aspinwall (1961), 'The Marketing Characteristics of Goods', reprinted in B.M. Enis and K.K. Cox (1977), *Marketing Classics*, 3rd edition, Allyn and Bacon, Boston, Mass.

33. B.M. Enis and K.J. Roering (1981), 'Services Marketing: Different Products, Similar Strategy', *Marketing of Services*, American Marketing Association Conference Proceedings.

34. J.A. Howard and J.N. Sheth (1967), 'A Theory of Buyer Behaviour', reprinted in B.M. Enis and K.K. Cox (1977), *Marketing Classics* (see note 32).

35. Sasser et al., *Management of Service Operations*.

36. C.H. Lovelock (1981), 'Why Marketing Management Needs to Be Different for Services' in *Marketing of Services*, AMA Conference, 1981.

37. L.M. Reneghan (1981), 'A New Marketing Mix for the Hospitality Industry', *Cornell Hotel and Restaurant Administration Quarterly*, August.

38. Grönroos, 'A Service-oriented Approach to Marketing of Services'.

39. W.H. Kaven (1974), 'Channels of Distribution in the Hotel Industry' in Rathmell, *Marketing in the Services Sector*.

40. J. Donelly (1976), 'Marketing Intermediaries in Channels of Distribution for Services', *Journal of Marketing*, vol. 40, no. 1, January.

41. V.T.C. Middleton (1980), 'Marketing Implications of Direct Selling in the Holiday Market', *International Tourism Quarterly*, no. 2.

42. M.J. Bitner and H.B. Booms (1981), 'Deregulation and Future of US Travel Agent Industry', *Journal of Travel Research*, vol. 20, no. 2.

Breaking Free from Product Marketing

G. *Lynn Shostack*

Service marketers urgently require concepts and strategies that are relevant to their actual situations. Traditionally, the marketing discipline has been overwhelmingly oriented to practices in the manufacturing sector, especially mass-produced, packaged consumer goods. The theme of this article is that many insights from goods (or 'product') marketing are not directly transferable to the service sector. **

New concepts are necessary if service marketing is to succeed. Service marketing is an uncharted frontier. Despite the increasing dominance of services in the US economy, basic texts still disagree on how services should be treated in a marketing context.[1]

The heart of this dispute is the issue of applicability. The classic marketing 'mix', the seminal literature and the language of marketing all derive from the manufacture of physical goods. Practising marketers tend to think in terms of products, particularly mass-market consumer goods. Some service companies even call their output 'products' and have 'product' management functions modelled after those of experts such as Procter and Gamble.

Marketing seems to be overwhelmingly product-oriented. However, many service-based companies are confused about the applicability of product marketing, and more than one attempt to adopt product marketing has failed.

Merely adopting product marketing's labels does not resolve the question of whether product marketing can be overlaid on service businesses. Can corporate banking services really be marketed according to the same basic blueprint that made *Tide* a success? Given marketing's historic tenets, there is simply no alternative.

Could marketing itself be 'myopic' in having failed to create relevant paradigms for the service sector? Many marketing professionals who transfer to the services arena find their work fundamentally 'different', but have a difficult time articulating how and why their priorities and concepts have changed. Often, they also find to their frustration and bewilderment that 'marketing' is treated as a peripheral function or is confused with one of its components, such as research or advertising, and kept within a very narrow scope of influence and authority.[2]

The situation is frequently rationalised as being due to the 'ignorance' of senior management in service businesses. 'Education' is usually recommended as the solution. However, an equally feasible, though less comforting, explanation is

* *Editor's note:* Marketing academics and practitioners increasingly use the word *product* as a generic term to describe both goods and services. In this article, however, the author equates the word *product* with *manufactured goods.*

Reprinted with permission from *Journal of Marketing*, vol. 41, April, pp. 73–80.
Copyright © 1977 by American Marketing Association, Chicago.

that service industries have been slow to integrate marketing into the mainstream of decision-making and control because marketing offers no guidance, terminology or practical rules that are clearly relevant to service.

MAKING ROOM FOR INTANGIBILITY

The American Marketing Association cites both goods *and* services as foci for marketing activities. Squeezing services into the Procrustean phrase 'intangible products'[3] is not only a distortion of the AMA's definition, but a complete contradiction in terms.

It is wrong to imply that services are just like products 'except' for intangibility. By such logic apples are just like oranges, except for their 'apple-ness'. Intangibility is not a modifier; it is a state. Intangibles may come with tangible trappings, but no amount of money can buy physical ownership of such intangibles as 'experience' (movies), 'time' (consultants) or 'process' (dry cleaning). A service is rendered. A service is experienced. A service cannot be stored on a shelf, touched, tasted, or tried on for size. 'Tangible' means 'palpable' and 'material'. 'Intangible' is an antonym, meaning '*im*palpable' and '*not* corporeal'.[4] This distinction has profound implications. Yet marketing offers no way to treat intangibility as the core element it is, nor does marketing offer usable tools for managing, altering or controlling this amorphous core.

Even the most thoughtful attempts to broaden the definition of 'that which is marketed' away from product synonymity suffer from an underlying assumption of tangibility. Not long ago, Philip Kotler argued that 'values' should be considered the end result of 'marketing'.[5] However, the text went on to imply that 'values' were created by 'objects', and drifted irredeemably into the classic product axioms.

To truly expand marketing's conceptual boundaries requires a framework which accommodates intangibility instead of denying it. Such a framework must give equal descriptive weight to the components of 'service' as it does to the concept of 'product'.

THE COMPLEXITY OF MARKETED ENTITIES

What kind of framework would provide a new conceptual viewpoint? One unorthodox possibility can be drawn from direct observation of the market-place and the nature of the market 'satisfiers' available to it. Taking a fresh look, it seems that there are really very few, if any, 'pure' products or services in the market-place.

Examine, for instance, the automobile. Without question, one might say it is a physical object, with a full range of tangible features and options. But another, equally important element is marketed in tandem with the steel and chrome – i.e. the service of transportation. Transportation is an *independent* marketing element; in other words, it is not car-dependent, but can be marketed in its own right. A car is only one alternative for satisfying the market's transportation needs.

This presents a semantic dilemma. How should the automobile be defined? Is General Motors marketing a *service*, a service that happens to include a *by*-product called a car? Levitt's classic 'Marketing Myopia' exhorts businessmen to think in exactly this generic way about what they market.[6] Are automobiles 'tangible services'? It cannot be denied that both elements – tangible and intangible – exist and are vigorously marketed. Yet they are, by definition, different qualities, and to attempt to compress them into a single word or phrase begs the issue.

Conversely, how shall a service such as airline transportation be described? Although the service itself is intangible, there are certain very real things that belong in any description of the total entity, including such important tangibles as decor, food and drink, seat design, and overall graphic continuity from tickets to attendants' uniforms. These items can dramatically affect the 'reality' of the service in the consumer's mind. However, there is no accurate way to lump them into a one-word description.

If 'either-or' terms (product versus service) do not adequately describe the true nature of marketed entities, it makes sense to explore the usefulness of a new *structural* definition. This broader

EXHIBIT 1:   DIAGRAM OF MARKET ENTITIES

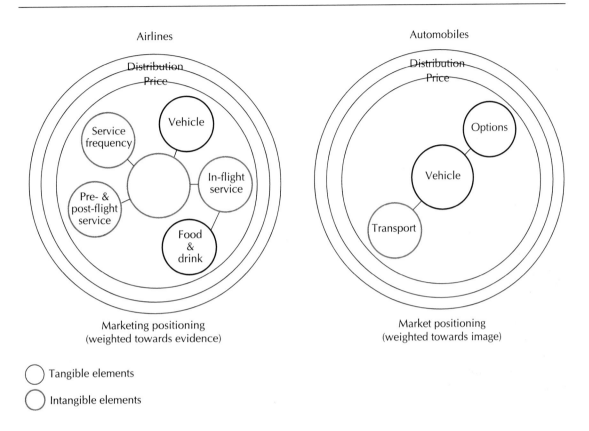

concept postulates that market entities are, in reality, *combinations* of discrete *elements* which are linked together in molecule-like wholes. Elements can be either tangible or intangible. The entity may have either a tangible or an intangible nucleus. But the whole can only be described as having a certain dominance.

MOLECULAR MODEL

A 'molecular' model offers opportunities for visualisation and management of a total market entity. It reflects the fact that a market entity can be partly tangible *and* partly intangible, without diminishing the importance of either characteristic. Not only can the potential be seen for picturing and dealing with multiple *elements*, rather than a *thing*, but the concept of dominance can lead to enriched considerations of the priorities

and approach that may be required of a marketer. Moreover, the model suggests the scientific analogy that if market entities have multiple elements, a deliberate or inadvertent change to a *single* element may completely alter the entity, as the simple switching of Fe_3O_2 to Fe_2O_3 creates a new substance. For this reason, a marketer must carefully manage all the elements, especially those for service-based entities, which may not have been considered previously within his domain.

DIAGRAMMING MARKET ENTITIES

A simplified comparison demonstrates the conceptual usefulness of a molecular modelling system. In Exhibit 1, automobiles and airline travel are broken down into their major elements. As shown, these two entities have different nuclei. They also differ in dominance.

EXHIBIT 2:   SCALE OF MARKET ENTITIES

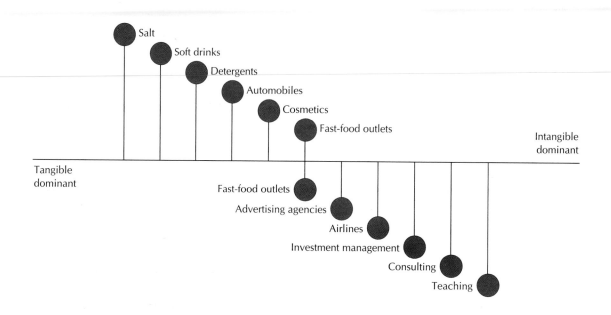

Clearly, airline travel is intangible-dominant; that is, it does not yield physical ownership of a tangible good. Nearly all of the other important elements in the entity are intangible as well. Individual elements and their combinations represent unique satisfiers to different market segments. Thus:

▷ For some markets – students, for example – pure transport takes precedence over all other considerations. The charter flight business was based on this element. As might be expected during lean economic times, 'no frills' flights show renewed emphasis on this nuclear core.

▷ For business travellers, on the other hand, schedule frequency may be paramount.

▷ Tourists, a third segment, may respond most strongly to the combination of in-flight and post-flight services.

As the market entity of airline travel has evolved, it has become more and more complex.

Ongoing reweighting of elements can be observed, for example, in the marketing of airline food, which was once a battleground of quasi-gourmet offerings. Today, some airlines have stopped marketing food altogether, while others are repositioning it primarily to the luxury markets.

AIRLINES VERSUS AUTOMOBILES

In comparing airlines to automobiles, one sees obvious similarities. The element of transportation is common to both, as it is to boats, trains, buses and bicycles. Tangible décor also plays a role in both entities. Yet in spite of their similarities, the two entities are not the same, either in configuration or in marketing implications.

In some ways, airline travel and automobiles are mirror opposites. A car is a physical possession that renders a service. Airline travel, on the other hand, cannot be physically possessed. It can only be experienced. While the inherent 'promise' of a car is service, airline transportation often promises a Lewis Carroll version of *'product'*, i.e. *destination*, which is marketed as though it were physically obtainable. If only tropical islands and redwood forests *could* be purchased for the price of an airline ticket!

The model can be completed by adding the remaining major marketing elements in a way that demonstrates their function *vis-à-vis* the organic core entity. First, the total entity is ringed and defined by a set value or price. Next, the valued entity is circumscribed by its distribution. Finally, the entire entity is encompassed, according to its core configuration, by its public 'face', i.e. its positioning to the market.

The molecular concept makes it possible to describe and array market entities along a continuum, according to the weight of the 'mix' of elements that comprise them. As Exhibit 2 indicates, teaching services might be at one end of such a scale, *intangible* or *I-dominant*, while salt might represent the other extreme, *tangible* or *T-dominant*. Such a scale accords intangible-based entities a place and weight commensurate with their true importance. The framework also provides a mechanism for comparison and market positioning.

In one of the handful of books devoted to services, the author holds that 'the more intangible the service, the greater will be the difference in the marketing characteristics of the service'.[7] Consistent with an entity scale, this axiom might now be amended to read: 'The greater the weight of intangible elements in a market entity, the greater will be the divergence from product marketing in priorities and approach.'

IMPLICATIONS OF THE MOLECULAR MODEL

The hypothesis proposed by molecular modelling carries intriguing potential for rethinking and reshaping classic marketing concepts and practices. Recognition that service-dominant entities differ from product-dominant entities allows consideration of other distinctions which have been intuitively understood, but seldom articulated by service marketers.

A most important area of difference is immediately apparent – i.e. that service 'knowledge' and product 'knowledge' cannot be gained in the same way.

A *product* marketer's first task is to 'know' his product. For tangible-dominant entities this is relatively straightforward. A tangible object can be described precisely. It is subject to physical examination or photographic reproduction or quantitative measure. It can be not only exactly replicated, but modified in precise and duplicate ways.

It is not particularly difficult for the marketer of *Coca-Cola*, for example, to summon all the facts regarding the product itself. He can and does make reasonable assumptions about the product's behaviour, e.g. that it is consistent chemically to the taste, visually to the eye, and physically in its packaging. Any changes he might make in these three areas can be deliberately controlled for uniformity since they will be tangibly evident. In other words, the marketer can take the product's 'reality' for granted and move on to considerations of price, distribution, and advertising or promotion.

To gain *service* 'knowledge', however, or knowledge of a service element, where does one begin? It has been pointed out that intangible elements are dynamic, subjective and ephemeral. They cannot be touched, tried on for size, or displayed on a shelf. They are exceedingly difficult to quantify.

Reverting to airline travel, precisely what is the service of air transportation to the potential purchaser? What 'per cent' of airline travel is comfort? What 'per cent' is fear or adventure? What is this service's 'reality' to its market? And how does that reality vary from segment to segment? Since this service exists only during the time in which it is rendered, the entity's true 'reality' must be defined experientially, not in engineering terms.

A NEW APPROACH TO SERVICE DEFINITION

Experiential definition is a little-explored area of marketing practice. A product-based marketer is in danger of assuming he understands an intangible-dominant entity when, in fact, he may only be projecting his *own* subjective version of 'reality'. And because there is no documented guidance on acquiring service knowledge, the chances for error are magnified.

CASE EXAMPLE

One short-lived mistake (with which the author is familiar) occurred recently in the trust department of a large commercial bank. The department head, being close to daily operations, understood 'investment management' as the combined work of hundreds of people, backed by the firm's stature, resources and long history. With this 'reality' in mind, he concluded that the service could be better represented by professional salesmen than through the traditional, but interruptive use of the portfolio manager as main client contact.

Three salesmen were hired, and given a training course in investments. They failed dismally, both in maintaining current client relationships and in producing new business for the firm. In hindsight, it became clear that the department head misunderstood the service's 'reality' as it was being experienced by his clients. To the clients, 'investment *management*' was found to mean 'investment *manager*' – i.e. a single human being upon whom they depended for decisions and advice. No matter how well prepared, the professional salesman was not seen as an acceptable substitute by the majority of the market.

VERSIONS OF REALITY

Clearly, more than one version of 'reality' can be found in a service market. Therefore, the crux of service knowledge is the description of the major *consensus realities* that define the service entity to various market segments. The determination of consensus realities should be a high priority for service marketers, and marketing should offer more concrete guidance and emphasis on this subject than it does.

To define the market-held 'realities' of a service requires a high tolerance for subjective, 'soft' data, combined with a rigidly objective attitude towards that data. To understand what a service entity is to a market, the marketer must undertake more initial research than is common in product marketing. More important, it will be research of a different kind than is the case in product marketing. The marketer must rely heavily on the tools and skills of psychology, sociology and other behav-

ioural sciences – tools that in product marketing usually come into play in determining *image*, rather than fundamental 'reality'.

In developing the blueprint of a service entity's main elements, the marketer might find, for instance, that although tax return preparation is analogous to 'accurate mathematical computation' within his firm, it means 'freedom from responsibility' to one segment of the consuming public, 'opportunity for financial savings' to another segment, and 'convenience' to yet a third segment.

Unless these 'realities' are documented and ranked by market importance, no sensible plan can be devised to represent a service effectively or deliberately. And in *new* service development, the importance of the service research function is even more critical, because the successful development of a new service – a molecular collection of intangibles – is so difficult it makes new-product development look like child's play.

IMAGE VERSUS EVIDENCE – THE KEY

The definition of consensus realities should not be confused with the determination of 'image'. Image is a method of *differentiating* and *representing* an entity to its target market. Image is not 'product', nor is it 'service'. As was suggested in Exhibit 1, there appears to be a critical difference between the way tangible- and intangible-dominant entities are best represented to their markets. Examination of actual cases suggests a common thread among effective representations of services that is another mirror-opposite contrast to product techniques.

In comparing examples, it is clear that consumer product marketing often approaches the market by enhancing a physical object through abstract associations. *Coca-Cola*, for example, is surrounded with visual, verbal and aural associations with authenticity and youth. Although *Dr Pepper* would also be physically categorised as a beverage, its *image* has been structured to suggest 'originality' and 'risk-taking'; while *7-up* is 'light' and 'buoyant'. A high priority is placed on linking these abstract images to physical items.

But a service is already abstract. To compound the abstraction dilutes the 'reality' that the marketer is trying to enhance. Effective service representations appear to be turned 180° *away* from abstraction. The reason for this is that service images, and even service 'realities', appear to be shaped to a large extent by the things that the consumer can comprehend with his five senses – tangible things. But a service itself cannot be tangible, so reliance must be placed on *peripheral* clues.

Tangible clues are what allow the detective in a mystery novel to surmise events at the scene of a crime without having been present. Similarly, when a consumer attempts to judge a service, particularly before using or buying it, that service is 'known' by the tangible clues, the tangible evidence, that surround it.

The management of tangible evidence is not articulated in marketing as a primary priority for service marketers. There has been little in-depth exploration of the *range* of authority that emphasis on tangible evidence would create for the service marketer. In product marketing, tangible evidence is primarily the product itself. But for services, tangible evidence would encompass broader considerations in contrast to product marketing, *different* considerations than are typically considered marketing's domain today.

FOCUSING ON THE EVIDENCE

In *product* marketing, many kinds of evidence are beyond the marketer's control and are consequently omitted from priority consideration in the market position process. Product marketing tends to give first emphasis to creating *abstract* associations.

Service marketers, on the other hand, should be focused on enhancing the differentiating 'realities' through manipulation of *tangible* clues. The management of evidence comes first for service marketers, because service 'reality' is arrived at by the consumer mostly through a process of deduction, based on the total impression that the evidence creates. Because of product marketing's biases, service marketers often fail to recognise the unique forms of evidence that they *can* normally control and fail to see that they should be part of marketing's responsibilities.

MANAGEMENT OF THE ENVIRONMENT

Environment is a good example. Since product distribution normally means shipping to outside agents, the marketer has little voice in structuring the environment in which the product is sold. His major controllable impact on the environment is usually product packaging. Services, on the other hand, are often fully integrated with environment; that is, the setting in which the service is 'distributed' *is* controllable. To the extent possible, management of the physical environment should be one of a service marketer's highest priorities.

Setting can play an enormous role in influencing the 'reality' of a service in the consumer's mind. Marketing does not emphasise this rule for services, yet there are numerous obvious examples of its importance.

Physicians' offices provide an interesting example of intuitive environmental management. Although the quality of medical service may be identical, an office furnished in teak and leather creates a totally different 'reality' in the consumer's mind from one with plastic slipcovers and inexpensive prints. Carrying the example further, a marketer could expect to cause change in the service's image simply by painting a physician's office walls neon pink or silver, instead of white.

Similarly, although the services may be identical, the consumer's differentiation between 'Bank A Service' and 'Bank B Service' is materially affected by whether the environment is dominated by butcher-block and bright colours or by marble and polished brass.

By understanding the importance of evidence management, the service marketer can make it his business to review and take control of this critical part of his 'mix'. Creation of an environment can be deliberate, rather than accidental or as a result of leaving such decisions in the hands of the interior decorators.

EXHIBIT 3:   PRINCIPLE OF MARKETING
             POSITIONING EMPHASIS

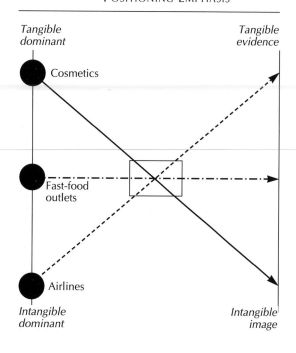

Tangible
dominant

Cosmetics

Fast-food
outlets

Airlines

Intangible
dominant

Tangible
evidence

Intangible
image

INTEGRATING EVIDENCE

Going beyond environment, evidence can be integrated across a wide range of items. Airlines, for example, manage and co-ordinate tangible evidence, and do it better than almost any large service industry. Whether by intuition or design, airlines do *not* focus on trying to explain or characterise the service itself. One never sees an ad that attempts to convey 'the slant of take-off', 'the feel of acceleration' or 'the aerodynamics of lift'. Airline transport is given shape and form through consistency of a firm's identification, its uniforms, the décor of its planes, its graphics, and its advertising. Differentiation among airlines, though they all provide the same service, is a direct result of differences in 'packages' of evidence.

Some businesses in which tangible and intangible elements carry equal weight emphasise abstractions and evidence in about equal proportions. McDonald's is an excellent example. The food *product* is associated with 'nutritious' (two all-beef, etc.), 'fun' (Ronald McDonald) and

'helpful' ('We Do It All for You', 'You Deserve a Break Today'). The main *service* element, i.e. fast-food preparation, is tangibly distinguished by uniformity of environment, colour and style of graphics and apparel, consistency of delivery (young employees), and the ubiquitous golden arches.

Using the scale developed in Exhibit 2, this concept can be postulated as a principle for service representation. As shown in Exhibit 3, once an entity has been analysed and positioned on the scale, the degree to which the marketer will focus on either tangible evidence or intangible abstractions for market positioning will be found to be *inversely related to the entity's dominance.*

The more intangible elements there are, the more the marketer must endeavour to stand in the consumer's shoes, thinking through and gaining control of *all* the inputs to the consumer's mind that can be classified as material evidence.

Some forms of evidence can seem trivial until one recognises how great their impact can be on service perception. Correspondence is one example. Letters, statements and the like are sometimes the main conveyers of the 'reality' of a service to its market, yet often these are treated as peripheral to any marketing plan. From the grade of paper to the choice of colours, correspondence is visible evidence that conveys a unique message. A mimeographed, non-personalised, cheaply offset letter contradicts any words about service quality that may appear in the text of that letter. Conversely, engraved parchment from the local dry cleaner might make one wonder about its prices.

PROFILE AS EVIDENCE

As was pointed out in the investment management example, services are often inextricably entwined with their human representatives. In many fields, a person is perceived to *be* the service. The consumer cannot distinguish between them. Product marketing is myopic in dealing with the issue of *people as evidence* in terms of market positioning. Consumer marketing often stops at the production of materials and programmes for salesmen to use. Some service industries, on the other hand, have long intuitively managed human evidence to larger ends.

Examples of this principle have been the basis for jokes, plays and literature. 'The Man in the Grey Flannel Suit', for example, was a synonym for the advertising business for many years. Physicians are uniformly 'packaged' in smocks. Lawyers and bankers are still today known for pinstripes and vests. IBM representatives were famous for adhering to a 'White Shirt' policy. Going beyond apparel, as mentioned earlier, McDonald's even achieves age uniformity – an extra element reinforcing its total market image.

These examples add up to a serious principle when thoughtfully reviewed. They are particularly instructive for service marketers. None of the above examples was the result of deliberate market planning. McDonald's, for instance, backed into age consistency as a result of trying to keep labour costs low. Airlines are the single outstanding example of consciously planned standards for uniformity in human representation. The power of the human evidence principle is obvious, and the potential power of more deliberately controlling or structuring this element is clear.

Lest this discussion be interpreted as an advocacy of regimentation, it should be pointed out that management of human evidence can be as basic as providing name-tags to service representatives or as complex as the 'packaging' of a political candidate, whose very words are often chosen by committee and whose hairstyle can become a critical policy issue. Or, depending upon what kind of service 'reality' the marketer wishes to create, human representation can be encouraged to display *non*conformity, as is the case with the 'creative' departments of advertising agencies. The point is that service marketers should be charged with tactics and strategy in this area, and must consider it a management responsibility.

SERVICES AND THE MEDIA
As has been previously discussed, service elements are abstract. Because they are abstract, the mar-

keter must work hard at making them 'real' by building a case from tangible evidence. In this context, media advertising presents a particularly difficult problem.

The problem revolves around the fact that media (television, radio, print) are one step removed from tangibility. Media, by their McLuhanesque nature, abstract the physical.

Even though product tangibility provides an anchor for media representation because a product can be *shown*, media still abstract products. A photograph is only a two-dimensional version of a physical object, and may be visually misleading. Fortunately, the consumer makes the mental connection between seeing a product in the media and recognising it in reality. This is true even when a product is substantially distorted. Sometimes, only part of a product is shown. Occasionally, as in recent commercials for *7-up*, the product is *not* shown. However, the consumer remembers past experience. He has little difficulty recognising *7-up* by name or remembered appearance when he sees it or wants to buy it.

Thus, media work *with* the creation of product image and *help* in adding abstract qualities to tangible goods. Cosmetics, for example, are often positioned in association with an airbrushed or soft-focus filmed *ideal* of beauty. Were the media truly accurate, the wrinkles and flaws of the flesh, to which even models are heir, might not create such an appealing product association.

MAKING SERVICES MORE CONCRETE
Because of their abstracting capabilities, the media often make service entities more hazy, instead of more *concrete*, and the service marketer must work *against* this inherent effect. Unfortunately, many marketers are so familiar with product-oriented thinking that they go down precisely the wrong path and attempt to represent services by dealing with them in abstractions.

The pages of the business press are filled with examples of this type of misconception in services advertising. In advertisements for investment managers, for instance, the worst examples attempt to describe the already intangible service with *more* abstractions such as 'sound analysis', 'careful portfolio monitoring', 'strong research capability', etc. Such compounded abstractions do *not* help the consumer form a 'reality', do *not* differentiate the service and do *not* achieve any credibility, much less any consumer 'draw'.

The best examples are those which attempt to associate the service with some form of *tangible evidence*, working against the media's abstracting qualities. Merrill Lynch, for instance, has firmly associated itself with a clear visual symbol of bulls and concomitant bullishness. Where Merrill Lynch does not use the visual herd, it uses photographs of *tangible physical booklets*, and invites the consumer to write for them.

Therefore, the final principle offered for service marketers would hold that effective media representation of intangibles is a function of establishing non-abstract manifestations of them.

CONCLUSION

This article has presented several market-inspired thoughts towards the development of new marketing concepts, and the evolution of relevant service marketing principles. The hypotheses presented here do not by any means represent an exhaustive analysis of the subject. No exploration was done, for example, on product versus service pricing or product versus service distribution. Both areas offer rich potential for creative new approaches and analysis.

It can be argued that there are many grey areas in the molecular entity concept, and that diagramming and managing according to the multiple-elements schema could present considerable difficulties by virtue of its greater complexity. It might also be argued that some distinctions between tangible- and intangible-dominant entities are so subtle as to be unimportant.

The fact remains that service marketers are in urgent need of concepts and priorities that are relevant to their actual experience and needs, and that marketing has failed in evolving to meet that demand. However unorthodox, continuing exploration of this area must be encouraged if marketing is to achieve stature and influence in the new post-Industrial Revolution services economy.

NOTES

1. See, for example, E. Jerome McCarthy (1971), *Basic Marketing: A Managerial Approach*, 4th edition, Richard D. Irwin, Homewood, Ill., p. 303; compared with William J. Stanton (1971), *Fundamentals of Marketing*, 3rd edition, McGraw-Hill, NY, p. 567.

2. See William R. George and Hiram C. Barksdale (1974), 'Marketing Activities in the Service Industries', *Journal of Marketing*, vol. 38, no. 4, October, pp. 65–70.

3. M. Halbert (1965), *The Meaning and Sources of Marketing Theory*, Marketing Science Institute Series, McGraw-Hill, NY, p. 88.

4. *Webster's New Collegiate Dictionary* (1974), G. & C. Merriam Company, Springfield, Mass.

5. Philip Kotler (1972), 'A Generic Concept of Marketing', *Journal of Marketing*, vol. 36, no. 3, April, pp. 46–54.

6. Theodore H. Levitt (1960), 'Marketing Myopia', *Harvard Business Review*, vol. 38, July–August, pp. 45–6.

7. Aubrey Wilson (1972), *The Marketing of Professional Services*, McGraw-Hill, NY, p. 8.

PART II

The Establishment
of the
Services Marketing Domain

THE ESTABLISHMENT OF THE SERVICES MARKETING DOMAIN

This part of the book focuses upon the key conceptual aspects of the services marketing literature which are built upon the earlier work of classifying and defining services as outlined in Part I. These aspects were developed and further refined during this 'second' stage in the evolution of the services marketing literature.

Throughout the 1980s and into the 1990s the concepts and activities of services marketing have been refined. This refinement has occurred through significant concentration and focus on aspects of service delivery, quality and satisfaction, and through exploration of services in different contexts. The extent of research into services and services marketing has created a clarity of definition within a wide and, as a consequence, complex range of circumstances.

The basic frameworks surrounding these approaches to and concepts of services marketing were largely determined by the late 1970s. Bateson (1977) grouped the work into three categories.

▷ Clarification of the problems facing management and their conceptualisation at a level above that of the individual firm or industry.

▷ Conceptualisation of the management decision process to produce 'classes' of decisions that all service managers can relate to.

▷ Development of new concepts for use by service marketers or modification of existing concepts and approaches.

Taking cognisance of these three categorisations we can address the commonly accepted concepts of services as well as the managerial aspects of the context in which services and services marketing operate in the specific situation of a firm's activities.

Essentially, the broad concepts are founded upon the distinctive characteristics originating out of the work of Regan, Rathmell and Judd referred to in Part I of this book. That is, the characteristics of services are adequately described as intangibility, heterogeneity of output, inseparability of production and consumption, and perishability. The synthesis of these characteristics is based upon Rathmell's comprehensive list of thirteen marketing characteristics of services as outlined earlier. In accepting these dimensions, much of the subsequent work has focused on determining their existence in a variety of circumstances and in measuring the impact or otherwise on services and services marketing. Good examples of classifying services are represented by Shostack (1977), Hill (1977), Chase (1978), Kotler (1980) and Lovelock (1980). A summary of this work can be found in Grönroos (1990).

The conceptual developments in the services marketing literature, which built upon the earlier work on the definitions and classifications of services, are summarised in this part. The managerial issues which stem from this work are addressed in Part III and the contextual aspects of these concepts are considered in relation to the functional aspects of services marketing in Part IV.

FIGURE II.1:   FULLY EXTENDED PRODUCT

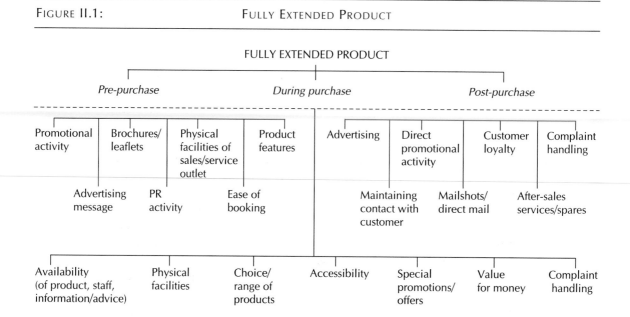

Source: A. Gilmore and D. Carson (1993), 'Quality Improvement in a Services Marketing Context', *Journal of Services Marketing,* vol. 7, no. 3, pp. 59–71.

The main conceptual developments in the services marketing literature during this second stage include: descriptions of the service product, identifying services marketing dimensions; marketing for a services-specific situation, and measuring service quality. Each of these areas is summarised below.

DESCRIPTIONS OF THE SERVICE PRODUCT

Grönroos (1977) reviews the concept of the 'augmented product' and finds it requires adaption for services situations; he argues that since the basic product concept of a service is totally intangible, it can be given meaning to the consumer only when it has a distribution system which covers the whole of the interaction between consumer and producer. Grönroos suggests that this interaction involves a form of personal marketing communication. Gummesson (1995) relates this notion to the consumer/producer 'relationship', and argues that relationships should be the focus of all marketing of services.

In the services literature the notion of the 'fully extended product' has been emphasised as a means of improving the overall service quality by considering all aspects of the product from the customer's point of view. Taking the complete customer's experience into account when planning all aspects of service delivery can facilitate the process of making improvements in a balanced and co-ordinated way. The concept of the fully extended product tries to take account of this need: a company's marketing offerings can be identified by detailed consideration of the fully extended service product, that is, the company's total offer to the customer. This can be described by taking account of the pre-purchase, during purchase and the post-purchase experience.

Figure II.1 serves to illustrate some of the key components of the purchase stages, although naturally these may vary according to the particular situation. Pre-purchase experience incorporates all those factors that lead the customer towards a decision of choosing and using the product/service. This may include his/her exposure to any advertising and promotional activity. Purchase experience encompasses everything that happens during the transaction or use of a product. Examples of this may include the current availability of the product/ service, staff accessibility and the quality of the information and advice given. Post-experience involves all post-purchase motivations and company contact to which the customer may be subjected. Direct customer contact such as the use of mailshots and customer loyalty schemes may be included at this stage.

Grönroos (1980) refers to the idea of a three-stage model which can be compared to the fully extended service product discussed above. Grönroos contends that the service organisation will have to consider three stages in the customer's opinion of the need-satisfying capabilities of the service offerings provided by the organisation. These are: 'interest in the organisation and its service offerings as possible means of satisfying the customer's needs; purchase of a service offering in order to get the particular need satisfied; and repeat purchase of the same or similar service offerings provided by the organisation whenever needed by the customer'. At each stage the objective of the marketing effort and the nature of marketing will be different.

IDENTIFYING SERVICES MARKETING DIMENSIONS

The multidimensional nature of services is a feature of much of the services marketing literature. Some of the dimensions frequently referred to include Lehtinen and Lehtinen's (1982) physical quality, corporate quality and interactive quality; the technical and functional aspects of services as described by Grönroos (1984); the dimensions of tangibles, reliability, responsiveness, assurance and empathy extolled by Parasuraman, Zeithaml and Berry (1985; 1988). Other dimensions such as tangibility and intangibility have been referred to by many other writers such as Shostack (1977) and Gilmore and Carson (1993), who identify and describe various dimensions of service quality.

Having explored customer relations with service firms, Grönroos (1984) defines how the quality of services is perceived by customers and how service quality is influenced. He proposes that customer expectations have both 'technical' and 'functional' components which are influenced by the company image as the dimensions relative to service quality. Swan and Combs (1976) also argue that customer expectations have two dimensions. They describe customer expectations as having both 'instrumental' and 'psychological' aspects. The 'instrumental' dimensions can be compared to the 'technical' aspects which Grönroos describes as the 'what' of the service delivery. The 'functional' or 'psychological' dimensions of expectations (the 'how' of service delivery) relate to the more intangible aspects of service such as customer feelings and perceptions about the service performance.

Citing Swan and Combs (1976), Carson and Gilmore (1989) write that principally customers have both instrumental and psychological expectations about a product or service performance, where expectations relate to both quantifiable, hard data and qualitative, soft data. Hard data are described by Smith (1987) as relating to performance and reliability standards or any tangible dimensions. Soft data are those concerned with descriptions of and knowledge about customers' feelings, perceptions and requirements. Consequently these aspects of service performance are more difficult to measure and more suited to the use of 'soft, qualitative data' (Carson and Gilmore, 1989).

Grönroos (1984) stresses the need for managers to create good 'functional' quality in order to satisfy customers. Carson and Gilmore (1989) warn against the tendency to concentrate on the more tangible aspects of the service delivery just because they are easier to measure, and highlight the neglect of the intangible aspects. The interrelationships between the tangible and intangible elements of service quality in a model are illustrated in Figure II.2. They argue that in order successfully to implement a market-led quality improvement initiative, an integrated approach focusing on the quality of both the tangible and intangible aspects of all marketing offerings is required.

The discussion so far has centred on the theories and concepts which can be deemed to be unique characteristics of services and services marketing. Whilst these theories and concepts may hold true at a general level of definition and description, how well do they translate to an industry or individual firm situation?

MARKETING FOR A SERVICES-SPECIFIC SITUATION

This is an issue which has concerned many scholars from the earliest stages of research in this area. Blois (1974) was one of the first to conceptualise the translating of general concepts and theories to individual products in the market. Focusing on buyer behaviour, Blois attempts to relate theories of services to what he calls 'levels of abstraction'; this approach also differentiates techniques of services marketing from consumer and industrial marketing and how these in turn apply to individual products. Rushton and Carson (1985) took Blois's concept of levels of abstraction and classified 'levels of generalisation'. At the most general level were general marketing concepts, approaches and theories. These can be distilled and refined by techniques and concepts which are specific to services marketing. Further refinement and distillation is brought about by consideration of industry-specific characteristics, for example, the characteristics of industrial or consumer markets. Eventually, complete refinement of a services marketing circumstance is achieved by consideration of a single firm's 'situation-specific' marketing circumstances. This framework can be applicable to any specific situation. Indeed, any studies which have looked at specific industries and firms within an industry implicitly apply this framework, for example, Bateson's (1977) consideration of airlines, Gummesson (1979) in relation to professional services, Lewis (1991) in her study of banking services, and Lewis (1987) and Lehtinen et al. (1994) in relation to hotel services. In particular many of these specific industry studies have focused on the measurement of service quality, which is addressed in the following section.

FIGURE II.2:   DIMENSIONS OF SERVICE QUALITY

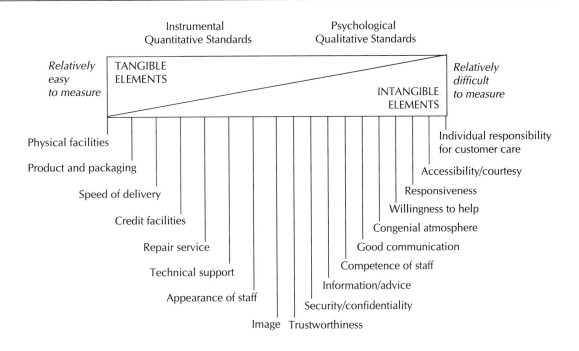

Source: Adapted from D. Carson and A. Gilmore (1989), 'Customer Care: The Neglected Domain', *Irish Marketing Review,* vol. 4, no. 3, pp. 49–61.

SERVICE QUALITY MEASUREMENT

In measuring the impact of services there are many examples. One of the first to attempt this was Bateson (1977), who looked at the positioning of tangible and intangible elements within the product/service offering. A recent examination by McDougall and Snetsinger (1990) focused on the intangibility dimension and tried to devise a scale to measure it in various areas of marketing. The most important contribution to this work, in terms of having attracted most attention and interest from a wide body of researchers, has been the work instigated by Parasuraman, Zeithaml and Berry on ways to measure the effects and efficiencies of services. Generally, a large proportion of the work in this area since the late 1970s has focused on the 'measurement' factor coupled with other dimensions, most importantly that of customer perceptions and satisfaction and how closely these relate to the product/service offering. In addition to the work of Parasuraman et al., much of the conceptual and empirical work in this area has stemmed from the so-called 'Nordic school of services', incorporating the work of Grönroos, Gummesson, Lehtinen and Normann.

The catalyst for much of the progressive research in the management domain of services was the conceptual model of 'SERVQUAL' presented by Parasuraman, Zeithaml and Berry (1985; 1988). The foundation and focus of this model lay in identifying the key components of service quality, namely customer expectations and perceptions and the service delivery associated with these. The basic premise of the model was that there existed a 'gap' between customer expectations and perceptions and the actual delivery of the service. In an attempt to measure service quality they identified ten dimensions which they then reduced to five to form the core of the SERVQUAL measuring instrument. The five final dimensions chosen were: tangibles, reliability, responsiveness, assurance and empathy. These are then measured using twenty-two items with respondents first giving their expectations of service and then their evaluation of the actual service. Satisfaction is calculated as the difference between perceptions and expectations (each item weighted according to its importance). Parasuraman et al. (1988) established that a mismatch between expectations and perceptions causes dissatisfaction, a 'performance gap', as they call it. As found with other writers the process of service delivery was considered to be a key feature in the assessment of quality (Cronin and Taylor, 1992, 1994; Liljander and Strandvik, 1994; Taylor, 1993).

Grönroos (1990) and Gilmore and Carson (1993) also identify the possible occurrence of performance gaps and in each case attribute the gap to a failure by marketing managers to balance the marketing mix in order that customers are not led to expect more than the organisation can offer.

The Parasuraman, Zeithaml and Berry (1985) conceptual SERVQUAL model was taken up by many researchers. Research using the model can be grouped into two broad aspects. Primarily, the widening of the scope of service situations, mostly industry-specific, by using the model for empirical research into measuring service quality in a specific industry. A secondary, but equally important, aspect centred on the issue of 'quality' and how to increase customer satisfaction by improving the quality of a service.

Thus the comparison of customer expectations with their perceptions of a service became the major focus of attention in the measurement of service quality from the early 1980s until the present day. Indeed, Buttle (1996) asserts that SERVQUAL has now been adopted by many industries. Examples of the widening and use of SERVQUAL are many and varied and are typified by the following:

▷ Lewis (1987) used SERVQUAL to examine hotel services from the perspective that quality can be measured more effectively and efficiently by focusing on the 'gaps' in service quality which are most easily measured where service is non-existent.

▷ Brown and Swartz (1989) used the model to evaluate aspects of professional and medical services from the perspective of both the provider and the client.

▷ Young et al. (1994) focused on the American airline industry by linking SERVQUAL with traditional industry-based measures.

▷ Lewis (1991) compared UK and US consumer expectations and perceptions of service quality in banks.

▷ Pitt et al. (1992) apply the model, with some modifications, to high-tech industrial services, specifically the computer software industry.

There are numerous other examples of industry-specific empirical studies using SERVQUAL (see, for example, Carman [1990], car retailing; Saleh and Ryan [1991], hotels; Fick and Ritchie [1991], travel and tourism; Johns [1993], hospitality).

Some researchers have begun to question aspects of the SERVQUAL application and signalled caution in some of its use. For example, many studies have illustrated that the number of service quality dimensions is dependent upon the particular service being offered (Babakus and Boller, 1992; Bouman and van der Weile, 1992). A recent review of the literature pertaining to Parasuraman, Zeithaml and Berry's and other studies replicating and testing SERVQUAL has concluded that contextual circumstances will have some bearing upon the suitability and the number of dimensions of service quality for any given situation (Buttle, 1996). Whether recognising such shortcomings or not, other research has attempted either to link the SERVQUAL model with other work or to offer alternative approaches. An alternative example is offered by Rouffaer's (1991) GOS model based on the notion that service can be defined as Goods, Objectively measured service elements, and Subjectively measured services components. Rouffaer applies his model to the hospitality industry.

Other research has attempted to take a broader view than simple SERVQUAL concepts in measuring service quality. Major studies have been undertaken, a notable example being the 'customer satisfaction barometer, (CSB) in Sweden (Fornell, 1992), which attempts to measure levels of service quality across 30 industries and 100 companies.

In the context of the foregoing discussion, the articles we include to represent the key aspects in the conceptual developments of the services marketing literature are:

Blois, K.J. (1974), 'The Marketing of Services: An Approach', *European Journal of Marketing,* vol. 8, no. 2, pp. 137–45.

Grönroos, Christian (1984), 'A Service Quality Model and its Marketing Implications', *European Journal of Marketing*, vol. 18, no. 4, pp. 36–44.

Parasuraman, A., Zeithaml, Valarie A. and Berry, Leonard L. (1985), 'A Conceptual Model of Service Quality and its Implications for Future Research', *Journal of Marketing*, vol. 49, Fall, pp. 41–50.

Blois's (1974) article begins by giving summaries of the current emphases of services marketing literature and concludes that the issues addressed, such as the development of taxonomies, the listing of types of services and the listing of differences between product marketing and the marketing of services, although useful, do not really come to terms with the problem of indicating possible marketing strategies. He argues that approaching the marketing of services through the use of already available general theories, such as those of buyer behaviour, can reduce the time and cost of developing a body of effective techniques.

Grönroos (1984) emphasises that there are two basic quality dimensions, the technical and functional aspects of service quality. He describes technical quality as *what* the customer receives or outcome of the process, and functional quality as *how* the customer receives the service.

Parasuraman, Zeithaml and Berry (1985) build upon the premise that although quality in tangible goods had previously been described and measured by marketers, quality in services had not. The conceptual model for service quality is presented as a result of an extensive exploratory investigation of quality in four service businesses. It is built upon the argument that quality is a comparison between expectations and performance and quality evaluations involve outcomes and processes. This study led to the identification of four gaps on the service provider's side that may affect service quality as perceived by the customer (with the fifth gap defined as the resulting difference between perceived and expected service).

KEY LEARNING QUESTIONS

1. Describe the fully extended service product. What implications do the different stages of customer experience have for marketing management?
2. What is meant by the 'multidimensional nature' of services?
3. Describe the SERVQUAL method of measuring service quality.

REFERENCES

Babakus, E. and G.W. Boller (1992), 'An Empirical Assessment of the SERVQUAL Scale', *Journal of Business Research*, 24, pp. 253–68.

Bateson, J. (1977), 'Do We Need Services Marketing?' in Pierre Eiglier et al., *Marketing Consumer Services: New Insights*, Marketing Science Institute, Cambridge, Massachusetts, Report No. 77–115, pp. 1–30.

Blois, K.J. (1974), 'The Marketing of Services: An Approach', *European Journal of Marketing*, vol. 8, no. 2, pp. 137–45.

Bouman, M. and T. van der Weile (1992), 'Measuring Service Quality in the Car Service Industry: Building and Testing an Instrument', *International Journal of Service Industry Management*, vol. 3, no. 4, pp. 4–16.

Brown, Stephen W. and Teresa A. Swartz (1989), 'A Gap Analysis of Professional Service Quality', *Journal of Marketing*, vol. 53, April, pp. 92–8.

Buttle, F. (1996), 'SERVQUAL: Review, Critique, Research Agenda', *European Journal of Marketing*, vol. 30, no. 1.

Carman, J.M. (1990), 'Consumer Perceptions of Service Quality: An Assessment of the SERVQUAL Dimensions', *Journal of Retailing*, vol. 66, no. 1, pp. 33–5.

Carson, D. and A. Gilmore (1989), 'Customer Care: The Neglected Domain', *Irish Marketing Review*, vol. 4, no. 3, pp. 49–61.

Chase, R.B. (1978), 'Where Does the Customer Fit in a Service Operation?', *Harvard Business Review*, November–December, pp. 137–42.

Cronin, J.J., Jr and S.A. Taylor (1992), 'Measuring Service Quality: A Re-examination and Extension', *Journal of Marketing*, 56, July, pp. 55–68.

Cronin, J.J., Jr and S.A. Taylor (1994), 'SERVPERF versus SERVQUAL: Reconciling Performance-based and Perceptions-minus-Expectations Measurement of Service Quality', *Journal of Marketing*, January, pp. 125–31.

Fick, G.R. and J.R.B. Ritchie (1991), 'Measuring Service Quality in the Travel and Tourism Industry', *Journal of Travel Research*, vol. 30, no. 3, pp. 2–9.

Fornell, C. (1992), 'A National Customer Satisfaction Barometer: The Swedish Experience', *Journal of Marketing*, 56, January, pp. 6–21.

Gilmore, A. and D. Carson (1993), 'Quality Improvement in a Services Marketing Context', *Journal of Services Marketing*, vol. 7, no. 3, pp. 59–71.

Grönroos, C. (1977), 'The Service Marketing Confusion and Service Oriented Approach to Market Planning', working paper, L'Institut d'Administration des Entreprises, Université de Droit, d'Economie et des Sciences d'Aix-Marseille, January.

Grönroos, C. (1980), 'Designing a Long Range Marketing Strategy for Services', *Long Range Planning*, 13, April, pp. 36–42.

Grönroos, C. (1984), 'A Service Quality Model and its Marketing Implications', *European Journal of Marketing*, vol. 18, no. 4, pp. 36–44.

Grönroos, C. (1990), *Service Management and Marketing: Managing the Moments of Truth in Service Competition*, Lexington Books, Mass.

Gummesson, E. (1979), 'The Marketing of Professional Services – An Organisational Dilemma', *European Journal of Marketing*, vol. 13, no. 5, pp. 308–18.

Gummesson, E. (1995), 'Relationship Marketing: Its Role in the Marketing Economy' in W.J. Glynn and J. Barnes (eds.), *Understanding Services Management: Integrating Marketing, Organisational Behaviour, Operations and Human Resource Management*, Oak Tree Press, Dublin.

Hill, T.P. (1977), 'On Goods and Services', *Review of Income and Wealth*, December.

Johns, N. (1993), 'Quality Management in the Hospitality Industry, Part 3, Recent Developments', *International Journal of Contemporary Hospitality Management*, vol. 5, no. 1, pp. 10–15.

Kotler, P. (1980), *Principles of Marketing*, Prentice-Hall, Englewood Cliffs, NJ.

Lehtinen, U. and J. Lehtinen (1982), 'Service Quality: A Study of Quality Dimensions', Research Report, Service Management Institute, Helsinki, Finland.

Lehtinen, U., J. Ojasalo and K. Ojasalo (1994), 'Consumers' Perceptions of Service Quality Dimensions', European Institute for Advanced Studies in Management, Quality In Services Management Conference Proceedings, Paris, May.

Lewis, B. (1991), 'Service Quality: An International Comparison of Bank Customers' Expectations and Perceptions', *Journal of Marketing Management*, 7, pp. 47–62.

Lewis, Robert C. (1987), 'The Measurement of Gaps in the Quality of Hotel Service', *International Journal of Hospitality Management*, vol. 6, no. 2, pp. 83–8.

Liljander, V. and T. Strandvik (1994), 'The Nature of Relationship Quality', European Institute of Advanced Studies in Management, Quality in Services Management Proceedings, Paris, May.

Lovelock, C.H. (1980), 'Towards a Classification of Services' in C.W. Lamb and P.M. Dunne (eds.), *Theoretical Developments in Marketing*, American Marketing Association, Chicago, Ill.

Lovelock, C.H. (1981), 'Why Marketing Needs to be Different for Services' in James H. Donnelly and William R. George (eds.), *Proceedings Series, AMA: Marketing Services*, pp. 5–9; and in Christopher Lovelock (1984), *Services Marketing*, Prentice-Hall, London, pp. 479–88.

Lovelock, C.H. (1983), 'Classifying Services to Gain Strategic Marketing Insights', *Journal of Marketing*, vol. 47, Summer, pp. 9–20.

McDougall, G.H.G. and D.W. Snetsinger (1990), 'The Intangibility of Services: Measurements and Competitive Perspectives', *The Journal of Services Marketing*, vol. 4, no. 4, Fall, pp. 27–40.

Parasuraman, A., Valarie A. Zeithaml and Leonard L. Berry (1985), 'A Conceptual Model of Service Quality and its Implications for Future Research', *Journal of Marketing*, vol. 49, Fall, pp. 41–50.

Parasuraman, A., Valarie A. Zeithaml and Leonard L. Berry (1988), 'SERVQUAL: A Multiple-item Scale for Measuring Consumer Perceptions of Service Quality', *Journal of Retailing*, vol. 64, no. 1, Spring, pp. 12–35.

Pitt, L.F., P. Oosthuizen and M.H. Morris (1992), 'Service Quality in a High-tech Industrial Market: An Application of SERVQUAL', American Marketing Association Proceedings, Summer, Chicago.

Rouffaer, B. (1991), 'In Search of Service: The "G.O.S" Model', *International Journal of Hospitality Management,* vol. 10, no. 4, pp. 313–21.

Rushton, Angela M. and David J. Carson (1985), 'The Marketing of Services: Managing the Intangibles', *European Journal of Marketing,* vol. 19, no. 3, pp. 19–40.

Saleh, F. and C. Ryan (1991), 'Analysing Service Quality in the Hospitality Industry Using the SERVQUAL Model', *Service Industries Journal,* vol. 11, no. 3, pp. 324–43.

Shostack, G. Lynn (1977), 'Breaking Free from Product Marketing', *Journal of Marketing,* vol. 41, April, pp. 73–80.

Smith, S. (1987), 'How to Quantify Quality', *Management Today,* October, pp. 86–8.

Swan, John E. and Linda Jones Combs (1976), 'Product Performance and Consumer Satisfaction: A New Concept', *Journal of Marketing,* vol. 40, April, pp. 25–33.

Taylor, S. (1993), 'The Roles of Service Quality Consumer Satisfaction and Value in Quinn's (1992) Paradigm of Services', *Journal of Marketing: Theory and Practice*, vol. 2, no. 1, Fall, pp. 14–25.

Young, C., L. Cunningham and M. Lee (1994), 'Assessing Service Quality as an Effective Management Tool: The Case of the Airline Industry', *Journal of Marketing: Theory and Practice*, Spring, pp. 76–95.

The Marketing of Services: An Approach

K.J. Blois

DEFINITIONS

One of the difficulties of discussing this topic is the lack of an agreed definition of a 'service'. Many writers have suggested definitions and the majority have revolved around the degree of tangibility of a good. Wilson,[1] after discussing several of the better-known ones, suggests that the one put forward by the American Marketing Association (that services are 'activities, benefits and satisfactions which are offered for sale or are provided in connection with the sale of goods')[2] is the most widely accepted. However, this particular definition could easily be construed to include goods not normally considered to be services. Surely, for example, a tin of peas offers benefits and satisfactions to consumers? In an attempt to overcome this objection this paper amends the AMA's definition as follows: 'A service is an activity offered for sale which yields benefits and satisfactions without leading to a physical change in the form of a good.'

Such a definition seems to include clearly those activities normally considered as services, e.g. insurance, banking, consultancy, distribution, transport, etc., without including items like tins of peas or machine tools. Its weakness lies in the fact that it excludes such activities, usually considered to be services, as hairdressing or restaurants. Furthermore, as with most definitions an infinite number of 'hair-splitting' problems can be considered – for example, an off-licence in a public house would be, by this definition, a service activity, while the public bar, by opening the bottles and pouring them out, would not! Nevertheless this definition does seem to discriminate between services and other activities in a way which more clearly matches the popular conception of services than most other definitions. For this very pragmatic reason this will be the definition adopted here.

SERVICES IN THE UK ECONOMY

Although there is little agreement on a definition of a service, there is little disagreement with the statement that the service sector of the UK economy is large and growing. Thus Smith (who defines services as comprising the 1958 SIC orders XX to XXIV – distribution, finance, professional services, miscellaneous services and public administration)[3] gives the employment data (which is one possible measure of the services' importance) shown in Table 1.

Many of the service industries have traditionally avoided any really positive marketing activity (e.g. stockbrokers were not allowed to advertise until recently but some did use special reports on particular industries as a form of publicity); nevertheless the expenditure on marketing in certain service industries has reached large sums.

Table 2 shows expenditure on TV and press

Reprinted with permission from *European Journal of Marketing*, vol. 8, no. 2, pp. 137–45.

TABLE 1:   PERCENTAGE OF UK WORKFORCE
EMPLOYED IN SERVICE INDUSTRIES

	1951	1961	1966
Services excluding transport	39.6	41.4	43.3
Services including transport	47.3	48.5	50.0

Source: Anthony D. Smith (1972), *The Measurement and Interpretation of Service Output Changes.*

advertising only in some service industries, and clearly indicates that overall expenditure on marketing must be high in some or all of the firms in these service industries at least.

In view of this situation in the UK and other economically developed nations it is surprising to find so little written about the marketing of services. Thus an examination of marketing journals such as the *European Journal of Marketing, Journal of Marketing* and *Journal of Marketing Research* indicates that few articles on this topic have been published. As far as textbooks are concerned, relatively few mention the topic at all and those that do often spare only a few paragraphs to it. For example, Kotler in 1967[4] does not comment at all, while the second edition of his book[5] has a chapter on 'metamarketing', but only two pages of it are about the marketing of services. Indeed few writers spare even a complete chapter to the subject (examples of authors who do are Stanton[6], and Converse et al.[7]) and Wilson[8] writes one of the few books concerned solely with the topic, although as his title, *The Marketing of Professional Services,* indicates, he is concerned with a particular subset of services.

THE CURRENT APPROACH

The paucity of marketing literature on this topic can be justified only if the problems of marketing services really are basically no different from the problems of marketing other products. However, examination of the available literature indicates that there are differences. Indeed, discussions with personnel concerned with the marketing of services make it apparent that they obtain relative-

ly little help from traditional marketing literature.

There appear to have been three main approaches to discussing this topic:

▷ the development of taxonomies, e.g. Wilson[9] and Stanton;[10]

▷ the listing of types of service, e.g. Kotler[11] and Converse;[12] and

▷ the listing of differences between product marketing and the marketing of services, e.g. Wilson[13] and Branton.[14]

Each of these approaches is helpful and can usefully be taken further than they have been to date. Thus Wilson, when using the taxonomic approach, suggests that services can be considered under the following three headings:

a. *Degree of durability.* This classification is based upon the concept that services purchased now provide benefits over differing periods of time. Thus attendance at a cinema show affords, in most cases, a fairly immediate satisfaction, while education provides benefits over a much longer period of time.

b. *Degree of tangibility.* Wilson suggests that this classification can be broken down further into:

▷ Services providing pure intangibles, e.g. museums, security;

▷ services providing added value to a tangible, e.g. car insurance, contract maintenance;

TABLE 2:   EXPENDITURE ON PRESS AND TV
ADVERTISING IN 1969

	£000s
Finance/HP companies	1,425
Foreign banks and travellers' cheques	768
Insurance companies	2,952
Joint stock banks	2,554
Holidays, travel and transport	12,607

Source: IPC Marketing Manual of the UK, 1970.

▷ services that make available a tangible, e.g., hire purchase, wholesaling.

c. *Degree of commitment.* This classification is closely linked with the fact that many services are purchased on a basis which implies or contractually binds the purchaser to a commitment through time. For example, mortgages and life insurance (although they can be terminated at a cost) usually imply a commitment over a long period. However, other services typically involve very short-term commitments in that they can be postponed or eliminated at very short notice. This latter category would include private education, direct payment private medicine.

However, other headings, not suggested by Wilson or Stanton, are useful. For example:

a. *Degree of essentiality.* Thus if you own a car then third-party insurance cover is legally essential while full cover is considerably less essential in that it is not legally obligatory.

b. *Degree to which one can postpone.* This is partially covered by Wilson's description of his classification 'degree of commitment', but there would seem to be two separate factors. Thus taking out life insurance can be delayed but once taken out implies a degree of commitment (in Wilson's sense). In some cases a service would be impossible to postpone because of its degree of essentiality, but some services can be postponed although essential. An example of this is regular attendance at the dentist – certainly essential if good teeth are to be maintained but easily able to be postponed while no pain occurs!

c. *Degree of cost.* Clearly services range widely in cost. In many cases where the cost is high interesting conflicts may arise for potential customers (and thus opportunities for creative marketing). For example, if a service is essential but costly, the need to raise the necessary finance might cause the purchase to be delayed in spite of that service's essentiality,

unless some form of financing arrangements are created.

Converse, one of the authors who produces lists of types of service, seems to be dating quickly as new product development (which tends to occur frequently in service industries) makes each of his types of service merely a group heading. For example, Converse lists insurance services and investment services as separate, but recent developments in the United Kingdom have led to the development of new forms of insurance – linked unit trusts which provide insurance cover, with tax benefits and investment opportunities.

The third approach, that of considering the differences between marketing services and marketing other products, is typified by Branton. It is suggested that critical differences occur with regard to quality assessment, promotional methods, the heterogeneity arising from the personality of the seller or producer, and the lack of distribution problems. All these factors can be illustrated by the situation of an osteopath. The service offered here is difficult to judge with regard to quality, and this makes for difficulties of promotion. The consumer's assessment of the quality of the service in most cases will be closely linked with their liking for or dislike of the practitioner, and the distribution problem is one of finding a mutually acceptable meeting place. However, there are services to which some of these differences are not applicable or non-service goods to which some of these factors do apply. An example of the former situation is life insurance, which is most frequently arranged by letter and form-filling with no personal contact; an example of the latter situation is any technologically complex product, such as a hi-fi system, where quality assessment is beyond the capabilities of the average purchaser.

In spite of these criticisms, the approaches outlined above have their uses – for example, classification enables facts and objects to be arranged in an orderly fashion so that their unifying principles can be discovered. Nevertheless, none of them really comes to terms with the problem of indicating possible marketing strategies.

FIGURE 1

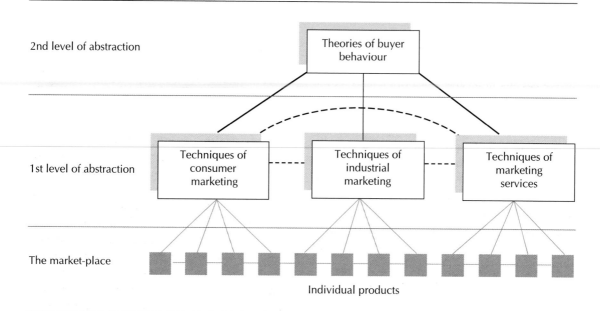

THE IMPORTANCE OF THEORIES OF
BUYER BEHAVIOUR IN MARKETING

It is generally accepted that one of the purposes of
theories is to provide a framework to enable
problems to be analysed and solutions suggested.
In the case of theories of buyer behaviour it is
apparent, from the following quotations, that
their originators see this as one of their objectives:

> The company policy maker at the marketing
> management level needs theory . . . the need
> for theory is to help the marketing executive in
> making the decision that alters product and
> promotion, in collecting the data on which to
> base the decisions in the first place, and in
> interpreting the data once he has collected
> them.[15]

> We hope . . . that research of this kind eventu-
> ally will be of direct utility to the marketing
> decision maker.[17]

In part, these claims are made on the basis of
the fact that they are seen as general theories. For
example, Howard and Sheth have suggested that
their theory of buyer behaviour operates at what
they call a 'second-order level of abstraction', in

that their theory 'encompasses description, explanation, and prediction of all types of buying
behaviours and is not limited to either a given
product class or even a type of product group such
as consumer durables or industrial products'.[18]
The aim of most originators of theories of buyer
behaviour is to operate at this level of abstraction.
(Thus the risk-taking approach to buyer behaviour is frequently referred to in the literature of
industrial marketing, even though the original
work was developed around consumer purchasing
patterns.)[19, 20, 21]

Thus, on these two grounds – their generality
and their intended utility – one would expect
these theories to be of interest to any marketing
manager, but particularly to a marketing manager
moving from one product field to another. For the
person moving into the field of marketing
services, it might be expected that these theories
could be extremely valuable as there is so little in
the way of established techniques and methods of
approach compared with other fields of marketing
– especially the marketing of consumer non-
durables. Furthermore, the differences such as
those considered by Branton[22] and Wilson[23]

between the marketing of services and the marketing of other products are sufficient to indicate that in general to seek to transfer the methods of marketing consumer products directly to the marketing of services could be dangerous. Indeed, the situation appears to be analogous to the relationship between industrial marketing and consumer marketing, where many of the techniques and approaches of consumer marketing have been found to be inapplicable in industrial marketing. The diagram shown in Figure 1 seeks to illustrate this. The dotted lines indicate the relatively weak links between, for example, the techniques and methods of marketing industrial products and consumer products (e.g., some cross-relationship does exist, but the differences are not so insignificant that they can be ignored) with the full lines indicating the strong links between the general theories.

BUYER BEHAVIOUR THEORIES AND THE MARKETING OF SERVICES

In an attempt to illustrate the claim made above, namely that theories of buyer behaviour can help in formulating marketing strategies, this section will outline one such theory and suggest its implication for the marketing of service.

The theory of consumer behaviour as risk-taking, deals with perceived risks which, it is suggested, can arise as a result of one or more of the following factors:[24]

TYPES OF PERCEIVED RISK
1. Uncertainty about buying goals.
2. Uncertainty about product's ability to satisfy goals.
3. Perception of adverse consequences if a purchase is made.

The theory suggests that consumers use various strategies to reduce perceived risks to an acceptable level, and typically these may include one or more of the following:

RISK-REDUCING STRATEGIES
1. Reliance on one's own personal experience.
2. Reliance on the personal experience of others.

3. Taking precautionary measures.
4. Choice avoidance.
5. Reliance on buying maxims.
6. Delegation of buying responsibility.

How then might such a theory assist a marketing manager in a service industry who is seeking to formulate a marketing plan? Firstly, the theory suggests that individuals may perceive risks in connection with products he is considering purchasing. Secondly, it suggests that one or more of a variety of strategies might be used to reduce the risks perceived. It follows that the marketing manager should seek to identify any such risks and then devise strategies which will help the consumer to reduce these perceived risks. Consider, for example, the case of a person responsible for running adult evening classes of a non-vocational nature. Such a person, on the basis of either his own experience or marketing research, may establish that the following risks are often perceived by potential 'customers' under the three headings suggested by the theory:

a. Uncertainty about buying goals: 'What do I want to achieve with my recreational activities? Social contact, increased skills or knowledge, fitness?'

b. Uncertainty about product's ability to satisfy goals: 'Will attending an evening class on modern French novelists satisfy my need for social contact and increased knowledge?'

c. Perception of adverse consequences if a purchase is made: 'Will the class be boring and badly presented – just like school?' 'Will the class close through lack of numbers after a few weeks, by which time I will have bought books and equipment?'

The methods which the theory suggests consumers might use to handle these risks may well guide the organiser in his marketing plans. For example, it may be believed (or established by market research) that many people consider adult education to be 'like school'. If this is the case then the following adverse consequences might be

perceived in attending adult education activities:
'It will be boring.'
'I'll be talked down to by the teacher.'
'It will be badly presented.'

Any attempt by an individual to reduce such perceived risks by reference to his own experience (risk-reducing strategy 1.), whether or not school was an enjoyable experience for that individual, is unlikely to provide attractive associations to an adult because of schools' and schooling's lack of adult connotations. Thus a marketing strategy which would suggest itself is to avoid the use of terms such as 'classes' and 'teacher' in publicity and the running of these activities, and to seek to use terms with neutral associations such as 'sessions' and 'centres'.

This type of risk, together with uncertainty about goals, may also be reduced by enabling consumers to take precautionary measures (strategy 3.). For example, attendance at the first, say, three classes would be free of charge, thus enabling people to sample the product with no financial commitment and the format and content of these 'sample' classes could be designed to emphasise the difference between them and formal education and to suggest satisfactions which might be achieved by attending the whole session.

Consideration of the other forms of the three types of perceived risk might lead to other types of strategy being suggested. However, this approach to developing plans through use of a theory is really useful only if it leads to the development of practical and more effective marketing policies than other approaches. At this stage of the development of the topic only a subjective judgement can be given and this, in the author's opinion, is that it is very difficult directly to trans-late the ideas and approaches of consumer or industrial marketing to the marketing of services. The only way in which it seems possible to do so is to appeal to theory which has been built on the experiences of others or to seek to generalise on the basis of one's own limited experience.

CONCLUSIONS

This paper has sought to suggest an approach to the marketing of services which has not been discussed in the literature. Without doubt, experienced marketing managers in these areas have worked instinctively in the manner suggested here. However, there seems to be a need to seek to explore a more general approach to this problem and it seems possible that such an approach might speed up the development of a body of knowledge and experience in the field of marketing of services.

Corey[26] pointed out: 'modern techniques of merchandising (product planning), advertising, and market research, for example, were widely applied in consumer goods marketing before being used to any great extent in the industrial goods area', and it would seem likely that the failure to apply these techniques to industrial marketing was partially because of their obvious inapplicability in many cases. At the time that industrial marketing was developing as a separate subject, general theories of buyer behaviour were hardly developed, and because of this the techniques of industrial marketing had to be built up from slow and sometimes costly experience of individual situations. It is hoped that by approaching the marketing of services through the available general theories, the time and cost of developing a body of effective techniques may be reduced.

ACKNOWLEDGEMENT
The author is indebted to D.W. Cowell for constructive comments on early drafts of this paper.

NOTES
1. A. Wilson (1972), *The Marketing of Professional Services*, McGraw-Hill, New York, p. 159.

2. Committee on Definitions (1960), *Marketing Definitions: A Glossary of Marketing Terms,* American Marketing Association, p. 21.

3. Anthony D. Smith (1972), *The Measurement and Interpretation of Service Output Changes*, National Economic Development Office, London, p. 10.

4. Philip Kotler (1967), *Marketing Management*, 1st edition, Prentice-Hall, Englewood Cliffs, New Jersey.

5. Philip Kotler (1972), *Marketing Management*, 2nd edition, Prentice-Hall, Englewood Cliffs, New Jersey.
6. William J. Stanton (1967), *Fundamentals of Marketing*, 2nd edition, McGraw-Hill, New York.
7. Paul D. Converse, Harvey W. Huegy, and Robert V. Mitchell (1958), *Elements of Marketing*, 6th edition, Pitman, London.
8. Wilson, *The Marketing of Professional Services*.
9. Wilson, *The Marketing of Professional Services*, pp. 6–9.
10. Stanton, *Fundamentals of Marketing*, pp. 572–4.
11. Kotler, *Marketing Management*, 2nd edition, pp. 870–72.
12. Converse et al., *Elements of Marketing*, pp. 500–17.
13. Wilson, *The Marketing of Professional Services*, p. 23.
14. Noel Branton (1969), 'The Marketing of Services', *Marketing World*, vol. 1, no. 2, October, p. 19.
15. John A. Howard and Jagdish N. Sheth (1969), *The Theory of Buyer Behavior*, Wiley, New York, p. 14.
16. James F. Engel, David T. Kollat and Roger D. Blackwell (1968), *Consumer Behavior*, Holt, Rinehart & Wilson, New York, p. 11.
17. Donald F. Cox (ed.) (1967), *Risk-taking and Information Handling in Consumer Behavior*, Boston Division of Research, Graduate School of Business Administration, Harvard University, p. 17.
18. Howard and Sheth, *The Theory of Buyer Behavior*, p. 17.
19. Patrick J. Robinson, Charles W. Faris and Yorman Wind (1967), *Industrial Buying and Creative Marketing*, Allyn & Bacon, Boston, p. 156.
20. Industrial Marketing Council (1968), *Industrial Marketing*, p. 60.
21. Keith J. Blois (1970), 'The Effect of Subjective Factors on Consumer/Supplier Relations in Industrial Marketing', *British Journal of Marketing*, vol. 4, no. 1, Spring, p. 19.
22. Branton, 'The Marketing of Services', p. 19.
23. Wilson, *The Marketing of Professional Services*, p. 23.
24. Cox, *Risk-taking and Information Handling in Consumer Behavior*, pp. 5–6.
25. Cox, *Risk-taking and Information Handling in Human Behavior*, pp. 54–65.
26. Raymond E. Corey (1962), *Industrial Marketing: Cases and Concepts*, Prentice-Hall, Englewood Cliffs, New Jersey, p. v.

A Service Quality Model and its Marketing Implications

Christian Grönroos

THE MISSING SERVICE QUALITY CONCEPT

In order to be able to develop service marketing models and service management models one has to have a clear picture of what customers in the market-place really are looking for and what they are evaluating in the customer relation of service firms. Nevertheless, publications on service marketing – research reports, scientific articles and books – do not include any explicit model of how the quality of a service is perceived and evaluated by consumers.[1] What we need is a model of service quality, i.e. a model which describes how the quality of services is perceived by customers. When we know this, and the components of service quality, we will be able to develop service-oriented concepts and models more successfully.

The term 'service quality' is frequently used by both academicians and practitioners. However, it is never defined in a way which could guide management decisions. Too often the term 'quality' is used as if it were a variable itself, and not a function of a range of resources and activities. To state that service firms, for instance, will have to develop the quality of their services to be able to compete successfully in the future is meaningless, unless one can: 1. define *how service quality is perceived* by the consumers; and 2. determine *in what way service quality is influenced.*

Today we have no service quality concept.

Therefore, the purpose of the present report is to develop a service quality model. This model is tested on a sample of service business executives.

EXPECTED SERVICE AND PERCEIVED SERVICE

To answer the first question of how service quality is perceived, we may find some guidance in the literature on consumer behaviour. However, theories and models of consumer behaviour and buying behaviour do not explicitly consider services. Still, literature from those areas is of some help to us.

Consumer researchers have not explicitly considered the effects of consumers' perceptions of a product after consumption to any considerable extent.[2] However, several researchers have studied the effect of expectations about product performance on post-consumption evaluations of the product.[3] Among other things, it has been found that higher levels of performance lead to higher evaluations, if expectations are held constant,[4] and that conflict arousal, in relation to the consumption of a product, depends on product performance relative to the expectations of the consumer.[5]

According to one writer[6] the outcome of a product will be more important to post-consumption evaluations, the higher the degree of the consumer's personal involvement in the con-

Reprinted with permission from *European Journal of Marketing*, vol. 18, no. 4, pp. 36–44.

sumption process. Higher involvement leads, for instance, to a greater degree of noticing.

Typically, services are products which require high consumer involvement in the consumption process. In the buyer–seller interactions, during the simultaneous parts of production and consumption, the consumer usually will find a lot of resources and activities to notice and evaluate. As an example we could think of an airline company or a provider of conference services. Hence, the consumer's experience of a service can be expected to influence his post-consumption evaluation of the service quality which he has experienced, i.e. the perceived quality of the service.[7]

Consequently, it is reasonable to state that the perceived quality of a given service will be the outcome of an evaluation process, where the consumer compares his expectations with the service he perceives he has received, i.e. he puts the *perceived service* against the *expected service*. The result of this process will be the *perceived quality of the service*.

Hence, the quality of the service is dependent on two variables: expected service and perceived service. Therefore, in a service quality model we need to know the resources and activities, under the control and outside the immediate control of the firm, that have an impact on these variables, i.e. an answer to the second question stated in the first section of this article. We shall turn to this question in the following sections.

PROMISES AND PERFORMANCE

Traditional marketing activities – advertising, field selling, pricing, etc. – can be used in order to give *promises* to target customers.[8] Such promises influence the expectations of the customers, and have an impact on the expected service. Moreover, traditions ('we have always done so') and ideology (religion, political involvement, etc.) may also have an effect on a given customer's expectations. The same goes for word-of-mouth communication.

Furthermore, previous experience with a service also influences the expectations of a customer. The perceived service, on the other hand,

is the result of the consumer's perception of the service itself. We shall now turn to the issue of how the service is perceived.

Swan and Combs have suggested that the perceived performance of a product can be divided into two sub-processes: namely, instrumental performance and expressive performance.[9] In empirical tests of these concepts and their impact on consumer satisfaction, made by these two researchers and by others,[10] mostly consumer goods have been considered. The tests and the results of them are, however, of considerable theoretical relevance to services, too.

The instrumental performance of a product is the technical dimension of the product. In the context of services, it would be the technical result of a service production process: e.g. a passenger has been transported from one place to another, a medical problem has been attended to in a hospital, financial transactions of a firm have been performed. It is, so to speak, what the customer is left with when the production process is finished. *Expressive performance* is related to a 'psychological' level of performance. In a service context, the expressive performance would be related to the buyer–seller interactions, i.e. to the contact the consumer has with various resources and activities of the service firm during the service production process when the technical outcome, the instrumental performance, is created. As an example, we may think of an airline passenger's contacts with the employees of the company; physical and technical resources such as in-checking desks; the plane itself, seats, meals; and the passenger's contacts with other passengers. The passenger's interactions with such human and non-human resources during the pre-flight, in-flight and post-flight production processes will clearly have an effect on his evaluations of the service, and on the service he perceives he has received.

Swan and Combs argue that satisfactory instrumental performance of a product is a prerequisite for consumer satisfaction, but that this is not enough. If the expressive performance of a product is not considered satisfactory, the consumer will still feel unsatisfied, irrespective of the degree of satisfaction caused by the instrumental performance.[11]

For example, a bank may manage the affairs of a customer perfectly in a technical sense – the instrumental performance is satisfactory – but if the customer is dissatisfied with the performance of the manager or the teller, or if he does not accept the idea of an automatic teller machine he is supposed to use, he will probably feel unhappy with the service he gets from the bank. Similar examples can easily be found from other areas of the service sector, such as hotels and restaurants, transportation, health care, repair and maintenance, shipping and consultancy.

In a service quality model, the different kinds of product performance ought to be translated into quality terms. In the next section we will develop the quality model.

TECHNICAL QUALITY AND FUNCTIONAL QUALITY

The service is basically immaterial and can be characterised as an activity where production and consumption to a considerable extent take place simultaneously. In the buyer–seller interactions the service is rendered to the consumer. Clearly, what happens in these interactions will have an impact on the perceived service.

The hotel guest will get a room with a bed to sleep in, the consumer of a restaurant's services will get a meal, the train passenger will be transported from one place to another, the client of a business consultant may get a new organisation scheme, a manufacturer may get its goods transported from its inventories to a customer by a transportation firm, a bank customer may be granted a loan, etc. As we have noticed earlier, this mere technical outcome of the production process corresponds to the instrumental performance of the service. And clearly, this technical outcome of the process, i.e. what the customer receives as a result of his interactions with a service firm, is important to him and to his evaluation of the quality of the service. This can be called the *technical quality* dimension. Frequently, it can be measured by the consumer in a rather objective manner, as any technical dimension of a product.

However, as the service is produced in interaction with the consumers, this technical quality dimension will not count for the total quality that the consumer perceives he gets. Obviously, he will also be influenced by the way in which the technical quality is transferred to him functionally.

The accessibility of a teller machine, a restaurant or a business consultant, the appearance and behaviour of waiters, bank tellers, travel agency representatives, bus drivers, cabin attendants, business consultants, plumbers, how these service firm employees perform, what they say and how they say it do also have an impact on the customer's view of the service. Furthermore, the more a consumer accepts self-service activities or other production-related routines, which he is expected to perform, the better he will, probably, consider the service. Moreover, the other customers simultaneously consuming the same or similar services may influence the way in which a given customer will perceive a service. Other customers may cause queues, disturb the customer, or they may, on the other hand, have a favourable impact on the atmosphere of the buyer–seller interactions.

In summary, the consumer is interested not only in what he receives as an outcome of the production process, but in the process itself. *How* he gets the technical outcome – or technical quality – functionally, is also important to him and to his view of the service he has received. This quality dimension can be called *functional quality.* Functional quality corresponds to the expressive performance of a service. Hence, we have two quality dimensions, which are quite different in nature: technical quality, which answers the question of *what* the customer gets, and functional quality, which, on the other hand, answers the question of *how* he gets it. Obviously, the functional quality dimension cannot be evaluated as objectively as the technical dimension. As a matter of fact, the functional dimension is perceived in a very subjective way.

The perceived service is the result of a consumer's view of a bundle of service dimensions, some of which are technical and some of which

FIGURE 1:   THE SERVICE QUALITY MODEL

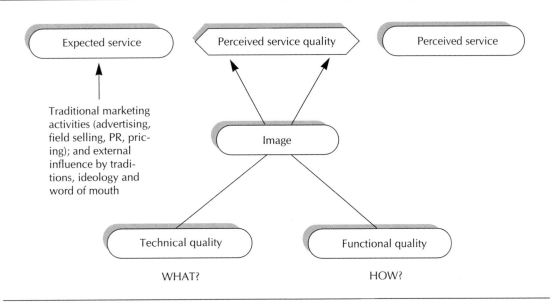

are functional in nature. When this perceived service is compared with the expected service, we get the perceived service quality. This is schematically illustrated in Figure 1. However, the figure includes a third quality dimension, the corporate image, which in some cases can be viewed as a third variable in the quality model. We shall turn to image as a quality dimension in the next section.

IMAGE AS A QUALITY DIMENSION

Usually, a service firm cannot hide behind brand names or distributors. In most cases the consumers will be able to see the firm and its resources during buyer–seller interaction. Therefore *corporate image*, or sometimes local image of an office or other organisational unit, is of utmost importance to most service firms.[12] The expectations of the consumers are influenced by their view of the company, i.e. by the image.

The corporate image is the result of how the consumers perceive the firm. The most important part of a firm, which its customers see and perceive, is its services. Therefore, the corporate image can be expected to be built up mainly by the technical quality and the functional quality of

its services. Of course, there are other factors, which also may influence the image, but they are normally less important. One may choose between two types of such factors: external factors, such as tradition, ideology and word of mouth, and on the other hand, traditional marketing activities, such as advertising, pricing and public relations.

When a service firm wants to inform new target markets about its image, traditional marketing activities like image advertising can be the most effective means of doing so. Moreover, if customers in an existing market, for some reason or another, have an image of the firm which does not correspond with reality, traditional marketing activities can again be expected to be an effective way of communicating the real image to the market. In our opinion, however, advertising campaigns, or other traditional marketing activities, should not be launched if the picture of the firm that is given to the customers does not reflect an existing technical quality and functional quality. All traditional marketing efforts have an impact on the expectations of the customer, and an advertising campaign which gives the impression that the technical and/or the functional quality of the service are better than they really are will result in an increased expected service level. If the perceived service remains on the same level as before, the gap between the expected service and the perceived service will grow, which may lead to conflict arousal. The firm will get disappointed customers. Finally, disappointed customers may cause the image to deteriorate.

However, the image may be a quality dimension. If a consumer believes that he goes to a good restaurant and the meal, for instance, is not perfect, or the behaviour of the waiter is irritating, he may still find the perceived service satisfactory. His positive image of the restaurant makes him find excuses for his negative experiences. Obviously, if he is disappointed many times, his image of the restaurant will deteriorate. In a corresponding manner, a negative image may easily increase perceived problems with service quality. Moreover, the bad image will probably become even more unfavourable.

SOME EMPIRICAL EVIDENCE CONCERNING THE SERVICE QUALITY MODEL

Tests in the instrumental performance and expressive performance of products indicate that the first kind of performance is a necessary, but not sufficient, condition for satisfaction.[13] Swan and Combs also argue that a satisfied consumer will be more likely to mention expressive attributes, rather than instrumental attributes, as a reason for his satisfaction.

As far as services are concerned, these observations would suggest that functional quality is more important to the perceived service than the technical quality, at least as long as the latter quality dimension is on a satisfactory level. Informal case-studies, which we have done as pilot studies, lead us to the same conclusion.

This is especially important to such service industries where the mere technical quality is very similar among firms in the market-place and is difficult to differentiate. As we know, this is the case for a very large number of services.

The hypothesis stated above was tested on a sample consisting of Swedish service firm executives in 1981. A random sample was drawn from a population consisting of persons participating in a series of service marketing seminars, and a questionnaire was mailed to the respondents on the average six months after the seminar. The respondents represent top management as well as marketing and other business functions, mainly internal training and personnel. Moreover, a wide range of service industries are included in the sample: e.g. banks, insurance companies, hotels, restaurants, shipping, airline companies, cleaning and maintenance, car rental companies, travel agencies, engineering consultants, architects, business consultants, advertising agencies, and a range of institutions from the public sector.

The items concerning service quality and corporate image are one part of the total questionnaire only. Approximately 60 per cent of the questionnaires were returned. This equals 219 respondents. As most service industries are very personnel-intensive, and are likely to stay so in the relevant future, the performance of the employees involved in buyer–seller interactions – the contact personnel – was used in order to operationalise the functional quality dimension. The terms contact personnel, technical quality and functional quality were familiar to the respondents.

The items used, as well as the results, are illustrated in Table 1. The answers were given on Likert-type scales with five points ranging from 'agree strongly' (5) to 'disagree strongly' (1). The scales were analysed separately, and the results are given separately. In the table the results for all respondents are given. The picture did not change when the data were broken down according to the background variables used, such as industry, size, position of the respondent, and type of customer.

As we may see from Table 1, a very large proportion of the respondents agree strongly or partly with the five first items. The buyer–seller interaction, where the functional quality emerges, is considered a more important part of marketing than traditional marketing activities. This stresses the view that the quality-generating process, and

TABLE 1: ITEMS AND RESULTS CONCERNING SERVICE QUALITY AND CORPORATE IMAGE

ITEM	Proportion agreeing strongly/partly (%)	n	No answer
In most cases the everyday contact with customers (the buyer–seller interaction) is a more important part of marketing than traditional marketing activities, such as advertising, mass communication, etc.	94.1	218	1
The corporate image is more the result of the customer's contacts with the company (the buyer–seller interaction) than the result of traditional marketing activities.	88.8	216	3
Traditional marketing activities are of marginal importance only to the view of the corporate image of the customers *the firm has today.*	74.0	218	1
Word-of-mouth communication has a more substantial impact on *potential customers* than traditional marketing activities.	83.5	216	3
The contact personnel's way of handling the contacts with the customers, if it is customer-oriented and service-minded, will compensate for *temporary problems* with the technical quality of the service.	91.3	219	0
The contact personnel's way of handling the contacts with the customers, if it is customer-oriented and service-minded, will compensate for an overall *lower technical quality level.*	37.9	217	2

especially the buyer–seller interaction, is of utmost importance to service marketing. We have, in other contexts, defined the management of the buyer–seller interaction as the *interactive marketing function*[14] of service firms as a complement to the traditional marketing function.

Items 2 through 4 indicate that traditional marketing activities are considered marginally important to corporate image, whereas the buyer–seller interaction and word of mouth is considered more effective. The fifth item indicates that functional quality (contact personnel performance) may compensate for temporary problems with the technical quality. One may also notice that more than one-third of the respondents agree strongly or partly with the sixth item, which says that good contact personnel performance may even compensate for an overall lower technical quality level.

CONCLUSIONS AND MARKETING IMPLICATIONS

We may conclude that the functional quality, in fact, seems to be a very important dimension of the perceived service. In some cases it is more important than the technical quality dimension. Successful service management may, therefore, mean that attention is paid to improving the functional quality of a firm's services. Managing the buyer–seller interaction, and thus creating good functional quality, may be a powerful marketing function (interactive marketing), more important than traditional marketing activities.

The importance of traditional marketing activities to corporate image should not be overestimated. The image is mainly the result of the perceived service. Moreover, the importance of word of mouth ought to be remembered.

Managing the perceived service quality means that the firm has to match the expected service and the perceived service to each other so that consumer satisfaction is achieved. In order to keep the gap between the expected service and the perceived service as small as possible, two things seem to be critical to the service firm:

1. The promises about how the service will perform given by traditional marketing activities, and communicated by word of mouth, must not be unrealistic when compared to the service the customers eventually will perceive.

2. Managers have to understand how the technical quality and the functional quality of a service are influenced, and how these quality dimensions are perceived by the customers.

The first consideration has implications for advertising and other traditional marketing efforts. By such activities a view of the service which is not based on reality should not be given to the customers. Moreover, for the firm's present customers such activities are probably far less effective than the impact of the customers' perceptions of the service. As far as potential customers are concerned, traditional marketing is more powerful.

The second consideration brings us back to the service quality model, illustrated in Figure 1. Management has to understand the importance of the functional quality, and how the two quality dimensions can be developed. The technical quality dimension is obviously a result of the know-how which the firm has. This means good technical solutions, technical abilities of the employees, etc. By appropriate use of machines and computer-based systems the technical quality may be improved.

However, as we have seen, this is not enough. To ensure that the consumers are satisfied an acceptable functional quality is demanded. The contact personnel are often of vital importance to functional quality. Moreover, customer-oriented physical resources and technical resources, as well as the accessibility of the firm's services, the consumer orientation of self-service systems, and the firm's ability to maintain a continuous contact with its customers are examples of ways of influencing the functional quality dimension.

In conclusion, one should notice that the quality dimensions are interrelated. An acceptable technical quality can be thought of as a prerequisite for a successful functional quality. On the other hand, it seems as if temporary problems with the technical quality may be excused, if the functional quality is good enough. Finally, the importance of the image should be recognised.

Of course, much more research is needed, especially research on the consumers' view of service quality.

NOTES

1. See, for example, publications by Wilson, Rathmell, Levitt, Eiglier and Langeard, Berry, Bateson, Gummesson, George, Thomas, Lovelock, Grönroos and others.
2. J.R. Bettman (1979), *An Information Processing Theory of Consumer Choice*, Addison-Wesley, Reading, Mass., p. 275.
3. See, for example, K. Lewin et al. (1994), 'Level of Aspiration' in J.M. Hunt (ed.), *Personality and Behavior Disorders*, vol. 1, Ronalds, New York; R.N. Cardozo (1965), 'An Experimental Study of Consumer Effort, Expectation and Satisfaction', *Journal of Marketing Research*, August; J. Cohen and M.E. Goldberg (1969), 'The Effects of Brand Familiarity and Performance upon Post-decision Product Evaluation', paper presented at the American Marketing Association's Workshop on Experimental Research in Consumer Behavior, Ohio State University; R.W. Olshavsky and J.A. Miller, (1972), 'Consumer Expectations, Product Performance and Perceived Product Quality', *Journal of Marketing Research*, February; R.E. Anderson (1973), 'Consumer Dissatisfaction: The Effect of Disconfirmed Expectancy on Perceived Product Performance', *Journal of Marketing Research*, February; R.L. Oliver (1977), 'Effect of Expectation and Disconfirmation on Post-exposure Product Evaluations: An Alternative Interpretation', *Journal of Applied Psychology*, August.
4. See Oliver, 'Effect of Expectation'.
5. F. Hansen (1972), *Consumer Choice Behavior: A Cognitive Theory*, The Free Press, New York, p. 179.
6. Bettman, *Information Processing Theory*, p. 272.
7. In the area of industrial services, Johnston and Bonoma have found that firms which successfully have rendered or currently render a service, often are the only one solicited when a repeat purchase is to be made. See W.J. Johnston and T.V. Bonoma (1981), 'Purchase Process for Capital Equipment and Services', *Industrial Marketing Management*, no. 4, p. 261.
8. H. Calonius (1980), 'Behövs begreppet löfte?',

Marknadsvetande, no. 1, and H. Calonius (1983), 'On the Promise Concept', unpublished working paper, Swedish School of Economics.

9. J.E. Swan and L.J. Combs (1976), 'Product Performance and Consumer Satisfaction: A New Concept', *Journal of Marketing*, April, p. 26.

10. See R.N. Maddox (1981), 'Two-factor Theory and Consumer Satisfaction: Replication and Extension', *Journal of Consumer Research*, June.

11. Swan and Combs, 'Product Performance', p. 26.

12. R.M. Bessom (1973), 'Unique Aspects of Marketing of Services', *Arizona Business Bulletin*, November, p.

78; and R.M. Bessom and D.W. Jackson Jr (1975), 'Service Retailing: A Strategic Marketing Approach', *Journal of Retailing*, Summer, p. 78.

13. Swan and Combs, 'Product Performance', pp. 27 and 32.

14. See C. Grönroos (1978), 'A Service-oriented Approach to Marketing of Services', *European Journal of Marketing*, vol. 12, no. 8, and Christian Grönroos, (1982), *Strategic Management and Marketing in the Service Sector*, Swedish School of Economics and Business Administration, Helsingfors, Finland, pp. 136ff.

A Conceptual Model of Service Quality and its Implications for Future Research

A. Parasuraman, Valarie A. Zeithaml and Leonard L. Berry

The attainment of quality in products and services has become a pivotal concern of the 1980s. While quality in tangible goods has been described and measured by marketers, quality in services is largely undefined and unresearched. The authors attempt to rectify this situation by reporting the insights obtained in an extensive exploratory investigation of quality in four service businesses and by developing a model of service quality. Propositions and recommendations to stimulate future research about service quality are offered.

> 'People want some wise and perceptive statement like, 'Quality is ballet, not hockey.'
>
> Philip Crosby (1979)

Quality is an elusive and indistinct construct. Often mistaken for imprecise adjectives like 'goodness', or 'luxury', or 'shininess', or 'weight' (Crosby, 1979), quality and its requirements are not easily articulated by consumers (Takeuchi and Quelch, 1983). Explication and measurement of quality also present problems for researchers (Monroe and Krishnan, 1983), who often bypass definitions and use unidimensional self-report measures to capture the concept (Jacoby, Olson and Haddock, 1973; McConnell, 1968; Shapiro, 1972).

While the substance and determinants of quality may be undefined, its importance to firms and consumers is unequivocal. Research has demonstrated the strategic benefits of quality in contributing to market share and return on investment (e.g. Anderson and Zeithaml, 1984; Phillips, Chang and Buzzell, 1983) as well as in lowering manufacturing costs and improving productivity (Garvin, 1983). The search for quality is arguably the most important consumer trend of the 1980s (Rabin, 1983) as consumers are now demanding higher quality in products than ever before (Leonard and Sasser, 1982; Takeuchi and Quelch, 1983).

Few academic researchers have attempted to define and model quality because of the difficulties involved in delimiting and measuring the construct. Moreover, despite the phenomenal growth of the service sector, only a handful of these researchers have focused on service quality. We attempt to rectify this situation by 1. reviewing the small number of studies that have investigated service quality; 2. reporting the insights obtained in an extensive exploratory investigation of quality in four service businesses; 3. developing a model of service quality; and 4. offering propositions to stimulate future research about quality.

EXISTING KNOWLEDGE ABOUT SERVICE QUALITY

Efforts in defining and measuring quality have come largely from the goods sector. According to the prevailing Japanese philosophy, quality is 'zero defects – doing it right the first time'. Crosby

Reprinted with permission from *Journal of Marketing,* vol. 49, Fall, pp. 41–50.

(1979) defines quality as 'conformance to requirements'. Garvin (1983) measures quality by counting the incidence of 'internal' failures (those observed before a product leaves the factory) and 'external' failures (those incurred in the field after a unit has been installed).

Knowledge about goods quality, however, is insufficient to understand service quality. Three well-documented characteristics of services – *intangibility*, *heterogeneity* and *inseparability* – must be acknowledged for a full understanding of service quality.

First, most services are intangible (Bateson, 1977; Berry, 1980; Lovelock, 1981; Shostack, 1977). Because they are performances rather than objects, precise manufacturing specifications concerning uniform quality can rarely be set. Most services cannot be counted, measured, inventoried, tested and verified in advance of sale to assure quality. Because of intangibility, the firm may find it difficult to understand how consumers perceive their services and evaluate service quality (Zeithaml, 1981).

Second, services, especially those with a high labour content, are heterogeneous: their performance often varies from producer to producer, from customer to customer, and from day to day. Consistency of behaviour from service personnel (i.e. uniform quality) is difficult to assure (Booms and Bitner, 1981) because what the firm intends to deliver may be entirely different from what the consumer receives.

Third, production and consumption of many services are inseparable (Carmen and Langeard, 1980; Grönroos, 1978; Regan, 1963; Upah, 1980). As a consequence, quality in services is not engineered at the manufacturing plant, then delivered intact to the consumer. In labour-intensive services, for example, quality occurs during service delivery, usually in an interaction between the client and the contact person from the service firm (Lehtinen and Lehtinen, 1982). The service firm may also have less managerial control over quality in services where consumer participation is intense (e.g. haircuts, doctor's visits) because the client affects the process. In these situations, the consumer's input (description of how the haircut should look, description of symptoms) becomes critical to the quality of service performance.

Service quality has been discussed in only a handful of writings (Grönroos, 1982; Lehtinen and Lehtinen, 1982; Lewis and Booms, 1982; Sasser, Olsen and Wyckoff, 1978). Examination of these writings and other literature on services suggests three underlying themes:

▷ Service quality is more difficult for the consumer to evaluate than goods quality.

▷ Service quality perceptions result from a comparison of consumer expectations with actual service performance.

▷ Quality evaluations are not made solely on the outcome of service; they also involve evaluation of the *process* of service delivery.

Service Quality More Difficult to Evaluate

When purchasing goods, the consumer employs many tangible cues to judge quality: style, hardness, colour, label, feel, package, fit. When purchasing services, fewer tangible cues exist. In most cases, tangible evidence is limited to the service provider's physical facilities, equipment and personnel.

In the absence of tangible evidence on which to evaluate quality, consumers must depend on other cues. The nature of these other cues has not been investigated by researchers, although some authors have suggested that price becomes a pivotal quality indicator in situations where other information is not available (McConnell, 1968; Olander, 1970; Zeithaml, 1981). Because of service intangibility, a firm may find it more difficult to understand how consumers perceive services and service quality. 'When a service provider knows how [the service] will be evaluated by the consumer, we will be able to suggest how to influence these evaluations in a desired direction' (Grönroos, 1982).

Quality Is a Comparison between Expectations and Performance

Researchers and managers of service firms concur that service quality involves a comparison of expectations with performance:

Service quality is a measure of how well the service level delivered matches customer expectations. Delivering quality service means conforming to customer expectations on a constant basis.

(Lewis and Booms, 1982)

In line with this thinking, Grönroos (1982) developed a model in which he contends that consumers compare the service they expect with perceptions of the service they receive in evaluating service quality.

Smith and Houston (1982) claimed that satisfaction with services is related to confirmation or disconfirmation of expectations. They based their research on the disconfirmation paradigm, which maintains that satisfaction is related to the size and direction of the disconfirmation experience where disconfirmation is related to the person's initial expectations (Churchill and Suprenaut, 1982).

Quality Evaluations Involve Outcomes and Processes

Sasser, Olsen and Wyckoff (1978) discussed three different dimensions of service performance: levels of material, facilities and personnel. Implied in this trichotomy is the notion that service quality involves more than outcome; it also includes the manner in which the service is delivered. This notion surfaces in other research on service quality as well.

Grönroos, for example, postulated that two types of service quality exist: *technical quality*, which involves what the customer is actually receiving from the service, and *functional quality*, which involves the manner in which the service is delivered (Grönroos, 1982).

Lehtinen and Lehtinen's (1982) basic premise is that service quality is produced in the interaction between a customer and elements in the service organisation. They use three quality dimensions: *physical quality*, which includes the physical aspects of the service (e.g. equipment or building); *corporate quality*, which involves the company's image or profile; and *interactive quality*, which derives from the interaction between contact personnel and customers as well as between

some customers and other customers. They further differentiate between the quality associated with the process of service delivery and the quality associated with the outcome of the service.

EXPLORATORY INVESTIGATION

Because the literature on service quality is not yet rich enough to provide a sound conceptual foundation for investigating service quality, an exploratory qualitative study was undertaken to investigate the concept of service quality. Specifically, focus group interviews with consumers and in-depth interviews with executives were conducted to develop a conceptual model of service quality. The approach used is consistent with procedures recommended for marketing theory development by several scholars (Deshpande, 1983; Peter and Olson, 1983; Zaltman, LeMasters and Heffring, 1982).

In-depth interviews of executives in four nationally recognised service firms and a set of focus group interviews of consumers were conducted to gain insights about the following questions:

▷ What do managers of service firms perceive to be key attributes of service quality? What problems and tasks are involved in providing high-quality service?

▷ What do consumers perceive to be the key attributes of quality in services?

▷ Do discrepancies exist between the perceptions of consumers and service marketers?

▷ Can consumer and marketer perceptions be combined in a general model that explains service quality from the consumer's standpoint?

Service Categories Investigated

Four service categories were chosen for investigation: retail banking, credit card, securities brokerage, and product repair and maintenance. While this set of service businesses is not exhaustive, it represents a cross-section of industries which vary along key dimensions used to categorise services (Lovelock, 1980, 1983). For example, retail banking and securities brokerage services are more 'high-contact services' than the other two types. The nature and results of the service act are more tangible for product repair and maintenance services than for the other three types. In terms of service delivery, discrete transactions characterise credit card services and product repair and maintenance services to a greater extent than the other two types of service.

EXECUTIVE INTERVIEWS

A nationally recognised company from each of the four service businesses participated in the study. In-depth personal interviews, comprised of open-ended questions, were conducted with three or four executives in each firm. The executives were selected from marketing, operations, senior management and customer relations because each of these areas could have an impact on quality in service firms. The respondents held titles such as president, senior vice-president, director of customer relations, and manager of consumer market research. Fourteen executives were interviewed about a broad range of service quality issues (e.g. what they perceived to be service quality from the consumer's perspective, what steps they took to control or improve service quality, and what problems they faced in delivering high-quality services).

FOCUS GROUP INTERVIEWS

A total of twelve focus group interviews was conducted, three for each of the four selected services. Eight of the focus groups were held in a metropolitan area in the south-west. The remaining four were conducted in the vicinity of the participating companies' headquarters and were therefore spread across the country: one on the West Coast, one in the Midwest and two in the East.

The focus groups were formed in accordance with guidelines traditionally followed in the marketing research field (Bellenger, Berhardt and Goldstucker, 1976). Respondents were screened to ensure that they were current or recent users of the service in question. To maintain homogeneity and assure maximum participation, respondents were assigned to groups based on age and sex. Six of the twelve groups included only males and six

included only females. At least one male group and one female group were interviewed for each of the four services. Consistency in age was maintained within groups; however, age diversity across groups for each service category was established to ascertain the viewpoints of a broad cross-section of consumers.

Identities of participating firms were not revealed to focus group participants. Discussion about quality of a given service centred on consumer experiences and perceptions relating to that service *in general*, as opposed to the specific service of the participating firm in that service category. Questions asked by the moderator covered topics such as instances of and reasons for satisfaction and dissatisfaction with the service; descriptions of an ideal service (e.g. ideal bank or ideal credit card); the meaning of service quality; factors important in evaluating service quality; performance expectations concerning the service; and the role of price in service quality.

INSIGHTS FROM EXPLORATORY INVESTIGATION

EXECUTIVE INTERVIEWS

Remarkably consistent patterns emerged from the four sets of executive interviews. While some perceptions about service quality were specific to the industries selected, commonalities among the industries prevailed. The commonalities are encouraging for they suggest that a general model of service quality can be developed.

Perhaps the most important insight obtained from analysing the executive responses is the following:

> A set of key discrepancies or gaps exists regarding executive perceptions of service quality and the tasks associated with service delivery to consumers. These gaps can be major hurdles in attempting to deliver a service which consumers would perceive as being of high quality.

The gaps revealed by the executive interviews are shown in the lower portion (i.e. the Marketer side) of Figure 1. This figure summarises the key insights gained (through the focus group as well as executive interviews) about the concept of service quality and factors affecting it. The remainder of

FIGURE 1:   SERVICE QUALITY MODEL

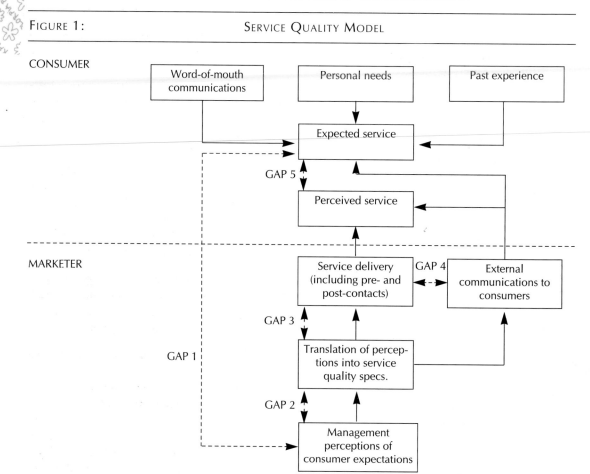

this section discusses the gaps on the service marketer's side (Gap 1, Gap 2, Gap 3 and Gap 4) and presents propositions implied by those gaps. The consumer's side of the service quality model in Figure 1 is discussed in the next section.

Consumer expectation–management perception gap (Gap 1): Many of the executive perceptions about what consumers expect in a quality service were congruent with the consumer expectations revealed in the focus groups. However, discrepancies between executive perceptions and consumer expectations existed, as illustrated by the following examples:

▷ Privacy or confidentiality during transactions emerged as a pivotal quality attribute in every banking and securities brokerage focus group. Rarely was this consideration mentioned in

the executive interviews.

▷ The physical and security features of credit cards (e.g. the likelihood that unauthorised people could use the cards) generated substantial discussion in the focus group interviews but did not emerge as critical in the executive interviews.

▷ The product repair and maintenance focus groups indicated that a large repair service firm was unlikely to be viewed as a high-quality firm. Small independent repair firms were consistently associated with high quality. In contrast, most executive comments indicated that a firm's size would signal strength in a quality context.

In essence, service firm executives may not always

understand what features connote high quality to consumers in advance, what features a service must have in order to meet consumer needs, and what levels of performance on those features are needed to deliver high-quality service. This insight is consistent with previous research in services, which suggests that service marketers may not always understand what consumers expect in a service (Langeard et al., 1981; Parasuraman and Zeithaml, 1982). This lack of understanding may affect quality perceptions of consumers:

Proposition 1: The gap between consumer expectations and management perceptions of those expectations will have an impact on the consumer's evaluation of service quality.

Management perception–service quality specification gap (Gap 2): A recurring theme in the executive interviews in all four service firms was the difficulty experienced in attempting to match or exceed consumer expectations. Executives cited constraints which prevent them from delivering what the consumer expects. As an example, executives in the repair service firm were fully aware that consumers view quick response to appliance breakdowns as a vital ingredient of high-quality service. However, they find it difficult to establish specifications to deliver quick response consistently because of a lack of trained service personnel and wide fluctuations in demand. As one executive observed, peak demand for repairing air-conditioners and lawnmowers occurs during the summer months, precisely when most service personnel want to go on vacation. In this and numerous other situations, knowledge of consumer expectations exists but the perceived means to deliver to expectations apparently do not.

Apart from resource and market constraints, another reason for the gap between expectations and the actual set of specifications established for a service is the absence of total management commitment to service quality. Although the executive interviews indicated a genuine concern for quality on the part of managers interviewed, this concern may not be generalisable to all service firms. In dis-

cussing product quality, Garvin (1983) stated: 'the seriousness that management attaches to quality problems [varies]. It's one thing to say you believe in defect-free products, but quite another to take time from a busy schedule to act on that belief and stay informed' (p. 68). Garvin's observations are likely to apply to service businesses as well.

In short, a variety of factors – resource constraints, market conditions and/or management indifference – may result in a discrepancy between management perceptions of consumer expectations and the actual specifications established for a service. This discrepancy is predicted to affect quality perceptions of consumers:

Proposition 2: The gap between management perceptions of consumer expectations and the firm's service quality specifications will affect service quality from the consumer's viewpoint.

Service quality specifications–service delivery gap (Gap 3): Even when guidelines exist for performing services well and treating consumers correctly, high-quality service performance may not be a certainty. Executives recognise that a service firm's employees exert a strong influence on the service quality perceived by consumers and that employee performance cannot always be standardised. When asked what causes service quality problems, executives consistently mentioned the pivotal role of contact personnel. In the repair and maintenance firm, for example, one executive's immediate response to the source of service quality problems was, 'Everything involves a person – a repair person. It's so hard to maintain standardised quality.'

Each of the four firms had formal standards or specifications for maintaining service quality (e.g. answer at least 90 per cent of phone calls from consumers within ten seconds; keep error rates in statements below 1 per cent). However, each firm reported difficulty in adhering to these standards because of variability in employee performance. This problem leads to a third proposition:

Proposition 3: The gap between service quality specifications and actual service delivery will affect service quality from the consumer's standpoint.

Service delivery–external communications gap (Gap 4): Media advertising and other communications by a firm can affect consumer expectations. If expectations play a major role in consumer perceptions of service quality (as the services literature contends), the firm must be certain not to promise more in communications than it can deliver in reality. Promising more than can be delivered will raise initial expectations but lower perceptions of quality when the promises are not fulfilled.

The executive interviews suggest another, perhaps more intriguing way in which external communications could influence service quality perceptions by consumers. This occurs when companies neglect to inform consumers of special efforts to assure quality that are not visible to consumers. Comments of several executives implied that consumers are not always aware of everything done behind the scenes to serve them well.

For instance, a securities brokerage executive mentioned a 'forty-eight-hour rule' prohibiting employees from buying or selling securities for their personal accounts for the first forty-eight hours after information is supplied by the firm. The firm did not communicate this information to its consumers, perhaps contributing to a perception that 'all the good deals are probably made by the brokers for themselves' (a perception which surfaced in the securities brokerage focus groups). One bank executive indicated that consumers were unaware of the bank's behind-the-counter, on-line teller terminals, which would 'translate into visible effects on customer service'. Making consumers aware of not readily apparent service-related standards such as these could improve service quality perceptions. Consumers who are aware that a firm is taking concrete steps to serve their best interests are likely *to perceive* a delivered service in a more favourable way.

In short, external communications can affect not only consumer expectations about a service but consumer *perceptions* of the delivered service. Alternatively, discrepancies between service delivery and external communications – in the form of exaggerated promises and/or the absence of information about service delivery aspects intended to serve consumers well – can affect consumer perceptions of service quality.

Proposition 4: The gap between actual service delivery and external communications about the service will affect service quality from a consumer's standpoint.

FOCUS GROUP INTERVIEWS

As was true of the executive interviews, the responses of focus group participants about service quality were remarkably consistent across groups and across service businesses. While some service-specific differences were revealed, common themes emerged – themes which offer valuable insights about service quality perceptions of consumers.

Expected service–perceived service gap (Gap 5): The focus groups unambiguously supported the notion that the key to ensuring good service quality is meeting or exceeding what consumers expect from the service. One female participant described a situation when a repairman not only fixed her broken appliance but explained what had gone wrong and how she could fix it herself if a similar problem occurred in the future. She rated the quality of this service excellent because it exceeded her expectations. A male respondent in a banking services focus group described the frustration he felt when his bank would not cash his payroll cheque from a nationally known employer because it was postdated by one day. When someone else in the group pointed out legal constraints preventing the bank from cashing his cheque, he responded, 'Well, nobody *in the bank* explained that to me!' Not receiving an explanation in the bank, this respondent perceived that the bank was *unwilling* rather than *unable* to cash the cheque. This in turn resulted in a perception of poor service quality.

Similar experiences, both positive and negative, were described by customers in every focus group. It appears that judgements of high and low service quality depend on how consumers perceive the actual service performance in the context of what they expected.

Proposition 5: The quality that a customer perceives in a service is a function of the magnitude and direction of the gap between expected service and perceived service.

TABLE 1:	DETERMINANTS OF SERVICE QUALITY

RELIABILITY involves consistency of performance and dependability. It means that the firm performs the service right first time. It also means that the firm honours its promises.
Specifically it involves:
- accuracy in billing;
- keeping records correctly;
- performing the service at the designated time.

RESPONSIVENESS concerns the willingness or readiness of employees to provide service. It involves timeliness of service:
- mailing a transaction slip immediately;
- calling the customer back quickly;
- giving prompt service (e.g. setting up appointments quickly).

COMPETENCE means possession of the required skills and knowledge to perform the service. It involves:
- knowledge and skill of the contact personnel;
- knowledge and skill of operational support personnel;
- research capability of the organisation, e.g. securities brokerage firm.

ACCESS involves approachability and ease of contact. It means:
- the service is easily accessible by telephone (lines are busy and they don't put you on hold);
- waiting time to receive service (e.g. at a bank) is not extensive;
- convenient hours of operation;
- convenient location of service facility.

COURTESY involves politeness, respect, consideration and friendliness of contact personnel (including receptionists, telephone operators, etc.). It includes:
- consideration for the consumer's property (e.g. no muddy shoes on the carpet);
- clean and neat appearance of public contact personnel.

COMMUNICATION means keeping customers informed in language they can understand and listening to them. It may mean that the company has to adjust its language for different consumers – increasing the level of sophistication with a well-educated customer and speaking simply and plainly with a novice. It involves:
- explaining the service itself;
- explaining how much the service will cost;
- explaining the trade-offs between service and cost;
- assuring the consumer that a problem will be handled.

CREDIBILITY involves trustworthiness, believability, honesty. It involves having the customer's best interests at heart. Contributing to credibility are:
- company name;
- company reputation;
- personal characteristics of the contact personnel;
- the degree of hard sell involved in interactions with the customer.

SECURITY is the freedom from danger, risk or doubt. It involves:
- physical safety (Will I get mugged at the automatic teller machine?);
- financial security (Does the company know where my stock certificate is?);
- confidentiality (Are my dealings with the company private?).

UNDERSTANDING/KNOWING THE CUSTOMER involves making the effort to understand the customer's needs. It involves:
- learning the customer's specific requirements;
- providing individualised attention;
- recognising the regular customer.

TANGIBLES include the physical evidence of the service:
- physical facilities;
- appearance of personnel;
- tools of equipment used to provide the service;
- physical representations of the service, such as a plastic credit card or a bank statement;
- other customers in the service facility.

A SERVICE QUALITY MODEL

Insights obtained from the executive interviews and the focus groups form the basis of a model summarising the nature and determinants of service quality as perceived by consumers. The foundation of this model is the set of gaps discussed earlier and shown in Figure 1. Service quality as perceived by a consumer depends on the size and direction of Gap 5, which, in turn, depends on the nature of the gaps associated with the design,

marketing and delivery of services:

Proposition 6: Gap 5 = f(Gap 1, Gap 2, Gap 3, Gap 4).

It is important to note that the gaps on the Marketer side of the equation can be favourable or unfavourable from a service quality perspective. That is, the magnitude *and direction* of each gap will have an impact on service quality. For instance, Gap 3 will be favourable when actual ser-

FIGURE 2:   DETERMINANTS OF PERCEIVED SERVICE QUALITY

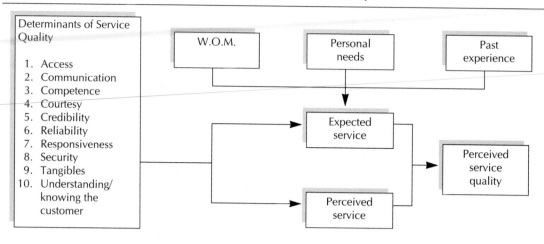

THE PERCEIVED SERVICE QUALITY COMPONENT

vice delivery exceeds specifications; it will be unfavourable when service specifications are not met. While Proposition 6 suggests a relationship between service quality as perceived by consumers and the gaps occurring on the marketer's side, the functional form of the relationship needs to be investigated. This point is discussed further in the last section, dealing with future research directions.

THE PERCEIVED SERVICE QUALITY COMPONENT

The focus groups revealed that, regardless of the type of service, consumers used basically similar criteria in evaluating service quality. These criteria seem to fall into ten key categories, which are labelled 'service quality determinants' and described in Table 1. For each determinant, Table 1 provides examples of service-specific criteria that emerged in the focus groups. Table 1 is not meant to suggest that the ten determinants are non-overlapping. Because the research was exploratory, measurement of possible overlap across the ten criteria (as well as determination of whether some can be combined) must await future empirical investigation.

The consumer's view of service quality is shown in the upper part of Figure 1 and further elaborated in Figure 2. Figure 2 indicates that perceived service quality is the result of the con-

sumer's comparison of expected service with perceived service. It is quite possible that the relative importance of the ten determinants in moulding consumer expectations (prior to service delivery) may differ from their relative importance vis-à-vis consumer perceptions of the delivered services. However, the general comparison of expectations with perceptions was suggested in past research on service quality (Grönroos, 1982; Lehtinen and Lehtinen, 1982) and supported in the focus group interviews with consumers. The comparison of expected and perceived service is not unlike that performed by consumers when evaluating goods. What differs with services is the *nature* of the characteristics upon which they are evaluated.

One framework for isolating differences in evaluation of quality for goods and services is the classification of properties of goods proposed by Nelson (1974) and Darby and Karni (1973). Nelson distinguished between two categories of properties of consumer goods: *search properties*, attributes which a consumer can determine prior to purchasing a product, and *experience properties*, attributes which can be discerned only after purchase or during consumption. Search properties include attributes such as colour, style, price, fit, feel, hardness and smell, while experience properties include characteristics such as taste, wearability and dependability.

Darby and Karni (1973) added to Nelson's two-way classification system a third category, *credence properties* – characteristics which the consumer may find impossible to evaluate even after purchase and consumption. Examples of offerings high in credence properties include appendectomies and brake relinings on automobiles. Few consumers possess medical or mechanical skills sufficient to evaluate whether these services are necessary or are performed properly, even after they have been prescribed and produced by the seller.

Consumers in the focus groups mentioned search, experience and credence properties when asked to describe and define service quality. These aspects of service quality can be categorised into the ten service quality determinants shown in Table 1 and can be arrayed along a continuum ranging from *easy to evaluate* to *difficult to evaluate*.

In general, offerings high in search properties are easiest to evaluate, those high in experience properties more difficult to evaluate, and those high in credence properties hardest to evaluate. Most services contain few search properties and are high in experience and credence properties, making their quality more difficult to evaluate than quality of goods (Zeithaml, 1981).

Only two of the ten determinants – tangibles and credibility – can be known in advance of purchase, thereby making the number of search properties few. Most of the dimensions of service quality mentioned by the focus group participants were experience properties: access, courtesy, reliability, responsiveness, understanding/knowing the customer, and communications. While customers may possess some information based on their experience or on other customers' evaluations, they are likely to re-evaluate these determinants each time a purchase is made because of the heterogeneity of services.

Two of the determinants that surfaced in the focus group interviews probably fall into the category of credence properties, those which consumers cannot evaluate even after purchase and consumption. These include competence (the possession of the required skills and knowledge to perform the service) and security (freedom from danger, risk or doubt). Consumers are probably never certain of these attributes, even after consumption of the service.

Because few search properties exist with services and because credence properties are too difficult to evaluate, the following is proposed:

Proposition 7: Consumers typically rely on experience properties when evaluating service quality.

Based on insights from the present study, perceived service quality is further posited to exist along a continuum ranging from ideal quality to totally unacceptable quality, with some point along the continuum representing satisfactory quality. The position of a consumer's perception of service quality on the continuum depends on the nature of the discrepancy between the expected service (ES) and the perceived service (PS):

Proposition 8: (a) When ES > PS, perceived quality is less than satisfactory and will tend towards totally unacceptable quality, with increased discrepancy between ES and PS; (b) when ES = PS, perceived quality is satisfactory; (c) when ES < PS, perceived quality is more than satisfactory and will tend towards ideal quality, with increased discrepancy between ES and PS.

DIRECTIONS FOR FUTURE RESEARCH

The proposed service quality model (Figure 1) provides a conceptual framework in an area where little prior research has been done. It is based on an interpretation of qualitative data generated through a number of in-depth executive interviews and consumer focus groups – an approach consistent with procedures recommended for marketing theory development. The conceptual model and the propositions emerging from it imply a rich agenda for future research.

First, there is a need and an opportunity to develop a standard instrument to measure consumers' service quality perceptions. The authors' exploratory research revealed ten evaluative dimensions or criteria which transcend a variety of services (Table 1). Research is now needed to generate items or statements to flesh out the ten dimensions, to devise appropriate rating scales to measure consumers' perceptions with respect to each statement, and to condense the set of statements to produce a reliable and comprehensive but concise instrument. Further, the statements generated should be such that with appropriate changes in wording, the same instrument can be used to measure perceived quality for a variety of services.

Second, the main thesis of the service quality model is that consumers' quality perceptions are influenced by a series of distinct gaps occurring on the marketers' side. A key challenge for researchers is to devise methods to measure these gaps accurately. Reliable and valid measures of these gaps will be necessary for empirically testing the propositions implied by the model.

Third, research is needed to examine the *nature* of the association between service quality as perceived by consumers and its determinants (Gaps 1–4). Specifically, are one or more of these gaps more critical than others in affecting quality? Can creating one 'favourable' gap – e.g. making Gap 4 favourable by employing effective external communications to create realistic consumer expectations and to enhance consumer perceptions – offset service quality problems stemming from other gaps? Are there differences across service industries regarding the relative seriousness of service quality problems and their impact on quality as perceived by consumers? In addition to offering valuable managerial insights, answers to questions like these may suggest refinements to the proposed model.

Fourth, the usefulness of segmenting consumers on the basis of their service quality expectations is worth exploring. Although the focus groups consistently revealed similar criteria for judging service quality, the group participants differed on the *relative importance* of those criteria to them, and their *expectations* along the various quality dimensions. Empirical research aimed at determining whether distinct, identifiable service quality segments exist will be valuable from a service marketer's viewpoint. In this regard, it will be useful to build into the service quality measurement instrument certain statements for ascertaining whether, and in what ways, consumer expectations differ.

Fifth, as shown by Figure 1, expected service – a critical component of perceived service quality – in addition to being influenced by a marketer's communications, is shaped by word-of-mouth communications, personal needs and past experience. Research focusing on the relative impact of these factors on consumers' service expectations, within as well as across service categories, will have useful managerial implications.

SUMMARY

The exploratory research (focus group and in-depth executive interviews) reported in this article offers several insights and propositions concerning consumers' perceptions of service quality. Specifically, the research revealed ten dimensions that consumers use in forming expectations about and perceptions of services, dimensions that transcend different types of service. The research also pinpointed four key discrepancies or gaps on the service provider's side that are likely to affect service quality as perceived by consumers. The major insights gained through the research suggest a conceptual service quality model that will hopefully spawn both academic and practitioner interest in service quality and serve as a framework for further empirical research in this important area.

REFERENCES

Anderson, Carl and Carl P. Zeithaml (1984), 'Stage of the Product Life Cycle, Business Strategy, and Business Performance', *Academy of Management Journal*, 27, March, pp. 5–24.

Bateson, John E.G. (1977), 'Do We Need Service Marketing?' in *Marketing Consumer Services: New Insights*, Marketing Science Institute, Cambridge, Mass., Report no. 77–115.

Bellenger, Danny N., Kenneth L. Berhardt and Jac L. Goldstucker (1976), *Qualitative Research in Marketing*, American Marketing Association, Chicago.

Berry, Leonard L. (1980), 'Services Marketing Is Different', *Business*, 30, May–June, pp. 24–8.

Booms, Bernard H. and Mary J. Bitner (1981), 'Marketing Strategies and Organisation Structures in Service Firms' in J. Donnelly and W. George (eds.), *Marketing of Services*, American Marketing Association, Chicago, pp. 47–51.

Carmen, James M and Eric Langeard (1980), 'Growth Strategies of Service Firms', *Strategic Management Journal*, 1, January–March, pp. 7–22.

Churchill, G.A. Jr. and C. Surprenant (1982), 'An Investigation into the Determinants of Customer Satisfaction', *Journal of Marketing Research*, 19, November, pp. 491–504.

Crosby, Philip B. (1979), *Quality Is Free: The Art of Making Quality Certain*, New American Library, New York.

Darby, M.R. and E. Karni (1973), 'Free Competition and the Optimal Amount of Fraud', *Journal of Law and Economics*, 16, April, 67–86.

Deshpande, Rohit (1983), '"Paradigms Lost": On Theory and Method in Research in Marketing', *Journal of Marketing*, 47, Fall, pp. 101–10.

Garvin, David A. (1983), 'Quality on the Line', *Harvard Business Review*, 61, September–October, pp. 65–73.

Grönroos, Christian (1978), 'A Service-oriented Approach to Marketing of Services', *European Journal of Marketing*, vol. 12, no. 8, pp. 588–601.

Grönroos, Christian (1982), *Strategic Management and Marketing in the Service Sector*, Swedish School of Economics and Business Administration, Helsingfors, Finland.

Jacoby, Jacob, Jerry C. Olson and Rafael A. Haddock (1973), 'Price, Brand Name and Product Composition Characteristics as Determinants of Perceived Quality', *Journal of Applied Psychology*, vol. 55, no. 6, pp. 570–79.

Langeard, Eric, John E.G. Bateson, Christopher H. Lovelock and Pierre Eiglier (1981), *Service Marketing: New Insights from Consumers and Managers*, Marketing Science Institute, Cambridge, Mass.

Lehtinen, Uolevi and Jarmo R. Lehtinen (1982), 'Service Quality: A Study of Quality Dimensions', unpublished working paper, Service Management Institute, Helsinki, Finland OY.

Leonard, Frank S. and Earl W. Sasser (1982), 'The Incline of Quality', *Harvard Business Review*, vol. 60, September–October, pp. 163–71.

Lewis, Robert C. and Bernard H. Booms (1982), 'The Marketing Aspects of Service Quality' in L. Berry, G. Shostack and G. Upah (eds.), *Emerging Perspectives on Services Marketing*, American Marketing Association, Chicago, pp. 99–107.

Lovelock, Christopher H. (1980), 'Towards a Classification of Services' in C. Lamb and P. Dunne (eds.), *Theoretical Developments in Marketing*, American Marketing, Chicago, pp. 72–6.

Lovelock, Christopher H. (1981), 'Why Marketing Management Needs to Be Different for Services' in J. Donnolly and W. George (eds.), *Marketing of Services*, American Marketing Association, Chicago, pp. 5–9.

Lovelock, Christopher H. (1983), 'Classifying Services to Gain Strategic Marketing Insights', *Journal of Marketing*, vol. 47, Summer, pp. 9–20.

McConnell, J.D. (1968), 'Effect of Pricing on Perception of Product Quality', *Journal of Applied Psychology*, vol. 52, August, pp. 300–3.

Monroe, Kent B. and R. Krishnan (1983), 'The Effect of Price on Subjective Product Evaluations', working paper, Virginia Polytechnic Institute, Blacksburg.

Nelson, P. (1974), 'Advertising as Information', *Journal of Political Economy*, vol. 81, July–August, pp. 729–54.

Olander, F. (1970), 'The Influence of Price on the Consumer's Evaluation of Products' in B. Taylor and G. Wills (eds.), *Pricing Strategy*, Brandon/Systems Press, Princeton, NJ.

Parasuraman, A. and Valarie A. Zeithaml (1982), 'Differential Perceptions of Suppliers and Clients of Industrial Services' in L. Berry, G. Shostack and G. Upah (eds.), *Emerging Perspectives on Services Marketing*, American Marketing Association, Chicago, pp. 35–9.

Peter, J. Paul and Jerry C. Olson (1983), 'Is Science Marketing?', *Journal of Marketing*, vol. 47, Fall, pp. 111–25.

Phillips, Lynn W., Dae R. Chang and Robert D. Buzzell (1983), 'Product Quality, Cost Position and Business Performance: A Test of Some Key Hypotheses', *Journal of Marketing*, vol. 47, Spring, pp. 26–43.

Rabin, Joseph H. (1983), 'Accent Is on Quality in Consumer Services this Decade', *Marketing News*, vol. 17, 4 March, p. 12.

Regan, William J. (1963), 'The Service Revolution', *Journal of Marketing*, vol. 27, July, pp. 57–62.

Sasser, W. Earl Jr, R. Paul Olsen and D. Daryl Wyckoff (1978), *Management of Service Operations: Text and Cases*, Allyn & Bacon, Boston.

Shapiro, Bensen (1972), 'The Price of Consumer Goods: Theory and Practice', working paper, Marketing Science Institute, Cambridge, Mass.

Shostack, G. Lynn (1977), 'Breaking Free from Product Marketing', *Journal of Marketing*, vol. 41, April, pp. 73–80.

Smith, Ruth A. and Michael J. Houston (1982), 'Script-based Evaluations of Satisfaction with Services' in L. Berry, G. Shostack and G. Upah (eds.), *Emerging Perspectives on Services Marketing*, American Marketing Association, Chicago, pp. 59–62.

Takeuchi, Hirotaka and John A. Quelch (1983), 'Quality Is More than Making a Good Product', *Harvard Business Review*, vol. 61, July–August, pp. 139–45.

Upah, Gregory D. (1980), 'Mass Marketing in Service Retailing: A Review and Synthesis of Major Methods', *Journal of Retailing*, vol. 56, Fall, pp. 59–76.

Zaltman, Gerald, Karen LeMasters and Michael Heffring (1982), *Theory Construction in Marketing: Some Thought on Thinking*, Wiley, New York.

Zeithaml, Valarie A. (1981), 'How Consumer Evaluation Processes Differ between Goods and Services' in J. Donnolly, and W. George (eds.), *Marketing of Services*, American Marketing Association, Chicago, pp. 186–90.

PART III

The Consolidation and Management of Service Quality

THE CONSOLIDATION AND MANAGEMENT OF SERVICE QUALITY

In this part the focus is primarily on the managerial aspects of service quality. Throughout the 1980s there was substantial consolidation of the services and services marketing concepts. Much of the definitional work had been established and most of the key characteristics unique to services were recognised. It is now universally recognised that services and services marketing are specialist management areas in their own right. Many scholars have attempted to illustrate how the management of services is different from goods marketing.

There is now a considerable body of work centred on the management aspects of services. Berry (1987), for instance, puts forward seven key aspects of services management. 1. Distinguish between the marketing department and the marketing function; 2. Leverage the freedom factor, by which he argues for freedom for services contact staff to make customer-contact decisions; 3. Market to employees, that is, internal marketing; 4. Market to existing customers, primarily to reduce the loss of current customers; 5. Be great at problem-solving; 6. Think high-tech and high-touch; and 7. Be a power brander by focusing on the corporation name.

In a similar fashion Grönroos (1990) advocates six 'principles of services management'. 1. The business logic and what drives profit; 2. Decision-making authority; 3. Organisational structure; 4. Supervisory control; 5. Reward systems; and 6. Measurement focus. This is illustrated in Table III.1.

To synthesise some of these aspects or principles of services management, writers and researchers have concentrated on three main areas of concern: designing systems for services management; managing marketing functions and tasks; and managing human performance and the use of internal marketing. This part of the book focuses on these aspects of managing in a services situation.

DESIGNING SYSTEMS FOR SERVICES MANAGEMENT

Some scholars have concentrated on 'designing' systems for services management. One of the most widely referenced articles on this topic is Shostack (1981), who argues that the first step towards rational service design is a system for visualising this phenomenon so that services can be given proper position and weight in the context of any market entity. Shostack's service designs use a molecular modelling approach which aids in the visualisation and management of a total market offering. It takes account of the fact that a market offering can be partly tangible and partly intangible. The benefit of using a molecular model is that it can lead to enriched consideration of the priorities and approach that may be required of a marketer, and recognition that a deliberate or inadvertent change in a single element may completely alter the offering. She uses the examples of an airline and an automobile offering. There are obvious similarities between these two service products – they are both transport products, where tangible décor is important. However, while a car is a physical possession that renders a service, airline travel cannot be physically possessed. Instead it can only be experienced. Thus while the inherent 'promise' of a car is service, airline transportation often promises a

TABLE III.1	PRINCIPLES OF SERVICE MANAGEMENT: A SUMMARY	
PRINCIPLE		REMARKS
1. The profit equation and the business logic	Customer-perceived service quality drives profit	Decisions on external efficiency and internal efficiency (customer satisfaction and productivity of capital and labour) have to be totally integrated
2. Decision-making authority	Decision-making has to be decentralised as close as possible to the organisation–customer interface	Some strategically important decisions have to be made centrally
3. Organisational focus	The organisation has to be structured and functioning so that its main goal is the mobilisation of resources to support the frontline operations	This may often require a flat organisation without unnecessary layers
4. Supervisory focus	Managers and supervisors have to focus on the encouragement and support of employees	As few legislative control procedures as possible, although some may be required
5, Reward systems	Producing customer-perceived quality has to be the focus of reward systems	All relevant facets of service quality should be considered, although all cannot always be built into a reward system
6. Measurement focus	Customer satisfaction with service quality has to be the focus of measurements of achievements	To monitor productivity and internal efficiency, internal measurement criteria may have to be used as well; the focus on customer satisfaction is continually benchmarked

Source: C. Grönroos (1990), *Service Management and Marketing: Managing the Moments of Truth in Service Competition,* Lexington Books, Mass., p. 119.

destination, which is marketed as though it were physically obtainable. Shostack argues that the molecular concept allows a manager to describe and display marketing offerings according to the weight of the 'mix' elements that comprise them.

From an operational perspective Chase (1981) focused on the 'customer contact approach to services' and proposed a classification scheme to categorise levels of customer contact and improve strategies for customer contact. Chase implicitly supports the feasibility of developing a general theory of services for operations management. The design of services linked to new technology is integral to the work of Harvey and Filiatrault (1991), who put forward four alternative service delivery processes involving the customer/server/backroom worker in the situation of a bank and its multiple branches. These four alternatives include designs which range from minimal to high contact between customer, front office and backroom staff. These designs also imply the use of relatively sophisticated technology.

Similarly, Olaisen and Revang (1991) focus on how information technology is rapidly becoming a necessary ingredient for service quality in the airline industry. Siehl and Bowen (1991) recognise the importance of information processing by designing 'integration mechanisms' for service delivery. Cohen and Lee (1990) emphasise the importance of a framework design for inventory management in after-sales service.

Shostack (1987), in discussing service positioning strategy, offers an approach where structural process design can be used to 'engineer' services on a more scientific, rational basis. Basing it on the notion that, 'though processes can be reduced to steps and sequences, services must be viewed as interdependent, interactive systems, not as disconnected pieces and parts', Shostack devises a series of 'blueprints' covering various consumer circumstances and presents these as illustrative 'maps' of how a service is consumed. The blueprint maps are presented as useful tools in consumer research. Perhaps the most comprehensive description of blueprinting is that of Kingman-Brundage (1989), who proposed 'The ABCs of Service System Blueprinting' for managing service systems in general. Kingman-Brundage advocates that although in simple terms, a service system blueprint is a picture of a service system, there may be different levels of blueprints for services management. For example, a concept blueprint is a macro-level blueprint which demonstrates how each job or department functions in relationship to the service as a whole; whilst a detailed blueprint is a micro-level blueprint which conveys the details of the service system identified but not described on the concept blueprint. Thus blueprinting can be a simple or more sophisticated means of designing a system for services management.

MANAGING MARKETING FUNCTIONS AND TASKS

Clearly it is important to ensure that all management activities and functions are integrated and co-ordinated in order to achieve service quality. Authors such as Grönroos (1980) and Lovelock (1983) emphasised the importance of long-range development of the service concept and the setting in place of appropriate strategies to achieve these long-term goals. For example Grönroos (1980) argued that in order to develop long-range strategies for services, marketers needed to consider all stages of a customer's experience of a service (as described in Part II).

Lovelock (1983) contends that in order to develop strategic plans, managers need to focus on the specific categories of services. He proposes five schemes for classifying these categories of services which would help to transcend industry boundaries. These categories are: the nature of the service act; the types of relationships service organisations have with customers; the scope of customisation; the nature of demand for the service; how the service is delivered; and the attributes of the service product, that is, are they people-based attributes or equipment-based attributes? These different categories of services marketing would have different implications for the development of long-term service strategies.

MANAGING HUMAN PERFORMANCE AND THE USE OF INTERNAL MARKETING

Berry (1980) recognises the importance of human performance in shaping the service outcome. From this he argues that in services, marketers need to be concerned with internal, not just external, marketing; and through good internal marketing a firm can upgrade its capabilities towards being a more effective service marketer. In a similar vein, Beckwith and Fitzgerald (1981) argue that the internal managerial dimensions of organisation, communications and planning are important in delivering services.

This is a theme which has attracted substantial research interest. Indeed much of contemporary research in services marketing examines the internal human relationship dimensions. A recent literature review on the scope and parameters of internal marketing emphasises that the management of internal marketing may involve:

▷ managing the internal and external marketing interface;

▷ the application of appropriate variables of the marketing mix to internal customers;

▷ using marketing training and internal communication to 'sell' staff their roles, involving and empowering staff to allow them to make decisions regarding customers and frontline operations;

▷ the development of managers' and staff's role responsibility and of cross-functional participation; and

▷ functional responsibility within the organisation for internal marketing integration (Gilmore and Carson, 1995).

Scholars such as Grönroos and Gummesson advocate a managerial approach to services and emphasise the interactive and 'people' dimensions of the domain. They argue that in order to deliver consistent service, quality management proponents need to recognise that the marketing function spreads beyond the marketing department. All employees in an organisation will have some impact upon the marketing activity despite their role within the organisation, thus an organisation's employees will be either full-time marketers or part-time marketers.

In linking the service product with an integrated management system, Gilmore and Carson (1993) review various service functions under the auspices of customer/staff interactions and position these in the context of the fully extended product. They argue that such interactions begin at initial product choice decisions, through pre-purchase and service purchase/experience stages to post-purchase evaluation and repeat purchase stages. Integral to this work is the service 'people' dimension. (As discussed earlier in Part II, this people dimension is considered central to services marketing.) Cowell (1984) emphasises the importance of the people dimension in all aspects of services and argues the importance of people management in providing effective and efficient services. As far back as the mid-1970s Sasser and Arbeit (1976) recognised the importance of the people factor. In a profound statement for its time they said, 'If service firm jobs are patterned after employee expectations, employee performance will improve. This factor, not advanced technology, is most critical to the success of a service enterprise.' Schlesinger and Heskett (1991) castigate service enterprises which fail to recognise the importance of the employee in service delivery and which perpetrate a cycle of failure by tolerating high employee turnover and an expectation of employee dissatisfaction.

In contrast, however, Heskett (1987) argues that goods marketing can learn from the lessons learned by services marketing. He argues that successful services have integrated functions, a strategic service perspective, inner-directed vision, a stress on the control of quality based on appropriate factors, as well as an understanding about economies of scale and the key role of information. In fact Heskett in 1987 was arguing that the quality of services management was, in many instances, more efficient and effective than some aspects of goods marketing.

In the light of the foregoing discussion, the articles we have chosen in relation to services marketing management are as follows:

Shostack, G. Lynn (1981), 'How to Design a Service' in J.H. Donnelly and W.R. George (eds.), *Marketing of Services,* American Marketing Association, pp. 221–9.

Lovelock, Christopher H. (1983), 'Classifying Services to Gain Strategic Marketing Insights', *Journal of Marketing,* 47, Summer, pp. 9–20.

Grönroos, Christian (1980), 'Designing a Long-range Marketing Strategy for Services', *Long Range Planning,* 13, April, pp. 36–42.

Gummesson, Evert (1991), 'Marketing-orientation Revisited: The Crucial Role of the Part-time Marketer', *European Journal of Marketing,* vol. 25, no. 2, pp. 60–75.

Heskett, James L. (1987), 'Lessons in the Service Sector', *Harvard Business Review,* March–April, pp. 118–26.

Shostack's (1981) article is based upon the premise that while products are tangible objects that exist in both time and space, services consist solely of acts or processes and exist in time only. Shostack argues that the first step towards rational service design is a system for visualising this phenomenon so that services can be given proper position and weight in the context of any market entity.

In his article Lovelock (1983) uses a matrix to illustrate the different types of service acts depending upon whether they are performed on people or things (one axis) by either tangible or intangible actions (the other axis).

Grönroos (1980) develops a framework of reference for long-range marketing strategy by using a three-stage model. In order to design a long range strategy, a service organisation will have to recognise the stages through which its customers proceed, from merely being interested in the company and its services to becoming loyal to the company. He argues that the marketing activities used in the different stages are not the same.

Gummesson (1991) argues that although marketing orientation as a theory is accepted and discussed by marketers, it is difficult to implement in organisations. His article emphasises the importance of the part-time marketer as marketing activities are carried out by all employees and all others who influence the organisation's customer relations directly or indirectly, irrespective of where they are positioned within the organisation.

Heskett (1987) argues that successful service organisations have much to teach other companies. He instances close co-ordination of the marketing-operations relationship; a strategy built around elements of a strategic vision; an ability to redirect the strategic service inward to focus on vital employee groups; a stress on the control of quality based on a set of shared values, peer group status, generous incentives, and a close relationship with the customer; appraisal of the effects of scale on both efficiency and effectiveness; substitution of information for other assets; and the exploitation of information to generate new business.

This area of managing services marketing highlights the uniqueness of the domain. There is an implicit recognition of the challenges of harnessing the 'people' dimension which is integral to management effectiveness. There is no doubt that this dimension will continue to evolve with the ever-changing marketing environment.

KEY LEARNING QUESTIONS

1. Describe a system for designing services.
2. What are the main classifications of service categories which will have an impact upon the development of long-term strategies?
3. What is meant by the term the 'people dimension' in services management?

REFERENCES

Beckwith, Neil E. and Thomas J. Fitzgerald (1981), 'Marketing of Services: Meeting of Different Needs' in Donnelly, James H. and George, William R. (eds.), *Marketing of Services*, AMA, pp. 239–51.

Berry, Leonard L. (1980), 'Services Marketing Is Different', *Business*, May–June, pp. 24–9.

Berry, Leonard L. (1981), 'The Employee as Customer', *Journal of Retail Banking*, vol. 3, no. 1, March, pp. 33–40.

Berry, L.L. (1987), 'Big Ideas in Services Marketing', *Journal of Services Marketing*, vol. 1, no. 1, Summer, pp. 5–7.

Chase, R.B. (1981), 'The Customer Contact Approach to Services: Theoretical Bases and Practical Expansions', *Operations Research*, v.

Cohen, M.A. and H.L. Lee (1990), 'Out of Touch with Customer Needs? Spare Parts and After Sales Service', *Sloan Management Review*, vol. 31, no. 2, pp. 55–65.

Cowell, Donald (1984), *The Marketing of Services*, Heinemann, Oxford, ch.11.

Gilmore, A. and D. Carson (1993), 'Improving Quality in Marketing: A Case Example', *Journal of Strategic Change*, 2, July–August, pp. 215–24.

Gilmore, A. and D. Carson (1995), 'Managing and Marketing to Internal Customers' in W.J. Glynn and J. Barnes (eds.), *Understanding Services Management: Integrating Marketing, Organisational Behaviour, Operations and Human Resource Management*, Oak Tree Press, Dublin.

Grönroos, C. (1980), 'Designing a Long-range Marketing Strategy for Services', *Long Range Planning*, 13, April, pp. 36–42.

Grönroos, C. (1990), *Service Management and Marketing: Managing the Moments of Truth in Service Competition*, Lexington Books, Mass.

Gummesson, E. (1991), 'Marketing-orientation Revisited: The Crucial Role of the Part-time Marketer', *European Journal of Marketing*, vol. 25, no. 2, pp. 60–75.

Harvey, J. and Filiatrault, P. (1991), 'Service Delivery Processes: New Technology and Design', *International Journal of Bank Marketing*, vol. 9, no. 1, pp. 25–31.

Heskett, James L. (1987), 'Lessons in the Service Sector', *Harvard Business Review*, March–April, pp. 118–26.

Kingman-Brundage, J. (1989), 'The ABC's of Service System Blueprinting' in M.J. Bitner and L.A. Crosby (eds.), *Designing a Winning Service Strategy,* American Marketing Association, Chicago.

Lovelock, C.H. (1983), 'Classifying Services to Gain Strategic Marketing Insights', *Journal of Marketing,* 47, pp. 9–20.

Olaisen, J. and Revang, O. (1991), 'The Significance of Information Technology for Service Quality: From Market Segmentation to Individual Service', *International Journal of Services Industry Management,* vol. 2, no. 3, pp. 26–46.

Sasser, W. Earl and Stephen P. Arbeit (1976), 'Selling Jobs in the Service Sector', *Business Horizons,* June, pp. 61–5.

Schlesinger, L.A. and J.L. Heskett (1991), 'Breaking the Cycle of Failure in Services', *Sloan Management Review,* 17, Spring, pp. 17–28.

Shostack, G. Lynn (1987), 'Service Positioning through Structural Change', *Journal of Marketing,* vol. 51, January, pp. 34–43.

Shostack, G. Lynn (1981), 'How to Design a Service' in James H. Donnelly and William R. George (eds.), *Marketing of Services,* AMA, pp. 221–9.

Siehl, C. and D.E. Bowen (1991), 'The Role of Rites of Integration in Service Delivery', *International Journal of Service Industry Management,* vol. 2, no. 1, pp. 15–34.

How to Design a Service

G. Lynn Shostack

INTRODUCTION

The difference between products and services is more than semantic. Products are tangible objects that exist in both time and space; services consist solely of acts or process(es) and exist in time only. The basic distinction between 'things' and 'processes' is the starting-point for a focused investigation of services. Services are rendered; products are possessed. Services cannot be possessed; they can only be experienced, created or participated in.

Though they are different, services and products are intimately and symbiotically linked. A box of cereal, for example, may appear to be a simple product. But it is the culmination of a very long series of marketed services and products, beginning with the service of farming. Or, services and products can act simultaneously to form a larger entity. A department store is a place in which the service of retailing is rendered. Yet retailing is not a complete entity without inclusion of products. A department store's image and clientele are a function of both retailing *and* merchandise, and these cannot be separated without sacrificing the unique definition of a department store.

Today, while 'that which is marketed' may still be a simple product or an unadorned service, it is often a more complex combination of products and services. And the first step towards rational service design is a system for visualising this phenomenon, so that services can be given proper position and weight in the context of any market entity.

THE MOLECULAR MODELLING APPROACH

Product/service combinations that form larger market entities can be quite complex. Since they are dynamic and have highly interrelated elements, it is useful to view them in an organic way, rather than as static bits and pieces. In fact, product/service combinations can be viewed very much like 'atoms' connected in unique 'molecular' configuration.

The molecular analogy has considerable merit. First, it allows full consideration of service elements as well as product elements. Second, it offers a framework for identifying and visualising all the parts of any complex market entity. Finally, it suggests the behavioural hypothesis that rearrangement or alteration of any element, whether by design or accident, will change the overall entity, just as changing the bonds or atoms in a molecule creates a new substance. This latter hypothesis has significant implications for both the planning and the management of complex market entities. Thus, scientific analysis can be applied in marketing to build models and to show structure and relationship.

FIGURE 1:   BASIC MOLECULAR MODELLING

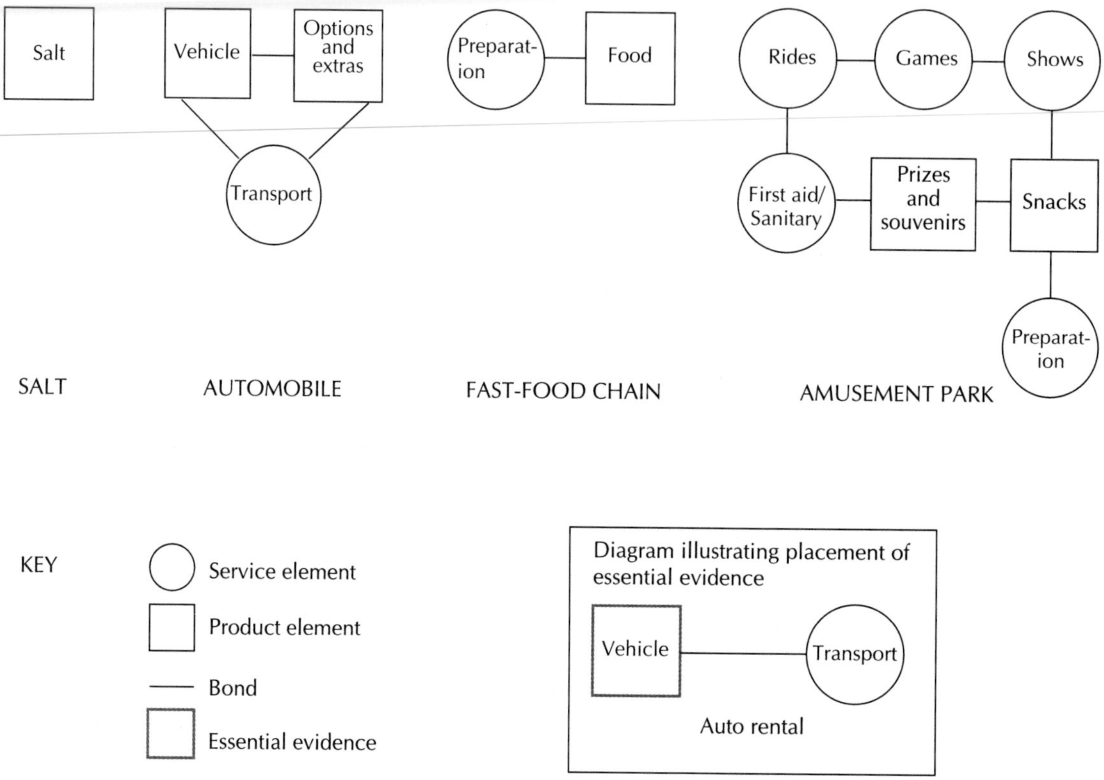

SALT   AUTOMOBILE   FAST-FOOD CHAIN   AMUSEMENT PARK

The system for doing so is called molecular modelling.

DIAGRAMMING COMPLEX ENTITIES

In practice, molecular modelling is a flexible, easily used tool which can help the marketer better understand any market entity. Figure 1 shows a range of entities diagrammed to illustrate the principles of molecular modelling. The system consists of two basic symbols denoting the key product and service elements of the entity; that is, the primary elements which will be purchased and/or used by the consumer. Only the most important elements have been shown in Figure 1. Within each of these, of course, a number of sub-products and sub-services may exist. Market research can be of assistance in

identifying and prioritising these elements, especially when an entity includes many products and services. While indirect or subordinate elements may be of some importance in a final market-ing strategy, they usually need not be addressed until the more detailed stages of analysis.

In Figure 1, the entities are arranged from product dominance to service dominance. Salt, for example, is an uncomplicated product. While salt is purchased to provide a benefit (i.e. seasoned food), no important services are purchased along with salt, only the very indirect services of mining, purifying, packaging and distributing the salt.

The automobile is, however, a more complex entity. While the main product element and its

FIGURE 2:   SCALE OF ELEMENTAL DOMINANCE

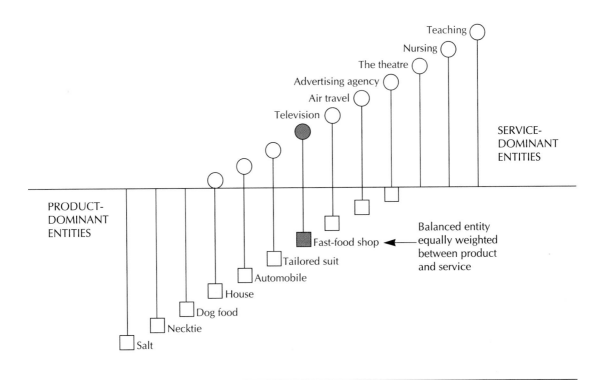

physical features are obvious and important, the entity includes the service of transportation as well. For some market segments the service of transportation is the *prime* purchase criterion. The automobile may be passed over in favour of an airline ticket or even a motorcycle by such a purchaser. Conversely, for some segments the product is paramount. The service characteristics of transportation are irrelevant. This segment will endure discomfort and inconvenience to drive an avant-garde or status vehicle.

In keeping with the hypothesis of molecular modelling, if one changes either the elements or their order, the entity is changed. For example, if transportation is removed from the automobile entity, it is clear that a non-functioning object is being marketed. An antique car, for display only, might be such an object. Conversely, removing the product elements from this model might

yield a pure transportation service such as parcel post.

At the far end of service-dominant complexity one might find banking, which is a host of services having little product context, or, as Figure 1 shows, an amusement park. Here, souvenirs and snacks may represent the only product elements in the entity, and these are clearly not the key variables in either the purchase decision or the usage experience.

RELATIONSHIPS AND PROPORTIONS OF ELEMENTS

In Figure 1, all elements have been shown at the same size. However, segmentation research can be applied to create prioritised models based on consumer preference. For example, in a complex entity such as an amusement park, first aid and food services will carry greater weight (and be drawn at proportionally larger size) for parents with young children than for teenagers. Similarly, research can be used to prioritise the bonds connecting various elements. These bonds may be used to signify clusters of elements having a high correlation in purchase decisions, or elements influencing usage of other elements or any other relationships deemed important by the marketer.

Using molecular modelling, a comparative scale of dominance can be created which arrays entities according to their overall make-up. As illustrated in Figure 2, entities at each end of the scale can, for convenience, be simply called 'products' or 'services', since their dominance is so pronounced. Hybrid entities, towards the middle of the scale, must be treated especially carefully by the marketer, for here product and service elements are almost balanced, and disrupting this balance can have a major impact on market perception of the overall entity.

THE ROLE OF SERVICE EVIDENCE

Services are often accompanied by physical objects which cannot be categorised as true product elements. These objects, or pieces of 'evidence', play the critical role of verifying either the existence or the completion of a service. A true product element, of course, never requires evidence. It is its own evidence.

There are two kinds of service evidence. The first is peripheral evidence. Typically, while peripheral evidence is actually possessed as part of purchase, it has little or no independent value. An example of peripheral service evidence is a cheque-book, which is useless without the funds transfer and storage service that it represents. Another example is the admission ticket to an amusement park or theatre. It serves only to confirm the service; it is not a surrogate for the service, nor is it purchased for its own sake. In a molecular model, peripheral evidence must be listed and fully described for each service element.

Essential evidence is the second type of service evidence. Unlike peripheral evidence, essential

evidence *cannot* be possessed by the consumer. Nevertheless, it may be so dominant in its impact on service purchase and use that it must be considered virtually an element in its own right. To a consumer who purchases transportation in the form of an airline ticket (peripheral evidence), the aircraft that 'facilitates' the service has a strong impact on service perceptions and even purchase. The marked resistance of Americans to flying in DC-10s after several of these craft crashed, and despite numerous safety tests, illustrates this phenomenon.

Because of its importance, essential evidence may be shown in a molecular model as a quasi-product element, defined by a broken-line border rather than the solid-line box that denotes a true product. In Figure 1, for example, the model shown for the automobile can be changed to a model for auto rental service simply by enclosing the vehicle component in a broken-line box.

MANAGING THE EVIDENCE

Whether peripheral or essential, service evidence is at the heart of service image, advertising and promotion. Evidence must be as carefully designed and managed as a service itself, for it is evidence that provides the clues and the confirmations (or contradictions) that the consumer seeks and needs in order to formulate a specific mental 'reality' for the service.

The management of service evidence goes beyond what is commonly thought of as 'packaging'. It extends to the control and design of *all* tangible evidence that the consumer might associate with the service. Typically, this includes objects that are not part of the product marketer's arsenal.

People, for example, are often essential evidence of a service. The way a service renderer is clothed or speaks can materially impact the consumer's perception of a service. Intuitively, many service firms recognise this phenomenon; thus the prevalence of uniforms of various kinds in service-dominant industries such as airlines, fast-food chains and hotels. Even in sophisticated service enterprises this rule applies. Somehow, no matter

FIGURE 3:   COMPONENTS OF A COMPLETED MOLECULAR MODEL

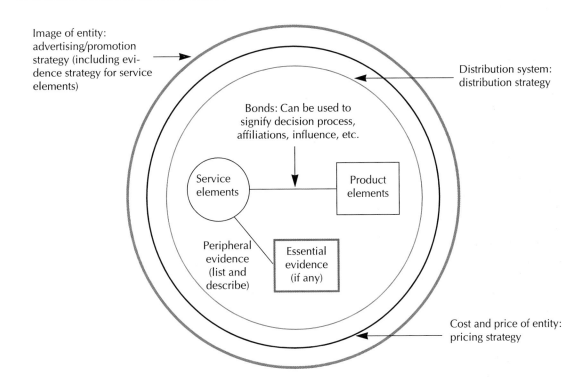

Image of entity: advertising/promotion strategy (including evidence strategy for service elements)

Distribution system: distribution strategy

Bonds: Can be used to signify decision process, affiliations, influence, etc.

Service elements

Product elements

Peripheral evidence (list and describe)

Essential evidence (if any)

Cost and price of entity: pricing strategy

how fine the service might be, one would have doubts entrusting one's health to a physician who wore cowboy boots and a neckerchief.

The environment in which a service is rendered is another example of potentially essential evidence. Often, it is controllable by the service marketer, and should be deliberately planned and managed. An attorney's office painted pink, for example, would probably not inspire confidence. In fact, the ideal environment for such a service (or any other) can be facilitated through market research, which allows designs and market opinions to be tested for suitability to the service. Of course, evidence management can include many other items, even the stationery used for a service. What is important is that every tangible clue be considered, for all of these have an impact on the service.

WHAT IS A BENEFIT?

The total real or perceived result of an entity upon the purchaser/consumer is its 'benefit'. The benefit of dry cleaning services, for example, might be described as 'clean clothes', and this, in fact, should be the result of purchase of the service. The benefit of toothpaste might be 'clean teeth', or 'fresh breath', which may or may not be a verifiable result. The benefits of a complex service such as tax return preparation might span a range and priority, depending on market segment, from 'accurate computation' to the less precise, but no less real, 'peace of mind'. It is vital that benefits not be confused with services or with image in diagramming, designing or managing an entity.

COMPLETING THE MOLECULAR MODEL

Figure 3 illustrates the structure of a completed

molecular model. All product and service elements have been identified. Bonds between elements have been described and drawn. The peripheral and essential evidence associated with each service element has been described. Finally, the remaining elements of the marketing equation have been added. They are shown as encompassing, or ringing, the entity, reflecting both their relationship to the entity and the order in which the marketer should logically deal with them.

First, the marketer must consider the entity's distribution system. Service elements can be difficult to distribute, since service uniformity is difficult to create and maintain. Second, the marketer must consider the entity's cost and set a proper price. Again, service elements present a problem. Services' 'raw materials' are often dominated by time, which, unless the service is carefully designed, can be difficult to measure or control. Finally, the marketer must consider the advertising and promotion of the entity. As previously described, service elements require close attention to evidence management, an area in which few advertising firms are fully versed.

Each of these rings in the marketing mix represents a field of discipline and detail in its own right. The problems presented by service elements in each ring will not be gone into in detail here, except to note that it is an area ripe for further inquiry, insight and research.

THE CONCEPT OF SERVICE BLUEPRINTING

After modelling the product and service elements of a complex entity, the marketer must thoroughly examine the structure of each element.

To 'know your product' is a fairly straightforward job. Engineering specifications, photographs, physical examination, even personal trial are all available to the marketer. If necessary, even more detailed data can be gathered, down to the formula for the paint on a bit of trim. There is little difficulty in making comparisons among products. Differences in raw materials, costs, finished appearance and functions can be ascertained.

To 'know your service' in any comparable sense is almost impossible. There is no 'service engineering' text to which the marketer can turn. There are no equivalents to help the marketer overcome the lack of photographic, physical or trial use documentation. There does not appear to be even common acknowledgement of the need to overcome these obstacles.

As a result, services are very often defined in terms of poorly articulated oral and written abstractions. From this subjective and superficial start, the conclusion is drawn that 'the service' is now documented and understood, that what is 'known' about the service can be communicated with precision and certainty to all those who will henceforth 'market' and manage it, and that the service has been 'fixed' in a way that allows rational minds to act rationally upon it.

Perhaps this is the reason so many services go awry, and why marketers so often seem limited to creating advertising programmes rather than actually creating and managing services. If a service cannot be completely and objectively dimensioned at the outset, how can it be adequately compared to other services, or intelligently planned or effectively changed or controlled?

What is required is a system which will allow the structure of a service to be mapped in an objective and explicit manner while also capturing all the essential functions to which marketing applies; in other words, a service blueprint.

THE NATURE OF SERVICES

Clearly a method for 'blueprinting' services is needed. This is no simple task, for among the many other intriguing characteristics of services is the fact that services 'exist' in two different states of being.

The best analogy for this phenomenon is electricity. Electricity exists in two states: as potential energy and as kinetic energy. A battery represents potential energy. For convenience, we say that electricity is *stored* in a battery, even though a battery is actually a fabrication of materials and chemicals possessing the *means for creating* electricity, not a repository for any physical substance.

Kinetic energy is the electric current itself. Kinetic refers to motion, thus kinetic electricity only exists during the time it is being rendered or while it is 'on'.

A service also exists in two states. In its potential state, a service may be 'stored' in ways that are analogous to batteries. For example, the potential service of haircutting is stored in the form of a trained barber. A potential service such as tax computation may be stored in the form of a program inside a computer.

In its potential state, a service can only be described in hypothetical terms, or as what will be called a 'blueprint'. For example, the potential service of haircutting consists of a series of steps which a barber should perform in a particular order and manner to yield a particular type of haircut. Many unique blueprints can be developed for any generalised service. In fact, many (if not most) underlying blueprints for services are developed through trial and error. One barber school may teach starting at the nape of the neck, while another may begin with the crown of the head, yet both will achieve satisfactory results.

Whatever the blueprint for the *potential* service, the *actual* rendering, or kinetic state, of the service will almost always deviate in some way. A battery is constructed to produce a given voltage. However, the actual current will always vary, within acceptable tolerances, from battery to battery because it is physically impossible to build absolutely identical batteries.

To the user, these variances are normally indistinguishable and unimportant, so long as the flashlight lights or the radio plays. Similarly, no two haircuts are exactly alike. They may differ in duration, in quality or in customer satisfaction, even when a specific blueprint has been followed. But unless the deviations exceed some level of tolerance, they will be accepted as part of satisfactory execution of the service. Of course, the more complex the service, the more likely the possibility of significant kinetic deviation. Also, the less specific the blueprint, the more room there is for deviation.

IMPLICATIONS OF POTENTIAL AND KINETIC SERVICE

Clearly, a service marketer cannot truly design a service without having a systematic way to build a service blueprint. Even with an existing service, it would seem foolhardy to think that any marketing plan or action could be taken without first thoroughly blueprinting the service in question. Yet, because marketing provides no blueprinting theory or tools, marketers very often plunge into action on the basis of nothing more than a paragraph on paper describing 'the service'.

Beyond a precise blueprint of the potential service, it seems equally clear that the marketer must be aware of and have a method for both setting and tracking the deviation tolerance of a service; that is, the degree to which the kinetic execution of the service can or will be allowed to vary from the blueprint.

THE ROOTS OF SERVICE BLUEPRINTING

Since a service is basically a process, service blueprinting rests, as it must, on systems that have been developed to deal with processes, acts and flows. Three systems are relevant: time/motion or methods engineering; PERT/project programming; and computer systems and software design. While none offers the complete answer, all offer tools and concepts which can be modified for service design.

TIME/MOTION ENGINEERING

Methods engineering offers an extremely precise and detailed system for process planning. While used mostly in planning the manufacture or assembly of products, it has also been applied effectively to service operations, typically 'back-office' operations, such as cheque processing and fast-food preparation.

At its most detailed level, methods engineering performs micro-motion studies of manual processes, analysing films of workers frame by frame in order to reduce or eliminate labour. Obviously, a discipline this precise and well-developed can and does have enormous utility in cost control, output and efficiency on the assembly line. It has equal applicability to services.

The basic tools of time/motion engineering are eight basic charts. They are visual and quantitative ways precisely and objectively to describe processes. Each charting method has a specific application. Of these, three are most relevant to service blueprinting.

First, the Operations Process Chart shows a chronological sequence of the operations, inspections, time allowances and materials used in a manufacturing process, and depicts the entrance of all components and sub-assemblies to the main assembly. In this system of description, specific symbology and visual rules apply – for example, a ⅜" circle is used to denote an operation, a ⅜" square is used to show an inspection.

The second kind of chart is called a Flow Process Chart. It is more detailed than an Operations Process Chart, and is used to show sub-processes. Again, specific symbols are used. For example, a small arrow signifies transportation of an item, a small triangle denotes storage.

A third chart, the Flow Diagram, puts these symbols and descriptions in order and pictorially shows the physical layout and location of all operations. Typically a factory floor plan is used, and the process is traced upon it.

PERT CHARTING

Allied with time/motion engineering, the PERT Chart is used for project scheduling, as opposed to process description. A PERT Chart shows time dimensions and costs for each part of a project. Its symbology is not visually detailed, but its method of visualising a project yields such concepts as critical pathing – which shows the minimum time needed to complete a project. PERT Charts are typically used in conducting cost/time trade-off analyses.

SYSTEMS AND SOFTWARE DESIGN

A computer program is nothing more than a series of instructions for executing binary choices. Within a computer system, various kinds of general programs exist that are conceptually and operationally relevant to services. There are application programs for processing data or transactions; there are supervisory programs to co-ordinate and schedule the work of application programs; there are support programs to maintain the functionality of other programs.

Multiprogramming, for example, is a name for a group of programs which tell a computer how to handle tasks involving erratic input, random timing and variable content. A task scheduler program decides which, of many tasks, will be done next. Task management is that part of an operating system that supervises units of work – maintains lists of tasks, controls the sequence and handles interruptions. Data management controls input and output. Of course, there are many other facets of systems design, but these serve to illustrate that what happens in a computer is often analogous to what must happen in order for a service to be successfully rendered.

MORE IS NEEDED

Conceptually, each of these three methodologies bears importantly on service blueprinting; yet each is incomplete in terms of the service marketer's needs. Time/motion engineering, for example, offers a descriptive system for manual human performance, but does not deal with other service functions such as evidence. Software design does not deal with time or cost in human terms, nor provide for alternative process execution. PERT does not offer an analogue for the consumer. None of the systems deals with distribution, pricing or promotion, or the interactiveness between marketer, service and consumer as an adaptive force.

NECESSARY ELEMENTS OF SERVICE BLUEPRINTING

The basic requirements of a service blueprint are three. First, since processes take place in time, the blueprint must, like PERT charting, show time dimensions in diagrammatic form.

Second, like methods engineering, the blueprint must identify all main functions (and subfunctions) of the service. Where these are performed by people, a work chart should be constructed. All input and output of functions must be shown. Like systems design, the blueprint must identify and handle errors, bottlenecks, recycling steps, etc.

Finally (usually after research), the blueprint must precisely define the tolerance of the model, i.e. the degree of variation from the blueprint standards that can be allowed in execution without affecting the consumer's perception of overall quality and timeliness.

TOLERANCES IN SERVICE EXECUTION
Tolerances may be expressed in terms of time, order or output. Typically, the deviation tolerance is a band, or range, around each function, which can be mathematically set. A model standard can thus be set for the service, and for all functions within it.

Deviation tolerances are used in many services already. McDonald's, for example, which revolutionised fast-food services, established a timer that signalled the moment the uniform-sized meat patty was to be turned on the griddle. A deviation tolerance of a few seconds obviously wouldn't make any perceivable difference to the consumer. Yet without this control, not only might the uniformity of the product element suffer (underdone or overdone), but consumer perceptions of 'fast' would be vulnerable to much greater swings and, not the least important, costs and profits would be directly affected.

Fast-food service is, when analysed, complex enough. Services such as legal clinics or accounting firms present much more difficult problems, partly because the service includes diagnosis and judgement, not just rote process. And yet these services are still created ad hoc, without anything analogous to the engineering that goes into equivalent products. A consulting service can be every bit as complex as a jet airplane; yet the difference in engineering effort that goes into designing these two entities represents total extremes.

If, however, all these criteria can be satisfied, the marketer (or service engineer) will at last be in a position materially to affect, knowledgeably to plan and strongly to control the service itself.

AN APPROACH TO BLUEPRINTING
A refined quantitative technique for service engineering does not exist. The marketer may find that a sub-function such as 'room cleaning' within the complex entity of 'hotel services' has been rather thoroughly worked out. But other functions (e.g. recreational services) will not have been so carefully mapped, nor will all functions have been linked together into a blueprint of the whole that satisfies criteria of deviation tolerance, consumer/back-office distinctions, competitive comparisons or consumer total image.

It is not possible to discuss in full all the details and nuances of a complete service blueprint. Only the most basic principles can be suggested here, with the intent of encouraging thoughtful inquiry and further research. Accordingly, Figure 4 illustrates a simple market entity, modelled according to principles described earlier, and Figure 5 displays a blueprint for the main service element of that entity.

IDENTIFYING SERVICE FUNCTIONS
In this example, four process steps have been identified proceeding left to right in time as constituting the primary blueprint for the service. The rectangular symbol signifying process is borrowed from computer systems design. The blueprint identifies one main error possibility, that is, application of the wrong colour of wax. An auxiliary, or recycling, process (i.e. clean shoes) is shown as being necessary in order to complete the service. (If the consumer himself renders part of the service, for example, with a do-it-yourself buffing machine, step 3 would be shown as a rectangle with a corner notched.)

The product element is an indirect facilitating good whose quality may be judged by the consumer as part of judging the entire service. This element is shown as being 'visible' to the consumer, but not part of the service process. Certain processes and evidence which are not visible to the consumer may also be shown. Purchase of supplies, for example, is shown below the 'line of visibility' of the service as a sub-service, necessary, but not seen by the consumer. For some services

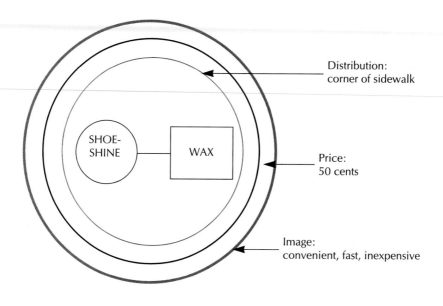

these back-office processes are important, since a change in them may change the service or entity. Thus, these may also require monitoring and consideration by the marketer. If, for example, a computer program is redesigned in such a way that a different account statement is produced for banking customers, this new piece of evidence may affect service image and may affect other perceptions of price/value as well.

In the example shown, there is no peripheral or essential service evidence. Even the single product element (a coat of wax) is virtually invisible.

IDENTIFYING BENEFITS

There are at least several consumer benefits derived from purchase of a shine. Shiny shoes is obvious. Self-confidence may also accrue, from the psychological uplift of a shine. Protection from dirt and wear may also be a benefit. Of these, two may be objectively verifiable. The benefits of the service may be listed below the blueprint, and should be researched both before and after a blueprint is changed.

IDENTIFYING STANDARDS AND TOLERANCES

The Figure 5 blueprint has a model execution time of two minutes. The deviation tolerance for this blueprint is shown at 180 seconds, or three additional minutes. Beyond five minutes, the consumer will show signs of dissatisfaction and begin to lower materially his judgement of quality.

As shown, the total tolerance is divided into two categories. Intracycle deviation occurs within the service process itself. For example, if buffing extends to sixty seconds, fifteen seconds of intercycle deviation will have taken place. Extracycle tolerance occurs outside the service process. Waiting two minutes in line for the service would be an example of extracycle deviation.

While both types of deviation affect consumer perception, usually only intracycle deviation affects profitability. Therefore, the marketer, in designing a service, should set service tolerances to relate directly to profit. The profit analysis for the Figure 5 blueprint is shown below.

FIGURE 5:   BLUEPRINT FOR A SIMPLE SERVICE CORNER SHOESHINE

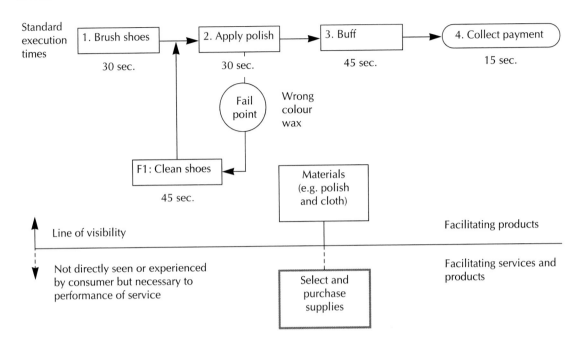

Standard execution time: 2 minutes

Deviation tolerance: 3 minutes   Intracycle tolerance = 1 minute
                                  Extracycle tolerance = 2 minutes

Total acceptable execution time: 5 minutes

TOTAL INTRACYCLE EXECUTION

	2 mins.	3 mins.	4 mins.
Price	50c.	50c.	50c.
Costs			
1. Time 9c. per minute	18c.	27c.	36c.
2. Wax	5c.	5–7c.	5–7c.
3. Other (brush, cloth, etc. – amortised)	7c.	7–8c.	7–8c.
Total costs	30c.	39–42c.	48–51c.
Pre-tax profit	20c.	8–11c.	2–(1)c.

Within the service cycle, an application of the wrong wax or spending too much time on any function can reduce the pre-tax profit by half or more. At the four-minute stage, the service loses money. This is true even though the customer will tolerate up to five minutes of total execution time. Thus the temptation to relax productivity to the customer's level of tolerance has been deliberately offset by the profit dynamics of doing so. When the marketer sets service standards and tolerances in this way, he establishes not only a basis for measuring performance, but a basis for managing uniformity and quality and for rational distribution of the process.

MODIFYING A SERVICE

While Figure 5 may appear to be a very simple service, it is subject to substantial changes by the marketer.

As Figure 6 shows, the marketer may add a repeat cycle of steps 2 and 3, thus creating a two-

FIGURE 6: MODIFIED DESIGN INCORPORATING NEW SERVICE CYCLE, SERVICE EVIDENCE AND
          PRODUCT ELEMENT

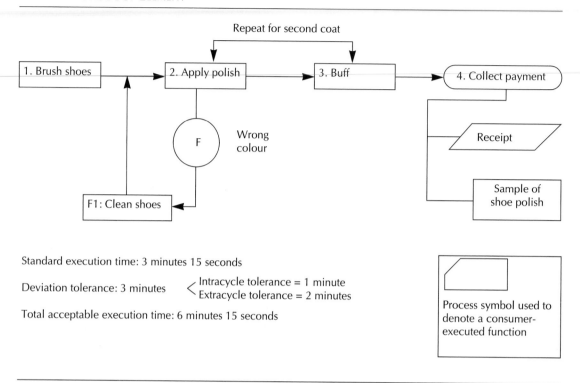

Standard execution time: 3 minutes 15 seconds

Deviation tolerance: 3 minutes $<$ Intracycle tolerance = 1 minute
                                      Extracycle tolerance = 2 minutes

Total acceptable execution time: 6 minutes 15 seconds

coat shine. This may be sufficient differentation to allow a 20c. price increase, thus increasing the margin by 1c. Or, a marketer might decide to add service evidence in the form of a receipt, or add product in the form of a sample of wax. Not only would the marketer create a 'reminder' of the service (by perhaps printing his name and address on the sample) but he might be able to raise prices even more. Or he might be able to maintain his price, yet increase his margin, by buying a machine that lets the customer buff his own shoes. The time saved would allow greater profit, provided no perceived diminishment in quality occurred on the customer's part.

In addition to the controlled change suggested by Figure 6, both the service blueprint and the molecular model can be used even more flexibly to 'engineer' market entities. Figure 7 shows how whole new market entities can be designed start-ing with a basic service element and adding other service and product elements to it. Clearly, a great deal of entity design can be done at the drawing-board well before expensive formal market intro-duction. Moreover, it can be done objectively, quantifiably and scientifically.

BENEFITS AND USES OF SERVICE
BLUEPRINTING

These principles can be applied to much more complex services than corner shoeshines. It is manifest that if changes in a service occur at random or without marketing as the controlling force, marketing cannot pretend to be exerting more than token influence on any service. Moreover, if no blueprint exists and customer behaviour towards the service changes, the marketer will be able neither to account for the change nor scientifically modify the service

FIGURE 7:   ALTERNATIVE DESIGNS FOR MORE COMPLEX ENTITIES

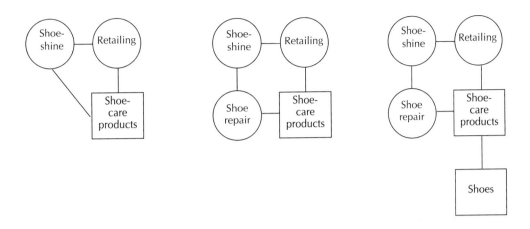

towards maximum efficiency.

Both molecular modelling and service blueprinting can materially improve the marketer's ability to design, manage and modify services, and are an important step towards rationalising the marketer's job and true scope of responsibility.

THE DESIGN OF ELEMENTS AND ENTITIES

At the design and planning stage, both molecular models and service blueprints help to encourage creativity, pre-emptive problem-solving and well-controlled implementation.

The service blueprint accomplishes a number of objectives. First, it provides both a visual and a quantitative description of any service element that is more precise than verbal definitions and less subject to interpretation or misinterpretation.

A service blueprint allows a service to be created on paper. Rather than resorting to subjective and imprecise concept-testing as a means of service development, an actual blueprint can be tested, in which the proposed service has been thoroughly and specifically worked out. A blueprint can even be mocked up into a prototype service which can be trial tested by potential consumers in ways that give the marketer concrete and actionable feedback. This feedback can be used to make rational modifications before the service is retested. All this is possible because the blueprint allows the marketer to know *exactly* what he is testing, be it deviation tolerances, fail points, consumer values associated with specific functions, evidence or any other feature.

IN MANAGING EXISTING SERVICES

The service blueprint provides a permanent benchmark against which execution can be measured, modification proposals analysed, competitors compared, prices established and cogent promotional plans developed.

When blueprints and deviation tolerances are established, service distribution becomes more controllable. A blueprint allows a service actually to be 'architected' at some remote location, yet conform exactly to model standards. A refined blueprint, the result of careful and continuous research and modification, can be literally distributed and implemented at any number of sites. Regular reporting systems can easily monitor performance of the service across its distribution system. This would be a significant step forward from today's unavoidable practice of shipping off trained *people* who supposedly understand a service to new sites and trusting that the same *service* will be created there.

With a blueprint, price changes, function changes, consumer input can all be evaluated for impact on the total entity. Diagnostics can be done on trouble spots, and market research on services can be made far more well-focused by being directly anchored to a specific visual and mathematical model.

Service evidence can be both created and managed in an integrated fashion; advertising and promotion can be intelligently linked to a total

evidence programme.

CONCLUSION

Finally, both modelling and blueprinting offer a system for the marketer that can lead to the kind of experimentation and management so necessary to service innovation and development. They give the marketer powerful professional tools and a discipline that allows the marketer a broader role and impact than has existed to this point. For marketers, and for service firms and industries, this is a necessary and surely welcome step forward.

Classifying Services to Gain Strategic Marketing Insights

Christopher H. Lovelock

The diversity of the service sector makes it difficult to come up with managerially useful generalisations concerning marketing practice in service organisations. This article argues for a focus on specific categories of services and proposes five schemes for classifying services in ways that transcend narrow industry boundaries. In each instance insights are offered into how the nature of the service might affect the marketing task.

INTRODUCTION

Developing professional skills in marketing management requires the ability to look across a broad cross-section of marketing situations, to understand their differences and commonalities, and to identify appropriate marketing strategies in each instance. In the manufacturing sector many experienced marketers have worked for a variety of companies in several different industries, often including both consumer goods and industrial firms. As a result, they have a perspective that transcends narrow industry boundaries.

But exposure to marketing problems and strategies in different industries is still quite rare among managers in the service sector. Not only is the concept of a formalised marketing function still relatively new to most service firms, but service industries have historically been somewhat inbred. The majority of railroad managers, for instance, have spent their entire working lives within the railroad industry – even within a single company. Most hoteliers have grown up in the hotel industry. And most hospital or college administrators have remained within the confines of health care or higher education, respectively. The net result of such narrow exposure is that it restricts a manager's ability to identify and learn from the experience of organisations facing parallel situations in other service industries – and, of course, from marketing experience in the manufacturing sector. Conversely, marketers from the manufacturing sector who take positions in service businesses often find that their past experience has not prepared them well for working on some of the problems that regularly challenge service marketers (Knisely, 1979; Lovelock, 1981; Shostack, 1977).

This article argues that development of greater sophistication in services marketing will be aided if we can find new ways to group services other than by current industry classifications. A more useful approach may be to segment services into clusters that share certain relevant marketing characteristics – such as the nature of the relationship between the service organisation and its customers or patterns of demand relative to supply – and then to examine the implications for marketing action.

After briefly reviewing the value of classification schemes in marketing, the article summarises past proposals for classifying services. This is followed by presentation and discussion of five classification schemes based on past proposals or on clinical research. In each instance examples are given of how various services fall into similar or different categories, and an evaluation is made of the resulting marketing insights and what they imply for marketing strategy development.

THE VALUE OF CLASSIFICATION IN MARKETING

Hunt (1976) has emphasised the usefulness of classification schemes in marketing. Various attempts have been made in the past by marketing theorists to classify goods into different categories. One of the most famous and enduring is Copeland's (1923) classification of convenience, shopping and specialty goods. Not only did this help managers obtain a better understanding of consumer needs and behaviour, it provided insights into the management of retail distribution systems. Bucklin (1963) and others have revised and refined Copeland's original classification and thereby been able to provide important strategic guidelines for retailers. Another major classification has been between durable and non-durable goods. Durability is closely associated with purchase frequency, which has important implications for development of both distribution and communications strategy. Yet another classification is consumer goods versus industrial goods; this classification relates both to the type of goods purchased (although there is some overlap) and to product evaluation, purchasing procedures and usage behaviour. Recognition of these distinctions by marketers has led to different types of marketing strategy being directed at each of these groups. Through such classifications the application of marketing management tools and strategies in manufacturing has become a professional skill that transcends industry divisions.

By contrast, service industries remain dominated by an operations orientation that insists that each industry is different. This mind-set is often manifested in managerial attitudes that suggest, for example, that the marketing of airlines has nothing at all in common with that of banks, insurance, motels, hospitals or household movers. But if it can be shown that some of these services do share certain relevant marketing characteristics, then the stage may be set for some useful cross-fertilisation of concepts and strategies.

HOW MIGHT SERVICES BE CLASSIFIED?

Various attempts have been proposed in the past for classifying services and are outlined, with brief commentaries, in Table 1. But developing classification schemes is not enough. If they are to have managerial value, they must offer strategic insights. That is why it is important to develop ways of analysing services that highlight the characteristics they have in common, and then to examine the implications for marketing management.

This article builds on past research by examining characteristics of services that transcend industry boundaries and are different in degree or kind from the categorisation schemes traditionally applied to manufactured goods. Five classification schemes have been selected for presentation and discussion, reflecting their potential for affecting the way marketing management strategies are developed and implemented. Each represents an attempt to answer one of the following questions:

1. What is the nature of the service act?
2. What type of relationship does the service organisation have with its customers?
3. How much room is there for customisation and judgement on the part of the service provider?
4. What is the nature of demand and supply for the service?
5. How is the service delivered?

Each question will be examined on two dimensions, reflecting my conclusion in an earlier study (Lovelock, 1980) that combining classification schemes in a matrix may yield better marketing insights than classifying service organisations on one variable at a time.

TABLE 1:   SUMMARY OF PREVIOUSLY PROPOSED SCHEMES FOR CLASSIFYING SERVICES

AUTHOR	PROPOSED CLASSIFICATION SCHEMES	COMMENT
Judd (1964)	1. Rented goods services (right to own and use a good for a defined period) 2. Owned goods services (custom creation, repair or improvement of goods owned by the customer) 3. Non-goods services (personal experiences or 'experiential possession')	First two are fairly specific, but third category is very broad and ignores services such as insurance, banking, legal advice and accounting.
Rathmell (1974)	1. Type of seller 2. Type of buyer 3. Buying motives 4. Buying practice 5. Degree of regulation	No specific application to services – could apply equally well to goods.
Shostack (1977)* Sasser et al.* (1978)	Proportion of physical goods and intangible services contained within each product 'package'	Offers opportunities for multi-attribute modelling. Emphasises that there are few pure goods or pure services.
Hill (1977)	1. Services affecting persons vs. those affecting goods 2. Permanent vs. temporary effects of the service 3. Reversibility vs. non-reversibility of these effects 4. Physical effects vs. mental effects 5. Individual vs. collective services	Emphasises nature of service benefits and (in 5.), variations in the service delivery/consumption environment.

Thomas (1978)	1. Primarily equipment-based
	  a. automated (e.g. car wash)
	  b. monitored by unskilled operators (e.g. movie theatre)
	  c. operated by skilled personnel (e.g. airline)
	2. Primarily people-based
	  a. unskilled labour (e.g. lawn care)
	  b. skilled labour (e.g. repair work)
	  c. professional staff (e.g. lawyers, dentists)
		Although operational rather than marketing in orientation, provides a useful way of understanding product attributes.

Chase (1978)	Extent of customer contact required in service delivery
	  a. high contact (e.g. health care, hotels, restaurants)
	  b. low contact (e.g. postal service, wholesaling)
		Recognises that product variability is harder to control in high-contact services because customers exert more influence on timing of demand and service features, due to their greater involvement in the service process.

Kotler (1980)	1. People-based vs. equipment-based 2. Extent to which client's presence is necessary 3. Meets personal needs vs. business needs 4. Public vs. private, for-profit vs. non-profit	Synthesises previous work, recognises differences in purpose of service organisation.

Lovelock (1980)	1. Basic demand characteristics
	  – object served (persons vs. property)
	  – extent of demand/supply imbalances
	  – discrete vs. continuous relationships between customers and providers
	2. Service content and benefits
	  – extent of physical goods content
	  – extent of personal service content
	  – single service vs. bundle of services
	  – timing and duration of benefits
	3. Service delivery procedures
	  – multi-site vs. single-site delivery
	  – allocation of capacity (reservations vs. first come, first served)
	  – independent vs. collective consumption
	  – time-defined vs. task-defined transactions
	  – extent to which customers must be present during service delivery
		Synthesises previous classifications and adds several new schemes. Proposes several categories within each classification. Concludes that defining object served is most fundamental classification scheme. Suggests that valuable marketing insights would come from combining two or more classification schemes in a matrix.

* These were two independent studies that drew broadly similar conclusions

FIGURE 1:   UNDERSTANDING THE NATURE OF THE SERVICE ACT

Who or what is the direct recipient of the service?

	PEOPLE	THINGS
What is the nature of the service act?		
Tangible actions	Services directed at people's bodies: ▷ health care ▷ passenger transportation ▷ beauty salons ▷ exercise clinics ▷ restaurants ▷ haircutting	Services directed at goods and other physical possessions: ▷ freight transportation ▷ industrial equipment repair and maintenance ▷ janitorial services ▷ laundry and dry cleaning ▷ landscaping/lawn care ▷ veterinary care
Intangible actions	Services directed at people's minds: ▷ education ▷ broadcasting ▷ information services ▷ theatres ▷ museums	Services directed at intangible assets: ▷ banking ▷ legal services ▷ accounting ▷ securities ▷ insurance

WHAT IS THE NATURE OF THE SERVICE ACT?

A service has been described as a 'deed, act or performance' (Berry, 1980). Two fundamental issues are at whom (or what) is the act directed, and is this act tangible or intangible in nature?

As shown in Figure 1, these two questions result in a four-way classification scheme involving 1. tangible actions to people's bodies, such as airline transportation, haircutting and surgery; 2. tangible actions to goods and other physical possessions, such as air freight, lawnmowing and janitorial services; 3. intangible actions directed at people's minds, such as broadcasting and education; and 4. intangible actions directed at people's intangible assets, such as insurance, investment banking and consulting.

Sometimes a service may seem to spill over into two or more categories. For instance, the delivery of educational, religious or entertainment services (directed primarily at the mind) often entails tangible actions such as being in a classroom, church or theatre; the delivery of financial services may require a visit to a bank to transform intangible financial assets into hard cash; and the delivery of airline services may affect some travellers' states of mind as well as physically moving their bodies from one airport to another. But in most instances the core service act is confined to one of the four categories, although there may be secondary acts in another category.

INSIGHTS AND IMPLICATIONS

Why is this categorisation scheme useful to service marketers? Basically it helps answer the following questions:

1. Does the customer need to be *physically* present:
   a. throughout service delivery?
   b. only to initiate or terminate the service transaction (e.g. dropping off a car for repair and picking it up again afterwards)?
   c. not at all (the relationship with the service supplier can be at arm's length through the mails, telephone or other electronic media)?

2. Does the customer need to be *mentally* present during service delivery? Can mental presence be maintained across physical distances through mail or electronic communications?

FIGURE 2:   RELATIONSHIPS WITH CUSTOMERS

Type of relationship between the service organisation and its customers

	'MEMBERSHIP' RELATIONSHIP	NO FORMAL RELATIONSHIP
Nature of service delivery Continuous delivery of service	▷ insurance ▷ telephone subscription ▷ college enrolment ▷ banking ▷ American Automobile Association	▷ radio station ▷ police protection ▷ lighthouse ▷ public highway
Discrete transactions	▷ long-distance phone calls ▷ theatre series subscription ▷ commuter ticket or transit pass	▷ car rental ▷ mail service ▷ toll highway ▷ pay phone ▷ movie theatre ▷ public transportation ▷ restaurant

3. In what ways is the target of the service act 'modified' by receipt of the service? And how does the customer benefit from these 'modifications'?

It's not always obvious what the service is and what it does for the customer because services are ephemeral. By identifying the target of the service and then examining how it is 'modified' or changed by receipt of the service act, we can develop a better understanding of the nature of the service product and the core benefits that it offers. For instance, a haircut leaves the recipient with shorter and presumably more appealingly styled hair, air freight gets the customer's goods speedily and safely between two points, a news radio broadcast updates the listener's mind about recent events, and life insurance protects the future value of the insured person's assets.

If customers need to be physically present during service delivery, then they must enter the service 'factory' (whether it be a train, a hairdressing salon, or a hospital at a particular location) and spend time there while the service is performed. Their satisfaction with the service will be influenced by the interactions they have with ser-

vice personnel, the nature of the service facilities, and also perhaps by the characteristics of other customers using the same service. Questions of location and schedule convenience assume great importance when a customer has to be physically present or must appear in person to initiate and terminate the transaction.

Dealing with a service organisation at arm's length, by contrast, may mean that a customer never sees the service facilities at all and may not even meet the service personnel face to face. In this sort of situation, the outcome of the service act remains very important, but the process of service delivery may be of little interest, since the customer never goes near the 'factory'. For instance, credit cards and many types of insurance can be obtained by mail or telephone.

For operational reasons it may be very desirable to get the customer out of the factory and to transform a 'high-contact' service into a 'low-contact' one (Chase, 1978). The chances of success in such an endeavour will be enhanced when the new procedures also offer customers greater convenience. Many services directed at things rather than people formerly required the customer's presence but are now delivered at arm's length.

Certain financial services have long used the mails to save customers the inconvenience of personal visits to a specific office location. Today, new electronic distribution channels have made it possible to offer instantaneous delivery of financial services to a wide array of alternative locations. Retail banking provides a good example, with its growing use of such electronic delivery systems as automatic teller machines in airports or shopping centres, pay-by-phone bill-paying, or on-line banking facilities in retail stores.

By thinking creatively about the nature of their services, managers of service organisations may be able to identify opportunities for alternative, more convenient forms of service delivery or even for transformation of the service into a manufactured good. For instance, services to the mind such as education do not necessarily require attendance in person since they can be delivered through the mails or electronic media (Britain's Open University, which makes extensive use of television and radio broadcasts, is a prime example). Two-way communication hook-ups can make it possible for a physically distant teacher and students to interact directly where this is necessary to the educational process (one recent Bell System advertisement featured a chamber music class in a small town being taught by an instructor several hundred miles away). Alternatively, lectures can be packaged and sold as books, records or videotapes. And programmed learning exercises can be developed in computerised form, with the terminal serving as a Socratic surrogate.

WHAT TYPE OF RELATIONSHIP DOES THE SERVICE ORGANISATION HAVE WITH ITS CUSTOMERS?

With very few exceptions, consumers buy manufactured goods at discrete intervals, paying for each purchase separately and rarely entering into a formal relationship with the manufacturer. (Industrial purchasers, by contrast, often enter into long-term relationships with suppliers and sometimes receive almost continuous delivery of certain supplies.)

In the service sector both household and insti-tutional purchasers may enter into ongoing relationships with service suppliers and may receive service on a continuing basis. This offers a way of categorising service. We can ask, does the service organisation enter into a 'membership' relationship with its customers – as in telephone subscriptions, banking and the family doctor – or is there no formal relationship? And is service delivered on a continuous basis – as in insurance, broadcasting and police protection – or is each transaction recorded and charged separately? Figure 2 shows the 2 x 2 matrix resulting from this categorisation, with some additional examples in each category.

INSIGHTS AND IMPLICATIONS

The advantage to the service organisation of a membership relationship is that it knows who its current customers are and, usually, what use they make of the services offered. This can be valuable for segmentation purposes if good records are kept and the data are readily accessible in a format that lends itself to computerised analysis. Knowing the identities and addresses of current customers enables the organisation to make effective use of direct mail, telephone selling and personal sales calls – all highly targeted marketing communication media.

The nature of service relationships also has important implications for pricing. In situations where service is offered on an ongoing basis, there is often just a single periodic charge covering all services contracted for. Most insurance policies fall in this category, as do tuition and board fees at a residential college. The big advantage of this package approach is its simplicity. Some memberships, however, entail a series of separate and identifiable transactions with the price paid being tied explicitly to the number and type of such transactions. While more complex to administer, such an approach is fairer to customers (whose usage patterns may vary widely) and may discourage wasteful use of what are perceived as 'free' services. In such instances, members may be offered advantages over casual users, such as discounted rates (telephone subscribers pay less for long-

FIGURE 3:   CUSTOMISATION AND JUDGEMENT IN SERVICE DELIVERY

Extent to which service characteristics are customised

	HIGH	LOW
Extent to which customer-contact personnel exercise judgement in meeting individual customer needs HIGH	legal service health care/surgery architectural design executive search firm real estate agency taxi service beautician plumber education (tutorials)	education (large classes) preventive health programmes
LOW	telephone service hotel services retail banking (excl. major loans) good restaurant	public transportation routine appliance repair fast-food restaurant movie theatre spectator sports

distance calls made from their own phones than do pay-phone users) or advance notification and priority reservations (as in theatre subscriptions). Some membership services offer certain services (such as rental of equipment or connection to a public utility system) for a base fee and then make incremental charges for each separate transaction above a defined minimum.

Profitability and customer convenience are central issues in deciding how to price membership services. Will the organisation generate greater long-term profits by tying payment explicitly to consumption, by charging a flat rate regardless of consumption, or by unbundling the components of the service and charging a flat rate for some and an incremental rate for others? Telephone and electricity services, for instance, typically charge a base fee for connection to the system and rental of equipment, plus a variety of incremental charges for consumption above a defined minimum. On the other hand, Wide Area Telephone Service (WATS) offers the convenience of unlimited long-distance calling for a fixed fee. How important is it to customers to have the convenience of paying a single periodic

fee that is known in advance? For instance, members of the American Automobile Association (AAA) can obtain information booklets, travel advice and certain types of emergency road services free of additional charges. Such a package offers elements of both insurance and convenience to customers who may not be able to predict their exact needs in advance.

Where no formal relationship exists between supplier and customer, continuous delivery of the product is normally found only among that class of services that economists term 'public goods' – such as broadcasting, police and lighthouse services, and public highways – where no charge is made for use of a service that is continuously available and financed from tax revenues. Discrete transactions, where each usage involves a payment to the service supplier by an essentially 'anonymous' consumer, are exemplified by many transportation services, restaurants, movie theatres, shoe repairs and so forth. The problems of such services is that marketers tend to be much less well informed about who their customers are and what use each customer makes of the service than their counterparts in membership organisations.

Membership relationships usually result in customer loyalty to a particular service supplier (sometimes there is no choice because the supplier has a monopoly). As a marketing strategy, many service businesses seek ways to develop formal, ongoing relations with customers in order to ensure repeat business and/or ongoing financial support. Public radio and television broadcasters, for instance, develop membership clubs for donors and offer monthly programme guides in return; performing arts organisations sell subscription series; transit agencies offer monthly passes; airlines create clubs for high-mileage fliers; and hotels develop 'exclusive service plans' offering priority reservations and upgraded rooms for frequent guests. The marketing task here is to determine how it might be possible to build sales and revenues through such memberships but to avoid requiring membership when this would result in freezing out a large volume of desirable casual business.

HOW MUCH ROOM IS THERE FOR CUSTOMISATION AND JUDGEMENT?

Relatively few consumer goods nowadays are built to special order; most are purchased 'off the shelf'. The same is true for a majority of industrial goods, although by permutating options it's possible to give the impression of customisation. Once they've purchased their goods, of course, customers are usually free to use them as they see fit.

The situation in the service sector, by contrast, is sharply different. Because services are created as they are consumed, and because the customer is often actually involved in the production process, there is far more scope for tailoring the service to meet the needs of individual customers. As shown in Figure 3, customisation can proceed along at least two dimensions. The first concerns the extent to which the characteristics of the service and its delivery system lend themselves to customisation; the second relates to how much judgement customer-contact personnel are able to exercise in defining the nature of the service received by individual customers.

Some service concepts are quite standardised. Public transportation, for instance, runs over fixed routes on predetermined schedules. Routine appliance repairs typically involve a fixed charge, and the customer is responsible for dropping off the item at a given retail location and picking it up again afterwards. Fast-food restaurants have a small, set menu; few offer the customer much choice in how the food will be cooked and served. Movies, entertainment and spectator sports place the audience in a relatively passive role, albeit a sometimes noisy one.

Other services offer customers a wide choice of options. Each telephone subscriber enjoys an individual number and can use the phone to obtain a broad array of different services – from receiving personal calls from a next-door-neighbour to calling a business associate on the other side of the world, and from data transmission to dial-a-prayer. Retail bank accounts are also customised, with each cheque or bank card carrying the customer's name and personal code. Within the constraints set down by the bank, the customer enjoys considerable latitude in how and when the account is used and receives a personalised monthly statement. Good hotels and restaurants usually offer their customers an array of service options from which to choose, as well as considerable flexibility in how the service product is delivered to them.

But in each of these instances, the role of the customer-contact personnel (if there are any) is somewhat constrained. Other than tailoring their personal manner to the customer and answering straightforward questions, contact personnel have relatively little discretion in altering the characteristics of the service they deliver: their role is basically that of operator or order-taker. Judgement and discretion in customer dealings is usually reserved for managers or supervisors, who will not normally become involved in service delivery unless a problem arises.

A third category of services gives the customer-contact personnel wide latitude in how they deliver the service, yet these individuals do not significantly differentiate the characteristics of their services between one customer and another. For instance, educators who teach courses by lectures and give multiple-choice, computer-scored exams expose each of their students to a potentially similar experience, yet one professor may elect to teach a specific course in a very different way from a colleague at the same institution.

However, there is a class of services that not only involves a high degree of customisation but requires customer-contact personnel to exercise judgement concerning the characteristics of the service and how it is delivered to each customer. Far from being reactive in their dealings with customers, these service personnel are often prescriptive: users (or clients) look to them for advice as well as for customised execution. In this category the locus of control shifts from the user to the supplier – a situation that some customers may find disconcerting. Consumers of surgical services literally place their lives in the surgeon's hands (the same, unfortunately, is also true of taxi services in many cities). Professional services such as law, medicine, accounting and architecture fall within this category. They are all white-collar 'knowledge industries', requiring extensive training to develop the requisite skills and judgement needed for satisfactory service delivery. Deliverers of such services as taxi drivers, beauticians and plumbers are also found in this category. Their work is customised to the situation at hand and in each instance, the customer purchases the expertise required to devise a tailor-made solution.

INSIGHTS AND IMPLICATIONS

To a much greater degree than in the manufacturing sector, service products are 'custom-made'. Yet customisation has its costs. Service management often represents an ongoing struggle between the desires of marketing managers to add value and the goals of operations managers to reduce costs through standardisation. Resolving such disputes, a task that may require arbitration by the general manager, requires a good understanding of consumer choice criteria, particularly as these relate to price/value trade-offs and competitive positioning strategy. At the present time, most senior

managers in service businesses have come up through the operations route; hence, participation in executive education programmes may be needed to give them the necessary perspective on marketing to make balanced decisions. Customisation is not necessarily important to success. As Levitt (1972, 1976) has pointed out, industrialising a service to take advantage of the economies of mass production may actually increase consumer satisfaction. Speed, consistency and price savings may be more important to many customers than customised service. In some instances, such as spectator sports and the performing arts, part of the product experience is sharing the service with many other people. In other instances the customer expects to share the service facilities with other consumers, as in hotels or airlines, yet still hopes for some individual recognition and custom treatment. Allowing customers to reserve specific rooms or seats in advance, having contact personnel address them by name (it's on their ticket or reservation slip), and providing some latitude for individual choice (room service and morning calls, drinks and meals) are all ways to create an image of customisation.

Generally, customers like to know in advance what they are buying – what the product features are, what the service will do for them. Surprises and uncertainty are not normally popular. Yet when the nature of the service requires a judgement-based, customised solution, as in a professional service, it is not always clear to either the customer or the professional what the outcome will be. Frequently, an important dimension of the professional's role is diagnosing the nature of the situation, then designing a solution.

In such situations those responsible for developing marketing strategy would do well to recognise that customers may be uneasy concerning the prior lack of certainty about the outcome. Customer-contact personnel in these instances not only are part of the product but determine what that product should be.

One solution to this problem is to divide the product into two separate components, diagnosis and implementation of a solution, that are executed and paid for separately. The process of diagnosis can and should be explained to the customer in advance, since the outcome of the diagnosis cannot always be predicted accurately. However, once that diagnosis has been made, the customer need not proceed immediately with the proposed solution; indeed, there is always the option of seeking a second opinion. The solution 'product', by contrast, can often be spelled out in detail beforehand, so that the customer has a reasonable idea of what to expect. Although there may still be some uncertainty, as in legal actions or medical treatment, the range of possibilities should be narrower by this point, and it may be feasible to assign probabilities to specified alternative outcomes.

Marketing efforts may need to focus on the process of client–provider interactions. It will help prospective clients make choices between alternative suppliers, especially where professionals are concerned, if they know something of the organisation's (or individual's) approach to diagnosis and problem-solving, as well as client-relationship style. These are considerations that transcend mere statements of qualification in an advertisement or brochure. For instance, some pediatricians allow new parents time for a free interview before any commitments are made. Such a trial encounter has the advantage of allowing both parties to decide whether or not a good match exists.

WHAT IS THE NATURE OF DEMAND AND SUPPLY FOR THE SERVICE?

Manufacturing firms can inventory supplies of their products as a hedge against fluctuations in demand. This enables them to enjoy the economies derived from operating plants at a steady level of production. Service businesses can't do this because it's not possible to inventory the finished service. For instance, the potential income from an empty seat on an airline flight is lost forever once that flight takes off, and each hotel daily room vacancy is equally perishable. Likewise, the productive capacity of an auto

repair shop is wasted if no one brings a car for servicing on a day when the shop is open. Conversely, if the demand for a service exceeds supply on a particular day, the excess business may be lost. Thus, if someone can't get a seat on one airline, another carrier gets the business or the trip is cancelled or postponed. If an accounting firm is too busy to accept tax and audit work from a prospective client, another firm will get the assignment.

But demand and supply imbalances are not found in all service situations. A useful way of categorising services for this purpose is shown in Figure 4. The horizontal axis classifies organisations according to whether demand for the service fluctuates widely or narrowly over time; the vertical axis classifies them according to whether or not capacity is sufficient to meet peak demand.

Organisations in Box 1 could use increases in demand outside peak periods, those in Box 2 must decide whether to seek continued growth in demand and capacity or to continue the status quo, while those in Box 3 represent growing organisations that may need temporary demarketing until capacity can be increased to meet or exceed current demand levels. But service organisations in Box 4 face an ongoing problem of trying to smooth demand to match capacity, involving both stimulation and discouragement of demand.

INSIGHTS AND IMPLICATIONS

Managing demand is a task faced by nearly all marketers, whether offering goods or services. Even where the fluctuations are sharp, and inventories cannot be used to act as a buffer between supply and demand, it may still be possible to manage capacity in a service business – for instance, by hiring part-time employees or renting extra facilities at peak periods. But for a substantial group of service organisations, successfully managing demand fluctuations through marketing actions is the key to profitability.

To determine the most appropriate strategy in each instance, it's necessary to seek answers to some additional questions:

FIGURE 4:   WHAT IS THE NATURE OF DEMAND FOR THE SERVICE RELATIVE TO SUPPLY?

Extent to which supply is constricted	Extent of demand fluctuations over time	
	WIDE	NARROW
Peak demand can usually be met without a major delay	1 electricity natural gas telephone hospital maternity unit police and fire emergencies	2 insurance legal services banking laundry and dry cleaning
Peak demand regularly exceeds capacity	4 accounting and tax preparation passenger transportation hotels and motels restaurants theatres	3 services similar to those in 2 but which have insufficient capacity for their base level of business

1. What is the typical cycle period of these demand fluctuations?
   ▷ predictable (i.e. demand varies by hour of the day, day of the week or month, season of the year).
   ▷ random (i.e. no apparent pattern to demand fluctuations).

2. What are the underlying causes of these demand fluctuations?
   ▷ customer habits or preferences (could marketing efforts change these)?
   ▷ actions by third parties (for instance, employers set working hours, hence marketing efforts might usefully be directed at those employers).
   ▷ non-forecastable events, such as health symptoms, weather conditions, acts of God and so forth – marketing can do only a few things about these, such as offering priority services to members and disseminating information about alternative services to other people.

One way to smooth out the ups and downs of demand is through strategies that encourage customers to change their plans voluntarily, such as offering special discount prices or added product value during periods of low demand. Another approach is to ration demand through a reservation or queuing system (which basically inventories demand rather than supply). Alternatively, to generate demand in periods of excess capacity, new business development efforts might be targeted at prospective customers with a counter-cyclical demand pattern. For instance, an accounting firm with a surfeit of work at the end of each calendar year might seek new customers whose financial year ended on 30 June or 30 September.

Determining what strategy is appropriate requires an understanding of who or what is the target of the service (as discussed in an earlier section of this article). If the service is delivered to customers in person, there are limits to how long a customer will wait in line; hence strategies to inventory or ration demand should focus on adoption of reservation systems (Sasser, 1976). But if the service is delivered to goods or to intangible assets, then a strategy of inventorying demand should be more feasible (unless the good is a vital necessity such as a car, in which case reservations may be the best approach).

FIGURE 5:   METHOD OF SERVICE DELIVERY

Nature of interaction between customer and service organisation	Availability of service outlets	
	SINGLE SITE	MULTIPLE SITES
Customer goes to service organisation	theatre barbershop	bus service fast-food chain
Service organisation comes to customer	lawn care service pest control service taxi	mail delivery AAA emergency repairs
Customer and service organisation transact at arm's length (mail or electronic communications)	credit card co. local TV station	broadcast network telephone co.

HOW IS THE SERVICE DELIVERED?

Understanding distribution issues in service marketing requires that two basic issues be addressed. The first relates to the method of delivery. Is it necessary for the customer to be in direct physical contact with the service organisation (customers may have to go to the service organisation, or the latter may come to the former), or can transactions be completed at arm's length? And does the service organisation maintain just a single outlet or does it serve customers through multiple outlets at different sites? The outcome of this analysis can be seen in Figure 5, which consists of six different cells.

INSIGHTS AND IMPLICATIONS

The convenience of receiving service is presumably lowest when a customer has to come to the service organisation and must use a specific outlet. Offering service through several outlets increases the convenience of access for customers but may start to raise problems of quality control as convenience of access relates to the consistency of the service product delivered. For some types of service the organisation will come to the customer. This is, of course, essential when the target of the service is some immovable physical item (such as a building that needs repairs or pest control treatment, or a garden that needs landscaping). But since it's usually more expensive to take

service personnel and equipment to the customer than vice versa, the trend has been away from this approach to delivering consumer services (e.g. doctors no longer like to make house calls). In many instances, however, direct contact between customers and the service organisation is not necessary; instead, transactions can be handled at arm's length by mail or electronic communications. Through the use of 800 numbers many service organisations have found that they can bring their services as close as the nearest telephone, yet obtain important economies from operating out of a single physical location.

Although not all services can be delivered through arm's length transactions, it may be possible to separate certain components of the service from the core product and to handle them separately. This suggests an additional classification scheme: categorising services according to whether transactions such as obtaining information, making reservations and making payment can be broken out separately from delivery of the core service. If they can be separated, then the question is whether or not it is advantageous to the service firm to allow customers to make these peripheral transactions through an intermediary or broker.

For instance, information about airline flights, reservations for such flights and purchases of tickets can all be made through a travel agent as well as directly through the airline. For those who prefer to visit in person, rather than conduct business by telephoning, this greatly increases the geographic coverage of distribution, since there are usually several travel agencies located more conveniently than the nearest airline office. Added value from using a travel agent comes from the 'one-stop shopping' aspect of travel agents; the customer can inquire about several airlines and make car rental and hotel reservations during the same call. Insurance brokers and theatre ticket agencies are also examples of specialist intermediaries that represent a number of different service organisations. Consumers sometimes perceive such intermediaries as more objective and more knowledgeable about alternatives than the various service suppliers they represent. The risk to the service firm of working through specialist intermediaries is, of course, that they may recommend use of a competitor's product!

DISCUSSION

Widespread interest in the marketing of services among both academics and practitioners is a relatively recent phenomenon. Possibly this reflects the fact that marketing expertise in the service sector has significantly lagged behind that in the manufacturing sector. Up to now most academic research and discussion has centred on the issue, 'How do services differ from goods?' A number of authors including Shostack (1977), Bateson (1979) and Berry (1980) have argued that there are significant distinctions between the two and have proposed several generalisations for management practice. But others such as Enis and Roering (1981) remain unconvinced that these differences have meaningful strategic implications.

Rather than continue to debate the existence of this broad dichotomy, it seems more useful to get on with the task of helping managers in service businesses do a better job of developing and marketing their products. We need to recognise that the service sector, particularly in the United States, is becoming increasingly competitive (Langeard et al., 1981), reflecting such developments as the partial or complete deregulation of several major service industries in recent years, the removal of professional association restrictions on using marketing techniques (particularly advertising), the replacement (or absorption) of independent service units by franchise chains, and the growth of new electronic delivery systems. As competition intensifies within the service sector, the development of more effective marketing efforts becomes essential to survival.

The classification schemes proposed in this article can contribute usefully to management practice in two ways. First, by addressing each of the five questions posed earlier, marketing managers can obtain a better understanding of the nature of their product, of the types of relationship their service organisations have with customers, of the factors underlying any sharp variations in demand, and of the characteristics of their service delivery systems. This understanding should help them identify how these factors shape marketing problems and opportunities and thereby affect the nature of the marketing task. Second, by recognising which characteristics their own service shares with other services, often in seemingly unrelated industries, managers will learn to look beyond their immediate competitors for new ideas as to how to resolve marketing problems that they have in common with firms in other service industries.

Recognising that the products of service organisations previously considered as 'different' actually face similar problems or share certain characteristics can yield valuable managerial insights. Innovation in marketing, after all, often reflects a manager's ability to seek out and learn from analogous situations in other contexts. These classification schemes should also be of value to researchers to whom they offer an alternative to either broad-brush research into services or an industry-by-industry approach. Instead, they suggest a variety of new ways of looking at service businesses, each of which may offer opportunities for focused research efforts. Undoubtedly there is also room for further refinement of the schemes proposed.

REFERENCES

Bateson, John E.G. (1979), 'Why We Need Service Marketing' in O.C. Ferrell, S.W. Brown and C.W. Lamb (eds.), *Conceptual and Theoretical Developments in Marketing*, American Marketing Association, Chicago, pp. 131–46.

Berry, Leonard L. (1980), 'Services Marketing Is Different', *Business Week*, May–June, pp. 24–9.

Bucklin, Louis (1963), 'Retail Strategy and the Classification of Consumer Goods', *Journal of Marketing*, 27, January, p. 50.

Chase, Richard B. (1978), 'Where Does the Customer Fit in a Service Operation?', *Harvard Business Review*, 56, November–December, pp. 137–42.

Copeland, Melvin T. (1923), 'The Relation of Consumers' Buying Habits to Marketing Methods', *Harvard Business Review*, 1, April, pp. 282–9.

Enis, Ben M. and Kenneth J. Roering (1981), 'Services Marketing: Different Products, Similar Strategies' in J.H. Donnelly and W.R. George (eds.), *Marketing of Services*, American Marketing Association, Chicago.

Hill, T.P. (1977), 'On Goods and Services', *Review of Income and Wealth*, 23, December, pp. 315–38.

Hunt, Shelby D. (1976), *Marketing Theory*, Grid, Columbus, OH.

Judd, Robert C. (1964), 'The Case for Redefining Services', *Journal of Marketing*, 28, January, p. 59.

Knisely, Gary (1979), 'Marketing and the Services Industry', *Advertising Age*, 15 January, pp. 47–50; 19 February, pp. 54–60; 19 March, pp. 58–62; 15 May, pp. 57–8.

Kotler, Philip (1980), *Principles of Marketing*, Prentice-Hall, Inc., Englewood Cliffs, NJ.

Langeard, Eric, John E.G. Bateson, Christopher H. Lovelock and Pierre Eiglier (1981), *Services Marketing: New Insights from Consumers and Managers*, Marketing Science Institute, Cambridge, Mass.

Levitt, Theodore (1972), 'Production Line Approach to Service', *Harvard Business Review*, 50, September–October, p. 41.

Levitt, Theodore (1976), 'The Industrialization of Service', *Harvard Business Review*, p. 54. September–October), pp. 63–74.

Lovelock, Christopher H. (1980), 'Towards a Classification of Services' in C.W. Lamb and P.M. Dunne, (eds.), *Theoretical Developments in Marketing*, American Marketing Association, Chicago, pp. 72–6.

Lovelock, Christopher H. (1981), 'Why Marketing Management Needs to Be Different for Services' in J.H. Donnelly and W.R. George (eds.), *Marketing of Services*, American Marketing Association, Chicago, Ill.

Rathmell, John M. (1974), *Marketing in the Services Sector*, Winthrop, Cambridge, Mass.

Sasser, W. Earl, Jr (1976), 'Match Supply and Demand in Service Industries', *Harvard Business Review*, 54, November–December, p. 133.

Sasser, W. Earl, Jr, R. Paul Olsen and D. Daryl Wyckoff (1978), *Management of Service Operations: Text and Cases*, Allyn & Bacon, Boston.

Shostack, G. Lynn (1977), 'Breaking Free from Product Marketing', *Journal of Marketing*, 41, April, pp. 73–80.

Thomas, Dan R.E. (1978), 'Strategy Is Different in Service Businesses', *Harvard Business Review*, 56, July–August, pp. 158–65.

Designing a Long-range Marketing Strategy for Services

Christian Grönroos

The purpose of the article is to develop a frame of reference for long-range marketing strategy, labelled the Three-stage Model, *which could benefit the attempts of service firms and institutions to introduce marketing successfully and eventually to achieve marketing-oriented operations. The author stresses some organisational aspects especially concerning the use of traditional marketing departments for handling an organisation's marketing function. The views on service marketing are supported by a substantial amount of empirical evidence from the industrial and the consumer service sector. The frame of reference and the organisational views of the marketing of services will be equally valid for industrial marketing of services and for marketing consumer services.*

INTRODUCTION

Marketing orientation means that a firm or organisation plans its operations according to market needs. The objectives of the firm should be to satisfy customer needs rather than merely to use existing production facilities or raw material. The organisation's marketing activities will be concerned with analysing and revealing customer needs, developing products which will satisfy those needs, and demonstrating the need-satisfying qualities of the products in order to make customers buy them.

In the goods-producing sector marketing activities have often been organised by establishing separate marketing departments, which have been made responsible for the marketing activities of the firm. The marketing department has been used as a means of making goods-producing companies marketing-oriented. In many cases, such firms have been accused of merely paying lip service to the so-called marketing concept. However, the organisational solution which has been used still seems to have a fair chance of succeeding.

At least this is the case for firms producing consumer goods. In the industrial sector there is a stronger interdependence between different departments of the companies, and therefore, the marketing activities cannot be as well planned and implemented within a marketing department as in the context of consumer goods.[1] Marketing seems to lead to some organisational problems.[2]

In the context of services there is very little explicit marketing knowledge today. Most frequently the marketing establishment, both academicians and practitioners, strongly resist the view that the marketing of services in any critical dimension could differ from that of physical goods. There are, however, some signs of a shift in thinking.[3-8] This will, in my opinion, benefit firms and institutions in the vast and growing service sector of Western economies. There the service sector counts for almost 50 per cent – and in some countries for much more – of total employment and gross national product. Indeed, we are moving into a post-industrial society, [9, 10] where the impact of services on welfare and the total economy is substantial, and yet we know almost nothing about how to manage marketing of services and about how to organise for marketing in service organisations.

Today, there is some evidence supporting the opinion that marketing is a difficult task in the service sector, and that service companies are less marketing-oriented than firms in the goods-producing sector.[3, 6, 11] Moreover, marketing executives who are experienced with consumer goods marketing in many cases seem to feel uncomfortable when coming into a service business. Marketing is often a small and marginal business function, and their past experience somehow does not seem quite applicable.[6, 7]

CHARACTERISTICS OF SERVICES

Services are immaterial and physically intangible. The customer cannot see, feel or taste a service, and therefore there will be substantial evaluation problems for him. As he is not able to evaluate the abstract service, he will look for tangible clues in the service context which he can use as a basis for an evaluation. Furthermore, services are frequently to a great extent consumed as they are produced. Because of this characteristic of services *buyer/seller interactions* emerge. The producing firm and its representatives gets in contact with its customers. In some cases one is confronted only with machines and other non-human attributes of the organisation, but most frequently human representatives of the service provider are also involved in the buyer/seller interactions.

Finally, services are activities, not things, although physical goods or things may be needed either to support or to facilitate the service consumption.[12] This means that a service is produced in a process which simultaneously *is* the service. The output of the production process cannot be separated – more than to some extent – from the process itself. Moreover, this process takes place in the presence of the consumer and with the co-operation of the consumer.[13]

The characteristics of services discussed above lead to some important conclusions about what actually is the service in the opinion of the consumer. His evaluation of a given service's capability of satisfying his needs will depend on several components in the service context.[4] *First* of all, the *means of production*, the technological resources and the human resources of the organisation, are important. A customer's preferences towards a given service will be influenced by the exterior and interior of offices, by the condition of transportation vehicles, by machines, documents and other items, as well as by the company employees. *Secondly*, the customer's opinion of a service depends on the *production process*, i.e. it depends on the way in which production resources are used in order to produce the service. For instance, the capabilities and behaviour of consultants, bank tellers and travel agency representatives, and their way of taking advantage of the other means of production, will have an impact on the customer's evaluation of the service. *Thirdly*, other people simultaneously purchasing or consuming a service may influence the preferences of a given customer. In the next section I shall discuss the marketing consequences of this view of the service offering content.

THE THREE-STAGE MODEL

In order to satisfy the needs of its target market the *Three-stage Model* holds that the service organisation will have to consider three stages in the customer's opinion of the need-satisfying capabilities of the service offerings provided by the organisation. These are:

1. *interest* in the organisation and its service offerings as possible means of satisfying the customer's needs;

2. *purchase* of a service offering in order to get the particular need satisfied; and

3. *repeat purchase* of the same or similar offering provided by the organisation whenever needed by the customer.

These three stages will have substantial consequences for the marketing of services, especially for designing a long-range marketing strategy. At each of the stages the objective of the marketing efforts and the nature of marketing will be different. The objective of marketing at each stage should be:

1. to *create interest* in the company and its service offerings;

2. to *turn the general interest into sales* by activities during the *purchasing process*, i.e. from the moment the potential consumer has come to the company or its representative up to the moment he has made the purchase decision; and finally

3. to *guarantee resales* by activities during the *consumption process*, i.e. when the service is consumed, usually in very close contact with the service provider and the production process.

There is a very clear difference between the marketing activities at the second and third stages as compared to the activities at the first stage. Interest is mainly created by developing an attractive company image, by advertising and other mass-marketing efforts, and in industrial marketing to firms and institutions by personal sales activities by more or less professional salesmen. Furthermore, interest can be created by offering services at a certain price level.

The mass-marketing activities cannot, however, result in much more than customer interest. A potential traveller may decide to get in contact with a given travel agency, a company may get interested in approaching a particular advertising agency, or a factory manager may find it suitable to ask for an offer from a security and maintenance company. Such an interest is also heavily influenced by external sources such as colleagues, family members and friends. The personal selling by professional salesmen, on the other hand, cannot lead to more than the creation of interest and perhaps sales. Resales are not, however, guaranteed by such efforts. One should notice that

this kind of personal selling normally exists only in industrial marketing of services, and not in marketing to ultimate consumers.

In most cases sales and certainly resales are achieved by other marketing activities than those which have been considered so far. These activities are frequently not thought of as marketing today, but nevertheless they do influence the preferences of the consumers towards a given service offering and therefore they are marketing activities. I here refer to activities in the buyer/seller interactions, which emerge in the buying and selling of services.

When a potential customer has come to the service company or its representative and is about to make up his mind about buying the service or not, he is confronted with the point of purchase, the employees, various kinds of document, etc. These certainly have an impact on his opinion of the service. For example, when choosing among administrative consultants the buyer will be influenced by the consultants themselves, their capabilities and behaviour, by the technological resources provided by the consulting agencies, etc.; when choosing among different banks the potential customer will be influenced by the location of bank offices, the capabilities, appearances and behaviour of the tellers, the supporting technological resources, documents, etc.

When the customer finally is consuming the service, he is in close contact with the service provider. He will be confronted with the means of production – both human and non-human – and with the production process. The means of production consist of *resources* and in the production process *these resources are utilised*. The consumer's future purchasing behaviour, i.e. possible resales, is to a great extent influenced by what happens during the consumption process.

Consequently, managing the buyer/seller interactions of the purchasing and consumption process is a marketing task and not solely an operational, technological or personnel problem. It can be labelled the *interactive marketing function* of service organisations. In the following sections I shall turn to the problem of fitting together the

FIGURE 1:   THE MARKETING AND NEED-ADAPTATION CIRCLE

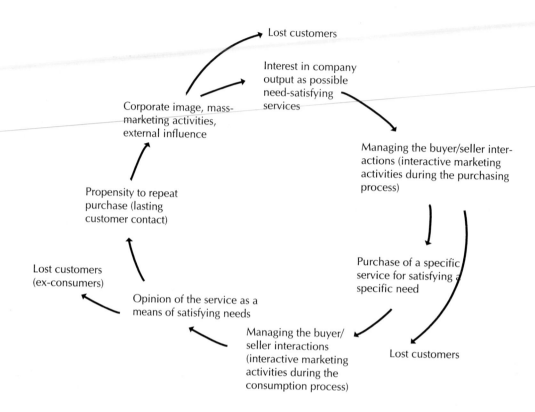

THE MARKETING AND NEED-ADAPTATION CIRCLE

objectives and activities of marketing at the various stages into a long-range marketing strategy for services.

According to the *Three-stage Model* the service company has to respond to the needs of its customers throughout the process. When interest is created, the customer in many cases has a rather vague idea of his actual needs. He is looking for some kind of transportation or bank account in general, or for some sort of factory maintenance or office cleaning. In the purchasing process, the scope of the needs is narrowed, and finally the customer decides to buy a certain service offering as the 'best' means of satisfying the needs he feels that he has at the moment. During the consump-

tion process he can evaluate how the service which he gets actually corresponds to his perceived needs. As a result he will be satisfied enough to come back, or he will be disappointed and become an ex-customer.

Figure 1 illustrates this process and demonstrates the place of the marketing functions in the process. In order to attract customers and turn an initial interest in the service offerings into sales and finally into resales and lasting customer contacts, a *continuous adaptation* of the operations to the customers' needs is required. Throughout the whole process the organisation will have to demonstrate its capabilities to offer services, which really can satisfy these needs. This fact leads to substantial marketing consequences.

The marketing and need-adaptation circle in Figure 1 illustrates the need for various kinds of activity throughout the process. By these activities the service firm tries to create customer interest in the services, turn the interest into sales, and in the long run establish lasting business contacts with satisfied customers and clients. The traditional mass-marketing activities and the personal selling by professional salesmen are by no means unimportant to the success of a service organisation, but in my opinion, managing the buyer/seller interactions – i.e. the interactive marketing function – is the most important marketing function in service organisations. Neglecting them may in the future be disastrous, in the increasingly competitive environment of many service industries.

It should be noticed that managing the interactive marketing function is not only handling the human resources of the firm. The buyer/seller interactions involve technological resources as well. Planning such resources should also be a marketing task, so that, for instance, the location and interior of offices, computer systems, fee-collection systems, transportation vehicles, and documentation systems benefit marketing instead of restricting or even counteracting it, as often is the case today. Moreover, the buyer/seller interactions also involve contacts between customers. Other customers may have an immense impact on a person's opinion of a service which he is about to buy or which he is consuming. They may, by their appearance or behaviour, increase the quality of a service but their influence can also be very undesired. Then their activities lead to a deterioration of service quality. Clearly, managing the interactions between customers should be a marketing task, too.

As an illustration of a long-range marketing strategy based on the marketing and need-adaptation circle concept, let us consider the activities of a transportation company offering transportation services by sea. The company is operating on a consumer market as well as on industrial markets, offering both transportation services and conference arrangements to business firms and other organisations. This example describes the company's marketing of conference services.

Through advertising efforts and various kinds of PR activity the company attempts to make potential clients interested in it as a possible conference operator. Occasionally, personal selling efforts are also used. Moreover, it relies heavily on external influence on potential clients by satisfied customers promoting the idea of using its ships as a possible conference site. The marketing activities used at this stage are mostly mass-marketing efforts and indirect promotion drawing on the company's reputation and on word-of-mouth communication.

When a potential client contacts the transportation company, the marketing activities become more specifically directed towards the unique needs of the client. The purchasing process starts. At this stage a conference service which corresponds to the wishes of the client and to his conference budget must be designed. Here the output of the process, sales, is to a great extent a result of personal selling efforts. The salesman will have to find out what the client really desires. His ability to negotiate is considered critical to the success of the marketing efforts. The client should be offered a conference design, which he will feel satisfied with during and after the conference, rather than merely a minimum budget design which seems to correspond to his initially expressed needs but in the long run will be a disappointment to him. The salesman is, therefore, encouraged to think of himself more as a consultant than as anything else.

If the purchasing process comes to a successful end the potential client will buy a conference service from the company. The marketing manager does not, however, stop being concerned with the client as soon as the purchase decision has been made. Marketing activities are carried out until the end of the conference. The company attempts to produce a service which corresponds to the expectations of the client. The conference facilities, arrangements for meals and accommodation, the appearance and performance of the personnel on board, etc. are considered to be of utmost importance to the success or failure of the company as a conference operator in the mind of the client. By appropriately designing the conference facilities as well as other necessary technological resources – e.g. cabin design, access to telex and telephone communication – and by conducting internal marketing programmes in order to improve the marketing performance of various categories of employee, the company tries to guarantee that the client, the conference participants, and of course other passengers too, leave the ship in a state of satisfaction and with a favourable image of the transportation company and its services in mind. Eventually, the client and conference participants will probably return to the company when the need for conference services or transportation services occurs. Moreover, they are expected to have a considerable impact on the word-of-mouth influence on potential customers that exists about the company, resulting in increased interest in the company and its service.

Thus, generally speaking, marketing services can be viewed as a continuous process, a circle. Successful marketing attracts customers who get into the circle and stay there, because they are satisfied with the performance of the firm. A customer may, however, break out at any stage of the process if the company is not capable of giving him what it has promised to do. A client may be lost because the company in an advertising campaign makes promises which the inactive marketing function cannot keep, or because the organisation cannot successfully manage the buyer/seller interactions of the purchasing and/or consumption processes. Moreover, external influence by colleagues or friends may also have an impact on the customer's behaviour.

The marketing and need-adaptation circle concept demonstrates how the preferences of a customer towards a certain service depends on an enormous part of the service company and on the operations of the company. Consequently, it demonstrates the importance of the marketing function in the context of service. In the next section of the article I shall turn to the question of how marketing has been introduced in service companies and how one could organise for successful marketing in the service sector.

THE MISUSE OF MARKETING DEPARTMENTS

When service companies have introduced marketing to any great extent, separate marketing departments have frequently been established. The model has been taken from the goods-producing sector – especially consumer goods – where the marketing activities of the firm to a high degree can be initiated, planned and implemented by and within the marketing department. What has happened in service firms? Other departments, such as operations, personnel, technology – as well as top management in many cases – have given up all their responsibility for the marketing performance. Before the marketing department was established, more or less spontaneous initiatives by various departments and persons in the firm were taken in improving the quality of the service and meeting the wishes and expectations of the consumers. Such activities tend to disappear in the new era of the marketing department.

What earlier was service production combined with often unconscious marketing efforts tends to become just plain service production. The firm has a separate department of specialists in marketing, so let them handle the marketing function and be responsible for the marketing performance of the organisation. At this moment the real problems of the company start. It is now that the firm will start losing customers. What has happened?

It is my opinion that the main reason for the company becoming increasingly production-oriented instead of marketing-oriented is a failure to see the nature of service marketing. The marketing of physical goods has been applied to service firms without noticing that the marketing of services seems to be different. Indeed such a difference is not commonly recognised even today.

The difference between the *marketing function* of an organisation and its *marketing department* should first of all be distinguished. The marketing function, as has been said in the article, is all activities which influence the preferences of the consumers towards the offerings and, therefore, also the success of the company and its chances of staying alive in the long run. The marketing

FIGURE 2:   THE RELATIONSHIP BETWEEN THE MARKETING FUNCTION AND THE MARKETING
DEPARTMENT

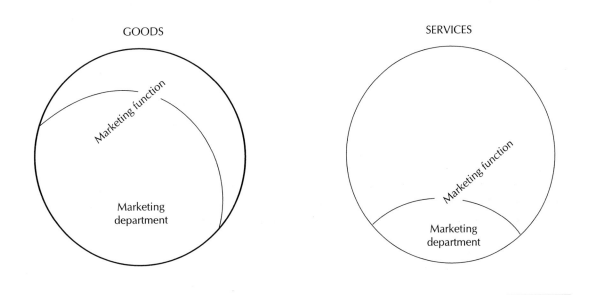

GOODS

SERVICES

Marketing function

Marketing
department

Marketing function

Marketing
department

department, on the other hand, is the organisational entity which is responsible for some but not necessarily all marketing activities performed by the firm. In Figure 2 the relationship between the marketing function and the marketing department of goods-producing firms and service companies, respectively, is illustrated.

In the goods sector, and especially as far as consumer goods are concerned, the marketing department can plan and implement most of the marketing activities, i.e. the marketing department is able to control almost the total marketing function. It can, therefore, also be given a total marketing responsibility. Only personal selling efforts by top management are normally outside the marketing department. In the industrial sector of goods-producing industries the situation is somewhat different, because of the greater interdependence between different business units.[1]

In the service sector the situation is entirely different. A traditional marketing department can control only a minor part of the marketing function. The marketing manager is in an offside position in the organisation. Usually he does not have

the necessary authority to manage the buyer/seller interactions. He cannot, therefore, plan and especially not implement activities within the interactive marketing function during the purchasing and consumption processes. Furthermore, people in the personnel department, operations department and other departments often are quite prejudiced against their activities simultaneously being the concerns of the marketing department and the marketing manager.

Consequently, the marketing department is mainly engaged in mass-marketing activities: planning advertising campaigns, designing brochures, etc. Moreover, personal selling to industrial buyers, some pricing decisions, and sometimes also some marketing research and analysis are performed by the marketing department. This means that the department which has been made responsible for the marketing activities mainly is concerned with creating customer interest. Those parts of the marketing function which influence sales are the responsibility of others, who are not particularly interested in marketing. Clearly, this is a most unhappy situation, but it is merely a consequence of the misuse of an organisational arrangement which has been developed for the goods-producing sector and not for service companies.

ORGANISING FOR MARKETING

It is quite clear that establishing marketing departments is not a useful means of introducing marketing in a service organisation. It must be realised, though, that *the marketing function is a key function in the service sector. Even if the term marketing is not used in connection with the activities in the buyer/seller interactions, managing these activities is a marketing function.* The responsibility for this marketing function must, therefore, be taken by someone who is concerned with the total marketing performance of the organisation. This person may be the marketing manager but as the head of a traditional, decentralised marketing department he will probably continuously come into conflict with other departments and their heads. It will, for instance, be difficult for him to avoid conflicts with the personnel department, but nevertheless, the personnel policy, including hiring, training and promoting almost every employee, as well as the design of job descriptions, should be a marketing task like, for instance, advertising.[3, 14, 15]

Successful service companies often do not have any marketing department at all, or they have very small marketing departments. In both cases the total marketing function is not expected by top management or by any part of the organisation to be initiated and implemented within a marketing department. If there is no marketing department, top management will take the responsibility for the marketing performance of the firm and there will be a fair chance that the different parts of the organisation accept their duty to assist top management in serving the customers. Of course, the managing director must realise the importance of the total marketing function, and especially of the interactive marketing function.

If the marketing department is comparatively small and top management keeps the total marketing responsibility, the other departments of the organisation may accept that they still have marketing tasks to perform, although there are marketing people in the company. It is essential that such a small marketing department either is concerned with the overall co-ordination of marketing activities and assisting other parts of the organisation to perform their marketing tasks, or is treated only as a specialist on some marketing activities and not as marketing specialists responsible for the total marketing function. As soon as the rest of the organisation, and indeed top management, starts to think of the marketing department as overall marketing specialists, the movement towards production-orientation begins.

As a conclusion, top management should never delegate the responsibility for the total marketing function to any department head. Preferably the top executive should keep it with himself. Unfortunately, when the company grows, the managing director will be so busy with other duties that it will be quite difficult for him to give the marketing function as much attention as would be necessary. It seems as if it would be almost impossible to solve the problem which follows within the organisational structure of today's service companies. Perhaps this is not so surprising, because the organisational structure has also been inherited from the goods-producing sector.

In order to illustrate the organisational aspects of service marketing, let us consider another transportation company which is engaged in urban mass transit. When the company in the past started to perform organised marketing activities, a traditional marketing department was established. The marketing activities of the company were delegated to this organisational unit headed by a marketing manager. What could the new department do? Mainly it was made responsible for advertising, some public relations activities and some market research. The marketing department became a rather weak unit within the organisational structure. Other parts of the company stopped being particularly concerned with the ways in which the company responded to the customers' wishes and transportation needs. A change in a production-oriented direction seems to have occurred.

The marketing department's attempts to influence the operational and personnel functions in a more marketing-oriented direction were resisted. The marketing manager's colleagues, to whom the responsibility for other business functions had been delegated, could, of course, not be expected to report to him and to be managed by him.

Eventually, the organisational structure was changed. The various functions were regrouped and as part of this process the status of the marketing department was changed. It became merely an information department responsible for both external information, such as advertising, PR and personal selling, and internal information. On the other hand, the marketing manager was removed from the marketing department to the board of directors, where he became a member responsible for co-ordinating the activities of all company functions and units in a marketing-oriented manner. Thus, the reduced marketing department *and* other organisational units are now expected to report to him. Instead of merely preparing marketing plans within the former marketing department, he is now responsible for developing a corporate plan of operations including advertising, pricing and other traditional marketing activities according to a goods-oriented philosophy, as well as technological resources, personnel planning, corporate image activities, etc. The new organisational structure is considered a more appropriate means of marketing-orienting the transportation company than the structure of the past.

In general, some sort of *organisational innovation* seems to be needed. As the managing director most frequently is too busy and the head of the marketing department is in an offside position, some kind of marketing co-ordinator on the top management level may be the solution: a person to whom a possible manager of market research, advertising and other mass-marketing activities, professional salesmen, and those responsible for personnel, operations, technology, etc., are all reporting. Then not only the traditional mass marketing and personal selling activities but the interactive marketing function could be managed with a responsibility for their marketing consequences. In such a case the result might be a mar-

keting-oriented service organisation, where not only lip service is paid to the marketing philosophy, but where the company really is adapting its operations to satisfying the needs of its target market.

SUMMARY

In order to design a long-range marketing strategy a service organisation will have to recognise the stages through which its customers proceed, from merely being interested in the company and its services to becoming loyal to the company. The marketing activities to be used in the different stages are not the same. Traditional mass-marketing efforts and personal selling by professional salesmen can only create customer interest and in some cases, when marketing to industrial buyers, also turn this interest to sales. However, sales, and, above all, resales and lasting customer contacts, cannot be achieved by these means. In spite of this fact, the traditional marketing activities from goods marketing mentioned above are usually the only activities of the service company which are considered to be marketing tasks.

Much more important to success are the activities performed in the buyer/seller interactions, which emerge during the purchasing and consumption processes. By these activities, which have been labelled the interactive marketing function of the service organisation, sales, and eventually, resales, are promoted.

Establishing traditional marketing departments does not seem to be an appropriate way of handling the total marketing function, because such a department usually cannot plan and implement activities within the interactive marketing function. As a matter of fact, marketing departments seem to be a bad means of making a service company marketing-oriented. Instead of becoming marketing-conscious the rest of the organisation rather tends to become production-oriented, thus leaving the total marketing responsibility to the marketing manager, who generally has not the necessary authority for such a responsibility. Therefore, an organisational innovation may be needed, if marketing-orientation is to be successfully introduced in service organisations.

NOTES

1. E. Frederick Webster Jr (1978), 'Management Science in Industrial Marketing', *Journal of Marketing*, January.

2. Håkan Håkansson and Claes Östberg (1975), 'Industrial Marketing, An Organisational Problem', *Industrial Marketing Management*, nos. 2–3.

3. Christian Grönroos (1978), 'A Service-oriented Approach to Marketing of Services', *European Journal of Marketing*, vol. 12, no. 8.

4. Christian Grönroos (1978), *The Nature of Service Marketing*, Swedish School of Economics and Business Administration, Helsingfors, Finalnd, working papers, no. 11 (report presented at the Seventh Annual Workshop on Research in Marketing, European Academy for Advanced Research in Marketing, Stockholm, May 1978).

5. Evert Gummesson (1978), 'Towards a Theory of Professional Services Marketing', *Industrial Marketing Management*, April.

6. Christian Grönroos (1979), 'An Applied Theory for Marketing Industrial Services', *Industrial Marketing Management*, no. 1.

7. G.L. Shostack (1977), 'Breaking Free from Product Marketing', *Journal of Marketing*, April.

8. Pierre Eiglier, E. Langeard, C.H. Lovelock and J.E.G. Bateson (1977), *Marketing Consumer Services: New Insights*, Marketing Science Institute, Cambridge, Mass.

9. Peter K. Mills (1977), *New Perspectives on Post-industrial Organizations*, Akademilitteratur, Stockholm.

10. Victor P. Fuchs (1968), *The Service Economy*, Columbia University Press for National Bureau of Economic Research, NY.

11. William R. George and Hiram C. Barksdale (1974), 'Marketing Activities in the Service Industries', *Journal of Marketing*, October.

12. John M. Rathmell (1974), *Marketing in the Services Sector*, Winthrop Publishers, Cambridge, Mass.

13. Pierre Eiglier and Eric Langeard (1975), 'Une approche nouvelle pour le marketing des services', *Revue Française de Gestion*, no. 2.

14. William R. George (1977), 'The Retailing of Services – A Challenging Future', *Journal of Retailing*, Fall.

15. David S. Davidson (1978), 'How to Succeed in a Service Industry ... Turn the Organization Chart Upside Down', *Management Review*, April.

Marketing-orientation Revisited: The Crucial Role of the Part-time Marketer

Evert Gummesson

THE PART-TIME MARKETER VS. THE FULL-TIME MARKETER

Marketing-orientation is an old issue. It has been written about in a stream of books and articles and is a major theme of conferences and consulting assignments. It is often a key issue in a company turn-around. It has been stated over and over again that the customer is the starting-point for successful business. It supposedly originated in the US but has probably been common knowledge among successful tradesmen throughout the world for ages. Production-orientation and product-orientation have been put up as its opposites with sales-orientation in between. Tables have been presented claiming that we have gone from production-orientation, where our resources and products were the focal point of interest, to marketing-orientation, putting the customer in focus; even the years when such a transition took place are sometimes given. The world, however, at this very moment, contains both extremes of these stages and variations in between them; even in a single company both extremes might coexist.

It is far more difficult to implant marketing-orientation in an organisational culture than textbook authors and university professors usually realise. Marketing-orientation does not occur because management preaches its gospel; it occurs when a customer notices the difference between now and before. Marketing-orientation becomes alive only when all members of an organisation have asked themselves, 'How do I contribute to excellence in customer relations and to revenue?', have answered the question and implemented the answer. It has to reach the firing-line in each specific department, function and organisational tier.

From this vantage point we could pose the question: 'What do the following people have in common: a telephone operator connecting a customer with a salesperson; an installation team from the supplier spending two weeks on the buyer's premises installing and testing new equipment; a management consultant presenting a progress report in an assignment; a customer telling a friend how badly she was treated at a seaside resort hotel; a managing director having dinner with a customer?'

The answer is that all these people influence customer relations, customer satisfaction, customer perceived quality, and revenue, they are all *part-time marketers* (PTMs). They carry out marketing activities but, in contrast to the full-time marketers, the FTMs, they do not belong to the marketing or sales department.

In Scandinavia, the Volvo CEO Gyllenhammar frequently (meaning every week) appears in the media to comment on traffic policy, environmental issues, unemployment, wages, leadership, the future of Europe, abusive methods in the training of horses, etc., assuming the role of statesman,

FIGURE 1: THEORIES AND CONCEPTS CONTRIBUTING TO THE EMERGENCE OF THE PTM CONCEPT

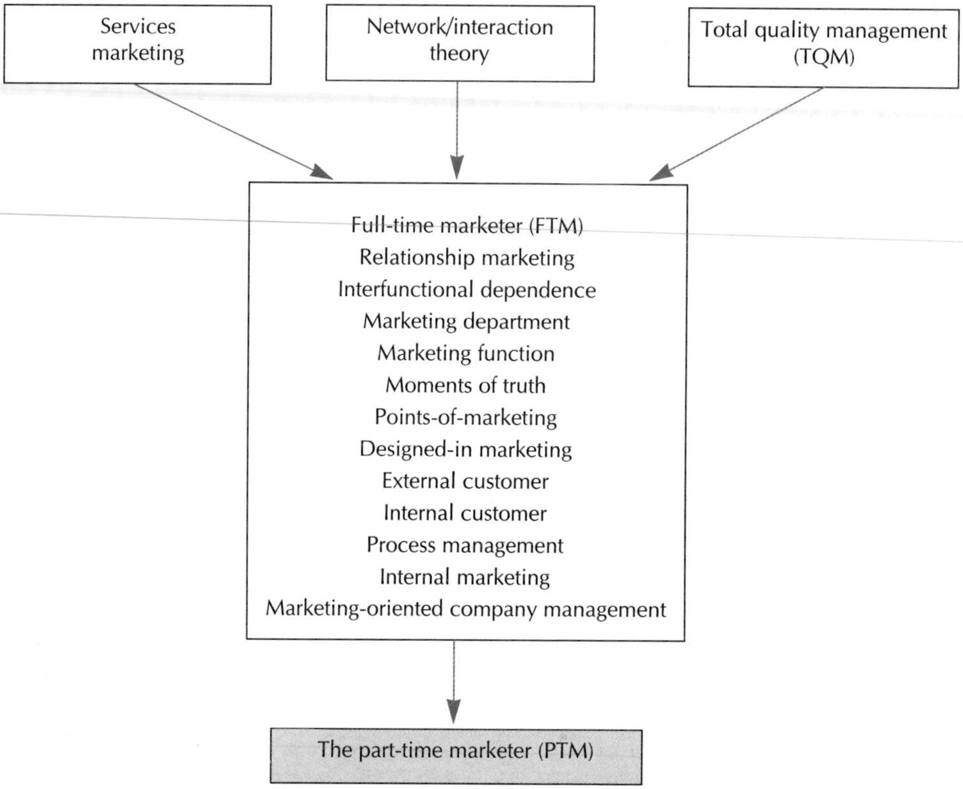

```
┌──────────────┐   ┌──────────────┐   ┌──────────────────┐
│   Services   │   │Network/inter-│   │ Total quality    │
│  marketing   │   │action theory │   │ management (TQM) │
└──────┬───────┘   └──────┬───────┘   └────────┬─────────┘
       └──────────────┐   │   ┌───────────────┘
                      ▼   ▼   ▼
      ┌──────────────────────────────────────────┐
      │         Full-time marketer (FTM)          │
      │         Relationship marketing            │
      │         Interfunctional dependence        │
      │            Marketing department           │
      │             Marketing function            │
      │              Moments of truth             │
      │             Points-of-marketing           │
      │             Designed-in marketing         │
      │              External customer            │
      │              Internal customer            │
      │             Process management            │
      │              Internal marketing           │
      │   Marketing-oriented company management   │
      └─────────────────────┬────────────────────┘
                            ▼
            ┌──────────────────────────────┐
            │  The part-time marketer (PTM) │
            └──────────────────────────────┘
```

indirectly promoting the cars by making Volvo a household word and reinforcing its image. On US television a totally different appearance is made by Chrysler's CEO Iacocca presenting the new car models in commercials. He exercises influence on customer relations by assuming the role of Chrysler's number one car salesman. In both cases the appearances are deliberate and well prepared and directed. The two CEOs know that they influence customer relations and revenue. But do others in the organisation understand their marketing role? All too often they don't. Even if they understand: how well do they handle it? This ignorance is reflected in inefficient action and eventually in the bottom line.

The importance that business attaches to a marketing-oriented approach is uncovered in a study made by the executive training centre INSEAD, France. In this study 128 major European companies ranked 18 strategic marketing issues for the 1990s.[1] Four of the issues directly concerned marketing-orientation and the organisation of marketing. They ranked as follows: 'Creating a marketing culture throughout the organisation', came no. 3; 'Adapting company structure to evolving changes in market strategies', no. 4; 'Recruiting and maintaining the necessary quality of marketing professionals', no. 5; and 'Improving the interface between marketing and technological resources', no. 8.

This article will explore the notion of the PTM and present concepts that can act as vehicles in renewing the approach to marketing-orientation. These concepts also influence organisational structure, decision-making and execution of marketing decisions; they are all interrelated and help to shed light on different facets of the same phenomenon. The PTM is chosen as the central concept supported by a number of auxiliary concepts. The primary theoretical base for generating the concepts is the recent developments in services marketing, industrial marketing (the network/interaction theory) and total quality management, TQM (see summary in Figure 1).

The approach to marketing in this article is conceptual and integrative. Its purpose is to contribute to theory generation grounded on qualitative, empirical data and not quantitative theory testing.[2,3] The concept of the PTM must be validated in action, and in action alone. A number of examples are presented, not as evidence, but in order to make the PTM concept come alive. The conclusions are based on a series of research projects carried out over a fifteen-year period. As research in marketing is fragmented, results have to be glued together with the practical experience and judgement of the researcher if a more integrated view is to be achieved.

The article will proceed to deal first with the theories on which the PTM concept is based; second, interfunctional dependency and the marketing function; third, the internal customer and internal marketing. The last section is a summary of conclusions.

NEW THEORETICAL DEVELOPMENTS AFFECTING THE PART-TIME MARKETER

This article will not look back into the history of marketing-orientation; others have already done that. The author's interest is the present and the future. What current approaches to marketing-orientation are there that might be of assistance for the 1990s?

There are two recent developments in marketing theory that emphasise the significance of the PTM although they neither use the term nor fully realise the consequences for marketing organisation. These are *services marketing theory* and the *network/interaction theory of industrial marketing*. A third non-marketing area whose implications for marketing have grown is *total quality management* (TQM).

These developments will be used as theoretical references in spelling out the concept of the PTM. They will be used because they contribute something new which is not as yet part of the marketing textbook. The author recognises that there may be other concepts and theories that are useful in approaching the PTM, for example the corporate strategy and organisation theory, but these are not explored here.

SERVICES MARKETING

Services marketing has grown into an independent field for marketing during the 1980s. Of the number of articles, reports and books on services marketing, according to the database Servmark, which stores references in English, 3 are from the 1950s, 98 from the 1960s, 885 from the 1970s, and 2,984 from the 1980s.[4] The influx of new references is almost exponential and since 1988 the Servmark organisation has not found it possible to enter new references. There are probably one or two thousand more in other languages. In industrialised countries in the western hemisphere the service sector (private and public together) accounts for two-thirds of the GNP, a slightly higher ratio of employment, and almost the whole net increase in jobs.[5,6] In services marketing it has been shown that the production, delivery and marketing are partially simultaneous and are partially carried out by the same employees who are partially in direct contact with the customer who partially consumes the service in interaction with the service provider. *Interaction* has become a key concept referring to the contact between the service provider's staff and the consumer. This creates another type of marketing than the traditional consumer product case where personal contact is handled by a salesperson and the impersonal contact by advertising. Thus another view on marketing organisation is warranted for service operations. European scholars and above all those from Northern Europe ('The Nordic School of Services'), France and the UK, have together with US scholars been active in developing services marketing theory.[7-11]

NETWORK/INTERACTION THEORY OF INDUSTRIAL MARKETING

This has been well documented in the 1980s.[12-14] It emanates primarily from Europe and is little known in the United States. A quotation from Ford et al.[15] will describe its basic vantage point:

> A company can be viewed as a node in an ever-widening pattern of interactions, in some of which it is a direct participant, some of which affect it indirectly and some of which occur independently of it. This web of interactions is so complex and multifarious as to deny full description or analysis. Indeed, the interaction between a single buyer and a selling company can be complex enough.

The complex networks of relations that exist in markets have many forms. They include dealers and distribution channels, franchise and licence agreements, joint ventures, strategic partnerships, social contracts, etc. A current phenomenon which stresses the significance of networks and long-term relationships is single sourcing and the just-in-time logistic system (JIT). Networks are the result of ideas and negotiations from many different units in a company; they can stem from the board, top management, R&D, the purchasing department, the marketing department, etc. The relations become strategic issues as they set an infrastructure, a network, in which the marketing game is played daily. Although the empirical background of the network/interaction theory is industrial markets it has wider application; it applies more generally to concentrated markets. Consumer goods marketing, when selling through a limited number of wholesalers or central purchasing departments of retail chains, is such an application. The buyer may, for example in the case of clothing, work out product specifications and the fashion design together with designers from the textile company and also inspect the progress of design work and production. A network is gradually built around a long-term interactive relationship.

TOTAL QUALITY MANAGEMENT (TQM)

The third body of knowledge is TQM. Quality started to become the focal point of interest among companies in Europe and North America in the 1980s, the driving force being the aggressive Japanese attacks on world markets. The literature on quality has grown at a rate similar to that of services literature.[16] Conceptual developments have emerged where quality, having been seen as a technological issue associated with specifications, blueprints, prototypes and manufacturing, is promoted to a strategic issue with corporate as well as marketing implications. Total quality is viewed as *customer-perceived quality* incorporating the internal capability of managing quality and the consideration of customer needs and customer satisfaction; quality has become part of marketing-orientation. The most striking and sensational contribution from TQM is that quality has become the integrator between production-orientation and marketing-orientation, between technology-driven and market-driven behaviour. It is the first time that these two extremes converge towards the same goal: customer-perceived quality and customer satisfaction. However, the impact of TQM on marketing textbooks so far has been little. The exception is services marketing, which has made quality a priority issue and has developed its own unique concepts and approaches.[17-19]

Services marketing, the network/interaction theory and TQM will be referred to subsequently as 'the three theories' although they are not fully-fledged theories but rather three baskets of new concepts, categories and models. 'The three theories' will be used as the springboard for developing the notion of the PTM. All three put the customer in focus. The basis for the two marketing 'theories' – although sprung from different sets of empirical data – is relationships, interactions and networks, and TQM contributes in the same direction. The term relationship marketing captures the essence of the contribution from 'the three theories'.

RELATIONSHIP MARKETING

Relationship marketing is different from manipulating customers by means of the four 'Ps' (product, price, promotion and place) which constitute the core of the reigning marketing mix 'theory'.[20] Efforts have been made to extend it into more 'Ps' in order to incorporate additional factors that are essential marketing management. In the author's view this is a detour and forces new marketing thinking into the strait-jacket of existing theory. Failure to market-orient companies may be due to the narrow perspective provided by traditional marketing mix theory, which is primarily based on a manipulative approach to mass marketing of packaged consumer goods to large US markets. Criticism of this approach to marketing has come from many directions. Gummesson[21] in Sweden talks about 'colonisation of marketing thought' through the US marketing textbook paradigm; Grönroos[22] in Finland recently attacked the marketing definition provided by the American Marketing Association; Robins[23] in Australia concludes that: 'there is an unmistakable feeling among marketing educators that the "4Ps" are fading'; the French/British marketing consultant de Ferrer[24] expresses his dissatisfaction with the European reverence towards US marketing thinking and its preachers: 'we fail to notice how much is not relevant to us, or how much that is of vital importance to Europeans is not treated at all'.

'The three theories' have proven themselves during the 1980s. Yet they are still in their infancy and in the author's view they will continue to grow in importance during the 1990s. The integration between 'the three theories' and the marketing mix 'theory', and the contribution of such an approach to marketing in general, has only just begun.[25]

INTERFUNCTIONAL DEPENDENCY AND THE MARKETING FUNCTION

Marketing organisation as presented in textbooks shows little development with regard to interfunctional dependency. The subject is sometimes touched upon but not as a central issue. Yet it is a fact that all activities in a company are interrelated; if they were not, what would they be doing in the same company? Consequently marketing

cannot live an isolated life. When companies do not consider the linkages between all functions they end up with 'broken chains'[26] and 'tribal warfare' in which each specialist department is a tribe with loyalty towards its own members and not towards the company as a unified entity.[27] Unfortunately, very little research is done directly on execution and on marketing organisation. In the author's experience, most academic researchers prefer the intellectual play with decision models and statistical techniques and duck the tricky issues of turning analysis into action. There are exceptions, such as Piercy's analysis of certain aspects of marketing organisation[28] and Rackham's studies on the efficiency of sales organisation.[29]

The transition of general organisation theory from a high level of abstraction – or a superficial level, if you prefer – to a specific function is far from automatic. There is a lack of empirical, inductive research geared specifically towards marketing and sales organisation. The major contribution comes from TQM, which stresses processes irrespective of organisational structure. 'The three theories', however, are primarily holistic, ecological and systemic in their perspective as opposed to traditional marketing management research, which is primarily reductionistic, fragmented and patched.

In order to make both the need for specialisation and the need for a broader view of marketing manageable the author has, since the early 1970s, used the distinction between the marketing department (including sales) and the marketing function. The marketing department is the unit designated to work solely with marketing and sales activities; it contains the FTMs whose job is to influence customer relations and generate revenue. Add to this all the others who influence customer relations and revenue, i.e. the PTMs inside the organisation; they are found in top management as well as in all other departments of the company. Add also outside PTMs: dealers, consultants (marketing strategy consultants, market research institutes, advertising agencies, etc.), customers, media, investors and

FIGURE 2:   PRINCIPAL COMPONENTS OF THE MARKETING FUNCTION OF A MANUFACTURER
OF INDUSTRIAL EQUIPMENT

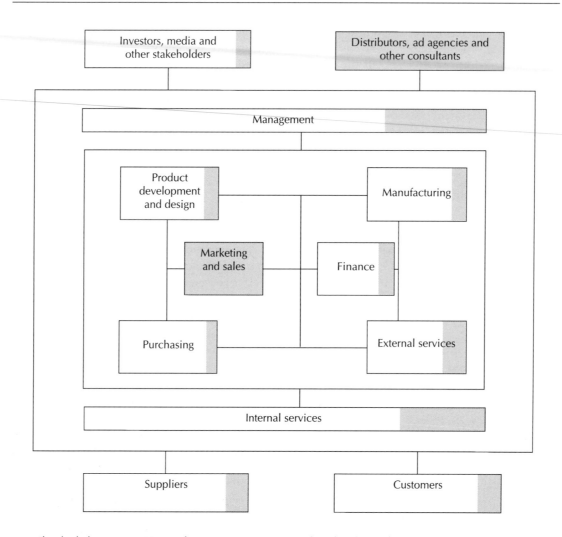

The shaded areas represent marketing activities. FTMs are found in the marketing department and in the group of reinforcing specialists; PTMs in the other boxes.

other stakeholders and you have the marketing function. Two examples of marketing organisation will illustrate the notion of the marketing function.

EXAMPLE 1: MARKETING ORGANISATION FOR COMPLEX INDUSTRIAL EQUIPMENT
The first example is based on an empirical study of the marketing of complex industrial equip-

ment.[30] A generalised version of organisation from this study is shown in Figure 2. The shaded areas that indicate the marketing function completely cover the marketing and sales department and its external reinforcement of distributors and consultants. These are the FTMs. The other boxes are inhabited by PTMs.

▷ *Management* spends time on such activities as

the design of marketing strategies, negotiation of major contracts, and entertaining of important visitors.

▷ *Product development*, including R&D, design and engineering departments, has to understand the needs of customers, design quality into the specifications and blueprints, and prepare for the user-friendly operation of the finished equipment.

▷ *Production,* including operations management and manufacturing, influences customer relations indirectly by keeping delivery times, keeping quality at the set standard, but also directly, for example when customers visit the plant for inspection.

▷ *Purchasing* affects customer relations as the end supplier has the responsibility of the equipment irrespective of who manufactured single components.

▷ *France* is often an important, sometimes decisive, factor in major deals, above all for developing countries and the Soviet bloc. Those countries may be forced to buy from a supplier that offers an attractive solution rather than looking at the quality of the equipment.

▷ *External services* are important as facilitators and as augmentations of the equipment to increase differentiation and uniqueness, and ultimately competitiveness. There are a large number of services connected with industrial equipment, both before-sales services (such as custom design, solutions in a tender), and after-sales services (installation, training and education of customer personnel, operations support, updating of software, emergency support, maintenance, etc.), and general services such as the telephone exchange.

▷ *Internal services* are computer services, legal services, canteen services, etc. which indirectly affect customer relations by constituting supporting 'back-office' functions.

These were all PTMs within the organisation. There are also several external PTMs among whom customers – through word of mouth and referrals – are particularly important. Through partnership strategies, which are currently expanding in business worldwide, suppliers may develop or provide components or services. This is obvious in the Japanese just-in-time concept, where the continuous and punctual flow of deliveries is a prerequisite for the buyer's manufacturing and marketing.

EXAMPLE 2: MARKETING ORGANISATION FOR SERVICES

In traditional marketing literature the salesforce is responsible for the personal contacts with customers. For most service companies the majority of face-to-face contacts are not handled by salespersons; they are handled by those who produce and deliver the service or part of it – for example the contact between a waiter and the guest.

The direct contacts between the customer and an employee of the service firm are referred to as the service encounters or moments of truth. These are natural opportunities emerging in the production/delivery process; for example the interaction between a doctor and a patient, a bank manager and a client, a flight attendant and a passenger. The doctor, the bank manager and the flight attendant all become PTMs and the customer becomes a co-producer. Looking at it from an opposite angle the term part-time employee can be used to signify the customer's role. If the customer does not co-operate – the patient does not take the prescribed medication, the bank client does not give the correct information to the bank manager, the airline passenger does not appear at the gate on time – the services cannot be reliably produced and delivered. The moments of truth for Scandinavian Airlines System (SAS) were estimated by its CEO Carlzon to be 50 million per annum.[31] The estimate for the Swedish State Railways was even higher: 250 million moments of truth per annum.[32] Moments of truth have primarily become associated with the person-to-person interaction between the service provider's staff and the customer. In order to broaden the concept for marketing purposes, the author has introduced the term of point-of-marketing. A point-of-marketing is an opportunity to influence favourably the customer's present and future purchases.[33] These influences go beyond person-to-person contacts.

Research shows that the customer will judge the quality of the service and form an attitude to the provider from the experience of both the production/delivery process and the future benefits of the service.[34] During the production/delivery process the service providers stand unique chances of influencing the customers' present and future purchases as they are in direct contact with the customer; natural points-of-marketing occur which may be used to the advantage of the service provider.

Four types of interaction, which all hold potential points-of-marketing, can be identified as part of the service production and delivery process. The first and second interactions are people-to-people contacts; the third and fourth are contacts between a human and non-human phenomenon:

1. interaction between the service provider's contact persons (the front-line employees) and the customer;

2. interaction between customers with the consequence that even the customers become PTMs within the process;

3. interaction between the customer and the provider's physical environment and tangible products: buildings, machinery, furniture, etc. and consumables associated with the service;

4. interaction between the customer and the provider's systems and routines.

The service production/delivery process is also referred to as the 'servuction' process.[10, 35] The word servuction, a parallel to production, implies that services are different from goods and that new concepts are needed to deal with services in their own right, rather than in terms of manufacturing. The servuction process as described above is actually designed-in marketing. It means that the more marketing is built into the servuction process and the more the opportunities provided by the points-of-marketing are utilised, the less you have to worry about the marketing department – a major part of the marketing will occur as a result of natural customer contacts during the servuction process.

A specific type of service is the professional services offered by such as management consultants, chartered accountants and architects.[7] It is common for professionals to see themselves as producers of qualified services, negotiating contracts during a limited part of their time. In small professional firms, partners and senior professionals are PTMs and they often perceive marketing as a nuisance that steals time from 'productive' work. In large professional service firms there is usually also a specialised marketing and sales department. This department has to include experienced professionals who have a gut feeling for the servuction process. In order to get leads and introductions to prospective clients, information on competitors, etc., the department has to draw on the skills and contacts of those professionals and assistants who do not belong to the marketing department. They also have to rely heavily on the professionals creating long-term relationships with clients leading to extended assignments. Present and former clients are instrumental in enhancing or degrading the image of the professional service firm. So are former employees and letting them leave gracefully, creating 'beautiful exits', may be an important long-term marketing strategy.

Figure 3 illustrates the application of the FTM and the PTM concepts on professional services.

THE EXTERNAL CUSTOMER VS. THE INTERNAL CUSTOMER

Traditionally marketing is focused on the external

FIGURE 3:   THE MARKETING FUNCTION OF A PROFESSIONAL SERVICE FIRM

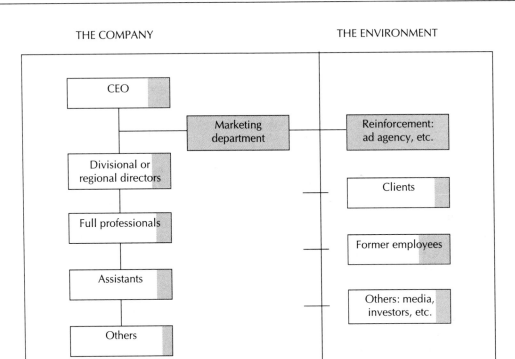

The shaded areas indicate marketing function.

customer. 'The three theories', however, also stress the significance of the internal customer. There are at least four phenomena that can be labelled internal marketing and where internal customers exist:

1. The customer–supplier relationship between employees inside a company. In TQM this is referred to as process management, viewing the organisation as a set of administrative and manufacturing processes which consist of chains of internal customers.

2. The application of marketing know-how, originally developed for external marketing, to the internal market, i.e. the personnel. This is what is labelled internal marketing in services marketing.

3. Activities to get a company marketing-oriented. In services marketing this is often the purpose of internal marketing.[8]

4. Marketing that takes place between profit centres inside a decentralised company, for example a manufacturing division selling to a subsidiary overseas, or a data-processing unit selling computer services to an operating division.

How do these uses of the terms internal customer and internal marketing concern the PTM? 1. above will be further discussed as the internal customer and 2. and 3. will be discussed together as internal marketing. (In the fourth use of internal marketing, market mechanisms have been brought inside the organisation and a profit centre may have the others as internal customers

FIGURE 4:   INTERNAL AND EXTERNAL MARKETING AND THEIR INTERDEPENDENCE

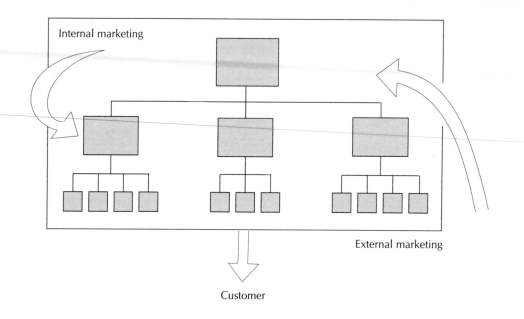

Internal marketing

External marketing

Customer

---

with whom it has to market its products and negotiate deals in much the same way as with outside customers; as the analysis of this case does not add substantially to the understanding of the role of the PTM, it is left out of the discussion.)

Although the first case emanates from TQM and the second case is an offspring of services marketing, the author's working hypothesis is that they apply to marketing in general.

CASE 1: THE INTERNAL CUSTOMER IN PROCESS MANAGEMENT

The first case brings customer–supplier relationships into everybody's job. All employees should see themselves as customers of other employees from whom they receive products, decisions, documents, messages, etc., and should see themselves as suppliers to other internal customers. Only when the internal customers are satisfied (it is the satisfied customers that count irrespective of whether they are external or internal) has a job

been properly executed. This means that every employee becomes an internal PTM.

The concepts of internal customer and process management have arisen in the area of operations management and quality. Kaoru Ishikawa, one of the fathers of TQM, used the slogan 'the next process is your customer' back in the 1950s 'to resolve fierce hostility between workers from different production processes of a steel mill' and 'still uses it today in his lifelong effort to break through the barriers of sectionalism in business organisations'.[36]

This statement is a direct reflection of interfunctional dependency, although here we have a concept to be used in facilitating the linkage between different functions. By making everyone a customer in his relations to others inside the organisation we begin to see what happens in a firm as a proper process. Principles of process management have been used for many years in manufacturing and these principles are now also being applied to services and administrative operations, for example at IBM.[37]

CASE 2: INTERNAL MARKETING: EXTERNAL MARKETING KNOW-HOW APPLIED TO THE INTERNAL CUSTOMER

Internal marketing is a widening of the ideas of training, education, information and communication. It is part of successful leadership. It is a recognition that the internal market is heterogeneous and needs to be segmented, that internal customers are exposed to a stream of 'noise' (euphemistically referred to as 'information') and only the data that are communicated properly will eventually have an impact, that a media mix must be selected, that timing is important, etc.

In service firms where the interface with the customer is particularly broad and intense, it is essential that all contact personnel are well attuned to the mission, goals, strategies and systems of the company. Otherwise they cannot represent their firm well and successfully handle all those natural points-of-marketing that occur in the interaction with customers. It is equally important that management and supporting personnel are well informed or the internal customer–supplier relationship will be inhibited.

Even though the need for internal marketing may be more evident in services marketing there is no reason to see it as limited to pure service firms. For example the interface between a firm's employees and its customers is extensive also in firms that market customised equipment or systems, whether to consumers or to businesses. But even if the interface is limited, companies look for better ways of preparing their employees for changes in the company's business concept, organisational changes, the introduction of new products and services, new technologies, etc.

Any company with a large staff – tens of thousands or even hundreds of thousands of employees, sometimes spread around the world – has an internal marketing problem. Employees may even outnumber customers. This is, for example, the case with Alcatel, AT&T, Ericsson, NEC, Northern Telecom and Siemens in their sales of switching equipment to telecommunications administrations: the number of customers in most countries is just one or a few.

The methods used to reach employees, using internal memos and magazines, meetings, kick-offs, training courses and video and computer techniques, involve applying marketing know-how to the internal market. They help you to reach the FTM, which in itself can be tough in a company with a large salesforce spread in many geographical locations, but they are absolutely necessary to reach the PTM.

Internal marketing is supported by the external marketing which is illustrated by the 'side-loop' in Figure 4: the personnel may be the most keen watchers of the employer's TV commercials and readers of its advertising or interviews with the CEO.

CONCLUSIONS: FROM MARKETING MANAGEMENT TO MARKETING-ORIENTED COMPANY MANAGEMENT

Initially it was advocated that marketing-orientation, although discussed for decades, is difficult to implement in organisations. The article has spelled out a number of approaches to marketing-orientation with the PTM as the central concept and with 'the three theories' as sources to novel concepts and approaches.

Several conclusions of significance to marketing practice can be drawn from the above discussion:

1. Marketing activities are carried out by all employees and all others who influence an organisation's customer relations directly or indirectly, irrespective of which organisational unit they belong to; they are carried out both with own personnel and outside support.

2. Marketing and sales departments are not able to handle more than a limited portion of the marketing as its staff cannot be at the right place at the right time with the right customer contact. Thus companies need both FTMs and PTMs. This has to be recognised by management as well as by each individual employee; both recruitment and training have to be

geared towards this fact.

3. The fact that it is hard to allocate all the marketing activities to one single department may be perceived as an organisational dilemma. Although it gives rise to a less clear and less simple structure it may also be turned into an advantage: the fact that so many people have direct or indirect influence on customers creates multiple marketing opportunities, points-of-marketing.

4. The servuction process is an instance of designed-in marketing. During the servuction process the service provider stands a unique chance of influencing the customers' present and future purchases as the employees are in direct contact with the customer. The more marketing is built into a production/delivery process and the points-of-marketing are utilised, the less the need for a marketing and sales department. Instead of regarding the marketing department as the apex of marketing activities it could be viewed as a supplement to points-of-marketing providing overall strategies and resources.

5. 'The three theories' stress that marketing can be viewed as the building, maintenance and liquidation of networks and interactive relationships between the supplier and the customer, often with long-term implications. As a consequence marketing becomes first and foremost relationship marketing.

6. Through the concepts of internal customer and process management, TQM (which is traditionally not part of marketing) has become an integrator between production-orientation and marketing-orientation, between technology-driven and market-driven behaviour. This is the first time that these two approaches have converged towards the same goal: customer-perceived quality and customer satisfaction.

Eventually the author would like to venture some recommendations for the design of marketing organisation:

▷ Identify where the FTM would be superior in fulfilling marketing tasks, and where the PTM would be superior.

▷ Define the role of external FTMs, such as dealers and advertising agencies.

▷ When the need for internal FTMs has been established, one or several marketing departments could be organised.

▷ Recruit employees that have a potential to take on the role of PTM as well as the professional role of their core job.

▷ Develop their understanding for their role in influencing customer relationships and building and maintaining networks by asking them to answer the question: 'How do I contribute to customer relations and revenue?'

▷ Motivate them through various incentives to strengthen long-term customer relationships as well as to exploit points-of-marketing and other sales opportunities.

▷ Design all the company's processes and structures to be supportive of excellence in customer relations.

▷ Use the external PTMs, customers, media, etc. to their full potential.

The author's overall conclusion is that marketing in the future must be presented and taught in a holistic perspective and be truly integrated with the other functions of the firm. Marketing mix manipulation becomes relationship marketing and marketing management is replaced by marketing-oriented company management.

NOTES

1. J.C. Larréché, W.W. Powell and H.D. Ebeling (1987), *Key Strategic Marketing Issues for the 1990s*, INSEAD, Fontainebleau.

2. B.G. Glaser and A.L. Strauss (1967), *The Discovery of Grounded Theory*, Aldine, Chicago.

3. B.G. Glaser (1978), *Theoretical Sensitivity*, The Sociology Press, Mill Valley, CA.

4. According to a hand-out from the American Marketing Association's Eighth Conference on Services Marketing, October 1988.

5. J.B. Quinn and C.E. Gagnon (1986), 'Will Services Follow Manufacturing into Decline?', *Harvard Business Review*, November–December, pp. 85–103.

6. J.B. Quinn, J.J. Baruch and P.C. Paquette (1987), 'Technology in Services', *Scientific American*, vol. 257, no. 6, December, pp. 50–58.

7. E. Gummesson (1979), 'The Marketing of Professional Services – An Organisational Dilemma', *European Journal of Marketing*, vol. 13, no. 5, pp. 308–18.

8. C. Grönroos (1983), *Strategic Management and Marketing in the Service Sector*, Marketing Science Institute, Cambridge, Mass.

9. R. Normann (1983), *Service Management*, Wiley, Chichester, UK.

10. P. Eiglier and E. Langeard (1987), *Servuction*, McGraw-Hill, Paris.

11. J.E.G. Bateson (1989), *Managing Services Marketing*, The Dryden Press, Chicago.

12. H. Håkansson (ed.) (1982), *International Marketing and Purchasing of Industrial Goods*, Wiley, Chichester, UK.

13. H. Håkansson (ed.) (1987), *Industrial Technological Development*, Croom Helm, London.

14. J. Johansson and L.G. Mattsson (1987), 'Interorganisational Relations in Industrial Systems: A Network Approach Compared with the Transaction-cost Approach', *International Studies of Management & Organisation*, vol. XVII, no. 1, Spring.

15. D. Ford, H. Håkansson and J. Johansson (1986), 'How Do Companies Interact?', *International Marketing & Purchasing*, vol. 1, no. 1, pp. 34–48.

16. One book that provides an overview of total quality management is D.A. Garvin (1988), *Managing Quality*, The Free Press, New York. The book, however, is limited in its perspective as it is solely concerned with product quality thus omitting two-thirds of economic activity (services as peripherals to goods are mentioned though); it is also concerned with quality from a US and Japanese perspective and Europe is not mentioned.

17. B. Edvardsson and B. Thomasson (eds.) (1989), *Kvalitetsutveckling i privata och offlentiga tjänsteföretag* (Quality Development in Private and Public Service Organisations), Natur och Kultur, Stockholm.

18. V.A. Zeithaml, A. Parasuraman and L.L. Berry (1990), *Delivering Quality Service*, The Free Press, New York.

19. S.W. Brown, E. Gummesson, B. Edvardsson and B. Gustavsson (eds.) (1991), *Service Quality: Multidisciplinary and Multinational Perspectives*, Lexington Books, Lexington, Mass.

20. J.E. McCarthy (1964), *Basic Marketing*, Richard D. Irwin, Homewood, Ill.

21. E. Gummesson (1988), 'Falsk bild från USA invaderer Europa' (A False Picture from the US Invades Europe), *Ledarskap*, no. 12, December, pp. 46–50.

22. C. Grönroos (1989), 'Defining Marketing: A Market-oriented Approach', *European Journal of Marketing*, vol. 23, no. 1, pp. 52–60.

23. F.D. Robins (1989), 'The 4 Ps – In the 1990s it May Be 4 Cs', paper presented for the Australian Marketing Educators' Conference.

24. R.J. de Ferrer (1986), 'A Case for European Management', *International Management Development Review*, vol. 2, pp. 275–81.

25. E. Gummesson (1987), 'The New Marketing – Developing Long-term Interactive Relationships', *Long Range Planning*, vol. 20, no. 4, pp. 10–20.

26. R. McKenna (1985), *The Regis Touch*, Addison-Wesley, New York.

27. P.C. Neuhauser (1988), *Tribal Warfare in Organisations*, Ballinger, New York.

28. N. Piercy (1985), *Marketing Organisation*, George Allen & Unwin, London.

29. N. Rackham (1986), *Making Major Sales*, Gower, Aldershot.

30. E. Gummesson (1985), *Marketing Public Telecommunications*, Ericsson, Stockholm.

31. J. Carlzon (1987), *Moments of Truth*, Ballinger, New York.

32. An estimate made by the author together with representatives of the railways.

33. This is a wider concept than point-of-sale or point-of-purchase, which appear in the marketing communica-

tion literature. It also stresses the opportunity to build relationships for the future and to reinforce existing relations without necessarily selling anything at each contact.

34. This and similar distinctions are found in J.R. Lehtinen, (1985), 'Improving Service Quality by Analyzing the Service Production Process' in C. Grönroos and E. Gummesson (eds.), *Service Marketing – Nordic School Perspectives*, University of Stockholm, Department of Business Administration, Research Report R 1985:2; and C. Grönroos (1990), *Service Management and Marketing*, Lexington Books, Lexington, Mass.

35. P. Eiglier, E. Langeard, C.H. Lovelock and J.E.G. Bateson (1977), *Marketing Consumer Services: New Insights*, Marketing Science Institute, Cambridge, Mass.

36. D.J. Lu (1985), 'Translator's Introduction' in K. Ishikawa, *What Is Total Quality Control? The Japanese Way*, Prentice-Hall, Englewood Cliffs, NJ.

37. E.J. Kane (1986), 'IBM's Quality Focus on the Business Process', *Quality Progress*, April, pp. 24–32.

Lessons in the Service Sector

James L. Heskett

▷ A large food and lodging company creates and staffs more general management jobs than any ten manufacturers of comparable size. This company, like many others dispensing high customer-contact services, has eliminated functional lines of responsibility between operations and marketing. In its planning the company routinely combines operations and marketing with what I call a strategic service vision.

▷ The most profitable large American company assumes daily the tasks of managing a work-force of window-washers, cooks, and maintenance personnel. An almost single-minded concentration on people – their jobs, their equipment, their personal development – accounts for much of its success.

▷ The quality control process in a decentralised oilfield services business involves careful selection, development, assignment and compensation of employees working under varying conditions and in widespread locations where close supervision is impossible. In this prosperous company, the process builds shared values and bonds people together.

▷ An international airline, by paying more attention to market economies than to production scale economies, reduces the average size of its aircraft and increases its net income.

▷ Products introduced since 1982 by a well-known financial service generated 10 per cent of its revenues in 1985. The raw material for these products is data already existing in other forms in the company's vast database.

These examples give a glimpse of forward-looking management practice. When examined closely, they offer insights into the ideas on which successful competitive strategies have been fashioned in the much-maligned and little-understood service sector.

It's no coincidence that dominant industries have cutting-edge management practices. Some US railroads in the nineteenth century pioneered in divisionalised management of their far-flung systems and in good procurement procedures to support their sizeable construction and operational needs. At the turn of the century, basic industries led the way in experimenting with scientific management. Then the rise of the large consumer goods manufacturer, epitomised by the auto industry, spawned concepts of decentralisation and a full product line aimed at carefully segmented markets.

Today service industries have assumed the mantle of economic leadership. These industries, encompassing trade, communications, transportation, food and lodging, financial and medical services, education, government, and technical services to industry, account for about 70 per cent of the national income and three-fourths of the non-farm jobs in the United States. In generating forty-four million new jobs in the past thirty years, they have absorbed most of the influx of women and minorities into the workforce, softened the effects of every post-World War II recession, and fuelled every recent economic recovery.

In view of this leadership role, now is a good time to look at the exemplars in the service sector for insights into ways of boosting productivity and altering competitive strategies. Despite their diversity, leading companies in many service industries display some common themes and practices. And they yield lessons for managers in any sector of business. Let's look first at the way the best service companies are structured.

INTEGRATED FUNCTIONS

Most goods-producing businesses follow the traditional organisational pattern of separate and equally important marketing and manufacturing functions, with co-ordinating authority at high levels. Some service businesses do the same thing, but the pattern is much less common in service companies where contact with customers is close, as in retailing, passenger transport, and food and lodging. In these businesses, service is marketed and produced at the same place and time, and often by the same person. Naturally, close co-ordination between marketing and operations management in these cases, regardless of reporting relationships, is essential.

Integration of marketing and operations is often found at very low levels in these organisations. In fact, more than 90 per cent of all field managers in four multi-site service companies surveyed in one study claimed responsibility for operations, personnel and marketing, could not say which was most important, and paid great attention to each.[1]

Even where operations are buffered from marketing activities in organisations offering little customer-contact service, there are ways to break down the traditional functional barriers. Several years ago, the Chase Manhattan Bank launched

an effort to upgrade its non-loan products, improve its external communications and customer service, and make its back-office (production) operations more market-based. A weak spot was Chase's international business. In the highly visible 'product' of international money transfer, differences of viewpoint between marketing – embodied in the account relations manager in the field – and the back office in New York had frustrated communication. Errors were frequent, a large backlog of inquiries about balances and transactions had piled up, and morale in the operations group was poor.

A study ordered by the executive put in charge showed that headquarters accounted for operational errors in only about one-third of all the inquiries and that the marketing people had little idea what operations could offer the bank's customers. The executive traced the backlogged errors to their sources, often a correspondent bank, and resolved them. He launched a campaign to improve operations staff morale around the theme 'We make it happen' and formed a new group, the customer mobile unit, consisting of the bank's most experienced international operations people. The unit visited Chase customers at their businesses to help resolve problems and smooth operations. The executive brought the marketing and back-office people together to talk about ways to improve the flow of information. Perhaps most important, the bank revised reporting relationships so that operations units serving specific market segments reported to both the customer relationship manager and the head of operations – a move that improved functional co-ordination.[2]

The product manager's job was created in many manufacturing organisations to address the problem of co-ordinating manufacturing and marketing. But in most cases, product managers have had profit responsibility without the authority to co-ordinate. Assignment to these positions has been regarded as temporary, which encourages decisions with a short-term orientation.

Because of their importance, the high-contact service company makes a point of developing

TARGET MARKET SEGMENTS	POSITIONING	SERVICE CONCEPT	VALUE–COST LEVERAGING	OPERATING STRATEGY	STRATEGY-SYSTEMS INTEGRATION	SERVICE DELIVERY SYSTEM
What are common characteristics of important market segments?	How does the service concept propose to meet customer needs?	What are important elements of the service to be provided, stated in terms of results produced for customers?	To what extent are differences between perceived value and cost of service maximised by:	What are important elements of the strategy? Operations? Financing? Marketing? Organisation? Human resources? Control?	To what extent are the strategy and delivery system internally consistent?	What are important features of the service delivery system, including: The role of people? Technology? Equipment? Layout? Procedures?
What dimension can be used to segment the market? Demographic? Psychographic?	How do competitors meet these needs?	How are these elements supposed to be perceived by the target market segment? By the market in general? By employees as a whole?	Standardisation of certain elements? Customisation of certain elements?	On which will the most effort be concentrated? Where will investments be made?	Can needs of the strategy be met by the delivery system?	What capacity does it provide? Normally? At peak levels?
How important are various segments?	How is the proposed service differentiated from competition?		Emphasising easily leveraged services?	How will quality and cost be controlled? Measured? Incentives? Rewards?	If not, what changes must be made in: The operating strategy? The service delivery system?	To what extent does it: Help ensure quality standards? Differentiate the service from competition? Provide barriers to entry by competitors?
What needs does each have?	How important are these differences?	How do customers perceive the service concept?	Management of supply and demand?			
How well are these needs being served?	What is good service?	What efforts does this suggest in terms of the manner in which the service is: Designed? Delivered? Marketed?	Control of quality through: Rewards? Appeal to pride? Visibility and supervision? Peer group control? Involving the customer? Effective use of data?	What results will be expected versus competition in terms of: Quality of service? Cost profile? Productivity? Morale and loyalty of servers?	To what extent does the co-ordination of operating strategy and service delivery system ensure: High quality? High productivity? Low cost? High morale and loyalty of servers?	
In what manner? By whom?	Does the proposed service concept provide it? What efforts are required to bring customer expectations and service capabilities into alignment?		To what extent does this effort create barriers of entry to potential competition?		To what extent does this integration provide barriers to entry to competition?	

Basic element   Integrative element

numbers of marketing-operations managers, often carrying the title of store or branch manager. At hand, therefore, is a large cadre of talent from which the company can draw senior managers already trained for administrative responsibilities.

STRATEGIC SERVICE VISION

The need of most service organisations to plan as well as direct marketing and operations as one function has led to the formation in leading companies of what I call strategic service vision. Its elements consist of identification of a target market segment, development of a service concept to address targeted customers' needs, codification of an operating strategy to support the service concept, and design of a service delivery system to support the operating strategy. These basic elements are shaded darker in Exhibit 1.

A company naturally tries to position itself in relation to both the target market and the competition. The links between the service concept and the operating strategies are those policies and pro-

EXHIBIT 2: INTERNALLY ORIENTED STRATEGIC SERVICE VISION

TARGET EMPLOYEE GROUP	POSITIONING	SERVICE CONCEPT	VALUE–COST LEVERAGE	OPERATING STRATEGY	STRATEGY-SYSTEMS INTEGRATION	SERVICE DELIVERY SYSTEM
What are common characteristics of important employee groups? What dimensions can be used to describe these employee groups? Demographic? Psychographic? How important are each of these groups to the delivery of the service? What needs does each group have? How well are these needs being served? In what manner? By whom?	How does the service concept propose to meet employee needs? How do competitors meet such needs? How are relationships with employees differentiated from those between competitors and their employees? How important are these differences? What is 'good service' to employees? Does the proposed service concept provide it? What efforts are required to bring employee expectations and service capabilities into alignment?	What are important elements of the service to be provided, stated in terms of results produced for employees and the company? How are these elements supposed to be perceived by the targeted employee group? How are these elements perceived? What further efforts does this suggest in terms of the manner in which the service is: Designed? Delivered?	To what extent are differences between returns to employees and the level of effort put forth maximised by: The design of the service concept? The design of the elements of the operating strategy? Job design? The leveraging of scarce skills with a support system? The management of supply and demand? Control of quality through: Rewards? Appeal to pride? Visibility? Supervision? Peer group control? Involving the customer in the delivery of the service? Effective use of data?	How important is direct human contact in the provision of the service? To what extent have employees been involved in the design of the service concept and operating strategy? How desirable is it to: Increase employee satisfaction? Increase employee productivity? What incentives are provided for: Quality? Productivity? Cost? How does the strategy address employee needs for: Selection? Assignment? Development? Evaluation? Compensation? Association?	To what extent are the strategy and the delivery system for serving important employee groups internally consistent? To what extent does the integration of operating strategy and service delivery system ensure: High quality? High productivity? Low cost? High morale and 'bonding' of the target employee group?	What are important features of the service delivery system, including: The role of people? Technology? Equipment? Layout? Procedures? What does it require of target employee groups? Normally? At peak periods of activity? To what extent does it help employees: Meet quality standards? Differentiate their service from competitors? Achieve expectations about the quality of their work life?

Basic element   Integrative element

cedures by which the company seeks to maximise the difference between the value of the service to customers (the service concept) and the cost of providing it. This difference, of course, is a primary determinant of profit. And the link between the operating strategy and the service delivery system is the integration achieved in the design of both. These integrative links are shaded lighter in Exhibit 1.

To see how the strategic service vision works, examine the Hartford Steam Boiler Inspection & Insurance Company. For many years, HSB has been in the business of insuring industrial and institutional equipment. Its market targets are organisations using boilers and related pieces of equipment with high operating risk. It offers the same risk reduction as many other insurance companies but positions itself against the competition by emphasising cost reduction as well.

HSB concentrates on a few types of equipment and has built a large database on their operating and performance characteristics. (Manufacturers of the equipment often turn to HSB to get wear and maintenance data.) The information furnishes the actuarial base on which HSB prices its insurance. The company's engineers, who inspect customers' equipment before and after it is insured, are also qualified to give advice on preventing problems and improving utilisation rates, and through many years of association they often get very close to their customers. As a service manager of one HSB client told me, 'If I tried to replace that insurance contract, my operating people in the plant would let me know about it.'

This practice enhances the perceived value of the service to the customer at little extra cost to HSB. Of course, by reducing the risk to the customer HSB can improve its own loss ratio.

HSB has a larger cadre of engineers than any of its competitors. These engineers, in tandem with the big database, make up a service delivery system that capitalises on the knowledge of marketing and operating managers at all levels of the organisation.

The net result is a strategic service vision (though HSB doesn't use the term) that is highly valued by its customers and very profitable for its provider. It addresses implementation issues as part of the strategic plan, and it requires agreement and co-ordination among marketing and operating managers throughout the organisation.

INNER-DIRECTED VISION

High-performance service companies have gained their status in large measure by turning the strategic service vision inward: by targeting important groups of employees as well as customers. In the head offices of these organisations, questions such as those listed in Exhibit 2 are heard often. The questions parallel those in Exhibit 1; but in asking them about employees, management shows that it's aware that the health of the enterprise depends on the degree to which core groups of employees subscribe to and share a common set of values and are served by the company's activities.

The basic elements, shaded darker as in Exhibit 1, start with the service concept designed with employees' needs in mind. The operating strategy is set to meet these needs in a superior fashion at the lowest cost, a result often achieved through the design of the service delivery system.

The integrative elements, shaded lighter, include positioning of a service concept, which it is hoped will lead to low turnover, low training costs, and the opportunity to develop shared goals and values. High-performance service organisations invariably have operating strategies designed to maximise differences between operating costs and value perceived by employees in their relations with the company. And delivery systems designed with the operating strategy in mind can form the foundation for remarkable gains in productivity.

A case in point is the ServiceMaster Company, based in Downers Grove, Illinois, which manages support services for hospitals, schools and industrial companies. It supervises the employees of customers' organisations engaged in housekeeping, food service and equipment maintenance. These are services that are peripheral to the customers' businesses and therefore get little management attention.

Many of the people whom ServiceMaster oversees are functionally illiterate. To them, as well as its own managers, ServiceMaster directs a service concept centred on the philosophy stated by its CEO, 'Before asking someone to do something you have to help them be something.' ServiceMaster provides educational and motivational programmes to help these employees 'be something'.

To its own supervisors the company offers training leading to an ambitious 'master's' programme taught in part by the chief executive. New responsibilities and opportunities present themselves via the rapid growth of the company, approximating 20 per cent per year, nearly all of it from expansion of existing operations rather than acquisition. Elaborate training aids and a laboratory for developing new equipment and materials enhance the employee-managers' 'be something' feeling.

For customers' employees ServiceMaster tries to build the 'be something' attitude and improve their productivity by redesigning their jobs and by developing equipment and pictorial, colour-coded instructional material. In most cases it is the first time that anyone has paid attention to the service of which these employees are a part. ServiceMaster also holds weekly sessions to exchange ideas and offers educational programmes to, among other things, develop literacy. ServiceMaster also recruits up to 20 per cent of its own managers from the ranks in jobs it handles. The service concept clearly is improved self-respect, self-development, personal satisfaction and upward mobility.

Another company slogan, repeated often, is 'to help people grow'. When a hospital served by the company decided to hire a deaf person, ServiceMaster's local head didn't object. Instead he authorised three of his supervisors to take a course in sign language.

It should be no surprise that the turnover rate among ServiceMaster's 7,000 employees is low. Further, the turnover rate in organisations it services is much lower than the averages for their industries. And when ServiceMaster takes a job, the productivity achieved by supervised support workers invariably rises dramatically.

Now a billion-dollar company, ServiceMaster has a return on equity from 1973 through 1985 that was the highest of all the largest service or industrial companies in the United States, averaging more than 30 per cent after taxes. It oversees the support service employees for fifteen hospitals in Japan, which probably makes it the largest exporter of managerial talent to Japan. According to one ServiceMaster executive, 'The Japanese immediately recognise and identify with what we do and how we do it.' This company turns its strategic service vision inward with dramatic results.

THE VISION APPLIED

In addition to building a strategic service vision, the best service companies apply it to customers and to those who deliver the service and oversee its delivery – in new or different ways. From my study of organisations like Hartford Steam Boiler and ServiceMaster, I've gathered a series of lessons useful for service providers to consider. These lessons can furnish goods producers food for thought too.

RETHINK QUALITY CONTROL

Executives whose careers have spanned service as well as manufacturing agree that reaching a consistently high quality level is tougher in services. In high-contact (so-called high-encounter) services, the interaction between two people or more varies with each transaction. In low-contact services, people many miles from the customer have to rely on their own judgement in handling orders and other transactions and in fielding complaints.

Those who have tried to solve the quality control problem by adding more supervision have found that it limits effectiveness. A service transaction cannot be halted, examined and recycled like a product.

The most effective approaches to the problem have included restructuring of incentives to emphasise quality, designing jobs to give service providers higher visibility in dealing with customers, and building a peer group to foster teamwork and instil a sense of pride.

One incentive that is often effective in organisations ranging from rapid transit companies to hotels is the employee-of-the-month award – especially if based on customer feedback. Both monetary and non-monetary incentives have been used successfully. What's more, the cost is low.

Making the person who delivers the service more visible is another technique. In England, at the Lex Service Group's luxury auto dealerships, the customer is encouraged to go directly to the mechanic working on the car. The Shouldice Hospital near Toronto, Canada specialises in the repair of hernias using only local anaesthetic – a practice that allows the doctor to talk with the patient during the operation. Defective work is referred to the doctor responsible. The remission rate for hernias performed at Shouldice is less than one-tenth that of the average North American hospital. At Benihana, the US chain of Japanese-style steak-houses, the chef cooks at a grill in front of the restaurant guests. The chef's visibility and proximity to customers promote a consistently high quality of service and a consistently high level of tips.

EXHIBIT 3: HOW SUCCESS BUILDS HIGH-CONTACT SERVICES

Incentives and visibility may be insufficient for those tasks performed without supervision and out of view of the customer. In these cases, some companies rely on careful selection and thorough training of employees and the development of programmes to build both a sense of pride in the service and a sense of identification with the company. This bonding process can be hard for rivals to emulate and can thereby contribute to competitive advantage.

Schlumberger's wire-line service has roughly 2,000 geological engineers, each responsible for a mobile rig equipped with more than $1 million worth of computers and electronic gear that helps predict the outcome of petroleum producers' drilling efforts. Each year the company recruits those it considers the brightest of the crop of college engineering graduates, spends months teaching them how to use the equipment, and goes to great lengths to make them feel a part of a special tradition. As one engineer put it recently, 'Indoctrination is just as important as technical training.' This is all in preparation for an assignment to represent Schlumberger in the field, without direct supervision, often in a remote part of the world. Two measures of the success of this programme are Schlumberger's dominant share of the world's wire-line business and the profit-to-sales ratios for this company, which consistently exceed others in its industry in good times and bad.

Often effective in achieving and maintaining quality is peer group control, supported by incentives, training, job design, and service delivery system design. In cases where professional standards have been established for a task, they reinforce peer group control.

In an architectural firm, the mere existence of a policy requiring partners' review of every piece of work can keep partners and associates on their toes. Surgeons are sometimes assigned in teams to foster the learning process and encourage peer group control. A partner of a leading real estate development company told me, 'There are three things I'm most concerned about in my work. In this order, they are not to embarrass my colleagues, not to cast a bad light on the company by inadequately serving my clients, and making money.' It's not surprising that this company has a strong sense of shared values, reinforced by a policy of encouraging partners to invest in the projects that they propose and carry out.

Recent research suggests that the internal strategic service vision, quality control and success are connected, especially in those providers of high-encounter service requiring judgement in delivery. I show it as the 'quality wheel' in Exhibit 3. Studies directly link customer satisfaction and the resulting sales volume to the satisfaction derived by the person serving the customer.[3] Naturally the more motivated the employee, the better the service.

The selection and development of employees, care in assignment, and the layout and equipment of the facility (in a high-contact environment) are all integral elements of the design of the service encounter, which in turn is based on the company's assessment of customer needs. Preconditioning of the customer may also be a part of the design of the service encounter. Review and redesign of the encounter go on continually as the organisation assesses how well it is meeting those needs.

A part of the internal service vision is the design of policies and performance measures that further the fulfilment of customers' needs. For example, the server's well-being in the job apparently depends, at least in part, on the extent to which his or her superiors emphasise the solution of problems for customers rather than strict adherence to a set of policies and procedures.[4]

Driving the self-reinforcing elements of the wheel of quality takes a great deal of executive time and requires an honest interest in people across the organisation. The senior vice-president for finance of Delta Airlines, an organisation well regarded for its service and employee programmes, remarked recently, 'I would guess that 25 per cent of the time of the finance department officers is spent listening to people's problems.'

For most service companies, people obviously are more important than machines in the control of quality. But even where the machines employed carry an unusually high value, as in Schlumberger and Delta, developing and building the dedication of people takes precedence.

REASSESS THE EFFECTS OF SCALE

In service organisations, scale economies are often much more important at the company level than at the operating unit level. This is particularly true for companies that have many units over wide areas connected by a common identity. Such scale gives McDonald's and Hertz great purchasing clout and General Cinema the advantage of selling soft drinks of its own manufacture.

Large scale at the company level is important for exploiting network effects, a phenomenon much more important in the service than in the manufacturing sector. To a point, the addition of new network links augments volume for those parts already in place, thus building average network capacity utilisation. The addition of service to Las Vegas from its Memphis hub gave Federal Express more volume on the Memphis–New York link. When Visa adds a large retailer to its network of card-accepting establishments, it increases the attractiveness of its credit card to present and potential cardholders and the potential volume to be realised by retailers already accepting the card.

Bigger is not better in those service industries in which the factory must be taken into the market-place to sell a more accessible, visible and convenient product that meets customers' needs. Factories operated by the Hyatt and Marriott organisations (called hotels) have not, on average, grown in size for years. These companies have settled on a range of hotel dimensions that can be designed, located and operated effectively to achieve the capacity utilisation, quality of service, and financial performance they want. The range describes sizes at which diseconomies resulting from poor supervision and inflexibility tend to outweigh advantages of larger scale. In the design and siting of hotels, Hyatt and Marriott give the less quantifiable advantages of market flexibility weight equal to operating economies of scale.

At the unit operating level, many service companies have found that the loss of flexibility and greater difficulty in supervising those delivering the service far outweigh any savings realised in operating costs as unit size grows. In the rush to cut costs per seat-mile, for example, many of the world's airlines bought large, wide-bodied aircraft like the Airbus 300 and McDonnell DC-10. While these planes performed admirably, their effective utilisation required funnelling large numbers of passengers into the airline's hub. Moreover, because business travellers, who represent the most attractive market segment, are prone to choose an airline on the basis of times and frequency of flights, the load and schedule consolidation necessary for effective employment of wide-bodied aircraft worked against the goal of building traffic.

When Jan Carlzon became CEO of Scandinavian Airlines System in 1980, wide-bodied aircraft were used extensively between the airline's hub at Copenhagen and major cities like London and Paris. With smaller DC-9s, SAS funnelled travellers between the hub and other Scandinavian cities. To reclaim the business travellers SAS had lost, Carlzon relegated most of the wide-bodies to charter work and offered non-stop flights using DC-9s between Scandinavian and principal European cities.

A size question confronts nearly every power utility in the United States today. For years it was industry gospel that the more power-generating capacity concentrated in one place, the greater the economies of scale. This was the case until the 1970s, when ever-larger units began encountering reliability problems. Furthermore, construction schedule stretch-outs, at times fomented by environmental groups' agitation against big plants, caused the expected power-generating economies to vanish. Finally, an improved capability for transmitting excess energy from one market to another made it possible to buy energy for less than the big units could afford to charge. So many utilities today are meeting the needs of smaller markets' fluctuating demands more economically through new means.

REPLACE AND CREATE ASSETS WITH INFORMATION

For decades, manufacturers have sought ways of substituting information for assets. Foremost among these are forecasting and inventory control techniques. For many service operations, information offers creative new ways to substitute for assets.

Heating oil dealers, by maintaining data on the capacity of their customers' tanks, on habitual consumption rates, and on weather, programme fuel oil deliveries to provide 100 per cent availability while reducing delivery times and the number of trucks and drivers. These companies substitute information for assets.

The Rural/Metro Fire Department extends effective fire protection at a fraction of the cost of most municipally run fire departments. This Scottsdale, Arizona-based company analyses data on past fires and uses much smaller, less expensive trucks staffed with smaller crews and equipped with a large-diameter hose that can shoot a lot of water on a fire very fast. On the way to a fire, a truck crew can learn the floor plan of the building to which it is going. While speeding through the streets, the crew examines a microfiche of the layout on a screen. Rural/Metro substitutes information for assets.

Many service industries are information-driven, beginning with familiarity between the server and the served. In many (not all), assets have never been allowed to become dominant, perhaps because of limited capital. But with the development of new technologies for processing and communicating information, companies in these industries have advanced far beyond the use of information as a substitute for assets. They are instead using the information they have collected in one business as the basis for new services.

Companies servicing manufactured goods, for example, have built databases on the types, wear rates and failure rates of various parts of a furnace, appliance or automobile. A company can use this information for sending timely service reminders to customers and also to manage parts inventories to reflect the age and condition of the particular machine serviced. In the process, the data have taken on great value for the producers of the goods – and they're willing to pay for the information.

A credit card service builds expenditure profiles for its customers; broken patterns may signal a problem like stolen cards. Theft is sometimes suspected when a large expenditure is made far from the cardholder's address. Instead of outright disallowance of a retailer's request for a big charge, one major travel card issuer tries to determine whether the cardholder indeed is travelling in the retailer's area. Information collected for this service yields person-specific data about travel patterns that often is valuable to airlines and hotel chains (to name two businesses). But the company limits the use of such information to ways that benefit its cardholders.

Dun & Bradstreet's $2.7 billion enterprise is centred on its database, a file of credit information describing businesses in thirty countries. Through development and acquisition, the file steadily grows. D&B has consistently realised about 10 per cent of its revenue from business that did not exist three years before. Nearly all of these services use the same data base but package the information in different ways. A potential competitor would have to spend an estimated $1 billion – nearly half of D&B's net asset value – to duplicate the database.

Though a database may constitute a service provider's most important asset, it doesn't appear on the balance sheet and can't be depreciated. But the degree to which many such companies rely on an accumulation of knowledge as their chief competitive weapon and source of new business development suggests opportunities for their counterparts in the manufacturing sector.

Harlan Cleveland has pointed out that information, unlike most manufactured products, is often infinitely expandable (as it is used), com-pressible, substitutable (for capital, labour or physical materials), transportable, diffusive (hard to keep secret) and sharable (as opposed to exchangeable).[5] If it is infinitely expandable, those who possess it are limited only by their imagination in creating new ideas, revenue sources and job opportunities. As the demand for creative exploitation of information grows, so will job creation in the service sector.

THE SERVICE ECONOMY

Many successful service providers have strategies in common that offer lessons to other companies. Among these are:

▷ Close co-ordination of the marketing-operations relationship.

▷ A strategy built around elements of a strategic service vision.

▷ An ability to redirect the strategic service inward to focus on vital employee groups.

▷ A stress on the control of quality based on a set of shared values, peer group status, generous incentives, and, where possible, a close relationship with the customer.

▷ A cool appraisal of the effects of scale on both efficiency and effectiveness.

▷ The substitution of information for other assets.

▷ The exploitation of information to generate new business.

Why these particular lessons among all I might cite? For one reason: they feature characteristics that distinguish many service industries from goods-producing industries. Notice the emphasis on people, ideas and information instead of things. For another, they promise twin benefits as part of a business strategy. Each can further differentiation of the service product as well as lower costs.

These lessons have significance for the economy too. While the service economy has wrought a gigantic social restructuring of the United States, it has come in for unwarranted criticism for its low rate of productivity gains. Companies like those I have described, however, have created new jobs while raising productivity. If other companies learn these lessons, job opportunities in the service sector will continue to expand and produc-tivity continue to rise. These developments will ease the pressures for the inflation of service prices, sharpen the already respected competitive-ness abroad of US-based services, and contribute to the partnership between services and manufac-turing that is crucial to a healthy, balanced national business base.

NOTES

1. Christopher H. Lovelock, Eric Langeard, John E.G. Bateson and Pierre Eiglier (1981), 'Some Organisational Problems Facing Marketing in the Service Sector' in James H. Donnelly and William R. George (eds.), *Marketing of Services*, American Marketing Association, Chicago, p. 168.

2. See James E. Loud (1980), 'Organizing for Customer Service', *The Bankers' Magazine*, November–December, p. 41.

3. Benjamin Schneider and David E. Bowen (1985), 'New Services Design, Development, and Implementation and the Employee' in William R. George and Claudia Marshall, *New Services*, American Marketing Association, Chicago, Ill., p. 82; and Eugene M. Johnson and Daniel T. Seymour (1985), 'The Impact of Cross Selling on the Service Encounter in Retail Banking' in John A. Czepiel, Michael R. Solomon and Carol F. Surprenant (eds.), *The Service Encounter*, D.C. Heath, Lexington, Mass., p. 243.

4. This is the implication of John J. Parkington and Benjamin Schneider (1979) in 'Some Correlates of Experienced Job Stress: A Boundary Role Study', *Academy of Management Journal*, June, p. 270.

5. Harlan Cleveland (1982), 'Information as a Resource', *The Futurist*, December, p. 37.

PART IV

The Functional Aspects of Services Marketing

THE FUNCTIONAL ASPECTS OF SERVICES MARKETING

The previous parts of this book have described how services and services marketing have evolved. They have examined the key aspects of research in the domain that has covered the establishment of broadly accepted definitions and concepts and the characteristics that surround these. Part II traced the burgeoning literature on the key conceptual developments and Part III focused on the managerial issues involved in services marketing. This part concentrates on the main functional areas of services marketing. The universally accepted variables within the services marketing function are product, price, communication, place and customer service.

In the early 1980s there was some discussion in the literature about the suitability of McCarthy's 4P marketing mix for services. For example, Renaghan (1981) argues that the marketing mix for hospitality services could be better described in terms of a combination of three mixes. The product-service mix offers simultaneously a blend of products and services; the presentation mix includes the physical plant, the location, atmospherics, price and employees as combining to create the overall presentation; and the communications mix seeks to persuade the customer and make the intangible qualities of the service more tangible to the customer.

Building on Renaghan's work, Booms and Bitner (1992) argue that in order to modify the marketing mix to suit service firms three further Ps, physical evidence, participants and the process of service assembly, need to be added to the traditional 4Ps marketing mix. In this part of the book the research in relation to the traditional aspects of the marketing mix is reviewed in the context of services and a concentration given to customer service as a main focus of services marketing.

PRODUCT ASPECTS

The Service Product – Much of the early research into services focused on product dimensions, and indeed there is still a strong bias towards aspects of the service product in research today. Much of this work is concerned with how the performance of the service product can improve customer satisfaction. One of the most comprehensive examinations of this factor goes back to the mid-1970s and the work of Swan and Combs (1976). As described earlier these authors determined that product performance was crucially influenced by a combination of physical and psychological dimensions. They argued that whilst the physical, or tangible, dimensions may be relatively easily addressed for aspects of improvement, such improvement would be undermined if aspects of psychological, or largely intangible, performance were not also addressed with equal importance and attention. It is interesting to note that whilst subsequent meaningful research in this area recognises this crucial combination in some form or other, there are many examples of research pertaining to the service product that are incomplete because they do not recognise these wider dimensions of the psychological aspects.

Product/Market Strategies – Still with the focus on customer satisfaction and product performance, there has also been some interesting work carried out in the area of product-market strategies. Good examples of research here are Slater and Narver (1993), who examine the business characteristics which lead to superior performance for different strategies. This work builds on the earlier work of Miles and Snow (1978) and their strategy criteria of prospector, analyser and defender strategies. Jacobson and Aaker (1987) look at the strategic advantages of improving product performance and achieving a comparative advantage. They use the PIMS database to detect feedback interactions between product quality and other strategic variables.

Product Quality – Much of the remaining research in the service product area centres on product quality. Cravens et al. (1988) link the competitive strategic dimension with marketing's role in product and service quality. In examining the definition and measurement of service product quality and marketing's quality improvement responsibilities they use Garvin's (1984) frameworks for types of product quality. Garvin describes five approaches to product quality: the transcendent approach, whereby quality is synonymous with innate excellence; the product-based approach, whereby quality is defined as a precise and measurable variable; the user-based approach, whereby quality consists of the capacity to satisfy wants; the manufacturing-based approach, whereby quality means conformance to requirements; and the value-based approach, defining quality as the degree of excellence at an acceptable price but with acceptable cost controls. This cost dimension coupled with overall business competitiveness is the focus of research by Phillips et al. (1983). These authors dispute the view that high relative quality position is incompatible with achieving a low relative cost position in an industry. The issue of quality and costs relationships is addressed by Bajpai and Willey (1989) in a review of the costs of quality. They suggest that a new emphasis should be placed on the benefits of quality rather than the costs.

PRICING ASPECTS

Price and its relationship with quality perceptions has long been an aspect of interest, if not a fascination, in marketing in general. Surprisingly there is relatively little research in services marketing literature on this relationship, although it is acknowledged that many of the issues surrounding this relationship are dealt with in the central themes of services marketing. Of some indirect relevance is the work of Chernatony et al. (1992), who examined prices of brands versus own labels, perceived quality, and market structures and positive price, and found that quality relationships do exist but concluded that management needs to have courage to support these in times of adversity. Curry and Reisz (1988) also looked at the relationship between price and quality over a longitudinal period and concluded that as price flexibility declines it is more likely that competition will centre on promotional dimensions rather than relative quality improvements.

COMMUNICATION ASPECT

The definitive research in the area of communications is that of Zeithaml et al. (1988), who examined reasons why it is difficult to deliver consistent service.

Their argument is centred on clarity about the role and responsibilities of contact personnel and the conflicts therein, but they stress the importance of good communication in overcoming such problems. Communications outside the organisation, principally advertising, which is important to any marketing effort, is addressed in the services marketing context. George and Berry (1981) offer guidelines for the advertising of intangible services. Similarly, Crask and Laskey (1990), focusing on the advertising message, discuss choosing the general message type: informational messages, messages on intangible cues, frequency of messages and messages on the product. They advocate using the various message types for market positioning.

PLACE ASPECTS

The most comprehensive work in this area is that of Bitner (1990), who argues that the service encounter is the service from the customer's point of view, as the evaluation of a service firm often depends on the evaluation of the 'service encounter' or the period of time when the customer interacts directly with the firm. Covering a wide range of instances, including airlines, hotels and restaurants, Bitner isolates the particular events and related behaviours of contact employees that cause customers to distinguish very satisfactory encounters from very dissatisfactory ones.

CUSTOMER SERVICE

The term customer service has been given many meanings and often is used as an 'umbrella' term for the other aspects of marketing which do not fit comfortably under the headings of product, price, place and communication. The term 'customer service' often has different meanings in different companies and different situations. Carson and Gilmore (1989) define customer service as a combination of the following: advice and information for customers in regard to a product or service's technical specifications; product quality in relation to standards and measures set to ensure that a product conforms to specifications and is fit for purpose; and after-sales back-up arrangements and procedures such as after-sales enquiries, complaints, repair and maintenance procedures.

Christopher (1986) writes that, 'ultimately customer service is determined by the interaction of all those factors that affect the process of making products and services available to the buyer'.

Thus customer service can take account of a variety of activities which may incorporate or 'tie up' some of the tangible and intangible aspects of during and post-purchase service. In addition, given the ease with which many services can be copied by competitors, good customer service can provide a service company with the competitive advantage it may find difficult to create with other aspects of its marketing activity.

Having considered some of the relevant literature surrounding the functional aspects of services marketing, it is appropriate to refer to the earlier discussion in Part III of this book which addresses the more recent services management issue of attention to quality in all aspects of the services marketing mix in order to deliver a consistent offering.

The keynote articles we have selected for Part IV come from particular functional areas of marketing in services in relation to product, product quality, communications, place and customer service.

Swan, J ohn E. and Linda Jones Combs (1976), 'Product Performance and Consumer Satisfaction: A New Concept', *Journal of Marketing,* 40, April, pp. 25–33.

Bitner, Mary Jo (1992), 'Servicescapes: The Impact of Physical Surroundings on Customers and Employees', *Journal of Marketing,* 56, April, pp. 57–71.

George, William R. and Leonard L. Berry (1981), 'Guidelines for the Advertising of Services', *Business Horizons,* July–August, pp. 52–6.

Christopher, Martin (1986), 'Reaching the Customer: Strategies for Marketing and Customer Service', *Journal of Marketing Management,* vol. 2, no. 1, pp. 63–71.

Swan and Combs (1976) report on a study which examined the instrumental and psychological dimensions of product performance in relation to customer expectations, performance and satisfaction. They describe 'instrumental performance' as the means to a set of ends or physical product, while 'expressive performance' is performance that the individual considers to be an end in itself, that is, the user's response to the product.

Bitner (1992) describes a study carried out to explore the impact of physical surroundings on the behaviour of both customers and employees. Bitner argues that despite the recognition and mention of atmospherics, physical design and décor elements in many marketing, retailing and organisational behaviour texts, and the fact that managers continually plan, build, change and control an organisation's physical surroundings, frequently the impact of a specific design change on ultimate users of the facility is not fully understood.

George and Berry (1981) argue that advertising intangible services is different from advertising physical goods. In particular, there is a different emphasis in relation to advertising to employees, the use of word of mouth, providing tangible cues, making the service understood, advertising continuity and promising what is possible.

Christopher's (1986) article describes how logistics and marketing can combine to create a means of achieving a sustainable competitive advantage. He argues that the combination of added-value through service and cost advantage through greater efficiency will provide more opportunities for profit improvement through superior marketing logistics than does any other source.

Of course, it should be remembered that functional aspects of marketing services cannot, indeed, should not, be confined to a few descriptive models of a services marketing mix. Such a mix of functions, tools, techniques, should be unique to any one service organisation. It is through this distinctive services marketing approach that an organisation can attractively differentiate itself from other competing organisations.

KEY LEARNING QUESTIONS

1. What do you consider to be an appropriate marketing mix for services?
2. How do the characteristics of services impact upon the management of the communication mix?
3. What is meant by the term 'service encounter'? What influences could physical surroundings and customer service have on the nature of the service encounter?

REFERENCES

Bajpai, A.K. and P.C.T. Willey (1989), 'Questions about Quality Cost', *International Journal of Quality and Reliability Management*, vol. 6, no. 6, pp. 9–17.

Bitner, Mary Jo (1990), 'Evaluating Service Encounters: The Effects of Physical Surroundings and Employee Responses', *Journal of Marketing*, vol. 54, April, pp. 69–82.

Bitner, Mary Jo (1992), 'Servicescapes: The Impact of Physical Surroundings on Customers and Employees', *Journal of Marketing*, vol. 56, April, pp. 57–71.

Booms, Bernard H. and Mary Jo Bitner (1992), 'Marketing Services by Managing the Environment', *The Cornell Hotel and Restaurant Administration (H.R.A.) Quarterly*, May, pp. 35–40.

Carson, D. and A. Gilmore (1989), 'Customer Care: The Neglected Domain', *Irish Marketing Review*, vol. 4, no. 3, pp. 49–61.

Chernatony, Leslie D., Simon Knox and Mark Chedgey (1992), 'Brand Pricing in a Recession', *European Journal of Marketing*, vol. 26, no. 2, pp. 5–14.

Christopher, M. (1986), 'Reaching the Customer: Strategies for Marketing and Customer Service', *Journal of Marketing Management*, vol. 2, no. 1, pp. 63–71.

Crask, Melvin R. and Henry A. Laskey (1990), 'A Positioning-based Decision Model for Selecting Advertising Messages', *Journal of Advertising Research*, August–September, pp. 32–8.

Cravens, David W., Charles W. Holland, Charles W. Lamb Jr and William C. Moncrief III (1988), 'Marketing's Role in Product and Service Quality', *Industrial Marketing Management*, vol. 17, pp. 285–304.

Curry, David J. and Peter C. Reisz (1988), 'Prices and Price/Quality Relationships: A Longtitudinal Analysis', *Journal of Marketing*, vol. 52, January, pp. 34–48.

Garvin, David A. (1984), 'What Does Product Quality Really Mean?', *Sloan Management Review*, Fall, pp. 25–43.

George, W.R. and L.L. Berry (1981), 'Guidelines for the Advertising of Services', *Business Horizons*, July–August, pp. 52–6.

Jacobson, Robert and David A. Aaker (1987), 'The Strategic Role of Product Quality', *Journal of Marketing*, vol. 51, October, pp. 31–44.

Miles, R.E. and C.C. Snow (1978), *Organisational Strategy, Structure and Process*, McGraw-Hill, NY.

Phillips, Lynn W., Dae R. Chang and Robert D. Buzzell (1983), 'Product Quality, Cost Position and Business Performance: A Test of Some Key Hypotheses', *Journal of Marketing*, vol. 47, Spring, pp. 26–43.

Renaghan, Leo M. (1981), 'A New Marketing Mix for the Hospitality Industry', *The Cornell Hotel and Restaurant Administration (H.R.A.) Quarterly*, August, pp. 31–5.

Slater, Stanley F. and John C. Narver (1993), 'Product-market Strategy and Performance: An Analysis of the Miles and Snow Strategy Types', *European Journal of Marketing*, vol. 27, no. 10, pp. 33–51.

Swan, John E. and Linda Jones Combs (1976), 'Product Performance and Consumer Satisfaction: A New Concept', *Journal of Marketing*, vol. 40, April, pp. 25–33.

Zeithaml, V.A., L.L. Berry and A. Parasuraman (1988), 'Communication and Control Processes in the Delivery of Service Quality', *Journal of Marketing*, vol. 52, April, pp. 5–48.

Product Performance and Consumer Satisfaction: A New Concept

John E. Swan and Linda Jones Combs

An empirical study examines the influence of physical and psychological dimensions of product performance on consumer satisfaction.

Even though knowledge of the processes that may determine consumer satisfaction should be of interest to both marketing theorists and practitioners, the topic has received little attention in the literature. A growing number of studies have analysed perceived product performance and expectations, but they have not considered the relationships between expectations, performance and satisfaction.[1] In addition, it is seldom clear which general dimensions of product performance are important to the consumer and how these dimensions are related to satisfaction.

The study reported in this article was designed to examine one aspect of the relationships between expectations, performance and satisfaction. In particular, the authors look at the expressive (non-material, psychological) and instrumental (physical) dimensions of a product, in this case clothing, to determine the extent of their influence on consumer satisfaction and dissatisfaction. Implications are given for the study of consumer behaviour and for marketing decision-making.

BACKGROUND
The hypotheses tested in this study evolved from two streams of research and conceptualisation: 1.

the concept that satisfaction results from the fulfilment of expectations; and 2. the idea that consumers judge products on a limited set of attributes, some of which are relatively important in determining satisfaction, while others are not critical to consumer satisfaction but are related to dissatisfaction when performance on them is unsatisfactory.

SATISFACTION AND THE FULFILMENT OF EXPECTATIONS
According to theoretical sources, when purchasing a product the consumer makes predictions (forms expectations) concerning the future performance of the item.[2] As the item is used, the consumer compares the quality of performance to his expectations. If the product performs as well as, or better than, expected he will be satisfied. If, however, performance is below expectations, dissatisfaction will result. Empirical research has established that judgements of the relative quality of product performance are related to expectations. The general finding is that products that meet or exceed expectations receive favourable ratings on product performance, while those that perform below expectations receive less favourable ratings.[3] Therefore, it is logical to assume that favourable judgements of performance would yield satisfaction and unfavourable judgements would lead to dissatisfaction. This last step, how-

ever, has not been empirically tested in reported research.

SALIENT PERFORMANCE ATTRIBUTES AND SATISFACTION

While product performance dimensions may appear to be 'natural' attributes of products, at least two lines of thought suggest that the salient product performance dimensions that are important to consumers are limited to consumer perceptions and conceptions. First, a natural attribute of a product (such as the fabric in the case of the clothing products included in this study) does not have a given set of performance dimensions; rather, performance dimensions are a property of human experience and thought.[4] For example, a consumer safety expert may be concerned because a particular fabric emits toxic gases when burned, but this dimension of product performance may not be salient to many consumers, who are not even aware that toxic gases result from the burning of some fabrics.

A second factor that serves to limit salient performance dimensions is that consumers appear to make implicit assumptions about some dimensions of product performance. Myers and Alpert have argued that only a limited set of attributes, the 'determinant attributes', play a critical role in determining choice between alternatives.[5] Determinant attributes are those that are important to consumers and are variable across alternatives. As an example, if all automobiles are safe enough to meet a buyer's requirements, then safety is not a determinant attribute; if, however, automobiles vary in styling and the buyer has styling preferences, then this would be a determinant attribute. The present study *extended* the concept of determinant attributes from choice behaviour, as discussed by Myers and Alpert, to satisfaction with post-purchase performance.[6]

Assuming that a limited set of salient product performance dimensions for which expectations are fulfilled results in consumer satisfaction, a central concern for marketing analysis is to identify the salient performance dimensions in that set. In the case of clothing items, which were the ref-

erence objects in this study, it was assumed that two qualitatively different categories of performance dimensions would be salient. One category, expressive performance, would be associated with satisfactory items; while the second category, instrumental performance, would be associated with dissatisfactory items. *Instrumental performance* refers to the *means* to a set of ends, while *expressive performance* is performance that the individual considers to be an end in itself. In the case of clothing, *instrumental performance* would correspond to the performance of the physical product *per se*; *expressive performance* would relate to a '*psychological*' level of performance, that is, the user's response to the item of clothing. As an example, the durability of an item of clothing would be an instrumental performance dimension, while styling would represent the expressive category.

Studies of factors resulting in dissatisfaction with clothing were summarised by Ryan, who suggested to the present authors that dissatisfaction appeared to be related to product failures at the *instrumental* level.[7] Ryan cited a study of clothing articles returned to a store, in which it was found that the items returned involved dissatisfaction with the physical product, fibre, seams, and the like. A study of complaints with clothing also involved aspects of the physical product, such as colour change. Reasons why people discarded clothing or did not use it for the purpose for which it had been purchased frequently involved physical product failures.

What end does clothing serve? That is, what performance results would correspond to *expressive* performance? In a comprehensive study of clothing, Horn wrote that clothing performs five major functions: modesty and/or enhancement of sexual attraction, protection from the environment, aesthetic and sensuous satisfaction, an indicator of status, and an extension of the self.[8] Except for protection from the environment, these functions are not direct properties of the physical product but are derived from consumer response to attributes of the physical product and, therefore, are expressive dimensions.

TABLE 1:   RELATIONSHIPS BETWEEN PERFORMANCE, THE FULFILMENT OF EXPECTATIONS, AND SATISFACTION

INSTRUMENTAL PERFORMANCE	EXPRESSIVE PERFORMANCE	RESULTING SATISFACTION OR DISSATISFACTION
Expectations fulfilled	Expectations fulfilled	Satisfaction
Expectations fulfilled	Expectations not fulfilled	Dissatisfaction
Expectations not fulfilled	Expectations fulfilled	Dissatisfaction
Expectations not fulfilled	Expectations not fulfilled	Dissatisfaction

INSTRUMENTAL PERFORMANCE AND MINIMUM LEVELS OF SATISFACTION

The main argument to be developed in this article is that satisfaction with an item of clothing involves the following processes: 1. instrumental performance (i.e. performance of the physical product) that meets or exceeds expectations, and 2. expressive performance that meets or exceeds expectations. However, satisfactory instrumental performance alone will not result in satisfaction to the consumer, since most of the functions of clothing that are important to consumers involve performance at a psychological level, such as an indicator of status or extension of the self.

After reviewing studies of consumer satisfaction–dissatisfaction with clothing, Ryan concluded that for a garment to be satisfactory it must perform well on the dimension that is most important to the consumer, and it must reach a certain minimum level on all of the other dimensions.[9] In the present study, it was predicted that instrumental performance is a necessary, but not sufficient, condition for satisfaction. Dissatisfactory items will involve primarily failures of instrumental performance to meet expectations. The relationships between expectations and performance resulting in satisfaction or dissatisfaction, as predicted in this study, are summarised in Table 1.

HYPOTHESES

The hypotheses tested in this study may be briefly stated as follows in terms of general hypotheses with subhypotheses:

H 1:   Satisfaction will tend to be associated with expressive outcomes, and dissatisfaction will tend to be associated with instrumental outcomes.

SUBHYPOTHESES:
S 1.1:
The relative frequency of instrumental performance outcomes will be higher than that of expressive outcomes in the case of dissatisfactory items.
S 1.2:
The relative frequency of expressive performance outcomes will be higher than that of instrumental outcomes for satisfactory items.
S 1.3:
Satisfactory items will be associated with a higher proportion of expressive outcomes than will dissatisfactory items.

H 2:   Satisfactory items will tend to be associated with performance outcomes equal to or above expectations, while dissatisfactory items will tend to be associated with performance outcomes below expectations.

H 3:   Satisfaction is based on a hierarchy of product performance dimensions in which the product must meet expectations in terms of instrumental performance first and expressive performance second.

SUBHYPOTHESES:

S 3.1:

Satisfactory items will tend to be associated only with outcomes equal to or above expectations.

S 3.2:

Dissatisfactory items will involve a mixture of outcomes above and below expectations.

S 3.3:

The frequency of reported dissatisfaction with any aspect of the satisfactory item will be less than the frequency of reported satisfaction with some aspects of the dissatisfactory item.

The first two main hypotheses were drawn from the research reviewed in the prior section, which suggested that satisfaction will tend to be associated with expressive outcomes and with performance above or equal to expectations, while dissatisfaction will be related to performance below expectations for instrumental outcomes. The third main hypothesis was drawn from the idea that in order to be satisfactory, a product must meet expectations on both instrumental and expressive dimensions. Dissatisfaction will result if any important performance outcome is below expectations; thus, a dissatisfactory product may be satisfactory in some ways.

METHODOLOGY

Following Herzberg, Mausner and Snyderman, this study used a modified form of the 'critical incidents' technique in which people discuss specific occurrences that they recall.[10] A semi-structured questionnaire was administered by the authors on an individual basis to sixty undergraduate student respondents, who were asked to 'think about a specific item of clothing that has been especially satisfactory and an item that has been especially dissatisfactory'. After these items had been named, the respondents were ques-

tioned about both. They were asked: 'What happened to make you satisfied [dissatisfied] with this item?' The responses were recorded by the interviewers, and later each experience or outcome was classified as instrumental or expressive by the authors.

An *outcome* was operationally defined as a separately identifiable performance result reported by a respondent. As an example, a respondent reported that the fabric of a shirt was what he liked because it was comfortable and in style. This was recorded as two outcomes because two identifiable performance results (comfortable, in style) were mentioned. Outcomes were classified as instrumental or expressive using the following decision rule:

1. All outcomes with reference to the physical product *per se* were classified as instrumental. Specific instrumental outcomes involved: durability, laundering properties, warm or cool to wear, retention of shape or colour, wrinkle-resistant, construction, and good or poor fit.

2. All outcomes that referred to performance dimensions other than the physical product *per se* (without reference to the physical product) were classified as expressive. Specific expressive outcomes included: styling, responses of other people to the item, comfort, and colour.

While the decision rule stated above provided a clear division between expressive and instrumental outcomes, the classification of comfort presented a problem. The decision rule considered comfort as an end, hence, an expressive outcome. However, some instrumental outcomes, such as warm or cool to wear, good or poor fit, are closely associated with comfort and provide sound grounds for classifying comfort as instrumental (means to an end). In addition, protection from the environment as a basic function of clothing was classified as instrumental by the present writers, and comfort would be closely related to this function. The problem was resolved as follows. In those cases where the analysis was based on the classification of outcomes as instrumental or expressive, an analysis with comfort as expressive was performed first and then a separate analysis with comfort reclassified as instrumental was run. Given the exploratory nature of the study and the limited prior application of the concepts to consumer behaviour, it was felt that this approach would provide more information both for the present study and for future research efforts.

The reliability of the classification of outcomes was measured by having two analysts, one of whom was unaware of the hypotheses of the study, independently classify a sample of outcomes. A coding agreement measure (C.R.) was used, and the coefficient of reliability was equal to 83 .6 per cent.[11]

Whether or not each outcome or performance dimension met the respondent's expectations was operationally measured by asking the respondents if the outcome was much better, better, about what expected, worse, or much worse than expected. The frequency of reported dissatisfaction [satisfaction] with the satisfactory [dissatisfactory] item was measured by responses to the following questions: 1. [Satisfactory Item] 'Were you dissatisfied with this item in any way?' yes _____ no_____. 2. [Dissatisfactory Item] Were you satisfied with this item in any way?' yes _____ no_____ .

Having the respondents discuss an especially satisfactory or dissatisfactory item was designed to enhance the respondent's recall. The use of especially satisfactory/dissatisfactory items reduces generalisations that can be made from the sample. However, one of the important steps in the critical incident technique used in this study is to focus on a specific situation to be studied. The especially satisfactory/dissatisfactory item and the respondent's recall of outcomes constituted the situation studied. The critical incident technique has had a long history of successful application, primarily in personnel psychology.[12]

It must be emphasised that this is only a preliminary study due to the use of a student sample and the use of clothing (which may be particularly sensitive to expressive dimensions) as the product. Students and clothing were used for a number of reasons. Clothing was used primarily because it was the only product that was found to have a substantial history of prior research on determinants of consumer satisfaction. While extensive work has been done on consumer choice, little research has appeared on satisfaction. Also, the central concepts tested in this study were drawn, in part, from prior research on clothing. Finally, it was assumed that clothing would be a product about which consumers could recall meaningful information because: 1. it is important enough for people to pay attention to it and thus to retain their experiences in memory; 2. it is used by both sexes and by the college students in the sample; and 3. individuals generally have a number of items of clothing, so it was likely that most members of the sample would have had experiences that were fairly recent and thus likely to be recalled accurately.

The main reason for using a sample of students was to maximise limited time available for interviewing. The use of a student sample always raises questions about generalising the results. Certainly, specific results cannot be generalised to a wider population. However, some writers have argued that basic processes may apply to both students and wider samples, and the central purpose of this study was to analyse a basic process.[13]

The student sample used in this study was composed of twenty-five students enrolled in a freshman general business course and thirty-five from a junior-level marketing course. Forty-six of the respondents were male, fourteen were female; sixteen were married, forty-four were single; twenty were between eighteen and twenty years of age, thirty-nine were twenty-one to twenty-five, and one was thirty years of age.

RESULTS
DEGREE OF SATISFACTION RELATED TO EXPRESSIVE/INSTRUMENTAL OUTCOMES
The first hypothesis predicted that satisfactory

TABLE 2:   CLASSIFICATION OF PERFORMANCE OUTCOMES ASSOCIATED WITH SATISFACTORY AND DISSATISFACTORY ITEMS BY PROPORTION OF EXPRESSIVE TO INSTRUMENTAL OUTCOMES

Items	Higher proportion of expressive outcomes than instrumental	Expressive outcomes equalled instrumental	Higher proportion of instrumental outcomes than expressive	Total	Chi-square
Comfort as expressive outcome					
Satisfactory items	31	12	17	60	9.7[b]
Dissatisfactory items	7	7	43	57[a]	45.5[c]
Comfort as instrumental outcome					
Satisfactory items	22	13	25	60	3.9
Dissatisfactory items	3	5	49	57[a]	64.8[c]

a. Three respondents did not report on a dissatisfactory item.
b. Probability of chi-square is less than .01.
c. Probability of chi-square is less than .001.

items would tend to be associated with expressive outcomes, and dissatisfactory items would tend to be associated with instrumental outcomes. In terms of the relative frequency of outcomes, with comfort classified as expressive, the satisfactory items tended to be associated with a higher or equal proportion of expressive outcomes relative to instrumental outcomes (72 per cent of the respondents), while for the dissatisfactory items the proportion of instrumental outcomes exceeded the expressive outcomes for 75 per cent of the respondents (Table 2). The results were significant assuming a null hypothesis of an equal distribution of respondents across the categories of outcomes in Table 2, and the first two subhypotheses were supported.

With comfort classified as an instrumental outcome, however, the results changed for the satisfactory items. No significant difference was found in the relative proportions of expressive outcomes to instrumental outcomes (as indicated in the lower part of Table 2). Thus, support for the second subhypothesis (which predicted a higher relative frequency of expressive to instrumental outcomes for satisfactory items) depends on the classification of comfort: the hypothesis is supported if comfort is expressive but is not sup-

ported if comfort is instrumental.

Support was found for the third subhypothesis, which predicted a higher proportion of expressive outcomes for the satisfactory than the dissatisfactory items (Table 3). This subhypothesis was tested using the Wilcoxon matched-pairs signed-ranks test to compare two observations on the same respondent (comparison of the satisfactory to the dissatisfactory item).[14] Each item was given a score as follows: score of 3 if all outcomes were expressive, score of 2 if outcomes were both instrumental and expressive, and a score of 1 if all outcomes were instrumental (Table 3). The classification of comfort did not influence this result (Table 3). The actual distribution of the data called for a modification of this third subhypothesis. The dissatisfactory items were most frequently associated with only instrumental outcomes (63 per cent or 67 per cent of the respondents, depending on whether comfort was classified as expressive or instrumental), while the satisfactory items involved a mix of expressive and instrumental outcomes (77 per cent or 83 per cent of the respondents, with comfort as expressive or instrumental). Dissatisfactory items were often linked to a failure of the physical product, an instrumental failure. A number of satisfactory outcomes did

TABLE 3:   WILCOXON RANK ORDER TEST RESULTS: PROBABILITY OF NO SIGNIFICANT DIFFERENCE BETWEEN SATISFACTORY AND DISSATISFACTORY ITEMS

Test	Z	p(Z)
Satisfactory items have higher proportion of expressive outcomes than dissatisfactory items:		
1. Comfort classified as expressive	−4.44	.000
2. Comfort classified as instrumental	−5.38	.000
Satisfactory items have higher proportion of outcomes equal to or above expectations than dissatisfactory items	−6.45	.000

involve the physical product *per se*. Since the outcomes involving the physical product were almost three times as great as the expressive outcomes for the dissatisfactory item, a restatement of the process may be in order: A satisfactory product may involve both expressive and instrumental outcomes, while the dissatisfactory item is likely to involve more instrumental than expressive outcomes.

FULFILMENT OF EXPECTATIONS AND SATISFACTION

Hypothesis 2 stated that a satisfactory item would be associated with performance outcomes equal to or above expectations, while a dissatisfactory item would be associated with performance outcomes below expectations. To test this hypothesis, the outcomes for each item were ranked on the proportion of outcomes related to expectations: all outcomes greater than or equal to expectations (score of 3); some outcomes greater than or equal to expectations and some outcomes less than expectations (score of 2); and all outcomes below expectations (score of 1). The proportion of outcomes related to expectations for the satisfactory and dissatisfactory items was compared across respondents.

The satisfactory items had a significantly higher proportion of outcomes equal to or above expectations, which supports the hypothesis (see Table 3, third Wilcoxon test). In fact, the data revealed that for all respondents for the satisfacto-

ry item all outcomes were greater than or equal to expectations, while for 91 per cent of the respondents for the dissatisfactory item all outcomes were below expectations.

A HIERARCHY OF PRODUCT PERFORMANCE DIMENSIONS AND SATISFACTION

The third hypothesis stated that satisfaction is based on a hierarchy of product performance dimensions in which the product must meet expectations in terms of instrumental performance first and expressive performance second. This hypothesis would imply subhypothesis 3.1 and 3.2; that is, that a dissatisfactory item could involve a mixture of outcomes above and below expectations, while a satisfactory item would involve only outcomes with expectations fulfilled. These subhypotheses were examined using two different sets of the data.

First, all outcomes were greater than or equal to expectations for all respondents for the satisfactory item, but the dissatisfactory item did not tend to involve a mixture of favourable and unfavourable outcomes. For fifty-two respondents (91 per cent), the unsatisfactory item was associated with only unfavourable outcomes; only three respondents (5 per cent) reported a mixture of favourable and unfavourable outcomes. The results were significant according to the Wilcoxon test for paired observations, Table 3.

A limitation of the previous analysis is that

TABLE 4:   RESULTS OF MCNEMAR TEST FOR SIGNIFICANCE OF CHANGES IN CLASSIFICATION OF RESPONDENTS

Response	Satisfied with the dissatisfactory item		Dissatisfied with the satisfactory item	
	N	%	N	%
Yes	34	59.6	12	21.1
No	23	40.4	45	78.9
	57	100.0	57	100.0

Chi-square = 16, probability of chi-square is less than .001.

for a satisfactory item, favourable outcomes (outcomes with expectations fulfilled) may tend to be salient and unfavourable outcomes not mentioned, with an opposite pattern for the dissatisfactory item. This limitation was anticipated, so the respondents were asked, for the satisfactory item, whether or not they were dissatisfied in any way and, for the dissatisfactory item, if they were satisfied in any way. The results shown in Table 4 suggest that for over 59 per cent of the respondents the dissatisfactory item did tend to involve mixed outcomes, while the satisfactory item involved mixed outcomes for only 21 per cent of the respondents. The differences were significant when the McNemar test for significant differences in changes was applied to the satisfactory as compared to the dissatisfactory item for each respondent.[15] Thus, subhypothesis 3.3 was supported.

APPLICATION OF THE CONCEPT TO OTHER PRODUCTS/SERVICES

The concept that consumer satisfaction is related to expressive and instrumental dimensions of product performance was developed and applied to clothing. The extent to which the concept may be applicable to other products is an empirical question that can be answered with confidence only by future studies on other products. However, evidence from the literature hints that for some products determinant attributes may involve primarily instrumental performance, while other products/services may be sensitive to both instrumental and expressive dimensions.

An example of a service that consumers may judge primarily on instrumental dimensions is air travel. The main instrumental dimension of air travel would be time saved, which is the factor respondents in one study liked most about flying. In contrast, only about one-third of the respondents mentioned comfort, the second most frequently cited characteristic; and only a few (5 per cent to 7 per cent) gave services (meals, drinks) as a response.[16] Myers and Alpert also did a study of consumer ratings of three airlines, and the airline with the most favourable overall ratings received relatively low ratings on expressive attributes of liquor, hostesses and food.[17]

A product that may be thought to involve primarily instrumental performance was found to illustrate a mixed case. Alpert related overall preference of ball-point pens to thirty-seven attributes, of which nine attributes classified as 'objective' would be termed instrumental attributes in this study.[18] Instrumental attributes included such dimensions as comfortable to hold, freedom from skipping, and convenience in refilling. The remaining three sets of attributes would be considered expressive: 1. seven aspects of the 'image' of the pen (old-fashioned–modern); 2. eight personality types of the typical user of the pen (careless–perfectionist); and 3. thirteen ratings of the likelihood that different occupational groups would use the pen (banker, housewife, etc.). Of the ten most important attributes in terms of a correlation with overall preference, five would be classified by the present authors as instrumental (e.g. smoothness while writing) and five as expressive (e.g. attractiveness of pen, typical user is a college student, athlete).[19]

A large number of store choice studies have reported that most aspects of store choice pertain to the merchandise, prices, convenience in shopping, and the like, which could be termed instrumental assuming that the primary end in shopping is purchasing wanted items.[20] However, some students of retailing have argued that other important choice dimensions are expressive, such as the type of person that shops at a store or the shopper's desire to command respect and attention rather than purchase goods.[21]

The purpose of discussing the application of the central concepts in this study to items other than clothing was to give the reader a basis for assessing the potential relevance of the process to consumer behaviour. If it can be assumed that choice and preference dimensions are related to satisfaction, then it appears that the instrumental-expressive concepts can be usefully applied to products and services other than clothing.

It should be noted that the idea that instrumental performance is only a means to an end was not tested directly in the non-clothing studies cited above and may not hold for some products/services. In fact, clothing may be a type of product where the model developed in this study is most likely to apply, since the functions performed by clothing are not direct attributes of the physical product. Other types of products and brands for which expressive dimensions would be important would be items where other people judge the consumer on the basis of what he purchases, such as furniture, magazines, cars and beer.[22] Other products, such as household glue, laundry soap and flashlight batteries, may essentially involve only instrumental attributes, in which case satisfaction would be contingent upon instrumental performance.

CONCLUSIONS

The findings concerning instrumental and expressive outcomes suggest that satisfaction and dissatisfaction are linked to qualitatively different kinds of outcomes. These outcomes form a hierarchy such that instrumental requirements must be satisfied first before satisfaction can occur. The distinction between instrumental and expressive outcomes suggests that consumers may judge products in a manner analogous to 'management by exception': as long as the product performs well on the instrumental dimensions, such performance is ignored. In describing the satisfactory item, no respondent said, 'I am satisfied because it did not rip, shrink or fade.' These kinds of experiences became salient only when they occurred and were linked to the dissatisfactory item. Thus, in applied research where consumers are questioned as to what they are seeking in a product, it is likely that the expressive, not the instrumental, attributes of the product will be mentioned if the respondent has been satisfied with the item. However, satisfactory instrumental performance is quite important, since instrumental requirements must be satisfied before satisfaction from expressive performance can occur.

This view of consumer satisfaction also suggests that the weights consumers attach to the importance of a set of attributes comprising a product are difficult to summarise and measure meaningfully, because such weights vary in perceived importance depending on the level of product performance. As an example, if respondents were asked to rank durability and appearance of clothing, most would probably put appearance first and durability second. However, this ranking may be based on the implicit assumption that durability will be 'satisfactory'. Relating the results of this study to the Myers and Alpert concept of determinant attributes, a determinant attribute leading to dissatisfaction may not be a determinant attribute resulting in satisfaction.[23]

The strong results supporting the hypothesis that satisfaction is associated with performance that fulfils expectations, while dissatisfaction occurs when performance expectations are not fulfilled, suggests that the determination of satisfaction involves relative rather than absolute judgements. Thus, future research should study the processes whereby expectations are formed, which dimensions of product performance consumers have expectations about, and the performance dimensions used by consumers to judge product performance.

IMPLICATIONS

The general implications of the model tested and the results of this study relate to: 1. knowledge of consumer behaviour, and 2. consumer analysis for marketing decisions.

CONSUMER BEHAVIOUR

In the area of consumer behaviour, the process of consumer response to product performance may be stated as follows:

> In judging the performance of a product, the consumer compares a set of performance outcomes to the outcomes that were expected for the item. If the performance of the physical product was below expectations, then the product is likely to be categorised as dissatisfactory. If both instrumental and expressive outcomes were equal to or exceeded expectations, the consumer will tend to judge the product as satisfactory.

The process is a multiattribute process; that is, the respondents tended to report a set of outcomes for each item (the mean number of outcomes was 3.4 for the satisfactory item and 2.0 for the dissatisfactory item). The limited set of attributes reported suggests that the salient attributes come closer to a 'satisficing' than an 'optimising' type of judgement, because a larger set of attributes could well be salient for an optimal judgement.

Since a majority (60 per cent) of respondents were satisfied in some way with the dissatisfactory item and only 21 per cent were dissatisfied with some aspect of the satisfactory item (Table 4), satisfaction/dissatisfaction does not appear to involve

some form of compensatory judgement where poor performance on one dimension is balanced by good performance on another, and vice versa. Also, learning probably plays an important role in consumer judgement of products. Since satisfaction/dissatisfaction was associated with various outcomes that buyers recalled in an interview, it is reasonable to assume that such outcomes are recalled and become what Howard and Sheth have labelled 'choice motives', or factors that buyers consider when similar items are repurchased.

Finally, the consumer's categorisation of an item as satisfactory or dissatisfactory constitutes an important attitude towards the item. Thus, another general implication of the present study is that attitude formation is subject to the processes incorporated in the satisfaction/dissatisfaction concept suggested by this study. That attitudes are sensitive to satisfaction/dissatisfaction may not be new information; however, this study has presented reasonably specific details concerning how degrees of satisfaction may be related to dimensions of product performance. Of course, only future research can specify the extent to which the implications drawn above are specific to the products, method and sample used in this study.

CONSUMER ANALYSIS FOR MARKETING DECISIONS

A number of general implications are also suggested for consumer analysis to suit managerial purposes. In a survey designed to determine what consumers like/dislike about a product, a useful research step may be to follow the procedure used here and ask consumers to talk about an especially satisfactory and dissatisfactory item, since salient outcomes have been shown to vary along such lines. Measurement of consumer expectations and determination of how well the firm's product may meet such expectations could be a useful step in helping to ensure consumer satisfaction. It is likely that an important source of expectations is promotion by the firm and members of the channel of distribution. Therefore, it would be useful to analyse which expectations are generated by promotion, since dissatisfaction may result if product performance cannot meet expectations.

A large-scale survey of users of a type of product, with a focus on both satisfied and dissatisfied users and the salient outcomes, may yield specific information with a number of applications. Areas for improvement of the physical product may be uncovered. Reports of kinds of outcomes associated with satisfactory items may provide ideas for promotional copy to create favourable attitudes towards the firm's brand. If some competitive products involve specific product failures, that information may be used in promotional copy illustrating why our brand is better. A knowledge of the kinds of outcomes that are likely not to meet widespread expectations may provide specific guidelines for developing warranties or other kinds of guarantee.

In summary, consumer satisfaction has been a neglected area of research and theory. It is hoped that the concepts used and results found in this study may be of use to marketing students and practitioners.

NOTES

1. Ralph E. Anderson and J.F. Hair (1972), 'Consumerism, Consumer Expectations, and Perceived Product Performance', *Proceedings of the 3rd Annual Conference of the Association for Consumer Research*, Chicago, pp. 67–79; Richard N. Cardozo (1965), 'An Experimental Study of Consumer Effort, Expectations, and Satisfaction', *Journal of Marketing Research*, vol. 2, August, pp. 244–9; and Richard W. Olshavsky and J.A. Miller (1973), 'Consumer Expectations, Product Performance, and Perceived Product Quality', *Journal of Marketing Research*, vol. 9, February, pp. 19–21.

2. James F. Engel, David T. Kollat and Roger D. Blackwell (1973), *Consumer Behavior,* 2nd edition, Holt, Rinehart & Winston, NY, pp. 529–43; John A. Howard and Jagdish N. Sheth (1969), *The Theory of Buyer Behavior*, John Wiley & Sons, NY, pp. 145–50; and Francesco M. Nicosia (1966), *Consumer Decision Processes*, Prentice-Hall, Englewood Cliffs, NJ, pp. 186–8.

3. Anderson and Hair, 'Consumerism, Consumer Expectations'; Cordozo, 'An Experimental Study of Consumer Effort'; Olshavsky and Miller, 'Consumer Expectations'.

4. Lee Thayer (1968), *Communication and Communication Systems*, Richard D. Irwin, Homewood, Ill., pp. 111–33.

5. James H. Myers and Mark I. Alpert (1968), 'Determinant Attributes: Meaning and Measurement', *Journal of Marketing*, vol. 32, October, pp. 13–20.

6. Myers and Alpert, 'Determinant Attributes'; and Mark I. Alpert (1971), 'Identification of Determinant Attributes: A Comparison of Methods', *Journal of Marketing Research*, vol. 8, May, pp. 184–91.

7. The studies noted in this paragraph are all mentioned by Mary S. Ryan (1966), *Clothing: A Study in Human Behavior*, Holt, Rinehart & Winston, NY, pp. 183–5.

8. Marilyn J. Horn (1968), *The Second Skin: An Interdisciplinary Study of Clothing*, Houghtin Mifflin Co., NY, p. 12.

9. Ryan, *Clothing: A Study in Human Behavior*, pp. 185–6, 150–1.

10. Frederick Herzberg, B. Mausner and B. Snyderman (1959), *The Motivation to Work*, 2nd edition, John Wiley & Sons.

11. The coefficient of reliability was computed as: C.R. = $2m/N_1 + N_2$ where m is the number of coding decisions on which the two analysts agreed and N_1 and N_2 are the number of coding decisions made by the ana-

lysts. In this study, m = 194 and N_1 + N_2 = 232. See Ole R. Holsti (1969), *Content Analysis for the Social Sciences and Humanities*, Addison-Wesley, Reading, Mass., p. 140.

12. John C. Flanagan (1954), 'The Critical Incident Technique', *Psychological Bulletin*, vol. 51, July, pp. 327–58.

13. Julian L. Simon (1969), *Basic Research, Methods in Social Science*, Random House, NY, p. 116.

14. Sidney Siegel (1956), *Nonparametric Statistics for the Behavioral Sciences*, McGraw-Hill Book Co., New York, pp. 75–83.

15. Siegel, *Nonparametric Statistics*, pp. 63–7.

16. Roger D. Blackwell, James F. Engel and David T. Kollat (1969), *Cases in Consumer Behavior*, Holt, Rinehart & Winston, NY, pp. 182–95.

17. Myers and Alpert, 'Determinant Attributes', pp. 14–15.

18. Alpert, 'Identification of Determinant Attributes', attributes 2–5 and 7–11, Table 1, p. 186.

19. Alpert, 'Identification of Determinant Attributes', Table 6, p. 190: instrumental attributes are numbers 3, 8, 2, 11, 7; expressive are numbers 6, 29, 38, 22, 16.

20. Engel, Kollat and Blackwell, *Consumer Behaviour*, pp. 442–56.

21. Engel, Kollat and Blackwell, *Consumer Behavior*, p. 451; and Edward M. Tauber (1972), 'Why Do People Shop?', *Journal of Marketing*, vol. 36, October, p. 48.

22. Engel, Kollat and Blackwell, *Consumer Behavior*, pp. 174–5.

23. Myers and Alpert, 'Determinant Attributes'.

Servicescapes: The Impact of Physical Surroundings on Customers and Employees

Mary Jo Bitner

A typology of service organisations is presented and a conceptual framework is advanced for exploring the impact of physical surroundings on the behaviours of both customers and employees. The ability of the physical surroundings to facilitate achievement of organisational as well as marketing goals is explored. Literature from diverse disciplines provides theoretical grounding for the framework, which serves as a base for focused propositions. By examining the multiple strategic roles that physical surroundings can exert in service organisations, the author highlights key managerial and research implications.

The effect of atmospherics, or physical design and décor elements, on consumers and workers is recognised by managers and mentioned in virtually all marketing, retailing and organisational behaviour texts. Yet, particularly in marketing, there is a surprising lack of empirical research or theoretically based frameworks addressing the role of physical surroundings in consumption settings. Managers continually plan, build, change and control an organisation's physical surroundings, but frequently the impact of a specific design or design change on ultimate users of the facility is not fully understood.

The ability of the physical environment to influence behaviours and to create an image is particularly apparent for service businesses such as hotels, restaurants, professional offices, banks, retail stores and hospitals (Baker, 1987; Bitner, 1986; Booms and Bitner, 1982; Kotler, 1973; Shostack, 1977; Upah and Fulton, 1985; Zeithaml, Parasuraman and Berry, 1985). Because the service generally is produced and consumed simultaneously, the consumer is 'in the factory', often experiencing the total service within the firm's physical facility. The factory (or the place where the service is produced) cannot be hidden and may in fact have a strong impact on customers' perceptions of the service experience. Even before purchase, consumers commonly look for cues about the firm's capabilities and quality (Berry and Clark, 1986; Shostack, 1977). The physical environment is rich in such cues (Rapoport, 1982) and may be very influential in communicating the firm's image and purpose to its customers. Research suggests that the physical setting may also influence the customer's ultimate satisfaction with the service (Bitner, 1990; Harrell, Hutt and Anderson, 1980).

Interestingly, in service organisations the same physical setting that communicates with and influences customers may affect employees of the firm (Baker, Berry and Parasuraman, 1988). Research in organisational behaviour suggests that the physical setting can influence employee satisfaction, productivity and motivation (e.g. Becker, 1981; Davis, 1984; Steele, 1986; Sundstrom and Altman, 1989; Sundstrom and

Reprinted with permission from *Journal of Marketing*, vol. 56, April, pp. 57–71.

Sundstrom, 1986; Wineman, 1986). The customer is left out of that research stream, however, just as the employee typically is ignored in the limited atmospherics research in marketing (e.g. Donovan and Rossiter, 1982; Kotler, 1973; Milliman, 1982, 1986). For example, in the Milliman experiments, music tempo was varied and the effect on a variety of consumer behaviours was measured; however, the effects on employee satisfaction and productivity were not explored. Because services generally are purchased and consumed simultaneously, and typically require direct human contact, customers and employees interact with each other within the organisation's physical facility. Ideally, therefore, the organisation's environment should support the needs and preferences of both service employees and customers simultaneously.

The purpose of this article is to take a first step towards integrating theories and empirical findings from diverse disciplines into a framework that describes how the built environment (i.e. the man-made, physical surroundings as opposed to the natural or social environment), or what is referred to here as the 'servicescape', affects *both* consumers and employees in service organisations. First, a typology of service organisations is presented that illuminates important variations in form and usage of the servicescape. Next, a conceptual framework is offered for explaining environment–user relationships in service organisations, and specific research propositions are advanced. The framework is anchored in the environmental psychology research tradition and also draws together relevant literature in marketing, organisational behaviour, human factors/ ergonomics, and architecture. Finally, the linkages between the service organisation typology and the framework are examined, and key managerial and research implications are discussed.

A TYPOLOGY OF SERVICESCAPES

'The way the physical setting is created in organisations has barely been tapped as a tangible organisational resource' (Becker, 1981, p. 130). Man-

agement of the physical setting typically is viewed as tangential in comparison with other organisational variables that can motivate employees, such as pay scales, promotions, benefits and supervisory relationships. Similarly, on the consumer side, variables such as pricing, advertising, added features and special promotions are given much more attention than the physical setting as ways in which customers can be attracted to and/or satisfied by a firm's services. A clear implication of the model presented here is that the physical setting can aid or hinder the accomplishment of both internal organisational goals and external marketing goals.

As is true of any organisational or marketing variable, the importance of physical setting depends on the nature of the job and the nature of the consumption experience. The position advanced here is that the physical surroundings are, *in general*, more important in service settings because customers as well as employees often experience the firm's facility. However, not all service firms and industries are alike (Lovelock, 1983; Schmenner, 1986), nor do they face the same strategic issues in planning and designing their servicescapes. Figure 1 is a typology categorising service organisations on two dimensions that capture important differences in the management of the servicescape. Firms that share a cell within the matrix face similar issues related to the design of their physical spaces.

The vertical dimension relates to *who* is performing actions within the servicescape – the customer, or the employee, or both. One extreme is represented by the 'self-service' organisation in which few if any employees are present and the level of customer activity is high. At the other extreme is the 'remote service' where there is little or no customer involvement in the servicescape and sometimes even little employee involvement, such as in fully automated voice-messaging services. Note from Figure 1 that 'interpersonal services' are positioned between the two extremes. In those organisations, both customers and employees are present and performing actions within the servicescape. The relative level of involvement of

FIGURE 1:   TYPOLOGY OF SERVICE ORGANISATIONS BASED ON VARIATIONS IN FORM AND USAGE OF THE SERVICESCAPE

TYPE OF SERVICE ORGANISATIONS BASED ON WHO PERFORMS ACTIONS WITHIN THE SERVICESCAPE	PHYSICAL COMPLEXITY OF THE SERVICESCAPE	
	Elaborate	*Lean*
Self-service (customer only)	Golf Land Surf 'n Splash	ATM Ticketron Post office kiosk Movie theatre Express mail drop-off
Interpersonal services (both customer and employee)	Hotels Restaurants Health clinic Hospital Bank Airline School	Dry cleaner Hot dog stand Hair salon
Remote service (employee only)	Telephone company Insurance company Utility Many professional services	Telephone mail order desk Automated voice-messaging-based services

customers and employees determines whose needs should be consulted in the design of the environment. In interpersonal servicescapes, special consideration must be given to the effects of the physical environment on the nature and quality of the social interaction *between* and *among* customers and employees.

Whether customers, employees or both are present within the servicescape also determines the types of objective a firm might expect to accomplish through use of its physical environment. In self-service settings, the creative use of physical design could support particular positioning and segmentation strategies and enhance specific marketing objectives, such as customer satisfaction and attraction. At the other extreme, for remote services, organisational objectives such as employee satisfaction, motivation and operational efficiency could be the primary goals in physical setting design, because few customers would ever see or experience the firm's physical setting. For interpersonal services, both organisational and market-

ing objectives could potentially be targeted through careful design of the servicescape. Even marketing goals such as relationship-building (Crosby, Evans and Cowles, 1990) could be influenced by the design of the physical setting.

The horizontal dimension of Figure 1 captures the complexity of the servicescape. Some service environments are very simple, with few elements, few spaces and few forms. They are termed 'lean' environments. Ticketron outlets and Federal Express drop-off kiosks would qualify as lean environments, as both provide service from one simple structure. For lean servicescapes, design decisions are relatively straightforward, especially in self-service or remote service situations in which there is no interaction between customers and employees. Other servicescapes are very complicated, with many elements and many forms. They are termed 'elaborate' environments. An example is a hospital with its many floors, rooms, sophisticated equipment, and complex variability in functions performed within the physical facility. In such an elaborate environment, the full range of marketing and organisational objectives theoretically can be approached through careful management of the servicescape. For example, a patient's hospital room can be designed to enhance patient comfort and satisfaction while simultaneously facilitating employee productivity. Figure 1 suggests that firms such as hospitals that are positioned in the elaborate interpersonal service cell face the most complex servicescape decisions.

CONCEPTUAL FRAMEWORK

Though the typology in Figure 1 highlights the relative complexity of environmental decisions across different types of service organisation, it does not explain what behaviours are influenced, or *why*, or how one would go about planning and designing an environment to achieve particular objectives. Figure 2 is a rich framework for addressing those questions and for exploring the role of physical environment in service organisations. The framework suggests that a variety of objective environmental factors are perceived by *both* customers and employees and that both groups may respond cognitively, emotionally and physiologically to the environment. Those internal responses to the environment influence the behaviour of individual customers and employees in the servicescape and affect social interactions between and among customers and employees. Though the model shares similarities with other models (e.g. Mehrabian and Russell, 1974), it is unique in its breadth of synthesis (for example, Mehrabian and Russell focus on emotional responses only), the incorporation of *both* customers and employees and their interactions, and its application to commercial settings. In the following sections, each of the components of the framework is defined and developed. Attention centres first on the behaviours that may be influenced by the servicescape and then on the internal responses and the controllable dimensions that constitute the servicescape. Propositions based on the framework are highlighted, and implications for firms within specific cells of the service typology are discussed.

BEHAVIOURS IN THE SERVICESCAPE

That human behaviour is influenced by the physical setting in which it occurs is essentially a truism. Interestingly, however, until the 1960s psychologists largely ignored the effects of physical setting in their attempts to predict and explain behaviour. Since that time, a large and steadily growing body of literature within the field of environmental psychology has addressed the relationships between human beings and their built environments (for reviews of environmental psychology, see Darley and Gilbert, 1985; Holahan, 1986; Russell and Ward, 1982; Stokols and Altman, 1987).[1] Here it is assumed that dimensions of the organisation's physical surroundings influence important customer and employee behaviours. The types of behaviours that are influenced are identified and discussed next.

INDIVIDUAL BEHAVIOURS

Environmental psychologists suggest that individuals react to places with two general, and opposite, forms of behaviour: approach and avoidance (Mehrabian and Russell, 1974). Approach behaviours include all positive behaviours that might be directed at a particular place, such as desire to stay, explore, work and affiliate (Mehrabian and Russell, 1974). Avoidance behaviours reflect the opposite, in other words, a desire *not* to stay, explore, work and affiliate. In a study of consumers in retail environments, Donovan and Rossiter (1982) found that approach behaviours in that setting (including shopping enjoyment, returning, attraction and friendliness towards others, spending money, time spent browsing, and exploration of the store) were influenced by perceptions of the environment. Milliman (1982, 1986) found that the tempo of background music can affect traffic flow and gross receipts in both supermarket and restaurant settings. In actual service settings, examples of environmental cues being used to change behaviour are abundant. At one 7-11 store, the owners played 'elevator music' to drive away a youthful market segment that was detracting from the store's image. Cinnamon roll

FIGURE 2:   FRAMEWORK FOR UNDERSTANDING ENVIRONMENT–USER RELATIONSHIPS IN
            SERVICE ORGANISATIONS

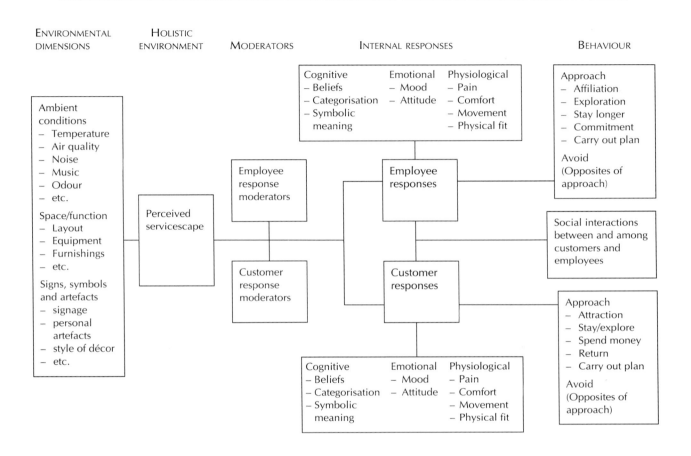

bakeries commonly pump the wonderful fragrance of their freshly baked products out into mall traffic areas to entice customers into the store.

In addition to attracting or deterring entry, the servicescape can actually influence the degree of success consumers experience in executing their plans once inside (Darley and Gilbert, 1985; Russell and Snodgrass, 1987). Each individual comes to a particular service organisation with a goal or purpose that may be aided or hindered by the setting. For example, assume that a traveller enters an airport and 1. is confused because he or she cannot find signage giving directions to the assigned gate; and 2. is emotionally distressed because of crowds, poor acoustics and high temperature. The traveller is unable to carry out the purpose for entering the environment, at least not very easily. Here the servicescape directly inhibits the accomplishment of the customer's goal. Similarly, physical surroundings and conditions could constrain an employee's ability to do his or her work and thereby detract from the purpose for being in the servicescape.

Clearly, firms want to encourage approach behaviours and the ability of customers and employees to carry out their plans while at the same time discouraging avoidance behaviours. As Figure 2 shows, the approach/avoidance behaviours of employees and customers are determined largely by individual internal responses (cognitive, emotional and physiological) to the environment. The three types of internal responses are discussed in greater detail subsequently. The basic assumption is that positive (negative) internal responses lead to approach (avoidance) behaviours.

P1: Positive (negative) internal responses to the servicescape lead to approach (avoidance) behaviours.

   a. For employees, approach includes such behaviours as affiliation, exploration, staying longer, expressions of commitment, and carrying out the purpose for being in the organisation. Avoidance is represented by the opposite behaviours.

   b. For customers, approach includes such behaviours as coming in, staying, spending money, loyalty, and carrying out the purpose for being in the organisation. Avoidance is represented by the opposite behaviours.

Social Interactions

In addition to its effects on their individual behaviours, the servicescape influences the nature and quality of customer and employee interactions, most directly in interpersonal services. Bennett and Bennett (1970) state that 'all social interaction is affected by the physical container in which it occurs'. They go on to suggest that the physical container affects the nature of social interaction in terms of the duration of interaction and the actual progression of events. In many service situations, a firm may want to ensure a particular progression of events (i.e. a 'standard script') and limit the duration of the service. Forgas (1979) suggests that environmental variables such as propinquity, seating arrangements, size and flexibility can define the possibilities and limits of social episodes, such as those between and among customers and employees.

He also suggests that physical environments represent a subset of social rules, conventions and expectations in force in a given behaviour setting, serving to define the nature of social interaction. In developing the concept of behaviour settings, Barker (1968) implies that recurring social behaviour patterns are associated with particular physical settings and that when people encounter typical settings, their social behaviours can be predicted.

Empirical studies confirm the impact of physical setting on the nature of social interaction. Behaviours such as small group interaction, friendship formation, participation, aggression, withdrawal and helping have all been shown to be influenced by environmental conditions (Holahan, 1982). Similarly, in studies of workplace design, researchers have found that communication patterns, group cohesion, and the formation of friendships and small groups can be influenced by the physical setting (Sundstrom and Sundstrom, 1986, Part III). By implication, those findings suggest that the servicescape influences the nature of social interactions between and among customers and employees.

Examples are again abundant in actual service settings. Even casual observation of a Club Med facility confirms that the highly complex setting is designed to encourage social interaction among and between guests and employees. Seating arrangements and the food preparation process at Benihana restaurants similarly encourage interactions among total strangers, as well as contact between patrons and the Japanese chef who prepares their meals in full view. In most airports, in contrast, research suggests that the arrangement of seating typically *discourages* comfortable conversation among travellers and their companions (Sommer, 1974).

One of the challenges in designing environments to enhance individual approach behaviours and encourage the appropriate social interactions is that optimal design for one person or group may not be the optimal design for others. Research in a bank setting suggests, for example, that employees and customers have different needs and desires for their physical surroundings (Baker, Berry and Parasuraman, 1988). Similarly, an environment that is conducive to an employee's individual work needs may not enhance the employee's ability to converse and interact interpersonally with customers.

P2: For interpersonal services, positive (negative) internal responses to the servicescape enhance (detract from) the nature and quality of social interactions between and among customers and employees.

P3: Optimal design for encouraging employee (customer) approach behaviour may be incompatible with the design required to meet customer (employee) needs and/or facilitate positive employee–customer interactions.

SERVICE TYPOLOGY AND BEHAVIOUR

Some research tradition in environmental psychology strongly suggests that the physical environment can influence behaviours in several ways. Therefore the first step in the purposeful design of the servicescape is to identify desirable customer and/or employee behaviours and the strategic goals that the organisation hopes to advance through its physical facility. For example, in designing its corporate headquarters offices, Scandinavian Airline Systems first identified particular goals that it wanted to achieve, among them teamwork and open and frequent communication with managers. The employee behaviours associated with these goals were identified and architects were commissioned to propose designs that would be conducive to the behaviours and ultimately support the strategic goals.

The typology (Figure 1) provides a structure for isolating the relevant behavioural issues. Self-service firms will be most interested in predicting and understanding *customer* behaviours (e.g. coming in, exploration, staying) in the physical setting and the potential achievement of marketing objectives such as customer attraction, satisfaction and retention. In contrast, firms that operate remote services will focus on *employee* behaviours (e.g. productivity, affiliation with co-workers) and the achievement of organisational goals such as teamwork, productivity and innovation. Organisations that are positioned in the interpersonal service cell will be concerned with both customer and employee behaviours, as well as the effects of physical setting on the *interactions* between and among customers and employees. There the strategist must understand the plans and goals of all participants and anticipate compatibility dilemmas in designing the servicescape. Once behaviours most likely to be influenced by the servicescape are identified, challenging questions emerge: What internal responses (e.g. feelings, beliefs) will lead to the desired behaviours and how should the environment be configured to bring about such responses? The next two sections address those questions.

INTERNAL RESPONSES TO THE SERVICESCAPE

One can infer from the environmental psychology literature that employees and customers in service firms respond to dimensions of their physical surroundings cognitively, emotionally and physiologically, and that those responses are what influence their behaviours in the environment. Hence, the perceived servicescape does not directly *cause* people to behave in certain ways. As Figure 2 shows, perceptions of the servicescape lead to certain emotions, beliefs and physiological sensations which in turn influence behaviours. Behaviours are thus mediated by a person's internal responses to the place. Though the internal responses (cognitive, emotional and physiological) are discussed independently here, they are clearly interdependent. For example, a person's beliefs about a place, a cognitive response, may well influence emotional response to the place and vice versa.

ENVIRONMENT AND COGNITION

As shown in Figure 2, the perceived servicescape may elicit cognitive responses (Golledge, 1987; Kaplan and Kaplan, 1982; Rapoport, 1982), influencing people's beliefs about a place and their beliefs about the people and products found in that place. In that sense, the environment can be viewed as a form of non-verbal communication (Broadbent, Bunt and Jencks, 1980; Rapoport, 1982), imparting meaning through what Ruesch and Kees (1956) called 'object language'. For example, particular environmental cues such as the type of office furniture and décor and the apparel worn by a lawyer may influence a potential client's beliefs about whether the lawyer is successful or not successful, expensive or not expensive, and trustworthy or not trustworthy. In a consumer study, variations in verbal descriptions of store atmospherics were found to alter beliefs about a product (perfume) sold in the store (Gardner and Siomkos, 1986). Another study showed that a travel agent's office décor affected customer attributions for the travel agent's behaviour (Bitner, 1990). Variations in environmental cues may also affect *employees'* beliefs. For example, office size and type of furnishings may affect an employee's beliefs about the importance of his or her function within the firm in relation to other employees. In all of those cases, perceptions of the servicescape influence beliefs about the environment itself, but also appear to affect beliefs about other, seemingly unrelated, service attributes.

In other cases, perceptions of the servicescape may simply help people to distinguish a firm by influencing how it is categorised. Categorisation is the process by which people assign a label to an object; when people see a feathered animal flying through the air, they categorise it as a 'bird' and not a 'fish' (Loken and Ward, 1990; Mervis and Rosch, 1981). Similarly, the overall perception of the servicescape enables the consumer or employee to categorise the firm mentally. For example, research shows that in the restaurant industry a particular configuration of environmental cues suggests 'fast food' whereas another configuration suggests 'elegant sit-down restaurant' (Ward, Bitner and Barnes, 1992). In such situations, environmental cues serve as a mnemonic or short-cut device enabling customers to categorise and distinguish among types of restaurant.

Because services are relatively intangible in comparison with most manufactured goods (Shostack, 1977) and because many services are high in experience and credence attributes (Zeithaml, 1981), they generally afford fewer intrinsic cues on which to form beliefs about service quality, particularly in initial purchase situations. Hence, in such situations consumers and employees tend to use extrinsic cues (such as the physical surroundings) to infer quality (Zeithaml, 1988). In other words, people may use their beliefs about the servicescape as surrogate indicators in forming beliefs about service quality and other attributes of the service and/or the people who work in the organisation.

P4:   Perceptions of the servicescape and associated positive (negative) cognitions can lead to positive (negative) beliefs and attributions associated with the organisation, its people, and its products.

P5:   Perceptions of the servicescape influence how people categorise the organisation; thus, the environment serves as a mnemonic in differentiating among firms.

P6:   The servicescape's influence on beliefs, attributions and categorisation of the organisation is stronger for inexperienced customers or new employees, and when few intrinsic cues are available on which to categorise or base beliefs.

ENVIRONMENT AND EMOTION

In addition to influencing cognitions, the perceived servicescape may elicit emotional responses that in turn influence behaviours. In a long stream of research, Mehrabian and Russell and their colleagues have programmatically explored emotional responses to environments (e.g. Mehrabian and Russell, 1974; Russell and Lanius, 1984; Russell and Pratt, 1980; Russell and Snodgrass, 1987). Through their research they have concluded that the emotion-eliciting qualities of environments are captured by two dimensions: pleasure–displeasure and degree of arousal (i.e. amount of stimulation or excitement). In other words, any environment, whether natural or man-made, can be located in a two-dimensional space reflecting people's emotional response to the place. Research shows that emotional response measured on those dimensions can predict behaviours with respect to the environment. For example, environments that elicit feelings of pleasure are likely to be ones where people want to spend time and money (Donovan and Rossiter, 1982; Mehrabian and Russell, 1974), whereas unpleasant environments are avoided. Similarly, arousing environments are viewed positively unless the excitement is combined with unpleasantness (Mehrabian and Russell, 1974). That is, unpleasant environments that are also high in arousal (lots of stimulation, noise, confusion) are particularly avoided. Hui and Bateson (1991) found that in the context of environmental crowding, increased perceptions of personal control are related positively to increased pleasure. Other environmental dimensions (e.g. clear signage, good ventilation, adequate space) may also increase perceptions of personal control.

Research also suggests that emotional responses to the environment may be transferred to people and/or objects within the environment (Maslow and Mintz, 1956; Mintz, 1956; Obermiller and Bitner, 1984). In the Obermiller and Bitner study, respondents who viewed retail products in an emotionally pleasing environment evaluated the products more positively than did subjects who viewed the same products in an unpleasing environment. Hence, perceptions of the servicescape appear to have influenced seemingly unrelated feelings about the products.

Other researchers also have emphasised the emotion-eliciting or affective qualities of environments, suggesting that environments can be viewed as aesthetic stimuli capable of eliciting affect (Wohlwill, 1976). In his work aimed at explaining the affective assessment of outdoor environments, Kaplan (1987) concluded that preference for or liking of a particular environment can be predicted by three environmental dimensions: complexity, mystery and coherence. Complexity (visual richness, ornamentation, information rate) has been found consistently to increase emotional arousal, whereas coherence (order, clarity, unity) has been found to enhance positive evaluation (Nasar, 1989). In addition, compatibility has been found to influence perceptions of order, and preference has been found to increase with compatibility (Nasar, 1987). Compatibility in natural settings refers to how well a place blends in with its surroundings and is related inversely to contrasts (in colour, texture, size and shape) with the natural background; in urban settings compatibility results from replication of features such as materials, style and overall shapes (Nasar, 1989). Other research has shown that people respond positively to nature and prefer natural to man-made elements (Kaplan and Kaplan, 1982), whereas the presence of what Nasar (1989) terms environmental 'nuisances' has been found to reduce preference and perceptions of quality in urban settings. In urban settings such things as poles, wires, signs, and dilapidated buildings and vehicles are classified as nuisances. Research is needed to define the cues that would determine compatibility and the objects that would be classified as nuisances in service settings.

P7: Customer and employee emotional responses to the servicescape can be captured by two dimensions, pleasure and arousal.
   a. Pleasure increases approach behaviours.
   b. Arousal, except when combined with unpleasantness, increases approach behaviours.

P8: Perceptions of greater personal control in the servicescape increase pleasure.

P9: Complexity in the servicescape increases emotional arousal.

P10: Compatibility, the presence of natural elements, and the absence of environmental nuisances in the servicescape enhance pleasure.

P11: Perceptions of the servicescape and associated positive (negative) emotions can lead to positive (negative) feelings associated with the organisation, its people and its products.

ENVIRONMENT AND PHYSIOLOGY

The perceived servicescape may also affect people in purely physiological ways. Noise that is too loud may cause physical discomfort, the temperature of a room may cause people to shiver or perspire, the air quality may make it difficult to breathe, and the glare of lighting may decrease ability to see and cause physical pain. All of those physical responses may in turn directly influence whether or not people stay in and enjoy a particular environment. For example, it is well known that the relative comfort of seating in a restaurant influences how long people stay. When they become uncomfortable (subconsciously or consciously) sitting on a hard surface in a fast-food restaurant, most people leave within a predictable period of time. Similarly, environmental design and related physiological responses affect whether a person can perform his or her job function (e.g. Riley and Cochran, 1984).

A vast amount of research in engineering and design has addressed human physiological responses to ambient conditions as well as physiological responses to equipment design (Bennett, 1977; Oborne, 1987; Sanders and McCormick, 1987). Such research fits under the rubric of human factors design or ergonomics. Human factors research systematically applies relevant information about human capabilities and limitations to the design of things and procedures people use. The primary focus and application of the research has been within the military, in space programmes, and in the design of computers, automobiles and employee workstations. Such research has great potential for application in the design of commercial environments, taking into account the effects of design on both customers and employees who coexist and interact in the environment.

In addition to directly affecting behaviour, physiological responses may influence seemingly unrelated beliefs and feelings about the place and the people there. Research has shown that when people are physically uncomfortable because of ambient temperature, their affective response to strangers is less positive than when they are physically comfortable (Griffitt, 1970). Mehrabian and

Russell (1974, ch. 4) review numerous studies of emotional reactions to sensory stimuli such as colour, thermal conditions, light intensity, sound and odours.

P12: Positive (negative) physiological responses to the servicescape can result in positive (negative) beliefs and feelings associated with the organisation, its people and its products.

SERVICE TYPOLOGY AND INTERNAL RESPONSES

Combining the typology of servicescapes (Figure 1) with the conceptual understanding of the internal responses of customers and employees leads to insights for designing and managing the servicescape. For example, a self-service firm that wants to enhance customer approach behaviours such as attraction and staying longer can assess the environmental dimensions or cues that may elicit particular cognitive, emotional or physiological responses. Attraction would most likely be facilitated by positive cognitive and emotional responses to the firm's exterior, whereas staying would depend more on positive emotional and physiological responses to the organisation's interior space. In measuring the emotion-eliciting qualities of a particular servicescape, attention might be given to emotional dimensions identified by Mehrabian and Russell (pleasure–displeasure and degree of arousal) as well as to perceptions of control (Hui and Bateson, 1991).

For interpersonal services, an effective servicescape design anticipates the likely responses of employees and customers to environmental conditions and creates the proper setting for the service encounter. In such cases, several goals and behaviours will be identified for both customers and employees as well as for their interactions. The desired behaviours then can be linked directly to their internal response counterparts. For example, what type of emotional response on the part of customers will be needed to encourage them to interact comfortably with each other as in the case of a Club Med? Or, in the case of a hospital, what beliefs, emotions and physiological responses will encourage patients to get up and walk around the facility if that is a desired behaviour for their recovery?

Because elaborate services (e.g. banks, hospitals, restaurants) consist of many forms and spaces, planning for compatibility and coherence is a particularly challenging task. In lean environments, coherence would be easier to achieve and measure and nuisances easier to identify and eliminate. Similarly, enhancing personal control is more straightforward in remote and self-service firms than in interpersonal service firms, where giving a sense of control to both employees and customers simultaneously may be difficult.

RESPONSE MODERATORS

In general, people respond to environments in the ways described here – cognitively, emotionally, physiologically – and their responses influence how they behave in the environment. As with all behavioural relationships, however, the strength and direction of the relation between variables is moderated by personal and situational factors. Here, and in Figure 2, those factors are referred to as 'response moderators'.

Studies have shown that individual personality traits influence a person's reaction to his or her physical surroundings (Mehrabian and Russell, 1974; Russell and Snodgrass, 1987). Arousal-seeking is one such trait. Arousal-seekers enjoy and look for high levels of stimulation, whereas arousal-avoiders prefer lower levels of stimulation. Thus, an arousal-avoider who found him- or herself in a loud, bright disco with flashing neon might show strong dislike for the environment whereas an arousal-seeker would be very happy. In a related vein, Mehrabian (1977) proposed that some people are better screeners of environmental stimuli than others. Screeners of stimuli would be able to experience high levels of stimulation, but not be affected by it. In other words, they can ignore external environmental stimulation. Non-screeners would be highly affected and might exhibit extreme responses even to low levels of stimulation.

An individual's response to an environment often depends on situational factors as well, such

as his or her plan or purpose for being in the environment (Russell and Snodgrass, 1987; Snodgrass, Russell and Ward, 1988). Though the individual differences in personality traits are *relatively* stable, plans and purposes for being in or seeking out a particular environment may vary from day to day or hour to hour. What the individual notices and remembers about the environment, as well as how he or she feels about it, is influenced by the purpose for being there. In a laboratory study, subjects' knowledge of environmental details and affective response to a place were found to be influenced by what they had planned to do while there – wait, explore, spy or redecorate (Ward et al., 1988).

In addition to the plan or purpose, each individual enters an environment in a particular mood state (e.g. happy, depressed, lonely, anxious, excited, impatient). Such mood states are likely to affect as well as be differentially affected by variations in physical surroundings (see Gardner, 1985). A person who is feeling anxious and fatigued after a frustrating day at work is likely to be affected differently by a highly arousing restaurant environment than he or she would be after a relaxing three-day weekend. Similarly, Harrell and Hutt (1976) suggest that people who are impatient or very time-sensitive on entering a retail store are more affected by crowding than those who are patient and not sensitive to time factors.

What an individual expects to find in an environment also affects how the individual responds to the place. In general, when expectations are negatively disconfirmed, the person is likely to dislike the place. The opposite occurs when expectations are met or when the environment exceeds expectations. Expectations vary across individuals on the basis of their past experiences in the environment or in similar environments, as well as what they have heard or read about the place.

P13: Personality traits (such as arousal-seeking tendencies and ability to screen environmental stimuli) moderate the relationship between the perceived servicescape and internal responses.

P14: Situational factors (such as expectations, momentary mood, plans and purposes for being in the servicescape) moderate the relationship between the perceived servicescape and internal responses.

DIMENSIONS OF THE SERVICESCAPE

A complex mix of environmental features constitutes the servicescape and influences internal responses and behaviours. Specifically, the dimensions of the physical surroundings include all of the objective physical factors that can be controlled by the firm to enhance (or constrain) employee and customer actions. Those factors include an endless list of possibilities, such as lighting, colour, signage, textures, quality of materials, style of furnishings, layout, wall décor, temperature, and so on. On the basis of a review of diverse literatures, three composite dimensions were identified as being particularly relevant to the present analysis: ambient conditions, spatial layout and functionality, and signs, symbols and artefacts (see Figure 2). Because the base of research findings is context-specific and therefore not easily generalised, the effect of a single dimension on customers and employees is difficult to forecast. However, relevant dimensions of the servicescape can be isolated and general patterns can be explored.

Environmental psychologists contend that people respond to their environments holistically. That is, though individuals perceive discrete stimuli, it is the total configuration of stimuli that determines their responses to the environment (Bell, Fisher and Loomis, 1978; Holahan, 1982; Ittelson et al., 1974). Hence, though the dimensions of the environment are defined independently here, it is important to recognise that they are perceived by employees and customers as a holistic pattern of interdependent stimuli. Note in Figure 2 that the holistic pattern is reflected in the perceived servicescape construct.

P15: Customers and employees perceive the environment holistically, as a composite of three dimensions: ambient conditions; spatial

layout and functionality; signs, symbols and artefacts. Each dimension may affect the overall perception independently and/or through its interactions with the other dimensions.

AMBIENT CONDITIONS

Several authors have identified ambient conditions as a factor that affects perceptions of and human responses to the environment (Baker, 1987; Baker, Berry and Parasuraman, 1988; Becker, 1981; Darley and Gilbert, 1985; Russell and Snodgrass, 1987; Sundstrom and Sundstrom, 1986; Wineman, 1982). Ambient conditions include background characteristics of the environment such as temperature, lighting, noise, music and scent. As a general rule, ambient conditions affect the five senses. However, sometimes such dimensions may be totally imperceptible (gases, chemicals, infrasound), yet may have profound effects (Russell and Snodgrass, 1987), particularly on employees who spend long hours in the environment.

A very limited number of empirical studies in consumer research confirm that ambient factors may influence customer responses. For example, in studies of restaurants and supermarkets, it has been illustrated that music tempo can affect pace of shopping, length of stay, and amount of money spent (Milliman, 1982, 1986). In another study, familiarity of music played in a department store setting was found to affect shoppers' perceptions of how long they spent shopping; when the music was unfamiliar to subjects, they believed they had spent more time shopping (Yalch and Spangenberg, 1988). Hundreds of studies of the workplace spanning many decades have shown that lighting, temperature, noise, music and colour can all influence employee performance and job satisfaction (see Sundstrom and Sundstrom, 1986, Part II, for a review).

P16: The effects of ambient conditions on the overall, holistic perception of the servicescape are especially noticeable when they are extreme (e.g. loud music, high temperature), when the customer or employee spends considerable time in the servicescape (e.g. hospital stay vs. visit to dry cleaner), and when they conflict with expectations (e.g. loud music in a law office).

SPATIAL LAYOUT AND FUNCTIONALITY

Because service encounter environments are purposeful environments (i.e. they exist to fulfil specific needs of consumers, often through the successful completion of employee actions), spatial layout and functionality of the physical surroundings are particularly important. Spatial layout refers to the ways in which machinery, equipment and furnishings are arranged, the size and shape of those items, and the spatial relationships among them. Functionality refers to the ability of the same items to facilitate performance and the accomplishment of goals. Much of the empirical research in organisational behaviour and psychology has illustrated effects of the spatial layout and functionality dimension, always from the employee's point of view (for reviews see Davis, 1984; Sundstrom and Sundstrom, 1986; Wineman, 1982, 1986). With the exception of some research on retail store layout, crowding (Harrell and Hutt, 1976; Harrell, Hutt and Anderson, 1980; Hui and Bateson, 1990, 1991), and use of orientation aids (e.g. Levine, Marchon and Hanley, 1984; Seidel, 1983; Wener, 1985), surprisingly little has been published about the effects of spatial layout and functionality on *customers* in commercial service settings. Logic suggests that spatial layout and functionality of the environment are highly salient to customers in self-service environments where they must perform on their own and cannot rely on employees to assist them. Similarly, if the tasks to be performed are very complex, efficiency of layout and functionality will be more important than when the tasks are mundane or simple. When either the employees or customers are under time pressure, they will also be highly conscious of the relative ease with which they can perform their tasks in the environment.

P17: The effects of spatial layout and functionality are particularly salient in self-service set-

tings, when the tasks to be performed are complex, and when either the employee or customer is under time pressure.

SIGNS, SYMBOLS AND ARTEFACTS

Many items in the physical environment serve as explicit or implicit signals that communicate about the place to its users (Becker, 1977, 1981; Davis, 1984; Wener, 1985; Wineman, 1982). Signs displayed on the exterior and interior of a structure are examples of explicit communicators. They can be used as labels (e.g. name of company, name of department), for directional purposes (e.g. entrances, exits), and to communicate rules of behaviour (e.g. no smoking, children must be accompanied by an adult). Signage can play an important part in communicating firm image. Signs have even been found to reduce perceived crowding and stress in a jail lobby setting (Wener and Kaminoff, 1982).

Other environmental objects may communicate less directly than signs, giving implicit cues to users about the meaning of the place and norms and expectations for behaviour in the place. Quality of materials used in construction, artwork, presence of certificates and photographs on walls, floor coverings, and personal objects displayed in the environment can all communicate symbolic meaning and create an overall aesthetic impression. Restaurant managers, for example, know that white tablecloths and subdued lighting symbolically convey full service and relatively high prices, whereas counter service, plastic furnishings and bright lighting symbolise the opposite. In office environments, certain cues such as desk size and placement symbolise status and may be used to reinforce professional image (Davis, 1984; McCaskey, 1979; Peters, 1978; Pfeffer, 1981; Sundstrom and Sundstrom, 1986). Studies of faculty office design indicate that desk placement, presence of diplomas on the wall, and tidiness of the office can influence students' beliefs about the person occupying the office (Campbell, 1979; Morrow and McElroy, 1981). In another study of faculty offices certain environmental cues were found to be symbolically associated with personality traits of the faculty member believed to occupy the office (Ward, Bitner and Gossett, 1989). Such symbolic and aesthetic communication is extremely complex – it may be intentionally conveyed or it may be accidental, it may be subject to multiple interpretations, and it may have intended and unintended consequences (Becker, 1977; Davis, 1984).

P18: Signs, symbols and artefacts are particularly important in forming first impressions, for communicating new service concepts, for repositioning a service, and in highly competitive industries where customers are looking for cues to differentiate the organisation.

SERVICE TYPOLOGY AND ENVIRONMENTAL DIMENSIONS

In a classic study, Whyte (1980) observed human activity in public spaces and found that even subtle changes in design (e.g. adding plants and flowers, providing comfortable perches) led to a rather dramatic increase in activity and utilisation. Similar results might be achieved by examining the direction and flow of activities in a particular servicescape. For example, changes in the layout and furnishings of the service facility can be made to speed the flow of transactions, encourage particular forms of interaction between and among customers and employees, or provide opportunities for customers to linger.

The importance of particular environmental dimensions is likely to vary across the typology of service organisations (Figure 1). For example, for self-service situations such as Ticketron facilities, ATMs or Golf Land, the spatial layout and functionality dimension of the servicescape is extremely important. Clear directions and simple layout aid the customer in completing the transaction. At the other extreme, for remote services, ambient conditions assume more importance because employees tend to spend extended periods of time in the servicescape. Their physical comfort (temperature level, lighting) and responses to noise level and/or music affect pro-

ductivity and overall satisfaction. Ambient conditions are similarly important to employee productivity in many interpersonal service businesses such as banks, hospitals and hotels, but in those cases employee preferences must be balanced against customer needs. These are just a few of many possible examples.

Rather than a single element, it is ultimately the total configuration of environmental dimensions that defines the servicescape.

MANAGERIAL IMPLICATIONS

By isolating the impact of the servicescape on both customers and employees, the theoretical framework raises several challenging managerial implications. The overall conclusion is that through careful and creative management of the servicescape, firms may be able to contribute to the achievement of both external marketing goals and internal organisational goals. Many specific implications are discussed in preceding sections; some general strategic observations are offered here.

The typology of service organisations combined with the theoretical framework suggests that the physical environment may assume a variety of strategic roles in services marketing and management. First, the servicescape provides a visual metaphor for an organisation's total offering. In other words, the dimensions of the servicescape act as a package, similar to a product's package, by conveying a total image and suggesting the potential usage and relative quality of the service (Solomon, 1985). Yet, the care given to product package design is commonly lacking in service 'package' design. Second, the servicescape can assume a facilitator role by either aiding or hindering the ability of customers and employees to carry out their respective activities. The floor plan, layout of equipment, and equipment design can have a major impact on the ability of users to complete their tasks and achieve their service goals. As a facilitator, the servicescape can also encourage and nurture particular forms of social interaction among and between employees and customers. Finally, the physical environment can serve as a differentiation in signalling the intended market segment, positioning the organisation, and conveying distinctiveness from competitors. Each of the roles can be shaped to a significant degree to support important services marketing and management objectives of the organisation.

The typology of service organisations (Figure 1) and the theoretical framework (Figure 2) help to direct managers to relevant issues and questions that should be asked in forming servicescape strategy around the basic roles. In addition, service organisations can gain strategic insights by examining how the servicescape is designed and managed in other industries that occupy the same cell in the typology and thus share similar characteristics.

To secure strategy advantages from the servicescape, the needs of ultimate users and the requirements of various functional units must be incorporated into environmental design decisions. The services marketing manager must be a strong advocate for using the servicescape as an element of the organisation's strategy. Yet, in most organisations, environmental management is a separate function performed by persons with titles such as 'environmental space manager', 'facility planner' and 'facility manager' (Becker, 1981; Davis and Szigeti, 1982). In many organisations, environmental decisions are made routinely without much attention to the impact on employee (or consumer) behaviour (Becker, 1981, p. 5).

A clear implication of the conceptual framework (Figure 2) is the need for cross-functional co-operation in decision-making about service environments. 'Facility planning and management ... is a problem-solving activity that lies in the boundaries between architecture, interior-space planning and product design, organizational [and consumer] behavior, planning and environmental psychology' (Becker, 1981, p. 7). As such, decisions about the physical facility can have an impact on human resource goals (e.g. worker retention, worker productivity), operations goals (e.g. efficiency, cost reduction) and marketing goals (e.g. consumer attraction, consumer satisfaction). Ideally, therefore, major

changes in physical design or the planning of new environments should benefit from input from managers in all three areas, grounded in direct input from actual users – that is, employees and customers.

RESEARCH IMPLICATIONS

The conceptual framework and the servicescape typology suggest a wide range of research possibilities. Given the scarcity of research reported in the consumer behaviour and marketing literature, there is a tremendous opportunity for theory building, empirical testing, development of better measures and methods, and application/replication of findings from other fields. Figure 2 and the preceding specific propositions provide numerous starting-points for research. The propositions are purposefully general. Each one could be explored and expanded through empirical research. For example, given a specific commercial environment, how does a consumer's or employee's purpose for being there affect the person's response to the place? That question addresses the moderating effects of situational factors in determining environmental responses. Alternatively, one could start with a particular social interaction behaviour such as teamwork among employees and work back through the framework to discover the types of internal responses and relevant environmental dimensions that would encourage such behaviour. In addition to the basic research suggested by the framework and propositions, there is a need for research that will illuminate the differential importance and differential effects of physical surroundings across types of service industries such as those identified in Figure 1. Research opportunities also are available in exploring the ability of the physical environment to achieve particular objectives of the firm, and at what cost.

In many cases, extensive work in environmental psychology and organisational behaviour (e.g. the stream of research by Russell and his colleagues and the review of workplace research by Sundstrom and Sundstrom, 1986) can be applied and extended into the consumer service setting.

In other cases, as in the effects of the environment on social interactions among customers and employees, the fact that there is relatively little empirical work in any field to draw on allows for true pioneering research to be done.

Given the complexity of environment/behaviour relationships, a variety of methods will be appropriate (see Bechtel, Marans and Michelson, 1987). Direct observation of environmental conditions and customer and employee behaviours may be most appropriate in some cases – for example, in research on the effect of facility layout options on customer/employee interaction patterns. The application of direct observation methods has just recently gained acceptance in the marketing literature (e.g. Belk, Sherry and Wallendorf, 1988; Belk, Wallendorf and Sherry, 1989), but has not yet been applied to the observation of consumption environments (for an exception, see Sherry and McGrath, 1989). Using observation methods, trained observers could make detailed accounts of current environmental conditions (i.e. environmental dimensions in Figure 2) and the actual behaviours of the occupants. Such observations could be extremely detailed and useful in an applied sense in redesigning a facility or in comparing environments. For theory development, direct observation could be the source of additional propositions.

Experimental methods and surveys also would be appropriate for assessing the impact of design dimensions on consumers and employees. Because of the expense involved in constructing actual environments, some form of simulated environment (verbal descriptions, photos/slides, scale models, videos) could be used in experimental studies (see Bechtel, Marans and Michelson, 1987, ch. 5). The environmental psychology tradition has shown that simulated environments work well in achieving generalisable results (Nasar, 1989). In designing experiments, the researcher should recall that people perceive environments holistically. It may be necessary to vary several environmental dimensions (e.g. artefacts, layout, colour, tidiness) simultaneously to achieve an overall perception of the surroundings that will significantly influence behaviour. User surveys are likely to be most appropriate in assessing basic customer/employee needs and preferences prior to the design of experimental simulations, and later for post-design evaluation.

For both experiments and surveys, applicable response measures are needed. If one uses Figure 2 as a guide, appropriate measures of cognitive, emotional and physiological responses to environments are needed, as well as measures of relevant individual differences. Though several standardised measures already are available (e.g. Lemke et al., 1979; McKechnie, 1974; Mehrabian, 1977; Russell and Snodgrass, 1987), most have not been applied to consumers in commercial settings, thus opening an opportunity for application and assessment of generalisability. Other, more novel approaches to measuring customer and employee responses to environments also could be considered. For example, Ward, Bitner and Gossett (1989) suggest an approach to measuring the symbolic meaning of service environments that adapts and extends ideas from research on object meaning (Kleine and Kernan, 1988; Szalay and Deese, 1978).

The typology, framework and propositions provide direction for research on a topic that is incredibly rich, and invite application of the full range of consumer and organisational methods and theories to gain a better understanding of its impact.

NOTE

1. Research on the built environment is only one aspect of environmental psychology. The field also encompasses the study of human beings and their relationships with the natural and social environment. What distinguishes environmental psychology from other areas of inquiry is its concern 'with the reciprocal and interactive influences that take place between the thinking and behaviour of an organism and the environment surrounding that organism' (Darley and Gilbert, 1985, p. 949).

REFERENCES

Baker, Julie (1987), 'The Role of the Environment in Marketing Services: The Consumer Perspective' in John A. Czepiel, Carole A. Congram and James Shanahan (eds.), *The Services Challenge: Integrating for Competitive Advantage*, American Marketing Association, Chicago, pp. 79–84.

Baker, Julie, Leonard L. Berry and A. Parasuraman (1988), 'The Marketing Impact of Branch Facility Design', *Journal of Retail Banking*, vol. 10, no. 2, pp. 33–42.

Barker, Roger G. (1968), *Ecological Psychology*, Stanford University Press, Stanford, Calif.

Bechtel, Robert B., Robert W. Marans and William Michelson (1987), *Methods in Environmental and Behavioral Research*, Van Nostrand Reinhold Co., NY.

Becker, Franklin D. (1977), *Housing Messages*, Dowden, Hutchinson & Ross, Inc., Stroudsburg, Pa.

Becker, Franklin D. (1981), *Workspace*, Praeger Publishers, NY.

Belk, Russell W., John F. Sherry Jr and Melanie Wallendorf (1988), 'A Naturalistic Inquiry into Buyer and Seller Behavior at a Swap Meet', *Journal of Consumer Research*, 14, March, pp. 449–70.

Belk, Russell W., Melanie Wallendorf and John F. Sherry Jr (1989), 'The Sacred and the Profane in Consumer Behavior: Theodicy on the Odyssey', *Journal of Consumer Research*, 16, June, pp. 1–38.

Bell, Paul, J.D. Fisher and R.J. Loomis (1978), *Environmental Psychology*, W.B. Saunders Co., Philadelphia.

Bennett, Corwin (1977), *Spaces for People, Human Factors in Design*, Prentice-Hall Inc., Englewood Cliffs, NJ.

Bennett, David J. and Judith D. Bennett (1970), 'Making the Scene' in G. Stone and H. Farberman (eds.), *Social Psychology through Symbolic Interactionism*, Ginn-Blaisdell, Waltham, Mass., pp. 190–96.

Berry, Leonard L. and Terry Clark (1986), 'Four Ways to Make Services More Tangible', *Business*, October–December, pp. 53–4.

Bitner, Mary Jo (1986), 'Consumer Responses to the Physical Environment in Service Settings' in M. Venkatesan, Diane M. Schmalensee and Claudia Marshall (eds.), *Creativity in Services Marketing*, American Marketing Association, Chicago, pp. 89–93.

Bitner, Mary Jo (1990), 'Evaluating Service Encounters: The Effects of Physical Surroundings and Employee Responses', *Journal of Marketing*, 54, April, pp. 69–82.

Booms, Bernard H. and Mary J. Bitner (1982), 'Marketing Services by Managing the Environment', *Cornell Hotel and Restaurant Administration Quarterly*, 23, May, pp. 35–9.

Broadbent, Geoffrey, Richard Bunt and Charles Jencks (1980), *Signs, Symbols and Architecture*, John Wiley & Sons Inc., NY.

Campbell, David E. (1979), 'Interior Office Design and Visitor Response', *Journal of Applied Psychology*, vol. 64, no. 6, pp. 648–53.

Crosby, Lawrence A., Kenneth R. Evans and Deborah Cowles (1990), 'Relationship Quality in Services Selling: An Interpersonal Influence Perspective', *Journal of Marketing*, 54, July, pp. 68–81.

Darley, John M. and Daniel T. Gilbert (1985), 'Social Psychological Aspects of Environmental Psychology' in Gardner Lindzey and Elliot Aronson (eds.), *Handbook of Social Psychology*, 3rd edition, vol. 11, Random House Inc., NY, pp. 949–91.

Davis, Gerald and Françoise Szigeti (1982), 'Planning and Programming Offices: Determining User Requirements', *Environment and Behavior*, vol. 14, no. 3, pp. 302–4, 306–15.

Davis, Tim R.V. (1984), 'The Influence of the Physical Environment in Offices', *Academy of Management Review*, vol. 9, no. 2, pp. 271–83.

Donovan, Robert and John Rossiter (1982), 'Store Atmosphere: An Environmental Psychology Approach', *Journal of Retailing*, 58, Spring, pp. 34–57.

Forgas, Joseph P. (1979), *Social Episodes*, Academic Press, Inc., London.

Gardner, Meryl P. (1985), 'Mood States and Consumer Behavior: A Critical Review', *Journal of Consumer Research*, 12, December, pp. 281–300.

Gardner, Meryl P. and George J. Siomkos (1986), 'Toward a Methodology for Assessing Effects of In-store Atmospherics' in Richard J. Lutz (ed.), *Advances in Consumer Research*, Association for Consumer Research, Ann Arbor, Mich., vol. 13, pp. 27–31.

Golledge, Reginald G. (1987), 'Environmental Cognition' in Daniel Stokols and Irwin Altman (eds.), *Handbook of Environmental Psychology*, John Wiley & Sons, Inc., NY, vol. 1, pp. 131–74.

Griffitt, William (1970), 'Environmental Effects on Interpersonal Affective Behavior: Ambient Effective Temperature and Attraction', *Journal of Personality and Social Psychology*, vol. 15, no. 3, pp. 240–44.

Harrell, Gilbert D. and Michael D. Hutt (1976), 'Crowding in Retail Stores', *MSU Business Topics*, Winter, pp. 33–9.

Harrell, Gilbert D., Michael D. Hutt and James C. Anderson (1980), 'Path Analysis of Buyer Behavior under Conditions of Crowding', *Journal of Marketing Research*, 17, February, pp. 45–51.

Holahan, Charles I. (1982), *Environmental Psychology*, Random House, Inc., NY.

Holahan, Charles I. (1986), 'Environmental Psychology', *Annual Review of Psychology*, pp. 381–407.

Hui, Michael K.M. and John E.G. Bateson (1990), 'Testing a Theory of Crowding in the Service Environment' in Marvin E. Goldberg, Gerald Gom and Richard W. Pollay (eds.), *Advances in Consumer Research*, Association for Consumer Research, Ann Arbor, Mich, vol. 17, pp. 866–73.

Hui, Michael K.M. and John E.G. Bateson (1991), 'Perceived Control and the Effects of Crowding and Consumer Choice on the Service Experience', *Journal of Consumer Research*, vol. 18, no. 2, pp. 174-84.

Ittelson, William H., Harold M. Proshansky, Leanne G. Rivlin and Gary H. Winkel (1974), *An Introduction to Environmental Psychology*, Holt, Rinehart and Winston, Inc., NY.

Kaplan, Stephen (1987), 'Aesthetics, Affect, and Cognition', *Environment and Behavior*, 19, January, pp. 3–32.

Kaplan, Stephen and Rachel Kaplan (1982), *Cognition and Environment*, Praeger Publishers, NY.

Kleine, Robert E. and Jerome B. Kernan (1988), 'Measuring the Meaning of Consumption Objects: An Empirical Investigation' in Michael J. Houston (ed.), *Advances in Consumer Research*, Association for Consumer Research, Provo, Utah, vol. 15, pp. 498–504.

Kotler, Philip (1973), 'Atmospherics as a Marketing Tool', *Journal of Retailing*, vol. 49, no. 4, pp. 48–64.

Lemke, S., R. Moos, B. Mehren and M. Ganvain (1979), *Multiphasic Environment Assessment Procedure (MEAP): Handbook for Users*, Social Ecology Laboratory, Palo Alto, Calif.

Levine, Marvin, Iris Marchon and Gerard Hanley (1984), 'The Placement and Misplacement of You-Are-Here Maps', *Environment and Behavior*, vol. 16, March, pp. 139–57.

Loken, Barbara and James Ward (1990), 'Alternative Approaches to Understanding the Determinants of Typicality', *Journal of Consumer Research*, 17, September, pp. 111–26.

Lovelock, Christopher H. (1983), 'Classifying Services to Gain Strategic Insights', *Journal of Marketing*, 47, Summer, pp. 9–20.

McCaskey, Michael B. (1979), 'The Hidden Messages Managers Send', *Harvard Business Review*, 57, November–December, pp. 135–48.

McKechnie, G.E. (1974), *Manual for the Environment Response Inventory*, Consulting Psychologists Press, Palo Alto, Calif.

Maslow, A.L. and N.L. Mintz (1956), 'Effects of Esthetic Surroundings', *Journal of Psychology*, vol. 1, no. 41, pp. 247–54.

Mehrabian, Albert (1977), 'Individual Differences in Stimulus Screening and Arousability', *Journal of Personality*, vol. 45, no. 2, pp. 237–50.

Mehrabian, Albert and James A. Russell (1974), *An Approach to Environmental Psychology*, Massachusetts Institute of Technology, Cambridge, Mass.

Mervis, C. and E. Rosch (1981), 'Categorization of Natural Objects' in M.R. Rosensweig and L.W. Porter (eds.), *Annual Review of Psychology*, Annual Reviews, Inc., Palo Alto, Calif., 32, pp. 89–115.

Milliman, Ronald (1982), 'Using Background Music to Affect the Behavior of Supermarket Shoppers', *Journal of Marketing*, 46, Summer, pp. 86–91.

Milliman, Ronald (1986), 'The Influence of Background Music on the Behavior of Restaurant Patrons', *Journal of Consumer Research*, 13, September, pp. 286–9.

Mintz, Norbett L. (1956), 'Effects of Esthetic Surroundings II: Prolonged and Repeated Experience in a "Beautiful" and an "Ugly" Room', *Journal of Psychology*, 41, pp. 459–66.

Morrow, Paula C. and James C. McElroy (1981), 'Interior Office Design and Visitor Response: A Constructive Replication', *Journal of Applied Psychology*, vol. 66, no. 5, pp. 646–50.

Nasar, Jack L. (1987), 'Effect of Sign Complexity and Coherence on the Perceived Quality of Retail Scenes', *Journal of the American Planning Association*, vol. 53, no. 4, pp. 499–509.

Nasar, Jack L. (1989), 'Perception, Cognition, and Evaluation of Urban Places' in Irwin Altman and Ervin H. Zube (eds.), *Public Places and Spaces*, Plenum Press, NY, pp. 31–56.

Obermiller, Carl and Mary Jo Bitner (1984), 'Store Atmosphere: A Peripheral Cue for Product Evaluation' in David C. Stewart (ed.), *American Psychological Association Annual Conference Proceedings, Consumer*

Psychology Division, American Psychological Association, pp. 52–3.

Oborne, David J. (1987), *Ergonomics at Work*, 2nd edition, John Wiley & Sons, Inc., NY.

Peters, Thomas J. (1978), 'Symbols, Patterns, and Settings: An Optimistic Case for Getting Things Done', *Organizational Dynamics*, 7, Autumn, pp. 3–23.

Pfeffer, Jeffrey (1981), 'Management as Symbolic Action: The Creation and Maintenance of Organizational Paradigms', *Research in Organizational Behavior*, 3, pp. 1–52.

Rapoport, Amos (1982), *The Meaning of the Built Environment*, Sage Publications, Inc., Beverly Hills, Calif.

Riley, M.W. and D.J. Cochran (1984), 'Dexterity Performance and Reduced Ambient Temperature', *Human Factors*, vol. 26, no. 2, pp. 207–14.

Ruesch, Jurgen and Weldon Kees (1956), *Nonverbal Communication*, University of California Press, Berkeley and Los Angeles.

Russell, James A. and U.F. Lanius (1984), 'Adaptation Level and the Affective Appraisal of Environments', *Journal of Environmental Psychology*, vol. 4, no. 2, pp. 119–35.

Russell, James A. and Geraldine Pratt (1980), 'A Description of the Affective Quality Attributed to Environments', *Journal of Personality and Social Psychology*, vol. 38, no. 2, pp. 311–22.

Russell, James A. and Jacalyn Snodgrass (1987), 'Emotion and the Environment' in Daniel Stokols and Irwin Altman (eds.), *Handbook of Environmental Psychology*, John Wiley & Sons, Inc., NY, vol. 1, pp. 245–81.

Russell, James A. and Lawrence M. Ward (1982), 'Environmental Psychology', *Annual Review of Psychology*, pp. 651–88.

Sanders, Mark S. and Ernest J. McCormick (1987), *Human Factors in Engineering and Design*, McGraw-Hill Book Company, NY.

Schmenner, Roger W. (1986), 'How Can Service Businesses Survive and Prosper?' *Sloan Management Review*, 27, Spring, pp. 21–32.

Seidel, A. (1983), 'Way Finding in Public Space: The Dallas Ft. Worth, U.S.A. Airport' in D. Aneseo, J. Griffen and J. Potter (eds.), *Proceedings of the Fourteenth International Conference of the Environmental Design Research Association*, Environmental Design Research Association, Lincoln, Nebr.

Sherry, John F., Jr and Mary Ann McGrath (1989), 'Unpacking the Holiday Presence: A Comparative Ethnography of Two Gift Stores' in Elizabeth C. Hirschman (ed.), *Interpretive Consumer Behavior*,

Association for Consumer Research, Provo Utah, pp. 148–67.

Shostack, G. Lynn (1977), 'Breaking Free from Product Marketing', *Journal of Marketing*, 41, April, pp. 73–80.

Snodgrass, Jacalyn, James A. Russell and Lawrence M. Ward (1988), 'Planning, Mood and Place-Liking', *Journal of Environmental Psychology*, vol. 8, no. 3, pp. 209–22.

Solomon, Michael R. (1985), 'Packaging the Service Provider', *Services Industries Journal*, 5, July, pp. 64–71.

Sommer, R. (1974), *Tight Spaces: Hard Architecture and How to Humanize It*, Prentice-Hall, Inc., Englewood Cliffs, NJ.

Steele, Fritz (1986), *Making and Managing High-quality Workplaces*, Teachers College Press, NY.

Stokols, Daniel and Irwin Altman (1987), *Handbook of Environmental Psychology*, John Wiley & Sons, Inc., NY.

Sundstrom, Eric and Irwin Altman (1989), 'Physical Environments and Work-group Effectiveness', *Research in Organizational Behavior*, 11, pp. 175–209.

Sundstrom, Eric and Mary Graehl Sundstrom (1986), *Work Places*, Cambridge University Press, Cambridge, UK.

Szalay, Lorand B. and James Deese (1978), *Subjective Meaning and Culture: An Assessment through Word Associations*, Lawrence Erlbaum Associates, Hillsdale, NJ.

Upah, Gregory D. and James N. Fulton (1985), 'Situation Creation in Services Marketing' in John Czepiel, Michael Solomon and Carol Surprenant (eds.), *The Service Encounter*, Lexington Books, Mass., pp. 255–64.

Ward, James C., Mary Jo Bitner and John Barnes (1992), 'Measuring the Prototypicality and Meaning of Retail Environments', *Journal of Retailing*, forthcoming.

Ward, James C., Mary Jo Bitner and Dan Gossett (1989), 'SEEM: Measuring the Meaning of Service Environments' in Mary Jo Bitner and Lawrence A. Crosby (eds.) *Designing a Winning Service Strategy*, American Marketing Association, Chicago, pp. 34–9.

Ward, Lawrence M., Jacalyn Snodgrass, Barry Chew and James A. Russell (1988), 'The Role of Plans in Cognitive and Affective Responses to Places', *Journal of Environmental Psychology*, vol. 8, no. 1, pp. 1–8.

Wener, Richard E. (1985), 'The Environmental Psychology of Service Encounters' in John Czepiel, Michael Solomon, and Carol Surprenant (eds.), *The Service Encounter*, Lexington Books, Mass., pp. 101–12.

Wener, Richard E. and Robert Kaminoff (1982), 'Improving Environmental Information: Effects of

Signs on Perceived Crowding and Behavior',
Environment and Behavior, vol. 14, no. 6, 671–94.

Whyte, William H. (1980), *The Social Life of Small Urban Spaces*, The Conservation Foundation, Washington, DC.

Wineman, Jean D. (1982), 'Office Design and Evaluation', *Environment and Behavior*, vol. 14, no. 3, pp. 271–98.

Wineman, Jean D. (1986), *Behavioral Issues in Office Design*, Van Nostrand Reinhold Co., NY.

Wohlwill, Joachim F. (1976), 'Environmental Aesthetics: The Environment as a Source of Affect' in Irwin Altman and Joachim F. Wohlwill (eds.), *Human Behavior and Environment*, vol. 1, Plenum Press, NY.

Yalch, Richard F. and Eric Spangenberg (1988), 'An Environmental Psychological Study of Foreground and Background Music as Retail Atmospheric Factors' in Gary Frazier et al. (eds.), *Efficiency and Effectiveness in Marketing, 1988 AMA Educators' Proceedings*, American Marketing Association, Chicago, pp. 106–10.

Zeithaml, Valarie (1981), 'How Consumer Evaluation Processes Differ between Goods and Services' in James H. Donnelly and William R. George (eds.) *Marketing of Services*, American Marketing Association, Chicago, pp. 186–90.

Zeithaml, Valarie (1988), 'Consumer Perceptions of Price, Quality, and Value: A Means–end Model and Synthesis of Evidence', *Journal of Marketing*, 52, July, pp. 2–22.

Zeithaml, Valarie, A. Parasuraman and Leonard L. Berry (1985), 'Problems and Strategies in Services Marketing', *Journal of Marketing*, 49, Spring, pp. 33–46.

Guidelines for the Advertising of Services

William R. George and Leonard L. Berry

Despite the growth and importance of service industries, there has been little work published specifically on the advertising of services. Given this lack of attention, one might conclude, incorrectly, that the problems of services advertising are no different from the problems of goods advertising. But, in some basic ways, goods and services are different and the advertising of each must reflect these differences.

This article presents six guidelines for services advertising based on some of the special characteristics of services. Service industries are, of course, quite heterogeneous and the intention is to present guidelines that will have relevance to a wide range of service industries, but not necessarily to all of them.

ADVERTISING TO EMPLOYEES

The most fundamental difference between a good and a service is that a good is an object and a service is a performance. When the performance is people-based (for example, real estate sales) rather than equipment-based (for example, telephone communications), the quality of the service rendered is inseparable from the quality of the service provider. A rude or slow waiter or a careless cook can ruin what otherwise might have been perceived as a fine meal. A testy stewardess means a testy airline to the consumer.

Not unlike goods advertising, services advertising will normally be directed towards one or more target markets. In addition, customer-contact personnel are a potentially important 'second audience' for services advertising. This is especially true for people-based service organisations. When the performances of people are what customers buy, the advertiser needs to be concerned not only with encouraging customers to buy, but with encouraging employees to perform.

When well conceived, advertising can have quite a positive effect on employees. A recent advertising campaign of a large bank promised 'person-to-person' banking. Bank employees were featured in radio and television commercials explaining in their own words what person-to-person banking meant. In follow-up research, over 90 per cent of the bank's contact employees reported paying attention to the bank's advertising. Just under 90 per cent felt that the personal service advertising set a job performance standard for them to follow. Nearly 75 per cent said that they had become more concerned with pleasing the customer and were more likely to go out of their way for customers.[1]

A recent Delta Airlines print advertisement includes employees in its audience with the headline: 'You never hear a Delta professional say, "That's not my job."' Underneath the headline, six Delta employees are pictured in work situations and identified. Smaller copy then reads:

You'll find a Delta Marketing Representative handling calls for reservations when the lines get hot. And a Line Mechanic lending a hand with the baggage to get a flight out on time. And a Passenger Service Agent rushing a wheelchair to the gate when all the Skycaps are busy. Delta is people helping other people help you. It's a family feeling. It's a spirit of service that just won't quit. It's men and women who know their jobs and love their work. And Delta has more than 34,000 of them.

Next trip go with the Delta professionals and have a great flight … Delta, the airline run by professionals.

The Delta advertisement, although ostensibly meant for the consumer, is also clearly aimed at Delta personnel. This advertisement not only shapes the perceptions and expectations of consumers by promising helpful, professional service, it helps define for employees management's perceptions and expectations of them – namely, that 'We think of you as professionals and expect you to perform as professionals.'

Sasser and Arbeit write: 'The successful service company must first sell the job to employees before it can sell its service to customers.'[2] Advertising is an important tool for 'selling' jobs; it is a tool for motivating, educating or otherwise communicating with employees.

CAPITALISING ON WORD OF MOUTH

The labour-intensiveness of many services introduces a degree of variability in the service provided which is not present when equipment dominates the production process. Such variability occurs because people providing services differ in their technical and customer relations skills, in their personalities, and in their attitudes towards their work; moreover, one individual worker may be inconsistent in the quality of service he or she provides.

The ever-present potential for variability in the provision of labour-intensive services is well understood by those who consume services, and contributes to the important role word-of-mouth communication plays in the selection of service suppliers.[3] When the consequences of buying a lower-quality service are perceived to be important, service consumers can be expected to be especially receptive to word-of-mouth communications. In brief, to find the right doctor, hairdresser, attorney, real estate agent, college professor or automobile mechanic, the consumer is often interested in the opinions of others with appropriate previous experience.

The importance for word-of-mouth communications in many service markets suggests the opportunity to use advertising (and other forms of promotion) to capitalise on this propensity. Making a conscious effort in advertising to leverage word of mouth might involve persuading satisfied customers to let others know of their experience, developing communication materials for customers to make available to noncustomers, targeting advertising to opinion leaders, or guiding prospective customers in soliciting word-of-mouth information. Yet another approach involves featuring the comments of satisfied customers in the advertising itself, a strategy which in effect merges conventional and word-of-mouth advertising.

Marketers of management development programmes sometimes ask satisfied programme participants for permission to reprint their comments in future advertisements. At the University of Wisconsin, Madison, each participant in a management development workshop receives a 'You can be a name dropper … and do a friend a favour' postcard asking for the names and addresses of up to three people who would be interested in receiving a catalogue listing of the various programmes offered. The recommender is given the choice whether or not to be identified in the cover letter. A successful Richmond, Virginia hairstylist prominently displays the following sign in his shop: 'If you like our service, please tell a friend; if you don't like it, please tell us.' E.F. Hutton emphasises the importance of word-of-mouth recommendation with its advertising message, 'People stop and listen when they know your broker is E.F. Hutton.'

What is important to glean from these examples is that it may be possible to design non-personal communications that capitalise on the service consumer's receptivity to more personal, word-of-mouth communications.

PROVIDING TANGIBLE CLUES

Because goods are tangible, and can be seen and touched, they are generally easier to evaluate than services. Consumers perceive service purchases to have a higher risk than goods purchases and to be a less pleasant buying experience.[4]

Word-of-mouth communication is prevalent in service consumption because it is a means to reduce risk. For the same reason, consumers tend to be attentive to tangibles associated with a service for 'clues' about the service's quality. Although a service is intangible in the sense that a performance rather than an object is purchased, there are tangibles associated with the service offered (for example, the facilities in which a service is performed), and these tangibles can provide meaningful evidence concerning the service itself.

Thus, one way advertisers can help lower the consumer's perception of uncertainty and risk-taking is by using tangibles in advertising in such a way as to convey appropriate signals about the service. Shostack has written about the need to use tangible clues in services advertising:

> it is clear that consumer product marketing often approaches the market by enhancing a physical object through abstract associations. *Coca-Cola*, for example, is surrounded with visual, verbal and aural associations with authenticity and youth ... A high priority is placed on linking these abstract images to physical items.
>
> But a service is already abstract. To compound the abstraction dilutes the 'reality' that the marketer is trying to enhance ... reliance must be placed on *peripheral* clues.[5]

Prior to his death, actor John Wayne was successfully used as advertising spokesman for California's Great Western Savings and Loan Association. Well known for his strong personal views as well as for his film characterisations of a rugged and honest cowboy who always stood tall against evil, Wayne represented tangibility and credibility in Great Western's advertising. The service conglomerate TransAmerica features prominently its large, pyramid-like headquarters building in its advertising. Merrill Lynch signifies its 'bullishness' about America through the continuing use of bulls in its advertising. Allstate and State Farm insurance companies, among others, have emphasised in advertising the tangible relationship between the insurance consumer and the insurance agent, who 'is presented as an all-around concerned counselor for the family'.[6] Some service advertisers rely on the tangibility of numbers in their advertising – for example, 'in business since 1910', or '70 per cent of the people taking this course pass the state exam'.

What these examples have in common is a visual concreteness that is often absent from services advertising. The tangibles used implicitly provide evidence about the service that the service itself cannot provide.

MAKING THE SERVICE UNDERSTOOD

One of the problems arising from the intangibility of services is that they are often difficult to define or grasp mentally.[7] Stephen Unwin captures the creative challenge intangibility presents services advertisers when he writes: 'The service advertiser ... is often left with describing the invisible, articulating the imaginary and defining the indistinct'.[8]

As suggested in the previous section, one method for dealing with intangibility is to use tangibles in advertising as evidence of the service's quality. Sometimes, however, it is possible to use tangibles for a different purpose: to make the service more easily understood.

Again, the insurance industry provides interesting examples. The insurance industry has made it easier for consumers to understand what is being sold by associating the intangible of insurance with relevant tangible objects more easily understood.

The following advertising themes illustrate:

'You are in good hands *with Allstate.'*
'Under the Travelers' umbrella.*'*
'The Nationwide blanket *of protection.'*

Insurance advertisers are using the images of hands, umbrellas and blankets to communicate more effectively the benefits of buying insurance. Tangible objects representing what consumers seek from insurance are used better to define and communicate the service.[9]

ADVERTISING CONTINUITY

With the exception of radio, all advertising media are visual media; that is, readers or viewers see pictures. Services, however, are non-visual by nature. American Airlines can picture its planes in advertising, or the planes' destinations, but not the service itself.

The intangibility of services undoubtedly adds to the frequent difficulty competing service firms have in differentiating themselves.[10] Whereas goods can often be made physically distinctive on the basis of design, packaging and branding, services have no physical appearance. Moreover, physically distinctive goods can be shown in advertising and associated with various forms of imagery.

Although differentiation is not easily attained by service firms, its achievement is by no means impossible. Advertising continuity is an important strategy in this regard because it involves the continual use in advertising of certain distinctive symbols, formats and/or themes to build and reinforce the desired image, regardless of any changes in specific advertising campaigns.

A master of advertising continuity is McDonald's, which, while using television advertising for different specific purposes (Big Macs, breakfast, special promotions, etc.), invariably uses the same image reinforcers in all advertisements: memorable tag lines, theme music, and pictures of upbeat, energetic employees and spotless facilities. Whatever the specific item advertised, the company's advertising consistently sends out the same signals: 'We are fast and efficient, we are friendly, we are superclean, we offer value, we are a family restaurant.'

The concept of advertising continuity is also epitomised by Harris Trust and Savings Bank in Chicago, which has used its cartoon lion mascot, Hubert, in its consumer advertising since the 1950s. Research shows that Hubert is one of Chicago's most recognised celebrities. Hubert is a device for tying Harris's past advertising efforts to its present campaign; Hubert is a means for 'branding' Harris's advertising, and, in the process, for helping the bank attain a distinctive image.

Advertising continuity gives a company's advertising a recognisability which continually communicates and reinforces its image. Ideally, consumers should be able to associate a specific firm with its advertising even if the firm's name is inadvertently left off a specific advertisement. If a tax-shelter annuities ad features a bull standing inside a cave, Merrill Lynch would immediately come to mind, even if the advertisement were anonymous.

PROMISING WHAT IS POSSIBLE

Since service buyers have only fulfilled promises to carry away from the service transaction, it is especially important that service firms deliver on advertising promises. Yet, as discussed earlier, the labour-intensiveness of many services introduces variability into the service offering. Accordingly, when making promises in services advertising, prudence and caution should rule.

When Holiday Inn's advertising agency used consumer research as the basis for a television campaign promising 'no surprises', top management accepted it while operations executives opposed it. Operating personnel knew that 'surprises' frequently occur in a complex company like Holiday Inn in which thousands of people are involved in the operations of facilities spread throughout the country and world. When it was aired, the campaign raised consumer expectations and provided dissatisfied customers with additional grounds on which to vent frustrations. It is not surprising that the 'no surprises' advertising had to be discontinued.

In advertising in general, and in services advertising in particular, it is better to promise only that which can be delivered a very high percentage of the time. It is better to foster realistic expectations than unrealistic expectations.

The six guidelines for more effective services advertising are based on certain special characteristics of services, most notably that services are performances rather than tangible objects and that frequently these performances are labour-intensive. Services advertisers can use these guidelines to make a checklist of considerations in designing effective advertising programmes.

▷ Does the advertising have positive effects on contact personnel?

▷ Does the advertising capitalise on word of mouth?

▷ Does the advertising provide tangible clues?

▷ Does the advertising make the service more easily understood?

▷ Does the advertising contribute to continuity?

▷ Does the advertising promise what is possible?

NOTES

1. Franklin Acito and Jeffrey D. Ford (1980), 'How Advertising Affects Employees', *Business Horizons*, February, pp. 58–9.
2. W. Earl Sasser and Stephen P. Arbeit (1976), 'Selling Jobs in the Service Sector', *Business Horizons*, June, p. 64.
3. Eugene W. Johnson (1969), 'Are Goods and Services Different? An Exercise in Marketing Theory', unpublished doctoral dissertation, Washington University, pp. 166, 201; and Duane Davis, Joseph P. Guiltinan and Wesley H. Jones (1979), 'Service Characteristics, Consumer Search and the Classification of Retail Services', *Journal of Retailing*, Fall, pp. 3–23.
4. Johnson, 'Are Goods and Services Different?', p. 166; and William F. Lewis (1976), 'An Empirical Investigation of the Conceptual Relationship between Services and Products', unpublished doctoral dissertation, University of Cincinnati, p. 82.
5. G. Lynn Shostack (1977), 'Breaking Free from Product Marketing', *Journal of Marketing*, April, p. 77.
6. James H. Donnelly, Jr (1980), 'Service Delivery Strategies in the 1980s – Academic Perspective' in Leonard L. Berry and James H. Donnelly, Jr (eds.), *Financial Institution Marketing Strategies in the 1980s*, Consumer Bankers Association, Washington DC, p. 148.
7. Leonard L. Berry (1980), 'Service Marketing Is Different', *Business*, May–June, p. 25.
8. Stephen Unwin (1975), 'Customized Communications: A Concept for Service Advertising', *Advertising Quarterly*, Summer, p. 28.
9. Donnelly, 'Service Delivery Strategies', pp. 147–8.
10. Pierre Eiglier and Eric Langeard (1977), 'A New Approach to Service Marketing' in Eiglier et al. (eds.), *Marketing Consumer Services: New Insights*, Marketing Science Institute, Cambridge, Mass., p. 39.

Reaching the Customer: Strategies for Marketing and Customer Service

Martin Christopher

The author suggests that logistics and marketing can combine to provide a sustainable means of competitive advantage. Many marketing executives never consider the very substantial contributions which effective logistics management could make to success in the market-place. 'Marketing Logistics' can lead to success by securing a cost advantage through increased efficiency and by maximising added value through customer service, providing high levels of service at lower cost.

Traditionally distribution has been viewed by many as a source of cost – admittedly a necessary cost, but a cost nevertheless. Inevitably such a viewpoint leads to a search for improvement in operating efficiency and a focus on cost reduction. Thus improving vehicle utilisation, warehouse throughput times, materials-handling methods and so on are the constant concern of many distribution managers.

Whilst not wishing to diminish the importance of cost containment, it can be argued that such a concern with *efficiency* can on occasion lead to a failure to recognise the real issue in distribution – that is, how *effective* is our distribution strategy?

The distinction between efficiency and effectiveness was most clearly defined by Peter Drucker, who argued that efficiency was a concern with 'doing things right', whilst effectiveness placed the emphasis on 'doing the right things'.

Such a statement could easily be dismissed as purely a clever play on words and yet it has a crucial significance for management. So often much of what we do is akin to rearranging the deck-chairs on the *Titanic* – we make the ship look tidier but neglect its overall direction. In other words operating efficiency takes precedence over strategy. On the other hand the successful companies – those who have developed leadership positions in their markets – tend to be those that have recognised that competitive advantage comes firstly from their strategic position and secondly from their operating efficiency. Clearly a combination of the two is better still.

How then does this philosophy relate to the management of the distribution task?

Firstly it must be recognised that logistics costs account for a large proportion of the sales value of many products. Thus it will follow that in a competitive market, particularly where substitutes are available and acceptable to the customer, a major advantage can be gained if logistics costs can be reduced whilst still maintaining the required service levels. A recent report (*Guardian*, 26 March 1986) stated that car industry experts are forecasting that each car made in Nissan UK's new Tyneside plant will be produced for about £600 less than it costs a British manufacturer to make. The report went on to state that the reason for this Japanese cost advantage is no longer primarily cheaper labour costs but is due to superior logistics management. Nissan will be managing the total material flow, from component source to final user, as an entity. As a result their inventory of materials, work in progress, goods in transit and finished goods will be kept to a minimum: throughput times will be reduced; transport costs will be low – yet their ability to service the end market will not be diminished.

Such an advantage will be difficult for competitors to overcome without the adoption of similar methods.

However, it must be recognised that the advantage in the market-place does not always go to the lowest cost producer. In the same industry as Nissan, Jaguar have achieved substantial success not so much by cutting costs but by adding value. Much has been said about the new approach to quality at Jaguar and how it has led to major improvements in the final product. Just as important, however, in their success has been their concentration on improving customer service, specifically in North America. A radical overhaul of their US dealer network plus a major emphasis on improving the logistics of spares support has transformed their market position.

Other examples of value-added strategies based around superior service could be cited; companies like DEC and IBM, for example, dominate the segments in which they compete as much through their service package as through their technology.

Evidence such as this suggests that it may be advisable for British companies to shift their emphasis towards the adoption of value-added strategies instead of struggling in vain to become the lowest cost producers. The relationship between market share and unit costs is well known but in so many markets UK companies have little chance of regaining lost volume except through offering the customer something over and above that provided by competitors.

If this is true what contribution can distribution and logistics management make in the search for value added?

MARKETING AND LOGISTICS CONVERGE

Most marketing executives probably have never considered the very real contribution to success in the market-place that can be made by more effective logistics management. Whilst many would acknowledge the sense of the old adage 'the right product in the right place at the right time', how many actually incorporate it explicitly into their marketing strategy?

On the other hand some of the more innovative companies recognise that if developing a position of sustainable competitive advantage is the name of the game, then a major source of that advantage is superior logistics performance.

Thus it can be argued that instead of viewing distribution, marketing and manufacturing as largely separate activities within the business, they need to be unified – particularly at the strategic level. One might be tempted to describe such an integrated approach to strategy and planning as 'Marketing Logistics'. Whatever we call it the important requirement is to understand that any business can only compete and survive through one or other of two options: by winning a cost advantage or by providing superior values and benefits to the customer.

Certain changes in the marketing environment make such a revised orientation even more appropriate. One such change has been the steady transition to 'commodity'-type markets. By this is meant that increasingly the power of the 'brand' is diminishing as technologies of competing products converge, thus making product differences less apparent. Faced with such situations the customer may be influenced by price or by 'image' perceptions, but overriding these aspects may well be 'availability' – in other words, is the product in stock. Nor is it only in consumer markets that we are encountering the force of customer service as a determinant of purchase; there is much evidence from industrial markets of the same phenomenon.

A second change is that the customer expectations of service have increased, thus in almost every market the customer is now more demanding, more 'sophisticated' than he or she was, say thirty years ago. Industrial buyers are more professional too, increasing use is made of formal vendor appraisal systems and suppliers are now confronted with the need to provide 'just-in-time' delivery performance.

The third change that has had a particularly severe impact in many industries is the trend for product life cycles to become shorter. The product life cycle represents the period of time that a brand or specific product model is an effective player in the market. There are many implications for management of shorter product life cycles but one in particular is worthy of note.

What we have witnessed in many markets is the effect of changes in technology and consumer demand combining to produce more volatile markets where a product can be obsolete almost as soon as it reaches the market. There are many current examples of shortening life cycles but perhaps the personal computer symbolises them all. In this particular case we have seen rapid developments in technology which have firstly created markets where none existed before and then almost as quickly have rendered themselves obsolete as the next generation of product is announced. Such shortening life cycles create substantial problems for logistics management. In particular shorter life cycles demand shorter lead-times – indeed our definition of lead-time may well need to change. Lead-times are traditionally defined as the elapsed period from receipt of customer order to delivery. However, in today's environment there is a second aspect to lead-time: how long does it take from the procurement of raw materials, sub-assemblies, etc. through to the delivery of the final product to the customer?

The same personal computer referred to earlier may have a total procurement-to-delivery lead-time of twelve months! In other words some of the components may remain in stock for several weeks before being incorporated in a sub-assembly or module. Those sub-assemblies may then be in transit to another location, possibly overseas, for another couple of weeks where they then, say, are held up pending customs clearance, then fur-

ther delays in storage and manufacturing and so on.

What we are now witnessing is a situation where the product life cycle, in some cases, is in danger of becoming shorter than the procurement-to-delivery lead-time with all the consequent problems for planning and operations that such a situation will create.

The answer to this problem must lie in greater attempts to manage the total materials lead-time throughout the entire system. So often it is found that a substantial proportion of this total lead-time is created through lack of insight and clearly defined managerial responsibilities at the interfaces between adjacent functions.

We have also identified a further trend in that because *production* lead-times are shortening through the use of new technology, this in effect means that a greater proportion of the total procurement-to-delivery lead-time is accounted for by transport and storage. Thus we see greater pressure for integrated distribution/logistics management arising as a result.

THE CUSTOMER SERVICE DIMENSION

These changes in the environment, previously described, have served to move logistics to centre stage and, in turn, to focus the spotlight on customer service.

Customer service is the thread that links the logistics and marketing processes because, in the end, the output of the logistics system is customer service. The skill lies in managing the twin arms of marketing and logistics in such a way as to maximise the value added through customer service whilst still seeking a cost advantage. It can be done, and perhaps one of the most intriguing examples of recent years has come from the world of high fashion – the Italian company Benetton. Benetton has become a world leader in the production and retailing of high-fashion casual wear – particularly knitwear. As this description of their approach indicates, they have found a way to gain a marketing edge through superior logistics management (Montgomery and Hausman, 1985).

Benetton's order system is 'just-in-time' as production runs are not started until orders have been received. A key aspect of its system is the dyeing of knitted goods after production rather than dyeing yarn prior to knitting. This allows Benetton outlets to delay commitment to particular colours until later in the production cycle. Since each selling season typically begins with about ten alternative colours with only about three usually resulting in high demand, the delay in colour choice affords Benetton an opportunity to respond directly to market demand. The retail system itself provides valuable information to Benetton for production planning via daily orders. These feed production with current demand, on which replenishment schedules for designs and colours may be based. The timeliness of this order data is crucial since popular colours will often sell out in the first ten days of a new season. This rapid response system gives Benetton retailers a competitive edge over their less responsive competitors. The order information is digested and fed back to those customers whose orders appear to be out of line with others in their area. Further, Benetton uses CAD for design and cutting in order to respond to dynamic demand as rapidly as possible. Finally, the company's marketing strategy promotes simple colour fashion with heavy advertising support, which in turn maximises the benefits from the delayed dyeing production process.

Examples such as this demonstrate the opportunities that exist for using a closely integrated logistics and marketing system in order to provide high levels of service at lowest cost. The competitive edge that Benetton have achieved through this means is considerable – they have both added value and achieved a cost advantage.

Given that the evidence to support the case for customer-service-driven strategies is so strong, where should those businesses that wish to travel down that road begin?

DEFINING AND MEASURING CUSTOMER SERVICE

It is sometimes suggested that the role of customer service is to provide 'time and place utility' in the transfer of goods and services between buyer and seller. Put another way, there is no value in a product or service until it is in the hands of the customer or consumer. It follows that making the product or service 'available' is what, in essence, the distribution function of the business is all about. Availability is in itself a complex concept, impacted upon by a galaxy of factors which together constitute customer service. These factors might include, for example, delivery, frequency and reliability, stock levels and order cycle time, as they impact upon availability. Indeed, it could be said that ultimately customer service is determined by the interaction of all those factors that affect the process of making products and services available to the buyer.

Many commentators have defined various elements of customer service, but the most commonly occurring seem to be:

▷ Order cycle time
▷ Invoicing procedures and accuracy
▷ Consistency and reliability of delivery
▷ Claims procedure
▷ Inventory availability
▷ Condition of goods
▷ Order-size constraints
▷ Salesman's visits
▷ Ordering convenience
▷ Order status information
▷ Delivery time and flexibility
▷ After-sales support

In any particular product/market situation, some of these elements will be more important than others and there may be factors other than those listed above which have a significance in a specific market. Indeed, the argument that will be developed in this paper is that it is essential to understand customer service in terms of differing requirements of different market segments and that no universally appropriate list of elements exists; each market that the company services will attach different importance to different service elements.

CUSTOMER SERVICE IS PERCEPTUAL

It is a common fault in marketing to fail to realise that customers do not always attach the same importance to product attributes as the vendor. Thus, it sometimes happens that products are promoted on attributes or features that are less important to the customer in reality than other aspects. A floor cleaner that is sold on its ease of application, for example, will not succeed unless 'ease of application' is a salient benefit sought by the customer. If 'shine' or the need for less frequent cleaning are important to the customer then we might be better advised to feature those aspects on our promotion. The same principle applies in customer service: which aspects of service are rated most highly by the customer? If a company places its emphasis upon stock availability but the customer regards delivery reliability more highly, it may not be allocating its resources in a way likely to maximise sales. Alternatively, a company that realises that its customers place a higher value on completeness of orders than they do on, say, regular scheduled deliveries, could develop this to its advantage.

There is, thus, a great premium to be placed on gaining an insight into the factors that influence buyer behaviour and, in the context of customer service, which particular elements are seen by the customer to be the most important. The use of market research techniques in customer service has lagged behind their application in such areas as product testing and advertising research, yet the importance of researching the service needs of customers is just as great as, say, the need to understand the market reaction to price. In fact, it is possible to apply standard, proven market research methods to gain considerable insight into the ways that customers will react to customer service. The first step in research of this type is to identify the relative source of influence on the purchase decision. If we are selling components to a manufacturer, for example, who will make the decision on the source of supply? This is not always an easy question to answer as, in many cases, there will be several people involved. The purchasing manager of the company to whom we

are selling may be acting only as an agent for others within the firm. In other cases, his influence will be much greater. Alternatively, if we are manufacturing products for sale through retail outlets, is the decision to stock made centrally by a retail chain or by individual store managers? The answers to these questions can often be supplied by the salesforce. The sales representative should know from experience who the decision-makers are.

Given that a clear indication of the source of decision-making power can be gained, the customer service researcher at least knows who to research. The question still remains, however – which elements of the vendor's total marketing offering have what effect on the purchase decision? Ideally, once the decision-making unit in a specific market has been identified, an initial, small-scale research programme should be initiated which would be based on personal interviews with a representative sample of buyers. The purpose of these interviews is to elicit, *in the language of the customers*, first, the importance they attach to customer service *vis-à-vis* the other marketing mix elements such as price, product quality, promotion and so on, and second, the specific importance they attach to the individual components of customer service.

ASSESSING THE CUSTOMER SERVICE CLIMATE

In our eagerness to develop a customer service strategy it would be a mistake to focus exclusively on the 'external' dimension of service, i.e. customer perceptions. Of equal importance is the 'internal' dimension, i.e. how do our own people, our managers and workforce, view service? What is their attitude to customers? Do they share the same concept and definition of service as our customers?

It would be a truism to suggest that ultimately a company's performance is limited more by the vision and the quality of its people than it is by market factors or competitive forces. However, it is perhaps only belatedly that we have come to recognise this.

Much has been written and spoken about 'corporate culture'. We have come to recognise that the shared values that are held throughout the organisation can provide a powerful driving force and focus for all its actions. More often than not though we have to admit that most organisations lack a cohesive and communicated culture – even if there is a defined philosophy of the business, it may be little understood. This lack of shared values can impact on the company in many ways, particularly its approach to customer service.

One viable way to assess the customer service 'climate' within the firm is to take the temperature by means of an employee survey. One such approach that has been developed begins with identifying all those personnel who have a direct or indirect impact upon customer service. A useful device here is to consider the complete 'order to cash' cycle and to ensure that we have identified all those people involved in all the different departments that influence the order flow. The focus of the survey should be upon these key people's perceptions of service: what do *they* think is important to the customers? and how do they think we perform service-wise?

What quite often emerges from these internal surveys is that employees hold quite different views as to what constitutes customer service. Similarly they may often overrate the company's actual performance compared with the customers' own rating. Making such comparisons between customers' perceptions and the employees' perceptions can provide a powerful means of identifying customer service problems and their sources.

This 'audit' of internal perceptions and attitudes towards service can form the basis of a programme of action aimed at developing a customer service culture. However, such a process, which almost inevitably will involve a major reorientation within the firm, cannot work without the total commitment of top management. The service culture must grow outwards from the boardroom and the chief executive must be its greatest champion.

Within the logistics function one very practical step is to set up the equivalent of a 'quality circle'. Such a scheme might involve looking at the total order-processing and invoicing cycle and selecting individuals from all the departments or sections involved. This group would meet at least once a week with the expressed objective of seeking improvements to customer service from whatever source they might come. A further task that might usefully be given to this group is to handle all customer complaints that relate to service.

Underpinning all of these initiatives should be a company-wide education programme. Increasingly, more and more organisations have come to recognise the key role that in-company education can have in developing a sense of shared values. Furthermore, because it is a basic tenet of psychology that attitude change must precede behaviour change, education can lead to measurably improved performance. One of the best examples recently has come from British Airways, whose 'Putting People First' campaign has resulted in a significant change in employee behaviour and thus in the company's market-place performance.

USING SERVICE TO SELL

Earlier it was stressed that it is important to establish those components of the total customer service mix which have the greatest impact on the buyer's perceptions of us as a supplier. This thinking needs to be carried right through into the design of the customer service offering. This offering can best be described as the customer service 'package', for it will most likely contain more than one component.

The design of the package will need to take account of the differing needs of different market segments so that the resources allocated to customer service can be used in the most cost-effective way. Too often, a uniform, blanket approach to service is adopted by companies which does not distinguish between the real requirements of different customer types. This can lead to customers being offered too little service or too much.

The precise composition of the customer service package for any market segment will depend on the results of the analysis described earlier. It will also be determined by budgetary and cost constraints. If alternative packages can be identified which seem to be equally acceptable to the buyer, it makes sense to choose the least-cost alternative. For example, it may be possible to identify a customer service package with high acceptability which enables the emphasis to be switched away from a high level of inventory availability towards, say, improved customer communications. Once a cost-effective package has been identified in this way, it should become a major part of the company's marketing mix – 'using service to sell' is the message here. If the market segments we serve are sensitive to service, then the service package must be actively promoted. One way in which this can be achieved with great effect is by stressing the impact on the *customer's* costs of the improved service package: for example, what improved reliability will do for his own stock planning; what shorter lead-times will do for his inventory levels; how improved ordering and invoicing systems will lead to fewer errors, and so on. All too often, the customer will not appreciate the impact that improved service offered by the supplier can have on his, the customer's, bottom line.

CONCLUSION

The main theme of this paper has been that logistics and marketing can combine to provide a powerful means of achieving a sustainable competitive advantage. The combination of added value through service and cost advantage through greater efficiency make a winning team wherever they are tried. There are probably more opportunities for profit improvement through superior marketing logistics than from any other source.

REFERENCE
Montgomery, D. and W. Hausman (1985), 'Managing the Marketing/Manufacturing Interface', *Journal of Management*, vol. 2, no. 2.

PART V

The Future of Services Marketing

THE FUTURE OF SERVICES MARKETING

Like all dynamic concepts, services marketing is continuously updating and changing. Whilst the principal concepts are well established there is continuing evolution and progression in both the existing domain and new developmental areas. Generally, it can be observed that there are two main thrusts of services marketing development. One aspect is the increasing sophistication of services in specific contexts, primarily in areas such as banking and not-for-profit circumstances. The other main thrust is in the development of new managerial aspects which reflect the service concept by focusing on aspects of people interactions within a firm's service operations.

SERVICES IN SPECIFIC CONTEXTS

There are several good examples of services development in the area of retail banking services. LeBlanc and Nguyen (1988) take the theories surrounding quality and customers' perceptions championed by a range of scholars and adapt them to the specific circumstances of financial institutions. A similar focus is taken by Kathawala and Johnson (1990) and Wong and Perry (1991) when they apply quality theories to financial retailing. Wong and Perry offer a useful four-step framework for improving customer service in this sector by attempting to segment the market for a service offering:

i. Establish commitment to the key components of customer service;
ii. Identify relative importance of service components to customers;
iii. Identify market segments by service requirements;
iv. Design customer service policies.

Wong and Perry argue that these four steps match recognised stages of development of marketing plans but they are modified for modern retail financial institutions. In the same vein of adaptation, Blois (1987) applies the principles of marketing to not-for-profit organisations and argues that such a marketing approach will improve the organisation's effectiveness and efficiency in dealing with its consumers. The potential for building upon Blois's work is immense, particularly from the standpoint of the adaptation of modern marketing concepts to this area.

Much of the more recent literature focuses on particular aspects of services marketing and marketing in specific service contexts. To illustrate this some examples are given below:

▷ Gwin (1995) writes about the prospects for the future of retail banking. He argues that the way forward involves electronic media. Therefore market segmentation should be on the basis of customers' technology life cycle, that is, the degree to which a consumer has moved from 'technophobia' towards 'technophilia'. Gwin predicts that this will become a meaningful and important strategic tool for those planning the direction for retail banking into the next century.

▷ Quinn (1994) describes an action-based framework to aid companies in understanding the key dimensions of service quality and in achieving a service advantage. The 'PROMPT' service approach includes: Prioritising customer needs, Reliability is critical, Organising for customers, Measuring customer satisfaction, Personnel training, and Technology focusing.

▷ Stewart (1994) focuses on the issue of customer loyalty and the reasons why customers break off their relationships with banks. She reports on a case-study of a major retail bank which was carried out using Hirschman's (1970) customer exit, voice and loyalty model. The study revealed that in only about half of the 'exit' cases did the bank query why a customer had closed an account.

THE DEVELOPMENT OF NEW MANAGERIAL ASPECTS

Much of the development in the managerial approach to services marketing has been led by the Scandinavians Grönroos and Gummesson. Grönroos (1990) argues for a 'relationship' approach to services marketing. He maintains that marketing in a services context is an organisational issue which reaches beyond the marketing department. He advocates the use of relationship marketing techniques for managers and employees of services organisations and the need to develop a 'service culture' and to recognise the importance of 'internal marketing'. Grönroos (1989) develops the relationship marketing theme by redefining the marketing concept to be more market-oriented than standard American definitions in textbooks. He suggests that the conventional marketing mix model has limitations and emphasises the importance of market-oriented management, customer relationships and managing 'promises' in marketing. In all of this he offers the 'Nordic school' definition of marketing, which is built upon mutual exchange and keeping promises.

Picking up the theme that services marketing concepts within an organisation must go beyond the marketing department, Gummesson (1991) introduces the notion of the 'part-time marketer' (as mentioned in Part III). In arguing that everyone in an organisation is involved in some aspect of marketing whether they work in the marketing department or not, he calls those outside the marketing department 'part-time marketers'. His thesis is closely linked with the developing 'new' theories of marketing, namely relationship marketing, interactive marketing and total quality management.

These theories are now being widely applied to services situations. For example, de Burca (1995) applies networking and relationship marketing theories to the management of services in the business-to-business sector and analyses the contribution and conflicts that the network perspective holds for the relationship marketing concept in this context.

Some scholars are now beginning to examine the implications of some of these new theories. Liljander and Strandvik (1994) examine the interactive dimension in the context of the nature of relationship quality. They do this by splitting relationship quality into two different concepts: service episode quality, defined as an event of interaction; and service relationship quality, determined as a relation consisting of a number of episodes.

Barnes (1994) analyses what the term relationship marketing really entails and asserts that there is little consensus on what the concept means and no consistency in how it is practised. Barnes reviews how the concept has been viewed by marketing authors and draws from psychology to shed light on the characteristics of relationships. He stresses the importance of the customer's views in determining what form of relationship, if any, s/he wants to have with a business. The intensity of a relationship is another issue increasingly under debate. Questions such as how relationships can be developed and maintained are being considered. In some aspects of small firms services marketing the connections within the 'personal contact network' of the entrepreneur or owner/manager are being assessed in the context of relationships. Carson et al. (1995) argue implicitly that networks and relationships exist along a continuum with networks representing loose relationships which can be developed over time towards genuinely tight relationships. The essence of this focus is on the nature and level of communication.

There is also emerging research into a 'holistic' view of services marketing. LeBlanc and Nguyen (1988) suggest that service quality should be viewed holistically. They produce a conceptual model incorporating five quality components, namely corporate image, internal organisation, physical support of the service producing system, customer/staff interaction and the degree of customer satisfaction. They base their model on previous schools of thought in relation to how customers evaluate quality, for example, the work of Shostack (1977), Berry (1980), Rathmell (1974) and Eiglier and Langeard (1987).

Glynn and Lehtinen (1995) offer an integrative approach to the management of services by taking account of the concept of exchange in services. By considering the traditional interactive, internal and relationship marketing concepts in a services context, they develop a more complex three-way interactive relationship involving the external customer.

Gilmore and Carson (1993) expand the holistic view of services marketing by considering services management dimensions in the context of the functional aspects of marketing. They argue that service quality must not only be managed across the organisation but it must be performed in a holistic way across all the dimensions of the services marketing function. They present a framework which explicitly recognises the need to focus managers' attention on improving the quality of all marketing activity and related functions. This is considered within the context of the tangible and intangible dimensions of service marketing activity as discussed in Part II; this again illustrates the need to address and balance the tangible and intangible nature of services management.

The way to achieve a holistic and balanced delivery of marketing activity which includes both tangibles and intangibles is through customer care. In services marketing activity in general, customer care and satisfaction will be of a prime concern in all aspects of marketing communications, sales incentives and motivation, quality improvements and value-added dimensions. However, the implementation of complete customer care will require some careful attention and management by service marketers. It is argued here that the future perspectives on service quality improvement will depend upon the management of all marketing activity by consistently focusing on the quality of management decision-making. This will entail the development of appropriate management competencies, as well as the proactive use of networking through communication, in relation to all aspects of customer care. These are discussed briefly below.

MANAGEMENT COMPETENCIES

It is widely recognised that developed management competencies are the key to improved management performance. From a management perspective it can be considered that competence is the ability to use knowledge and skills effectively in the performance of a specific task. Competencies may embrace a more tangible set of attributes, such as the ability to make sound judgements, willingness to take risks, decisiveness, ability to take initiative and a results orientation. When applied to services marketing the focus will be upon those competencies which are most appropriate to performing effectively in the context of managing people and customer care.

NETWORKING

As well as developing competencies, management must take account of proactive self-development and communication through networking. These competencies will be naturally enhanced by good networks, since they revolve around meaningful 'personal contacts'. The personal contact network defines any relationship, either direct, in terms of a particular impact upon the company/customer interface, or indirect, in that it may lead to further contact through and with other people. The density, reachability and diversity of a personal contact network will have considerable bearing on the impact it has on customer care. Thus people who are involved in the company/customer interface represent the richest sources of personal contact, for example, buyers, frontline supervisors and interface staff, telephonists and so on. By proactively nurturing and enhancing the relationship network with all of these individuals an employee with customer care responsibility will perform more effectively.

INTEGRATED 'HOLISTIC' MARKETING ACTIVITY

The ultimate way forward in the development of service quality management is a fully integrated package of activities and decision-making functions. This means focusing on key factors and linking these together into such an integrated package. The key factors drawn from this overview of the future development of service quality are:

1. Wide consideration of all marketing functional variables which include the

service product, advertising, promotion, personal selling, order processing and customer service.

2. Identification and enhancement of key marketing competencies and personal contact networks with particular attention to the nurturing and development of personal contacts in all aspects of service delivery.

3. Consistent and balanced delivery of all key service activities by taking account of all tangible and intangible aspects of the services marketing mix.

4. A consistent and balanced perspective on the customer/company interface – acknowledgement of all aspects of the interrelationships between a customer and a company, both in relation to hard instrumental and soft psychological dimensions.

By combining all four of these factors under clear and precise service quality objectives and policies an organisation will provide consistent and holistic service quality.

Considering the foregoing the keynote articles we have chosen for this final section of the book are:

Glynn, William J. and Uolevi Lehtinen (1995), 'Services Marketing and the Concept of Exchange: An Integrative Approach' in W.J. Glynn and J. Barnes (eds.), *Understanding Services Management: Integrating Marketing, Organisational Behaviour, Operations and Human Resource Management,* Oak Tree Press, Dublin, pp. 89–118.
Gilmore, Audrey and David Carson (1993), 'Quality Improvement in a Services Marketing Context', *Journal of Services Marketing,* vol. 7, no. 3, pp. 59–71.
LeBlanc, Gaston and Nha Nguyen (1988), 'Customers' Perceptions of Service Quality in Financial Institutions', *International Journal of Bank Marketing,* vol. 6, no. 4, pp. 7–18.
Liljander, V. and T. Strandvik (1994), 'The Nature of Relationship Quality', European Institute for Advanced Studies in Management (EIASM), Proceedings, Quality Management in Services IV, Paris, May.
Grönroos, Christian (1989), 'Defining Marketing: A Market-oriented Approach', *European Journal of Marketing,* vol. 23, no. 1, pp. 52–60.

Glynn and Lehtinen's (1995) article describes a more integrated approach to services marketing by reinterpreting and extending the traditional marketing concept and the concept of exchange which is fundamental to marketing. This article takes account of the relationship view of marketing, the interactive and traditional views of marketing and considers them in the context of services. The authors then present a model of the service exchange process (Figure 3 in the article) which illustrates the position of internal and external customers and their marketing relationship with the organisation. Finally a case-study description of relationship and interactive marketing intensity is given.

Gilmore and Carson (1993) consider the various definitions of 'quality' and how these definitions can be adapted to fit the characteristics and nature of services marketing. Taking cognisance of the tangible and intangible aspects of service marketing activity and the key marketing management functions for a services organisation they offer a 'holistic' model for quality improvement. This model illustrates the tangible and intangible nature of service managers' tasks and responsibilities. They use it to illustrate and describe a case-study of the operationalisation of quality improvement in a travel company.

LeBlanc and Nguyen (1988) provide a discussion and illustration of both marketing in a specific situation (banking) and consideration of the holistic nature of managerial issues. The authors present a 'conceptual model of service quality', taking account of previous studies into how customers evaluate quality. They carried out a study in a number of credit unions in the French population of New Brunswick in order to identify a set of factors capable of explaining perceived quality in financial institutions.

Liljander and Strandvik's (1994) article builds upon the theories of relationship marketing and perceived service quality. They identify two different concepts in the context of perceived quality, that of service episode quality and that of service relationship quality. Furthermore they describe different patterns of episodes in a relation and different relationship assortments and then consider these in the context of different types of services.

Grönroos (1991) focuses on redefining marketing from a European and Scandinavian context. He argues that traditionally marketing management texts were based on definitions to fit the marketing circumstances and environments of the United States. He argues that the marketing mix model needs to be adapted to become more market-oriented. He presents the Nordic approach to marketing research based upon qualitative research aimed at developing a deeper understanding of the marketing function, the nature of customer relations and marketing situations as they really exist.

As in anything, the future of services marketing is uncertain. Whether the trends and developments alluded to here will continue to grow and consolidate remains to be seen. However, there are two distinctive factors that we can state with certainty. One is that the domain of services marketing has seen rapid evolution to the point where it is now an established discipline in its own right. The other certainty is that new concepts and ideas will emerge which will enhance and develop this discipline in keeping with the new eras of the future. It might be speculated that the foundations of the services marketing philosophy will indeed become the ethos for all marketing regardless of circumstance. Such a notion we can observe with interest.

KEY LEARNING QUESTIONS

1. What is meant by relationship marketing? How does this contribute to the ideal of service quality?
2. What is integrated functional activity?
3. Describe the advantages of networking in the potential development of managers in a services context.
4. Could the fundamental philosophy of services marketing be applied to any marketing circumstance?

REFERENCES

Barnes, J.G. (1994), 'Close to the Customer: But Is it Really a Relationship?', *Journal of Marketing Management,* vol. 10, no. 7, pp. 561–70.

Berry, Leonard L. (1980), 'Services Marketing Is Different', *Business,* May–June, pp. 24–9.

Blois, Keith J. (1987), 'Marketing for Non-profit Organisations' in Michael J. Baker (ed.), *The Marketing Book,* pp. 404–12, Heinemann, London.

Carson, D., S. Cromie, P. McGowan and J. Hill (1995), *Marketing and Entrepreneurship in SMEs: An Innovative Approach,* Prentice-Hall, Hemel Hempstead.

de Burca, S. (1995), 'A Network Approach to Business to Business Exchange Relationships: Key Meta-theoretical Assumptions', *Irish Marketing Review,* 8, pp. 117–25.

Eiglier, P. and E. Langeard (1987), *Servuction, le marketing des services,* McGraw-Hill, Paris.

Gilmore, A. and D. Carson (1993), 'Quality Improvement in a Services Marketing Context', *Journal of Services Marketing,* vol. 7, no. 3, pp. 59–71.

Gilmore, A. and D. Carson (1993), 'Enhancing Service Quality: The Case of Sealink Stena', *Irish Marketing Review,* 6, pp. 64–9.

Glynn, W.J. and U. Lehtinen (1995), 'Services Marketing and the Concept of Exchange: An Integrative Approach' in W.J. Glynn, and J. Barnes (eds.), *Understanding Services Management: Integrating Marketing, Organisational Behaviour, Operations and Human Resource Management,* Oak Tree Press, Dublin, pp. 89–118.

Grönroos, C. (1990), 'Relationship Approach to Marketing in Service Contexts: The Marketing and Organisational Behaviour Interface', *Journal of Business Research,* 20, pp. 3–11.

Grönroos, C. (1989), 'Defining Marketing: A Market-oriented Approach', *European Journal of Marketing,* vol. 23, no. 1, pp. 52–60.

Gummesson, E. (1991), 'Marketing-orientation Revisited: The Crucial Role of the Part-time Marketer', *European Journal of Marketing,* vol. 25, no. 2, pp. 60–75.

Gwin, J.M. (1995), 'Prospects for the Future of Retail Banking', *Irish Marketing Review,* 8, pp. 48–52.

Hirschman, A. (1970), *Exit, Voice and Loyalty: Responses to Decline in Firms, Organisations and States,* Harvard University Press, Mass.

Kathawala, Yunus and Judy Johnson (1990), 'Quality Issues in Marketing: A Conceptual Approach', *International Journal of Bank Marketing,* vol. 8, no. 6, pp 35–9.

LeBlanc, G. and N. Nguyen (1988), 'Customers' Perceptions of Service Quality in Financial Institutions', *International Journal of Bank Marketing,* vol. 6, no. 4, pp. 7–18.

Liljander, V. and T. Strandvik (1994), 'The Nature of Relationship Quality', European Institute for Advanced Studies in Management (EIASM), Proceedings, Quality Management in Services IV, Paris, May.

Quinn, M. (1994), 'Winning Service Quality – The PROMPT Approach', *Irish Marketing Review,* 7, pp. 110–18.

Rathmell, J.M. (1974), *Marketing in the Service Sector,* Winthrop Publishers, Inc., Cambridge, Mass.

Shostack, G. Lynn (1977) 'Breaking Free from Product Marketing', *Journal of Marketing,* vol. 41, April, pp. 73–80.

Stewart, K. (1994), 'Customer Exit: Loyalty Issues in Retail Banking', *Irish Marketing Review,* 7, pp. 45–53.

Wong, Su Mon and Chad Perry (1991), 'Customer Service Strategies in Financial Marketing', *International Journal of Bank Marketing,* vol. 9, no. 3, pp. 11–16.

Services Marketing and the Concept of Exchange: An Integrative Approach

William J. Glynn and Uolevi Lehtinen

Exploring the concept of exchange in services marketing interprets traditional, interactive, internal and relationship marketing in the context of a more complex three-way interactive relationship involving the external customer, the internal customer and the service organisation. This reading proposes a model of service exchange depicting this relationship. A number of services marketing inferences are drawn from the model. Demonstrative case materials are also used to illustrate this material.

INTRODUCTION: EXTENDING THE MARKETING CONCEPT

Reinterpreting and extending the traditional marketing concept to cater more adequately for the services marketing challenge has proven to be a fruitful exercise. The marketing concept, which views marketing as a philosophy and extols the virtues of finding and filling customer wants, fits just as well in the services context as it does in its physical-product-oriented birthplace. Descriptions of the marketing concept centre on the fulfilment of needs and wants of target market segments and the adaptation of organisations to deliver desired satisfactions more efficiently and effectively than competitors (McKitterick, 1957; Borch, 1957).

The prevailing marketing philosophy revolving around the concept of exchange and the application of the marketing mix paradigm has always served as a good basis upon which to define marketing (Culliton, 1948; McCarthy, 1960; Borden, 1965; Levy and Zaltman, 1975; Bagozzi, 1975, 1979; Hunt, 1976). This definition has been updated by the American Marketing Association in 1985 to encompass services as well as goods (American Marketing Association, 1985):

'Marketing is the process of planning and executing the conception, pricing, promotion and distribution of ideas, goods and services to create exchange and satisfy individual and organisational objectives.'

Basing seller activities on consumer needs and wants in selected target markets is neither new nor controversial. However, several authors have expressed their dissatisfaction with the limitations of the American-based marketing concept in the context of both services and industrial marketing (de Ferrer, 1986; Gummesson, 1987). The established exchange and marketing mix view of marketing is considered to be still overly production-oriented in that it originates with the supplier and not the customer (Grönroos, 1990a). Limiting study to single isolated exchanges fails to recognise the need to build long-term relationships with customers (Houston and Gassenheimer, 1987). The marketing mix paradigm alone does not account for the many marketing-like activities, interactions and resources that go towards maintaining the customer relationship over time (Grönroos and Gummesson, 1986; Grönroos, 1990b). The relationship paradigm adds to the marketing mix paradigm in that it recognises the value of related exchanges and the need to maintain customer relationships over time. The relationship paradigm is best represented in the services literature under the heading of relationship marketing.

RELATIONSHIP VIEW OF MARKETING

During the 1980s, increasing competition and deregulation in many industries had, and still has, a number of far-reaching effects on the competitive environment. Firstly, the ability to replicate physical products at lower and lower costs facilitated price undercutting by domestic and international competitors. This encouraged many manufacturers to augment their physical products with services in order to compete and even survive. Many large firms have been transformed from predominantly manufacturing organisations into predominantly service organisations by bundling services with products (Peters, 1988; Chase and Garvin, 1989). Secondly, the need to keep existing customers became a priority in the face of intense competition and the higher comparative marketing costs of acquiring new customers. Thirdly, increased competition and deregulation in many service-dominated industries resulted in a concentration on service quality as a means of achieving a competitive advantage.

The term relationship marketing was first coined in the early 1980s in the services literature (Berry, 1983). Prior to that time several authors had discussed the need to concentrate on customer retention, customer loyalty and reselling efforts (George, 1977; Ryans and Wittink, 1977; Schneider, 1980; Grönroos, 1981). The Conference Board, as early as 1970, proposed that selling to the prospective customer was only half the battle and that winning repeat sales was the other half (Hopkins and Bailey, 1970). The need to develop and maintain profitable long-term relationships with customers has received particular attention both in the industrial net-

work interaction theory and in the services marketing theory (Håkansson, 1982; Rosenberg and Czepiel, 1984; Jackson, 1985; McKenna, 1985, 1991; Gummesson, 1987). The long-term holistic approach of relationship marketing can be contrasted with the short-term focus of transaction marketing and the predetermined structure of decision-making variables presented by the reductionist marketing mix approach (Jackson, 1985; Grönroos, 1990b). Relationship and transaction marketing have been opposed on a marketing strategy continuum and equated with the marketing of services and consumer packaged goods respectively (Grönroos, 1990c, 1991). This approach is illustrated and examined in the case-study material included in this chapter.

Keeping and improving customer relationships is important for a number of reasons.

1. There are higher marketing costs associated with generating interest in new customers as opposed to already informed existing customers.

    'The marketing costs involved in the creation of interest in an uninformed new customer far outweigh those involved in maintaining the relationship necessary to continue exchanges between buyer and seller' (Barnes and Glynn, 1992).

    Attracting new customers can cost up to six times as much as retaining existing customers (Desatnick, 1987; Sellers, 1989; Congram, 1991).

2. Close and long-term relationships with customers imply continuing exchange opportunities with existing customers at a lower marketing cost per customer (Grönroos, 1990b). As Reichheld and Sasser observe, 'Across a wide range of businesses, the pattern is the same: the longer a company keeps a customer, the more money it tends to make' (Reichheld and Sasser, 1990).

3. Viewing customer exchanges as a revenue stream, as opposed to a compendium of isolat-

ed transactions, enables cross-selling of related services over time and premium pricing as a result of the customer's confidence in the business (Reichheld and Sasser, 1990; Congram, 1991).

4. Strong customer relationships with a high degree of familiarity and communications on both sides can generate more practical new product ideas from customers and contact personnel (Kiess-Moser and Barnes, 1992).

5. Good relationships with customers can result in good word of mouth from successful exchanges and minimal bad word of mouth in the event of unsuccessful exchanges. Service quality cracks can often be papered over where good relationships have existed previously.

The relationship paradigm views marketing as revolving around relationships between the parties to the exchange. Exchanges take place in order to establish and develop these relationships. The relationship marketing approach also recognises the importance of fulfilment of promises in the maintenance of long-term relationships with customers (Calonius, 1986, 1988; Grönroos, 1990c, 1991). The establishment, maintenance and development of relationships by sellers involves giving and fulfilling promises concerning goods, services, systems, finances, information, materials, social contacts and future commitments (Grönroos, 1990b). Reciprocal promises concerning customer commitment to the relationship make for continuity over the long term. Customer and business relationships have been described as significant intangible marketing assets of the firm which need to be cultivated and sustained (Carson and Gilmore, 1989–90; Normann, 1991; Forsgren and Johanson, 1992).

The relationship paradigm also applies to other relationships with and among partners/stakeholders which are more or less peripheral to the central direct customer-seller exchange process. Relationships with and among customers, technology and people – employees,

peers, union officials and suppliers – are often critical and interrelated success factors in the competitive environment (Blount, 1988).

Grönroos's relationship definition of marketing endeavours to capture many of the concepts discussed above.

> Marketing is to establish, maintain and enhance [usually but not necessarily long-term] relationships with customers and other partners, at a profit, so that the objectives of the parties involved are met. This is achieved by a mutual exchange and fulfilment of promises.
> (Grönroos, 1990c, p. 138)

This definition is valuable in so far as it extends the list of resources and activities necessary in the application of the marketing concept. These activities include interactive marketing, service quality management and internal marketing. While emphasising the lack of empirical testing, Grönroos is eager to point out that the importance of the elements of the marketing mix is not diminished by the above definition. On a similar note, Lehtinen points out that the importance of the marketing mix is not diminished but rather completed and improved through the interactive approach (Lehtinen, 1983). However, the absence of reference to any element of marketing mix in the definition would seem to imply the contrary. The definition of marketing outlined below has been developed as a working definition and research guide for the purposes of this reading:

> Marketing is the establishment, maintenance and enhancement of mainly long-term profitable relationships with customers and other stakeholders. This is achieved by an ongoing mutually beneficial exchange process, including the fulfilment of promises, and is facilitated by the application of the marketing mix.

The relationship marketing paradigm places the activities of interactive marketing, between service provider and service consumer, at the heart of the services marketing function. Organising for the diverse interactive marketing roles played within and without the boundaries of the service organisation presents the organisation with a complex management task. This task will be explored in the remainder of this reading.

INTERACTIVE MARKETING AND TRADITIONAL MARKETING

The forging of exchange relationships necessarily involves buyers and sellers in interactive relationships. The literature dealing with the concepts of interactive relationships and interactive marketing/relationships marketing emanates from two sources: industrial marketing and services marketing. In the industrial context, empirical research has been carried out by the Industrial Marketing & Purchasing (IMP) Group at the University of Uppsala and the Stockholm School of Economics, Sweden, in the development of network interaction theory (Håkansson, 1982, 1987; Turnbull and Valla, 1986; Johansson and Mattsson, 1987; Lindquist, 1987). The IMP Group view the development of relationships over time, through an interactive network, as a core concept of industrial marketing, i.e. bilateral and multilateral supplier-customer activities to produce and deliver goods and services mainly through interpersonal communication. Bradley describes four underlying constructs of an interactive paradigm: organisations and individuals involved in interactions, the interaction/exchange process, the environment in which interactions take place, and the atmosphere of the interaction (Bradley, 1991).

In the service context, the Nordic School of Services, with researchers based in Sweden and Finland, have emphasised the importance of interactions and interactive marketing (Grönroos and Gummesson, 1985). The predominance of the characteristics of intangibility, inseparability and heterogeneity in service exchanges brings buyers and sellers into intimate and multiple contacts. These exchange occasions are often related either directly or indirectly over time, transaction and situation. Consequently they effect long-term relationships. The nature of the exchanges can also vary by taking the form of information, goods, service and social exchanges (Grönroos, 1990a).

These multiple contact points and exchange occasions have been popularly referred to as 'Moments of Truth or Opportunity' (Normann, 1984; Carlzon, 1987; Gummesson, 1987; Blount, 1988; Beatty and Gup, 1989; Albrecht and Zemke, 1990; George, 1990; Grönroos, 1988, 1990b; Mayo, 1990). All preparations, support, expectations and perceptions on both sides are confronted in individual moments of interpersonal contact. During these interactions the customer has the opportunity to form an impression of the service supplier. These interactions have both short-term effects and longer-term cumulative effects on the all-important customer relationship. Ensuring the successful outcome of every moment of truth through good interactive marketing is the primary objective of the services marketing strategy.

A number of interactive relationships have been identified (Lehtinen, 1985; Gummesson, 1987, 1991; Martin and Pranter, 1989):

▷ internal interactions within a marketing organisation;

▷ internal interactions within a customer organisation;

▷ interaction between the customer and the service provider's contact person (front-line employees);

▷ interactions between the buyer and the seller's systems, machinery and routines;

▷ interaction between the customer and service provider's physical environment and/or tangible products;

▷ interaction among customers who produce the service amongst themselves;

▷ interaction between the organisation, facilitating agencies and customer's customers;

▷ interaction between the organisation and its competitors.

Buyer–seller interactions utilise three main resources (Eiglier et al., 1977):

▷ the employees who come into contact with the customers (contact personnel);

▷ resources present in the physical environment

FIGURE 1: THE TRADITIONAL/INTERACTIVE MARKETING LINK IN SERVICES

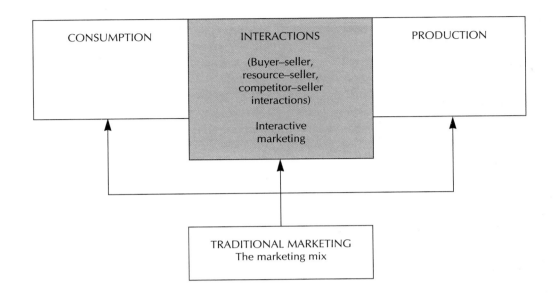

where the service is produced and consumed (physical/technical resources);

▷ the consumers.

Grönroos sees the management of interactions between these resources as a task of marketing which he calls interactive marketing (Grönroos, 1981). The total marketing function in services is composed of traditional marketing and interactive marketing (Grönroos, 1982). The interactive marketing tasks of handling the moments of truth differ significantly from those tasks involved in traditional marketing activities such as advertising and pricing (Grönroos, 1981). Traditional marketing activities can be managed separately from other functions in the company. These activities are normally planned and implemented by sales and marketing specialists.

Grönroos has described the interactive marketing function as the marketing activities outside the marketing mix (Grönroos, 1990b). The traditional marketing efforts are seen as occasional supports to the interactive marketing activities performed during the moments of truth

(Grönroos, 1990c). While this description attempts to differentiate the interactive marketing function from the traditional marketing mix, it fails to capture the marketing mix implementation role played by every employee in every customer interaction or moment of truth or indeed marketing's interest in influencing that role. Lehtinen describes the nature of service interaction as necessarily linking marketing with production and consumption on several levels (Lehtinen, 1985). Figure 1 illustrates the link between production, consumption, traditional marketing and interactive marketing in the context of services.

With the exception of the sales function, interactive marketing is carried out for the main part by contact personnel outside the marketing department, for example production, technical services, claims handling, accounts and deliveries. These non-marketing personnel have been referred to as 'Part-time Marketers' (George and Compton, 1985; Gummesson, 1987; George, 1990; Grönroos, 1990b). The part-time marketer concept places all non-marketing employees in the role of service marketers. The part-time mar-

FIGURE 2:   THE SERVICES MARKETING FUNCTION

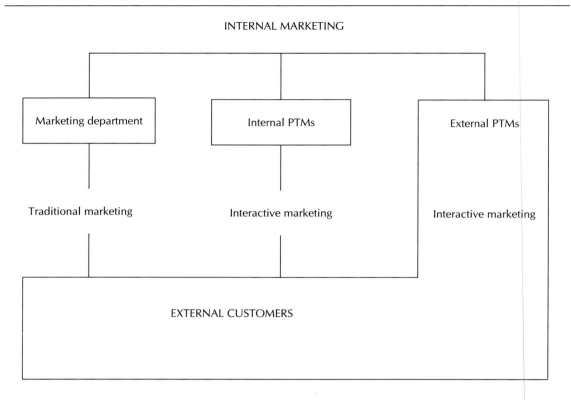

Note: Part-time marketers (PTMs)

keter tends to be a non-marketing specialist who predominates in the vast majority of interactive marketing tasks. Part-time marketers have been classified into internal and external groupings (Gummesson, 1990, 1991). Internal part-time marketers comprise top management, support personnel and front-line contact personnel other than the full-time marketers of the marketing department. External part-time marketers comprise marketing facilitation agencies, suppliers, investors, trade unions, environmentalists, the media and other stakeholders including customers. Services customers can also be classed as external part-time marketers in so far as they are often involved in the production, delivery and consumption of the service. The marketing department can best influence the interactive marketing function by directing marketing inter-

ventions internally at part-time marketers. Figure 2 interprets the marketing function in the context of traditional and interactive marketing and the relationship between internal and external part-time marketers and the marketing department.

A SERVICE EXCHANGE MODEL

The fundamental keystone of marketing theory has been identified as the broad exchange relationships including the theory of marketing transactions and the exchange of values between parties (Kotler and Levy, 1969; Kotler, 1972; Hunt, 1976). In proposing a formal theory of marketing exchanges, Bagozzi considers the basic subject-matter of marketing science to be the explanation and prediction of marketing exchanges (Bagozzi, 1974). Hunt's fundamental explanada of marketing science attempts to describe four interrelated

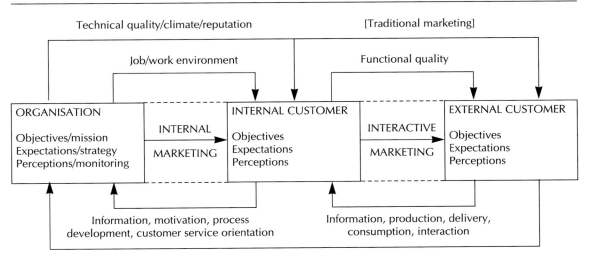

elements of exchange relationships, i.e. the behaviours of buyers, the behaviours of sellers, the facilitating institutional framework and the consequences on society (Hunt, 1983). This macro-perspective focuses on the organisation as synonymous with the seller and the institutions facilitating exchange as outside the organisation. In the context of the highly interactive people-oriented area of service exchange, this impersonal macro-level of abstraction is somewhat inadequate.

The model of service exchange proposed here can best be understood by considering the organisation as an involved exchange facilitator with service provider and service consumer interactions. The elements of the exchange process illustrated in the model are marketing-oriented in nature and form part of the exchanges. This model concentrates on the consideration of three of the four fundamental explanada proposed by Hunt (Hunt, 1983).

There remains considerable scope for theory development regarding the consequences on society of the interactive and interdependent behaviours of service customers, service providers and service facilitators. Viewed from the three-way

perspective of service organisations, internal customer and external customer, the overall service exchange process can be characterised by complexity, interaction and interdependence. All three exchanging parties are involved in a three-way exchange and it is not possible to isolate any party from the overall exchange process. Figure 3 offers a model of service exchange to integrate the service exchange process.

At the broadest level, the service organisation is exchanging technical service quality, a climate of interaction and a level-of-service reputation for patronage, information and recommendation. At this level exchange is mainly facilitated by the traditional 4Ps marketing mix. Each exchanging party brings objectives, expectations and perceptions to the exchange process. In the case of the service organisation, these objectives, expectations and perceptions are formalised in terms of a mission, strategies and monitoring/evaluations of exchange performance.

At another level, the service provider or internal customer exchanges a functional service quality for varying amounts of external customer involvement in the production, delivery and consumption of the service. This is a complex exchange process with unclear boundaries between service provider and service customer. In addition, the external customer provides information as to the nature of the service required and the delivery and production process. This information is part of the exchange process itself. Traditional market information is also gathered by the service provider during the exchange process. At this level of exchange, the service provider plays the role of part-time marketer in the interactive marketing mode. The relationship marketing paradigm is expressed through the application of traditional and interactive marketing activities over time. Again, the individual service provider brings objectives, expectations and perceptions to the external customer exchange process.

Additional objectives, expectations and perceptions are brought to the internal exchange process between the service organisation and the internal customer. These objectives, expectations and perceptions are reflected in the nature of the internal exchange process between the internal customer and the service organisation and between internal customers and internal suppliers. In the service organisation/internal customer exchange case, the organisation is exchanging a job and work environment for a customer service quality orientation, a holistic-based motivation, an informed input to service process development and external market information. At this level, the marketing process is mainly internal in nature with some related cross-market impact of external traditional marketing activities aimed at both external and internal customers.

From this model it can be seen that the traditional dividing lines between organisation, internal customer and external customer are to a large extent blurred. The service organisation itself is composed of its own internal customers, the external customers occupy boundary-spanning roles as part-time employees, and the internal customer occupies a part-time marketing role both in internal and in external exchange relationships.

In order to manage the service exchange process successfully, the service organisation needs to develop marketing intelligence, which not only endeavours to understand the needs of the external customer, but examines the needs of the internal customer in themselves, and their relationship to the needs of the external customer. The process of understanding needs, wants and demands is basic to marketing (Kotler, 1980). What is emphasised in relation to services marketing is the interrelationship between internal and external customers.

Examination of the process of exchange in the context of services marketing requires consideration of the notions of boundary spanning, employees as partial customers, customers as partial employees, and exchange between external customers, the service organisation and the individual service provider(s) (Parkinson and Schneider, 1979; Mills and Moberg, 1982; Mills, Chase and Marguilies, 1983; Bowen and Schneider, 1985; George and Compton, 1985; Bowen, 1986; Mills, 1986; Gummesson, 1987; Bowen and Schneider, 1988; George, 1990; Grönroos, 1990b).

Service marketing exchanges are complex in nature and occur at a number of levels: between the organisation and the external customer; between the service provider and the external customer; and between the organisation and the service provider or internal customer. Almost all services are provided, to some extent or other, by people. The following discussion examines the service exchange from the *people* perspective.

At the most basic level the external customer exchanges custom/patronage for technical service quality; the physical service encounter climate; and the organisation's service quality reputation. This exchange occurs against a background of the organisation's mission/objectives, strategy/expectations and evaluations/perceptions; and the customer's objectives, expectations and perceptions of the service exchange. At this service exchange level, traditional marketing is largely used to facilitate the exchange process.

However, the customer wants more from the exchange than mere technical service quality. In order for the service exchange to take place, a

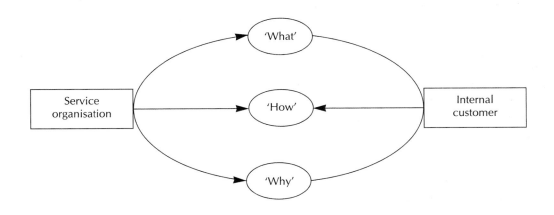

functional service quality must be provided and a personal interaction process must occur. This direct level of exchange occurs between the service provider, i.e. front-line employee, and the external customer. Each exchanging party brings their own objectives, perceptions and expectations to the service quality encounter. The exchange flows consist of functional quality, as delivered to the external customer, and varying levels of external customer inputs including production, delivery, consumption and information exchange. The variation is a function of the nature and dramaturgy of the service exchange (Grove and Fisk, 1983). This level of exchange is of vital importance to the retention of external customers through good interactive marketing by the service provider or part-time marketer (Grönroos, 1981, 1990b). Interactive marketing can be likened to the building blocks upon which the external customer relationship house is constructed over time. The service organisation needs to ensure that the individual builders, i.e. service providers, have adequate tools and instruction to enable them to build a customer relationship house that will last a lifetime.

INTERNAL MARKETING AND SERVICE EXCHANGE

Attention has been drawn to the need for the service organisation to achieve a level of control over the personal and dynamic exchange interaction between service provider/internal customer and external customer (Bowen and Schneider, 1988; Bowen, 1990). Acceptance of this principle draws attention to a third interrelated exchange between the service organisation and the internal customer, i.e. the front-line, support and management employees in the organisation. Again, each party brings their own objectives, expectations and perceptions to the internal exchange relationship. In this case, the exchange flow comprises a job and work environment in exchange for a desired level of customer service quality orientation, motivation, process development input and external customer market intelligence feedback. The role of internal marketing to internal customers is thus one of facilitating internal exchange within the context of the overall exchange process. Internal marketing consists of the organisation informing internal customers of target external customer service levels – the *'what service'* question; providing the means of service delivery, i.e. selection, training, internal communications and support – the *'how to serve'* question; and developing and communicating the exchange offer and external marketing plan to internal customers – the *'why serve'* question (Berry, Bennett and Brown, 1989, p. 147). The 'why serve' offer includes the external marketing plan, the job description itself, monetary reward, bonuses, non-monetary benefits-in-kind, promotion opportunities, new skills, prestige, status, recognition, power, authority, responsibility and job security, to name but a few. Figure 4 illustrates the 'what', 'how' and 'why serve' internal marketing function.

Once recognised and appreciated, the interactive and interdependent nature of the complex service exchange process can be facilitated, through a dedicated relationship marketing approach combining interactive, internal and traditional marketing, aimed at building long-term relationships with customers. The case materials summarised in the remainder of this reading provide evidence of the success of this approach.

A CASE-STUDY OF RELATIONSHIP/ INTERACTIVE MARKETING INTENSITY

The nature and methodological difficulties of empirical research in services has to a great extent given service marketing concepts a 'life of their own' in the literature. The research presented here makes an attempt to redress this imbalance with a view to testing the model of service exchange and its associated concepts in a number of diverse environments. The following case material is based on data collected in Finland in 1993. Five companies from different lines of business were selected for empirical study of the intensity of relationship/interactive marketing within the overall context of the model (Lehtinen, Hankimaa and Mittilä, 1994). Two of the companies were service firms (hotels) and the others were manufacturers (consumer durables, consumer non-durables and industrial goods). The inclusion of manufacturing organisations in the research study allowed the authors scope for additional comparisons and generalisability testing of the model.

In each company, a person responsible for marketing strategy formation and decision-making was interviewed in detail. Interviews were structured, semi-structured and theme-type in nature.

The study was theoretically based on the dimensional examination of the transaction (or traditional)–relationship/interactive marketing continuum. Dimensions evaluated to be suitable for empirical measurement of the intensity of relationship marketing were collected from the marketing theory literature. A number of sources, including Grönroos's marketing strategy continuum, were utilised to identify dimensions (or marketing and management implications) upon which to describe the intensity of relationship marketing in the five firms (Oldano, 1987; Frazier, Spekman and O'Neal, 1988; Grönroos, 1989, 1991; Copulsky and Wolf, 1990; Christopher, Payne and Ballantyne, 1991; Webster, 1992; Blomqvist, Dahl and Haeger, 1993).

The identified dimensions, which even theoretically are not clear continuums, are divided into three natural sections. Each section is then considered as an individual continuum on which the five companies can be placed. In the context of this research, the data is utilised in the examination of the exchange model from three basic viewpoints, i.e. organisation, interactive marketing and its exchange objects, and internal marketing and its exchange objects. The dimensions can then be approximately classified to the groups that belong to the different areas of examination.

Dimensions such as *time perspective*, *focus of marketing*, *marketing definition* and *target of marketing activities* as well as those of *customer service emphasis* and *quality* could be considered as dimensions concerning **organisation**, especially its strategic basis. Marketing dimensions such as *dominating marketing function*, *communication*, *advertising media* as well as *collecting, recording and utilising customer information* concern **interactive marketing**. Dimensions such as *the role of internal marketing* and even *interdependency between marketing and other functions of the firm* measure the intensity of **internal marketing**.

The main results of the case-study research are summarised in Figure 5. It is emphasised here, that in the case of manufactured durable and non-durable goods, it is possible to market directly to consumers and through intermediaries. This can differentiate the nature of marketing activity to a large extent. The remainder of this reading discusses a number of the dimensions in the context of the generalised service exchange model under the headings of organisation, interactive marketing and internal marketing.

FIGURE 5:   INTENSITY OF RELATIONSHIP/INTERACTIVE MARKETING EMPIRICAL RESULTS

	Transaction marketing		Relationship marketing
Time perspective	Short-term focus C(c), D(c) H(1), H(2)	I	Long-term focus C(b), D(b)
Focus of marketing	Product C D	Customer H(2)	H(1) I	Customer relationship
Marketing definition	Mass markets C(c)	Segments D(c) H(2) C(b), D(b)	I H(1)	Individual customer
Target of marketing activities	Gaining new customers D(a) H(2)	Maintaining old customers H(1) I C D(f)
Dominating marketing function	Marketing mix C(c), D(c)	Interactive marketing (supported by marketing mix activities) C(b), D(b) H(1), H(2), I
Price elasticity	Customers tend to be more sensitive to price C H(1), H(2) D	Customers tend to be less sensitive to price I
Communication	Campaigns C(c), D(c)	Ongoing H(1), H(2)	Interactive I, C(b), D(b)
Advertising media	Mass media C(c), D(c)	Direct media H(2) H(1)	Interactive direct media C(b), D(b)
Measurement of customer satisfaction	Monitoring marketing share (indirect approach) C(c) D(c)	Managing the customer base (direct approach) H(1), H(2) C(b), D(b), I
Customer information system	Ad hoc customer satisfaction surveys C(c), D(c)	Real-time customer feedback system H(1), H(2) I, C(b), D(b)
System of collecting customer information	Marketing research C(c), D(c)	Dialogue with customers H(1), H(2) I, C(b), D(b)
Recording of customer data	Disintegrated system C(c), D(c) H(2)	Integrated system H(1) I, C(b), D(b)
Main utiliser of customer information system	Marketing department C(c), D(c) H(2)	All customer-contact persons H (1) I,C(b), D(b)
Dominating quality dimension	Quality of output C(b), D(c), I	Quality of interactions C(b), D(b) H(2) H(1)
Production of quality	Primary concern of production C(c) D(c) I	The concern of all C(b), D(b) H(2) H(1)
Customer service emphasis	Low C(c), D(c)	High C(b), D(b) H(2), H(1), I
The role of internal marketing	No or limited importance to success	Substantial strategic importance to success C D I H(2) H(1)
Interdependency between marketing and other functions of the firm	Interface of no or limited strategic importance C D	Interface of substantial strategic importance H(2) H(1), I

I = Manufacturer of industrial goods
C = Manufacturer of non-durable consumer goods
D = Manufacturer of durable consumer goods

H(1) = Private hotel
b = business customers
a = abroad

H(2) = SBU of a chain of hotels
c = consumers
f = in Finland

ORGANISATION: DIFFERENT STRATEGIES AND MARKETING APPROACHES

The need for long-term marketing planning and strategies is obvious in every company, but the prevailing turbulent economic situation compels the companies towards increased flexibility and short-term decision-making. The *time perspective* is clearly illustrated in this respect. In this case, marketing to consumers is represented by short-term transaction marketing activity whereas marketing to business is a long-term relationship-based marketing activity. The hotels H(1) and H(2) can be placed between the two approaches. The difficulty faced by the researchers in the hotel case was one of customer differentiation, i.e. differentiating private from business customers. The business customer marketing approach in hotels can be considered more relationship-based marketing.

The dimensions labelled *focus of marketing* and *marketing definition* are more easily defined in so far as transaction marketing tends to be concentrated on products and mass markets, whereas relationship marketing, emphasising individual relationships with customers, dominates in the case of the private hotel H(1) and the manufacturer of industrial goods (I). In the case of the manufacturer of non-durable consumer goods (C) and the manufacturer of durable goods (D) the *focus of marketing* was on the product and its various characteristics including price. Customer relationships were important, but they were less emphasised than the product. For the manufacturer of industrial goods (I) the *focus of marketing* is on the customer relationship with some emphasis on the price/quality aspect of the product. Both of the hotels placed emphasis on customers, but in the private hotel H(1) customer relationships were more important than for the SBU hotel chain member H(2). The number of outlets/branches and the nature of the marketing channel are typical determinants of the nature of marketing activity along these dimensions. The dimension labelled *marketing definition*, in the firms manufacturing consumer non-durables (C) and consumer durables (D), is two-dimensional

in nature in that consumers were often seen as comprising a transactional mass market, or at most, segments, while business customers were treated as individuals. The private hotel H(1) individualised its marketing approach to a greater extent than any of the other four companies.

Responses to questions regarding the *target of marketing activities* dimension reflected a strong emphasis on maintaining existing (old) customers. In this context, comments such as 'this year' or 'at least at the moment' reveal, however, that the objectives of marketing activities are not always planned in the long-term perspective.

The five case companies described the *customer service emphasis* dimension as being primarily concerned with the building of bonds with customers to ensure long-term mutually advantageous relationships. Service was placed in a broader context as a multidimensional issue with an impact on relationships with specific target groups across a broad range of company activities. The line between the service as a core product or as a supplementary activity is purposefully somewhat blurred. As one interviewee dealing with consumer goods put it: 'Our whole activity is serving the customers.' The manufacturer of industrial goods (I) placed the highest emphasis on the physical aspects of customer service, e.g. installation, repair and maintenance services, licensed services, etc. In both hotels H(1) and H(2) a heavy emphasis was placed on customer service, which was considered to be bound to their image. This is to be expected in so far as service comprises the main part of the total product offering. The private hotel H(1) maintained the strongest desire to serve customers in all possible ways and situations. This desire was expressed as a willingness to tailor all services according to customer wants and thereby maximise service to the customer.

In the non-durable (C), durable (D) and industrial (I) manufacturing operations, the *dominating quality dimension* was described as technical (output) quality of the goods with some emphasis on the interaction between the buyer and the seller in the exchange process. The importance of interaction grew where manufacturers needed to co-operate with intermediaries on a regular basis.

In the case of both hotels H(1) and H(2) a large part of their services were produced in interaction between employees and customers. The interactive skills of employees were emphasised here.

The *production of quality* dimension was identified as the primary concern of production in the case of the manufacturer of non-durable consumer goods (C). While the first-buy of a consumer good is often influenced by the promotional elements of the marketing mix, e.g. advertising, subsequent re-buys are more influenced by technical quality. In the case of the manufacturer of durable consumer goods for consumer markets D(c), the customer-perceived quality was more influenced by the quality of the interaction. The manufacture of industrial goods (I) maintained that the *production of quality* was the concern of both production and all of those dealing with customers. Manufacturers of non-durable goods for business customers C(b) and durable goods for business customers D(b) saw functional quality to be the concern of all internal customers in the exchange process. In the case of the private hotel H(1), the *production of quality* was considered to be the concern of all employees in their roles as quality producers and marketers. The strong employee role as producer of quality in the private hotel can be attributed to the entrepreneurial spirit exhibited by the company. This perceived production role combined with job rotation served to encourage a strategic vision of quality among all employees of the private hotel. In the SBU hotel H(2), not all employees were considered to be in charge of quality to the same extent as those in the private hotel. The production of quality was primarily the concern of those employees actually providing the services and interacting with external customers. This difference can be attributed to the larger size and more functional structure of this hotel.

All case companies made use of both traditional transaction marketing and relationship marketing to varying degrees. However, the emphasis varied both between and within industries. In examining company profiles across dimensions, the private hotel H(1) can be considered to practise more relationship-type marketing than the SBU hotel H(2). On the basis of these results, it could be argued that the theoretical juxtapositioning of transaction marketing against relationship marketing is unjustified. All case firms utilised the broadest level of the exchange model, i.e. traditional or transaction marketing. Traditional marketing is most at home in firms manufacturing non-durable consumer goods and to a slightly lesser extent in those manufacturing durable goods. However, it is more difficult to evaluate the relative importance of traditional marketing in the case of services or industrial products. Variables such as numbers of customers and various strategic issues would influence any evaluation of the importance of traditional marketing in such cases.

Another consideration is the variation in exchange objects from firm to firm. In the case of the manufacturing firms, the emphasis seemed to be more on the technical quality and image/reputation of their products and services as the primary exchange offering. The hotels, and the private hotel H(1) in particular, considered the functional quality of the service and its consequent image and reputation as being of primary importance in addition to that of the technical quality exchange offering. In this case the image and climate of interaction were strongly associated in the minds of respondents.

INTERACTIVE MARKETING

Interactive marketing issues were emphasised by respondents in relation to the *dominating marketing function* dimension. Most service operations, by their nature, involve personnel and customer interaction in the simultaneous production, marketing and consumption of the service. Functional quality is a major exchange item in the service provider/customer exchange process, e.g. in both hotels. Technical service quality was also used to improve interactions between manufacturers and intermediaries, e.g. linked information technology. The level of interaction between consumer goods manufacturers and retailers was evidenced by in-store promotional stands in retail outlets. A greater level of interaction and co-operation was reported between consumer goods manufacturers and wholesalers. The level of interaction between the industrial goods manufacturing company (I) and its potential customers was high due to the customised nature of the jobbing process requiring extensive sales negotiation and planning on a job-by-job basis. The time factor was a feature of this interaction, e.g. some larger projects could take from three to five years to negotiate. The highly individualised nature of many projects often necessitated the formation of teams from both exchanging parties. Extensive and prolonged interaction and information exchange regarding production and delivery planning was the norm in industrial exchanges.

Interviewees from manufacturing firms singled out word of mouth as the most important way/*system of collecting business customer information*. Information was gathered from partners and co-operatives, salespersons and colleagues. However, there were big differences on all dimensions of information collection and utilisation regarding consumers and business customers. All five case companies utilised some kind of real-time customer feedback system. In the case of the hotels, customer information forms were placed in the guests' rooms on a daily basis.

The dimensions labelled *recording of customer data* and *main utiliser of customer information system* were represented to differing degrees in the two hotels. The private hotel H(1) maintained databases on contact level, use of services and special (individual) customer requirements. In addition to the individual hotel customer database, the SBU hotel H(2) utilised the chain's central register of larger customers and their usage patterns including meetings at any of the chain's hotels. It was interesting to note that the hotels also used feedback in different ways. In the private hotel H(1) the manager read each guest comment personally. Individual thank-you notes were dispatched to each guest and their requests are facilitated immediately. The private hotel H(1) interviewee mentioned that customers were more than willing to give positive and negative feedback. The main users of customer information in this hotel were marketing and reception. Marketers in such a small hotel were also customer-contact personnel. In contrast, the market-

ing department was more defined in the SBU hotel H(2). Customer comments were followed up by telephone or mail. In this respect, customers were also treated on an individual basis via the customer feedback system. Although both hotels could be said to possess real-time customer feedback systems, they did not systematically collect this data in databases. Neither of the hotels employed market research methods in the development of customer information, preferring instead to concentrate on personal interaction with customers. This personalised market intelligence system was crucially important to both hotels in the ongoing monitoring of external customer needs and wants. The same approach was used in the collection of internal customer intelligence and was used as input in the development of hotel marketing strategy. The nature, quantity and quality of external and internal customer information collection and utilisation can be a useful indicator of whether a company's marketing approach is transaction- or relationship-oriented.

In summary, the dimensions labelled *recording of customer data* and *main utiliser of customer information system* offered preliminary evidence of interactive marketing activity within the overall model of service exchange.

INTERNAL MARKETING

The *role of internal marketing* was clearly emphasised as a crucial success factor in all five case companies. The construction of a solid customer orientation requires the development of the new service-oriented attitude in the mind of every employee of the firm. Employees of both consumer goods manufacturers (C) and (D) were encouraged towards a greater customer orientation by their attendance at external and internal educational courses. Further evidence of internal marketing was uncovered in the non-durable consumer goods manufacturer (C) in the form of an in-company magazine. The durable consumer goods manufacturer (D) used an internal video system to broadcast part-time marketer contacts and negotiations with customers. The private hotel H(1) maintained good internal communications and high motivation levels among employees. The high motivation levels and consequent congruence of marketing thinking were achieved through a close co-operative work environment, management by example, i.e. full management participation in all customer service tasks, and a functioning job rotation scheme. The less personalised approach to internal marketing in the SBU hotel H(2) was considered to be a function of its larger size. Nevertheless, the educational course approach and interactive internal information flow was also strongly in evidence here.

Case companies were also examined for their level of *interdependency between marketing and other functions*. The marketing department of the non-durable consumer goods manufacturer (C) had firm connections with product development and some connections with the buying and production departments. In the durable consumer goods manufacturer (D) marketing and product development were also closely related. Marketing and production were particularly closely related due to the fact that the firm was a producer of raw material for the dynamic clothing industry. The financial and marketing departments worked together in the creation of franchising solutions to manage the intermediate customer base better . In the case of the industrial goods manufacturer (I) interaction was evident among all functions due to size and jobbing orientation of the company. The interdependency among functional areas was also strong in the private hotel H(1) due to the high level of commitment to job rotation. Similarly, in order to facilitate job rotation, the SBU hotel H(2) plans to increase co-operation between marketing, service production and finance. However, the size and more disintegrated organisational structure of the SBU hotel H(2) made for less interdependency than was the case in the private hotel H(1).

Although the case material presented here is limited in terms of the number of firms surveyed, the depth of the survey in each case offers useful illustration of the different elements of the proposed model of service exchange in action. For the same reason the researchers were also afforded the possibility of drawing some additional conclusions related to the nature of the service exchange process: 1. the importance of fulfilment of promises and trust was considered an important element in the marketing practice of all case companies; 2. although service marketing is considered to be close to the relationship juxtaposition of the transaction–relationship marketing continuum (Grönroos, 1990c), this study has positioned business-to-business marketing at the same extreme and in many cases even further along the continuum than the services companies surveyed. This second point would seem to argue that the service exchange model may have further application in the business-to-business exchange process.

CONCLUSIONS

The interactive and interdependent nature of the process of service exchange requires the service marketer to formulate interactive, internal and traditional marketing plans which themselves are integrated from first principles. Dependence on the traditional marketing planning approach alone, or the *post hoc* addition of interactive and/or internal marketing elements, fails to cater for the complexity of the three-way exchange relationship between service organisation, internal customer and external customer. A first step in this process is the establishment of an integrated marketing information system designed to understand and monitor internal and external customers' service demands in tandem. The proposed service exchange model and associated case research presents some argument against the juxtapositioning of transaction and relationship marketing in the context of service exchange. In addition, the preliminary evidence regarding business-to-business marketing activity places it at least beside services marketing in terms of its relationship focus and points to the possible extension and modification of the model to include the business-to-business exchange process. At a macro-level, there remains considerable scope for theory development regarding the consequences on society of the interactive and interdependent behaviours of service customers, service providers and service facilitators. Services marketing researchers have many challenging and exciting frontiers to cross in the future.

REFERENCES

Albrecht, Karl and Ron Zemke (1985), *Service America!: Doing Business in the New Economy*, Dow Jones-Irwin, Homewood, Ill; also Warner Books Edition (1990), NY.

'American Marketing Association Approves New Marketing Definition' (1985), *Marketing News*, no. 5, 1 March.

Bagozzi, R.P. (1974), 'Marketing as an Organised Behavioural System of Exchange', *Journal of Marketing*, vol. 38, October, pp. 77–81.

Bagozzi, R.P. (1975), 'Marketing as Exchange', *Journal of Marketing*, vol. 39, October, pp. 32–9.

Bagozzi, R.P. (1979), 'Towards a Formal Theory of Marketing Exchange' in O. Ferrel, S.W. Brown and C.W. Lamb, Jr (eds.), *Conceptual and Theoretical Developments in Marketing*, Proceedings Series, American Marketing Association, pp. 431–47.

Barnes, James G. and William J. Glynn (1992), 'Beyond Technology: What the Customer Wants Now Is Service', *Proceedings, 2nd International Research Seminar in Service Management*, Institut d'Administration des Enterprises, Université d'Aixmarseille III, L'Agelonde, France, pp. 25–41.

Beatty, Sharon E. and Benton E. Gup (1989), 'A Guide to Building a Customer Service Orientation', *Journal of Retail Banking*, vol. 11, no. 2, Summer, pp. 15–22.

Berry, Leonard L. (1983), 'Relationship Marketing' in L. Leonard Berry, G. Lynn Shostack and Gregory D. Upah (eds.), *Emerging Perspectives on Services Marketing*, Proceedings Series, American Marketing Association, Chicago, Ill., pp. 25–8.

Berry, Leonard L, David R. Bennett and Carter W. Brown (1989), *Service Quality: A Profit Strategy for Financial Institutions*, Dow Jones-Irwin, Homewood, Ill.

Blomqvist, R., I. Dahl and T. Haeger (1993), *Relationsmarknadssföring. Strategioch method för service konkurrens*, Göteborg.

Blount, W.F. (1988), 'AT&T Service Quality and Renewal', *AT&T Technology*, vol. 3, no. 1, pp. 2–7.

Borch, Fred J. (1957), 'The Marketing Philosophy as a Way of Business Life' in *The Marketing Concept: Its Meaning to Management*, Marketing Series, no. 99, American Management Association, NY, pp. 3–5.

Borden, N.H. (1965), 'The Concept of the Marketing Mix' in G. Schwartz (ed.), *Science in Marketing*, Wiley & Sons, NY.

Bowen, David E. (1986), 'Managing Customers as Human Resources in Service Organisations', *Human Resource Management*, vol. 25, pp. 371–84.

Bowen, David E. (1990), 'Interdisciplinary Study of Service: Some Progress, Some Prospects', *Journal of Business Research*, vol. 20, no. 1, January, pp. 71–9.

Bowen, David E. and Benjamin Schneider (1985), 'Boundary-spanning-role Employees and the Service Encounter: Some Guidelines for Management and Research' in John A. Czepiel, Michael R. Solomon and Carol F. Surprenant (eds.), *The Service Encounter: Managing Employee/Customer Interaction in Service Businesses*, D.C. Heath & Company, Lexington, Mass., pp. 127–47.

Bowen, David E. and Benjamin Schneider (1988), 'Services Marketing and Management: Implications for Organisational Behaviour', *Research in Organisational Behaviour*, vol. 10, pp. 43–80.

Bradley, M. Frank (1991), *Industrial Marketing Strategy*, Prentice-Hall International (UK) Ltd, Hertfordshire, England.

Calonius, Henrik (1986), 'A Market Behaviour Framework' in Kristian Moller and M. Paltschik (eds.), *Contemporary Research in Marketing*, proceedings of the 15th European Marketing Academy Conference, Helsinki, Finland.

Calonius, Henrik (1988), 'A Buying Process Model' in Keith Blois and Stephen Parkinson (eds.), *Innovative Marketing: A European Perspective*, proceedings of the 17th European Marketing Academy Conference, University of Bradford, England, pp. 86–103.

Carlzon, Jan (1987), *Moments of Truth*, Ballinger, NY.

Carson, David and Audrey Gilmore (1989–90), 'Customer Care: The Neglected Domain', *Irish Marketing Review*, vol. 4, no. 3, pp. 49–61.

Chase, Richard B. and David A. Garvin (1989), 'The Service Factory', *Harvard Business Review*, July–August, pp. 30–38.

Christopher, Martin, Adrian Payne and David Ballantyne (1991), *Relationship Marketing: Bringing Quality, Customer Service and Marketing Together*, Butterworth-Heinemann, Oxford, England.

Congram, Carole A. (1991), 'Building Relationships that Last' in Carole A. Congram and Margaret L. Friedman (eds.), *The AMA Handbook of Marketing for the Service Industries*, American Management Association, AMACOM, NY, pp. 263–79.

Copulsky, Jonathan R. and Michael J. Wolf (1990), 'Relationship Marketing: Positioning for the Future', *Journal of Business Strategy*, July–August, pp. 16–20.

Culliton, J.W. (1948), *The Management of Marketing Costs*, Andover Press, Andover, Mass.

de Ferrer, Robert J. (1986), 'A Case for European Management', *The Information Management Development Review*, 2, pp. 275–81.

Desatnick, Robert L. (1987), *Managing to Keep the Customer: How to Achieve and Maintain Superior Customer Service throughout the Organisation*, Jossey-Bass Inc., SF.

Eiglier, Pierre, Eric Langeard, Christopher H. Lovelock, John E.G. Bateson and Robert F. Young (1977), *Marketing Consumer Services: New Insights*, Report 77-115, Marketing Science Institute, Cambridge, Mass.,

December.

Forsgren, Mats and Jan Johanson (1992), 'Managing Internationalisation in Business Networks' in Mats Forsgren and Jan Johanson (eds.), *Managing Networks in International Business*, Gordon and Breech Science Publishing, Philadelphia, Penn., chapter 1, pp. 1–15.

Frazier, G.L., R.E. Spekman and C.R. O'Neal (1988), 'Just-in-Time Exchange Relationships in Industrial Markets', *Journal of Marketing*, vol. 52, October, pp. 52–67.

George, William R. (1977), 'The Retailing of Services: A Challenging Future', *Journal of Retailing*, vol. 53, Fall, pp. 85–98.

George, William R. (1990), 'Internal Marketing and Organisational Behaviour – A Partnership in Developing Customer-conscious Employees at Every Level', *Journal of Business Research*, vol. 20, pp. 63–70.

George, William R. and Fran Compton (1985), 'How to Initiate a Marketing Perspective in a Health Services Organisation', *Journal of Health Care Marketing*, vol. 5, no. 1, Winter, pp. 29–37.

Grönroos, Christian (1981), 'Internal Marketing: An Integral Part of Marketing Theory' in James H. Donnelly and William R. George (eds.), *Marketing of Services*, Proceedings Series, American Marketing Association, pp. 236–8.

Grönroos, Christian (1982), 'An Applied Service Marketing Theory', *European Journal of Marketing*, vol. 16, no. 7, pp. 30–41.

Grönroos, Christian (1988), 'Service Quality: The Six Criteria of Good Perceived Service Quality', *Review of Business*, vol. 9, no. 3, Winter, pp. 10–13.

Grönroos, Christian (1989), *A Relationship Approach to Marketing: The Need for a New Paradigm*, working papers, Svenska Handelshögskolan, Helsinki.

Grönroos, Christian (1990a), 'Marketing Redefined', *Management Decision*, vol. 28, no. 8, pp. 5–9.

Grönroos, Christian (1990b), 'Relationship Approach to Marketing in Service Contexts: Marketing and Organisational Behaviour Interface', *Journal of Business Research*, vol. 20, pp. 3–11.

Grönroos, Christian (1990c), *Service Management and Marketing: Managing the Moments of Truth in Service Competition*, Lexington Books, Mass.

Grönroos, Christian (1991), 'The Marketing Strategy Continuum: Towards a Marketing Concept for the 1990s', *Management Decision*, vol. 29, no. 1, pp. 7–13.

Grönroos, Christian and Evert Gummesson (eds.) (1985), *Service Marketing – Nordic School Perspectives*, research report no. R. 1985:2, Department of Business Administration, University of Stockholm.

Grönroos, Christian and Evert Gummesson (1986), 'Service Orientation in Industrial Marketing' in M. Venkatesan, Diane M. Schmalensee and Claudia

Marshall (eds.), *Creativity in Services Marketing: What's New, What Works, What's Developing*, Proceedings Series, American Marketing Association, Chicago, pp. 23–6.

Grove, Stephen J. and Raymond P. Fisk (1983), 'The Dramaturgy of Services Exchange: An Analytical Framework for Services Marketing' in Leonard L. Berry, G. Lynn Shostack and Gregory D. Upah (eds.), *Emerging Perspectives in Services Marketing*, Proceedings Series, American Marketing Association, Chicago, Ill., pp. 45–9.

Gummesson, Evert (1987), 'The New Marketing – Developing Long-term Interactive Relationships', *Long Range Planning*, vol. 20, no. 4, pp. 10–20.

Gummesson, Evert (1990), 'Marketing Organisation in Service Businesses: The Role of the Part-time Marketer' in R. Teare, Luiz Moutinho and Neil Morgan (eds.), *Managing and Marketing Services in the 1990s*, Cassell Education Limited, London, pp. 35–48.

Gummesson, Evert (1991), 'Marketing-orientation Revisited: The Crucial Role of the Part-time Marketer', *European Journal of Marketing*, vol. 25, no. 2, pp. 60–75.

Håkansson, Håken (ed.) (1982), *International Marketing and Purchasing of Industrial Goods*, John Wiley & Sons, Chichester, England.

Håkansson, Håken (ed.) (1987), *Industrial Technological Development*, Croom Helm, London.

Hopkins, D.S. and E.L. Bailey (1970), 'Customer Service – A Progress Report', The Conference Board, NY.

Houston, Franklin S. and J.B. Gassenheimer (1987), 'Marketing and Exchange', *Journal of Marketing*, vol. 51, October, pp. 3–18.

Hunt, Shelby D. (1976), 'The Nature and Scope of Marketing', *Journal of Marketing*, vol. 40, July, pp. 17–28.

Hunt, Shelby D. (1983), 'General Theories and the Fundamental Explananda of Marketing', *Journal of Marketing*, 46, Fall, pp. 9–17.

Jackson, Barbara Bund (1985), 'Build Customer Relationships that Last', *Harvard Business Review*, November–December, pp. 120–28.

Johansson, Jan and Lars Gunnar Mattsson (1987), 'Interorganisational Relations in Industrial Systems: A Network Approach Compared with the Transaction–Cost Approach', *International Studies of Management and Organisation*, vol. XVII, no. 1, Spring.

Kiess-Moser, Eva and James G. Barnes (1992), 'Emerging Trends in Marketing Research: The Link with Customer Satisfaction', Report 82–92, The Conference Board of Canada, Ottawa, Ontario.

Kotler, Philip (1972), 'A Generic Concept of Marketing', *Journal of Marketing*, 36, April, pp. 46–54.

Kotler, Philip (1980), *Marketing Management: Analysis, Planning and Control*, 4th ed., Englewood Cliffs, NJ.

Kotler, Philip and S.J. Levy (1969), 'Broadening the Concept of Marketing', *Journal of Marketing*, 33, January, pp. 10–15.

Lehtinen, Uolevi (1983), 'Changes in Interpreting International Marketing', *The Finnish Journal of Business Economics*, vol. 32, no. 1, pp. 94–6.

Lehtinen, Uolevi (1985), 'Functional Interactions and International Services Marketing', 2nd Open International IMP Research Seminar on International Marketing, Uppsala, September.

Lehtinen, Uolevi, Anna Hankimaa and Tuula Mittilä (1994), 'Measuring the Intensity of Relationship Marketing', unpublished working paper, University of Tampere.

Levy, S.J. and Gerald Zaltman (1975), *Marketing Society and Conflict*, Prentice-Hall, Englewood Cliffs, NJ.

Lindquist, Lars J. (1987), 'Quality and Service Value in the Consumption of Services' in Carol F. Surprenant (ed.), *Add Value to your Service*, American Marketing Association, Chicago, Ill.

McCarthy, E. Jerome (1960), *Basic Marketing*, Irwin, Homewood, Ill.

McKenna, Regis (1985), *The Regis Touch*, Addison-Wesley, Reading, Mass.

McKenna, Regis (1991), *Relationship Marketing: Successful Strategies for the Age of the Customer*, Addison-Wesley, Reading, Mass.

McKitterick, John B. (1957), *What Is the Marketing Management Concept? Frontiers of Marketing Thought and Action*, American Marketing Association, Chicago, Ill.

Martin, Charles L. and Charles A. Pranter (1989), 'Compatibility Management: Customer-to-Customer Relations in Service Environments', *Journal of Services Marketing*, vol. 3, no. 3, Summer, pp. 5–15.

Mayo, Michael C. (1990), 'The Services Marketing Literature: A Review and Critique, *Canadian Journal of Marketing Research*, vol. 9, pp. 33–41.

Mills, Peter K. (1986), *Managing Service Industries: Organisational Practices in a Post-industrial Economy*, Ballinger, Cambridge, Mass.

Mills, Peter K. and D.J. Moberg (1982), 'Perspectives on the Technology of Service Operations', *Academy of Management Review*, vol. 7, no. 3, pp. 467–78.

Mills, Peter K., Richard B. Chase and Newton Margulies (1983), 'Motivating the Client/Employee System as a Service Production Strategy', *Academy of Management Review*, vol. 8, no. 2, pp. 301–10.

Normann, Richard (1984), *Service Management: Strategy and Leadership*, John Wiley & Sons, Chichester, England.

Normann, Richard (1991), *Service Management: Strategy and Leadership in Service Businesses*, 2nd edition, John Wiley & Sons, Chichester, England.

Oldano, T.L. (1987), 'Relationship Segmentation' in Carol F. Surprenant (ed.), *Add Value to your Service*, American Marketing Association, Chicago, Ill., pp. 143–6.

Parkinson, J.J. and Benjamin Schneider (1979), 'Some Correlates of Experienced Job Stress: A Boundary Role Study', *Academy of Management Journal*, 22, pp. 270–81.

Peters, Tom (1988), 'New Products, New Markets, New Competition, New Thinking', *The Economist*, March, p. 20.

Reichheld, Frederick F. and W. Earl Sasser (1990), 'Zero Defections: Quality Comes to Services', *Harvard Business Review*, vol. 68, no. 5, September–October, pp. 105–11.

Rosenberg, Larry J. and John A. Czepiel (1984), 'A Marketing Approach for Customer Retention', *Journal of Consumer Marketing*, 1, pp. 45–51.

Ryans, Adrian B. and Dick R. Wittink (1977), 'The Marketing of Services: Categorisation with Implications for Strategy' in B. Greenberg and D. Bellinger (eds.), Proceedings series, American Marketing Association, Chicago, Ill. pp. 312–14.

Schneider, Benjamin (1980), 'The Service Organisation: Climate Is Crucial', *Organizational Dynamics*, Autumn, p. 54.

Sellers, Patricia (1989), 'Getting Customers to Love You', *Fortune*, 13 March, pp. 38–49.

Turnbull, Peter W. and Jean-Paul Valla (eds.) (1986), *Strategies for International Industrial Marketing*, Croom Helm, London.

Webster, F.E., Jr (1992), 'The Changing Role of Marketing in the Corporation', *Journal of Marketing*, vol. 56, October, pp. 1–17.

READING 18

Quality Improvement in a Services Marketing Context

Audrey Gilmore and David Carson

INTRODUCTION

Quality is a much abused term throughout aspects of business and by marketers in particular. Historically, when marketers talk of improving quality the focus has been on improving the features of the product or service. While this is a wholly acceptable objective, alone it displays a myopic view of the 'total marketing effort'. That is, marketing is not just concerned with the *product* dimension, it must maintain a *balance* with decisions on price, promotion and distribution.

Equally, when improving any aspect of marketing quality it is not enough to focus only on the prescriptive aspects of improvement but consideration must be given to the *implementation* of quality improvement. Thus, this article is concerned with two main issues, the full spectrum of 'quality improvement' in marketing and the implementation dimensions of decision-making on quality. This discussion uses conceptual models to develop both themes.

Many authors (Morgan and Piercy, 1991; Schmalensee, 1991; Witcher, 1990) argue that marketing practitioners' and academics' response to the quality issue has been unremarkable. Indeed they go so far as to say that the existing literature on the nature and focus of the interface between marketing and quality has been wholly inadequate.

IMPROVING PRODUCT QUALITY

Most of the literature which exists on the relationship between quality and marketing focuses primarily on the tangible aspects of quality improvement and deals with product quality in particular. Indeed, even this literature on product quality has been deemed inadequate. A recent article (Morgan and Piercy, 1991) quotes Phillips et al.'s comment in 1983 that 'in view of the importance of product quality it is surprising that so little attention has been paid to it by marketing scholars', and adds that there has been little evidence in the literature since to change that opinion. There has been scant attention given to the quality improvement of any other functions of marketing activity. There is evidence that this is the case in practice also. Using the example of recession-hit fast-food marketers Bonoma (1991) describes how they go about improving the quality of their marketing activity by adding more product features, rather than giving better service, changing the restaurant sites or improving the value for money.

TOTAL QUALITY MANAGEMENT AND MARKETING

To date, academics and practitioners in both services and physical goods marketing have focused on the 'product' aspect of the marketing mix when improving quality. Much of the recent development in this quality improvement has been as a result of Total Quality programmes which in many cases concentrated on improving systems and processes which then impact on product quality. Total Quality Management has also attempted to improve employees' perceptions pertaining to the performance quality of the systems and procedures and thereby the product offering. Examples of private companies in the USA which have adopted this philosophy are Ford, Hewlett Packard and McDonnell-Douglas. In these companies TQM has been described as the managerial philosophy which entails the involvement of the entire organisation in the quest for continual improvement (Juran, 1988).

THE FULLY EXTENDED PRODUCT AND QUALITY

However, improving the product offering is not enough for improving quality throughout the whole of the marketing function. Consider the fundamental concept of marketing in relation to the marketing mix function. This concept requires that marketing variables must be fully integrated for maximum impact and effect. If this is not so the marketing effort may be wasteful.

The marketing mix is essentially a balance of interrelating activities and techniques which must come together for proper efficiency and impact. If one component of the marketing mix is changed then it will have an effect on the other variables. Any changes made to the components of the marketing mix should be carried out with the total marketing picture in view. Each variable should be seen in the context of the other variables. A good product poorly distributed may never reach the market or a good product which is either priced too high or too low may have a limited appeal for its intended target market. Similarly, a change in promotional activity on its own will probably be counter-productive. Increasing promotional activity alone could create a mismatch through having insufficient stocks to meet customers' demand or using different promotional offers for the same product may confuse the customer.

Thus, if the quality of one component (the product) is substantially improved then one should naturally expect compatible improvement in quality in all other components of the mix. These issues sharpen considerably in the context of services marketing. In services at least theory has learned to accommodate the notion of the 'fully extended product' to improve the overall service quality by considering all aspects of the product by taking into account and making improvements in a balanced co-ordinated way. The concept of the fully extended product tries to take account of this need. A company's marketing offerings can be identified by detailed consideration of the fully extended service product, that is, the company's total offer to the customer. This can be described by taking account of the pre-purchase, during purchase and the post-purchase experience.

Figure 1, a model of the 'Fully Extended Product',[1] serves to illustrate some of the key components of the purchase stages although naturally these may vary according to the particular situation.

Pre-purchase experience incorporates all those factors that lead the customer towards a decision of choosing and using the product/service. This may include their exposure to any advertising and promotional activity.

Purchase experience encompasses everything that happens during the transaction or use of a product. Examples of this may include the current availability of the product/service, staff accessibility and the quality of the information and advice given.

Post-experience involves all post-purchase motivations and company contact to which the customer may be subjected. Direct customer contact such as the use of mailshots and customer loyalty schemes may be included at this stage.

The contention here is that in order to improve the quality of marketing it is vital to pay attention to detail in all aspects of a company's marketing offerings. The marketing mix concept needs to be expanded and adapted to suit the particular service situation. It is marketing management's task to determine how the marketing mix component parts may be brought together to make a complete whole, through committing

FIGURE 1:   FULLY EXTENDED PRODUCT

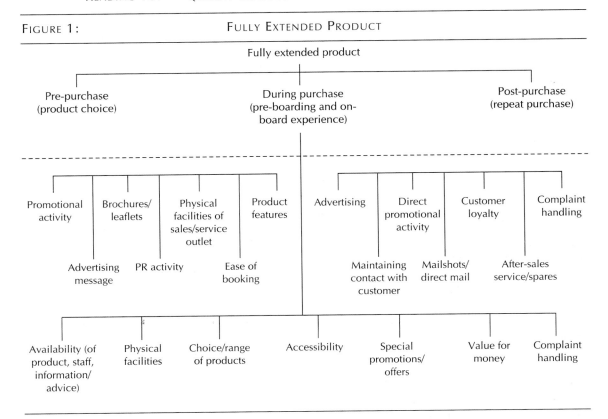

itself to a thorough decision-making process. The design and management of the marketing mix will depend on how the company perceives its strengths and weaknesses in relation to the threats and opportunities in the market and environment in which it is to compete.

THE MARKETING CONCEPT AND QUALITY

So far the discussion has focused on the tasks which marketing is involved with but the marketing function is not necessarily the same as the marketing department's task. The marketing function is spread over a large part of the organisation outside the marketing department and all the activities which have an impact on the current and future buyer behaviour of the customer cannot be taken care of only by marketing specialists. Many staff and support functions include an element of marketing as well. In most firms a large number of employees have something to do

with marketing. These people perform interfirm functions which require a service orientation similar to customer-contact functions. People involved in support functions such as production, technical servicing and invoicing have been called 'part-time marketers' (Grönroos, 1990a). Often these people do not know they have this role as well as their functional tasks and management may also fail to understand this dual role responsibility. However, because marketing is spread all over the organisation it has been argued that marketing specialists can take care of only part of the total marketing function and therefore the nature of the marketing cannot be only that of a specialist function (Grönroos, 1990b). The concept of marketing is market-oriented management rather than a separate function and this is particularly so in a services marketing situation. Thus, it is important to recognise that the marketing concept transcends all management functions and the whole organisation.

FIGURE 2: SPECTRUM OF KEY MARKETING
MANAGEMENT FUNCTIONS FOR QUALITY IN
CUSTOMER RELATIONS

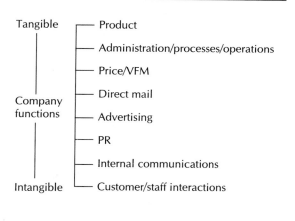

CUSTOMER RELATIONS AND QUALITY

Consequently, there is clearly a need for management to take account of all marketing functions and related activity when considering quality improvement. Therefore a deeper understanding of the marketing function based on the customer relations and marketing situations which actually exist is required in order to improve the quality of the company's marketing activity. It has been argued that the most important issue in marketing is to establish, strengthen and develop customer relations where they can be commercialised at a profit and where individual and organisational objectives are met(Grönroos, 1990a and b).

The size and shape of the marketing function depends on the nature of customer relations. Each service company should ensure its company functions are organised in such a way as to maximise on its customer relationships. The essence of customer relations is represented by the interaction points between a company's staff and its customers. These interaction points can happen obviously at the personal interface between individuals but also and less obviously at the intangible/impersonal interaction between company communication and customers. Thus, all company communication techniques including advertis-

ing, direct mail, public relations, etc. serve to contribute to customer relations. All these interactions need to be fully integrated if they are to be effective. The effectiveness of total service quality will depend on the quality of customer/staff interactions in all areas of marketing activity. The key generic marketing functions for a service situation are shown in Figure 2. These functions can be subdivided and extended according to the type of business activity in which a company operates and its company structure.

This model (Figure 2) recognises the need to focus managers' attention on improving the quality of *all* marketing activity and related functions. It can be related to any business circumstance and service as a 'descriptive' framework on this issue. However, in adopting this framework for the purpose of more penetrative understanding in a specific situation it is then necessary to elaborate on this simple framework in order to arrive at a more comprehensive picture. Some of the description so far acknowledges the activity of quality in the service context. Therefore to examine and develop this model in improving the quality of marketing in a services context it will be important to take account of the fundamental characteristics of services.

SERVICE CHARACTERISTICS AND QUALITY

The multidimensional nature of the quality construct is found in much of the services marketing literature. Various studies (Carson and Gilmore, 1989–90; Grönroos, 1982; Kuhn, 1962) identify and describe some dimensions of service quality. It is generally accepted that quality is about consistent conformance to customer expectations (Crosby, 1979) and 'fitness for purpose' (Juran, 1988). Principally customers have both instrumental and psychological expectations about a product or service performance (Swan and Combs, 1976), where expectations relate to both quantifiable, hard data and qualitative, soft data. Hard data have been described as relating to performance and reliability standards or any tangible dimensions whereas soft data are those concerned

FIGURE 3:   MARKETING MANAGEMENT DIMENSIONS OF SERVICE QUALITY

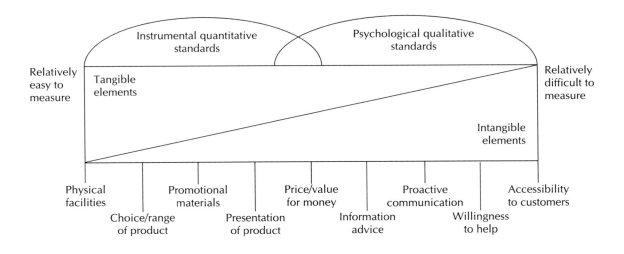

with descriptions of and knowledge about customers' feelings, perceptions and requirements (Smith, 1987). These are more difficult to measure because they are intangible.

The important elements of this issue are brought together in a conceptual model of the 'Dimensions of Service Quality' by Carson and Gilmore (1989–90). The scope of these dimensions ranges from the hard, tangible, relatively easy to measure and evaluate aspects, such as packaging and product range, to the soft, intangible, more difficult to measure and evaluate aspects such as the degree of courtesy and consideration experienced by the customer. A focus on both tangible and intangible dimensions of marketing offerings is necessary in order to improve the quality of these aspects of the marketing mix. Considering these elements from the perspective of marketing management the same continuum with its hard and soft, tangible and intangible, criteria can be used to produce a continuum as illustrated in Figure 3. This model shows that in order to implement a market-led initiative successfully emphasis must be placed on the intangible aspects of the total offering as well as dealing with the tangible aspects.

Consequently there is a need for an integrated approach to quality improvement in marketing management functions which needs to focus on the quality of the tangible and intangible aspects of the marketing offerings, in addition to focusing on the quality of all marketing activity and related functions. In order to do this we must therefore bring Figures 2 and 3 together in an integrated way. This is shown in the matrix model in Figure 4.

The quality improvement model serves to match marketing functions with the service quality dimensions showing how the marketing function and activity are influenced by the tangible and intangible nature of the service elements. Some of the company functions and activities have more tangible aspects than others. For example, product management focuses on issues such as the physical facilities and choice and range of products available. People and staff management functions are made up of predominantly intangible aspects such as being accessible and customer-friendly.

The main benefit of the matrix is twofold. First, the matrix format shows the interrelationships of the company functions with the service quality dimensions and as such demonstrates the importance of addressing both the tangible and intangible aspects of service quality improvement

FIGURE 4:   A HOLISTIC MODEL FOR QUALITY IMPROVEMENT

	Tangible								
Dimensions of service quality									**Intangible**
	Physical facilities	Choice/ range of products	Promotional materials	Presentation of product	Price/value for money	Information advice	Proactive communica-tion	Willingness to help	Accessibility to customers
Product management	●	●		●					
Administration, processes, operations		●		●					
Pricing strategy					●				
Advertising , direct mail, PR			●				●		
Internal communication						●	●		
Customer/ staff interaction						●	●	●	●

Tangible ⎫
           ⎬ Company functions
Intangible ⎭

   Denotes the dimensions of service quality which have most relevance to each company function

in an integrated way. Second, in illustrating that service quality is both tangible and intangible, it particularly emphasises the intangible dimensions and it enables the specific components of tangible and intangible to be positioned within the overall service quality concept.

To explain further it serves to emphasise the folly of improving only the product aspect of the marketing mix as has been the focus of many quality improvement programmes in the past. The product aspects of the marketing activity such as the physical facilities, layout of the service area, choice and range of products are shown in the top left quadrant of the matrix model. When illustrated in this way it emphasises how the tangible product aspects are only a fraction of the company's total marketing activity to be taken into account in order to improve overall service quality. Any quality programme which focuses on the product aspects alone neglects many of the more intangible aspects shown in the bottom

right quadrant. These are the more intangible aspects of marketing activity which impact strongly upon the internal and external communication dimensions and are the foundation-stone of good marketing performance.

It is vital to recognise that all the dimensions on the model have an important role to play and are all interactive. An overconcentration on one area to the neglect of the others may cause a serious imbalance of marketing activity and therefore result in a waste of resources and only minimal improvement.

OPERATIONALISATION OF THE MODEL FOR QUALITY IMPROVEMENT IN A SERVICES CONTEXT: A CASE EXAMPLE

The remainder of this article will focus on illustrating the model in practice by using the example of a car ferry ship company; that is, a description of the development of a quality improvement which is currently being implemented in the

FIGURE 5: QUALITY IMPROVEMENT IN OPERATION

	Personnel	Issues to address	Tasks
Product management Physical facilities Choice/range of products Presentation of product	Chefs/stewards	New items for menu Presentation of food	Create variety Lighter meals/snacks Special needs customers Items for lower price range Freshness Hotness Menu displays Serving presentation
Advertising management Promotional materials Proactive communication	Advertising, direct mail and PR managers	Passenger communication	Improve/standardise messages Promote offerings Creativity
Pricing management Price/value for money	Managers/cashiers/chefs	Pricing/value for money	Investigate costs/margins Special offers Family meals

largest ferry ship company in the world, Stena, with a particular focus on the company's Irish/Scottish route. Stena's ferry ships each have a variety of products and services on board. These include a restaurant/cafeteria, a bar with live entertainment, a video lounge/cinema, a children's play area, a snack bar, and comfortable lounges for each of the customer segments: foot passengers, motorists and freight drivers.

The impetus for improvement in the quality of its marketing activity stems from the Stena company's recent acquisition of Sealink British Ferries in the United Kingdom. Quality is the basis of Stena's management philosophy. This quality dimension is so important to Stena that the company has a main board director with responsibility for quality and also a functional department solely for monitoring quality improvements. The Stena philosophy requires all staff, regardless of function, to seek to improve the quality of the Stena service. The philosophy is translated to practice through the 'cruise ship' concept, whereby guests are encouraged to enjoy a cruise ship atmosphere while travelling. Quality 'standards' are set by performance ratings from guests using the service. The emphasis is always on striving to increase or improve the standards of

the quality of service. In contrast this philosophy would have been generally considered alien to Sealink's activities before the acquisition, hence there is a considerable challenge for the new company's management to implement a programme of quality improvement.

The first steps in improving the quality of services marketing began with an analysis of customer perceptions of the company's current service quality using the dimensions of service quality as seen in the model in Figure 4 and further identifying how management could improve the performance of the overall service. The analysis focused on the customers' perceptions and also took account of the opinions and perceptions of travel agents who acted as the company's distribution and sales network.

The analysis highlighted the quality dimensions, illustrated in Figure 3, which required immediate attention and were thought to be indicative of other factors which would emerge in the future and therefore needed to be tackled through appropriate mechanisms.

While the results of the comprehensive analysis showed a clear dissatisfaction with a wide range of marketing activity the underlying problem lay with functional management decision-making and staff performance. Both these dimensions would need to be addressed before significant improvement could be made in the actual quality of service.

The aim now was to enhance Stena Sealink's overall marketing performance by focusing on the key functions of the company's operations as defined in the model and improving the quality of each employee's contribution to the marketing activity.

The holistic model shown in Figure 4 is the conceptual foundation framework used to guide specifically the operationalisation and implementation of such a quality programme. The matrix can be used to identify the issues to be addressed and shows the responsibility of each particular company function in relation to each of the dimensions of service quality. The responsibility of each company function is identified and those issues requiring improvement can be allocated to the individual operators concerned. Each problem area can be examined and specific tasks identified. Figure 5 illustrates how the matrix (Figure 4) can be used as the mechanism for triggering action. Each company functions' problem area to be addressed is shown in the context of the dimensions of service quality. Thus the choice or range and presentation of product dimensions are the responsibility of product management, the promotional materials and activity are the responsibility of advertising management and the price/value for money dimensions are the responsibility of the pricing management team. The physical facilities and layout dimensions of the product management responsibility are not included in this operationalisation model because they incur capital expenditure and are improved on an annual basis when the ferries are in dry dock. The other columns show the personnel within each company function who have responsibility for that activity, the issue or problem to be addressed and the tasks involved.

Improving quality in marketing involves recognising that quality is about continual change. In a service organisation change is predominantly about behaviour. Changing behaviour involves a learning process and it is evident that adults learn because they want to learn (Quimby et al., 1991). Employees need to be involved in improving quality so that involvement will encourage motivation and lead to individuals taking an active role, therefore teamwork and participation at all levels needed to be encouraged. Developing and implementing a quality strategy demands the support not only of top management but of managers and staff at all levels in an organisation.

In implementing the quality model the principles of implementing the marketing concept were applied; that is, key staff were *involved* in confronting the problem/task and in subsequent decision-making.

Responsibilities and accountability were delegated widely to the operational and implementation staff who previously had not been given responsibility for decision inputs. The objective was that teams of staff involved in the delivery of that job function would therefore have responsibility for improving the quality of their performance where previously they had simply been directed to do so. Staff were encouraged to form 'self-support teams' consisting of those individuals who had an influence on the quality outcome of a given issue. The teamwork aspect is considered crucial to the implementation of quality improvement and as such it is worthwhile to take a moment to emphasise the teamwork issue. What are the foundations of this importance? Any staff development programme should enable each individual and team to learn through their work, recognise their current level of competence, develop new competences and be able to interpret them effectively in their job situation. Teamwork and participation are better ways to solve problems because knowledge, information and skills are distributed among a number of people (Revans, 1983). The involvement of those people who have the relevant knowledge, information and skills about the particular area requiring change is essential to real improvement. Teamwork is an integral part of this 'action learning' method of achieving company development, which is strongly advocated by Revans (1983). He writes that team meetings provide an opportunity for teams or individuals to seek help from other teams, they serve as an internal source of pressure on members of each team to keep their individual work moving and they provide mutual encouragement and support. Because learning is a social process managers learn more from their exchanges with each other than from an outsider. Consequently the involvement and participation of all staff concerned will lead to a consensus of opinion and agreement on necessary tasks. This results in a uniformity of tasks and everyone working towards the same goal.

IMPLEMENTING ACTION LEARNING

An intensive training workshop was set up. The aim of this workshop was to discuss the issues raised from the findings of the market research study. This workshop involved all the key personnel in Stena's Irish/Scottish route whose day-to-day responsibilities revolved around the actual management, planning and operational aspects of their functional roles in the company. These staff worked in close contact with customers and they agreed that the issues outlined in the analysis of customers' perceptions of current service quality were indeed the major causes of customer complaints. They were in the best position to determine what could be done to overcome these problems and raise the quality of on-board services.

These key personnel readily accepted – indeed were motivationally stimulated by – the responsibility for developing and building on the quality of service they already provided. This contributed to maintaining the commitment and enthusiasm of staff, particularly the key personnel, so that the quality improvement process could maintain momentum.

The staff organised themselves according to the key functions of the company's quality improvement operations denoted in the 'Operationalisation of Quality Improvement Model' (Figure 5). The emphasis of these decisions was twofold:

1. to improve the quality of the tangible aspect of their particular area/issue; thus, the product management team would seek to improve the menu in the ship's restaurant and the presentation of the food,

2. and most importantly, to improve the quality of the intangible aspect of these particular areas/issues. This meant taking account of *all* the intangible issues considered under the heading of internal communication and customer/staff interaction. These can be found in the bottom right quadrant of the 'Holistic Model for Quality Improvement' (Figure 4).

That is, the product management team incorporated all personnel who were involved in decisions relating to any aspects of the product such as hotel managers, stewards and chefs. The advertising management team involved the PR and advertising managers and the pricing management team involved cashiers, chefs and managers. Each of these functions involved management teams of two–six in number. Within this context each group addressed an identified and appropriate problem area focusing on issues to address and the tasks involved. These groups involved as many other staff from their functional area as possible in discussions charged with the responsibility of producing suggestions and solutions to problems. The counterpart groups from each service area would communicate with each other to compare ideas and agree which were the most feasible suggestions for implementation. It was crucial that as many staff as possible felt involved and participated in the service development process. Each group was responsible for coming up with realistic ideas and plans for improvement without incurring any capital or additional manpower expenditure within a specified time period. All groups agreed to formulate ideas for improvement and present them to the whole team.

The outcomes and agreements reached at these meetings were recorded on a single sheet of paper under the headings: Tasks; Action to be taken; Responsibility; Completion date.

At the next meeting this record sheet was produced with each completed item checked off, so highlighting any task which had not yet been resolved. This encouraged further discussions and plans for completing those tasks in relation to the progress they had made, problems they were encountering and the next stage in the way forward.

A key component of an effective programme was a co-ordinator/facilitator who could monitor the developments and ensure that progress was being made from one meeting to the next. This role was carried out by an independent consultant. Good planning, communication with the people involved and co-ordination played an important part in the development process, preventing pitfalls and poor participation. One of the vital priorities was to maintain close contact with the key decision-makers in order to ensure continued support for the quality improvement process and commitment to the goals.

SUMMARY

The quality improvement model has been used in the Stena Sealink Company as the basis of gradual and systematic improvement. The quest for continual improvement was maintained by means of discussions, team meetings and regular feedback sessions. Feedback from each of these planning workshops was important in order to monitor the progress of each team and measure the effectiveness of the quality improvement process over the longer term. This feedback accentuated any further changes that needed to be made and identified any group needing more encouragement or some outside advice before progressing to the next stage of development.

The monitoring of all suggestions was continuous and the responsibility of all team members. Staff involvement and responsibility for improving the tangible offerings of the company clearly encouraged and indeed necessitated increased internal communication in the planning and execution stage.

At the stage of performing and delivering the service product to customers external communi-cation was an integral part of monitoring customer perceptions of the new offerings. The measurement of results required staff to communicate proactively with customers. When new ideas had been implemented customers were made aware of these new products and services through tannoy announcements, posters and point-of-sale material.

Ongoing observation studies continued to monitor how customers responded to the new products and services on board. Many new ideas were refined to suit any observed or requested customer preferences. In addition to observing customers, members of each team were encouraged to talk proactively to customers more frequently throughout their visits on board and particularly when customers were using the new services and products offered.

This provided useful and immediate feedback to the staff who were involved in the creation and evolvement of providing improved services. Praise and appreciation from customers also provided encouragement to the staff who were initiating and implementing their new suggestions on board. This first-hand communication with customers led to a more pleasant atmosphere on board overall and a closer understanding of customer likes and dislikes than had been experienced prior to the changes on board.

MANAGERIAL IMPLICATIONS AND RECOMMENDATIONS

The Holistic Model (Figure 4) and the Operationalisation Model of Quality Improvement (Figure 5) serve to emphasise all the issues involved in quality improvement. There are a number of significant benefits of using these models, principally in relation to structure, focus, balance, consistency and organisation. To explain further:

▷ *Structure* – These models offer a systematic and structured approach to the enormous task of managing service marketing quality improvement.

▷ *Focus* – The use of the models can provide a

clear focus on the key aspects of service quality that require attention and also focus on how those aspects affect and interact with each other. As the quality programme progresses it can be expected that the developments will impact upon activities leading to further improvements and additional initiatives in other areas of the service marketing function. The Operationalisation of Quality Improvement Model lends itself to refinement and adaptation as a result of these developments. Indeed refinement and development of the model will help target main areas of quality weakness and in so doing contribute to the aim of achieving an overall level of quality on a consistent basis.

▷ *Balance* – By using these models marketing managers can ensure that quality improvements are made in a balanced way across the key marketing functions by recognising the tangible/intangible nature of these functions, particularly in a services operation. The value of using this model to measure and improve the overall quality is to ensure that it happens in a cohesive way.

▷ *Consistency* – In order to improve and maintain marketing quality it is important to recognise that it is a continuous and ongoing process. The main purpose must be continually to develop and improve all marketing activity and all dimensions of the service to customers.

▷ *Organisation* – As marketing quality improvement involves change and changing behaviour of staff in particular, it is vital to involve all staff in the changing process. Participation and involvement as shown in the Operationalisation Model will contribute to the commitment and co-operation of staff in the evolving work environment.

In the light of this dynamic environment the Holistic Model and the Operationalisation Model for Quality Improvement in a services context serve to provide a stable framework from which to work and since stability is a most desirable management circumstance this can only be of significant value to the management of marketing services.

NOTES

1. The term 'model' as used throughout this article stems from Kuhn's (1962) description that a model is a 'simplified representation of a concept, system or process' and that to be of value it must 'bear some measure of similarity to the structure or process being modelled' (George, 1968). Therefore the model must be suited to its purpose. The models described in this article were designed to show the interactions and integration of marketing concepts and management functions.

REFERENCES

Bonoma, T. (1991), 'How Are we Doing? Not Too Bad Overall', *Marketing News*, vol. 25, no. 20, 30 Sept, p. 17.

Carson, D and A. Gilmore (1989–90), 'Customer Care: The Neglected Domain', *Irish Marketing Review*, vol. 4, no. 3, pp. 49–61.

Christopher, M., A. Payne and D. Ballantyne (1991), 'Relationship Marketing: Bringing Quality, Customer Service and Marketing Together', *Marketing Educators Conference Proceedings*, Cardiff, vol. 1.

Crosby, P. (1979), *Quality Is Free, The Art of Making Quality*, McGraw-Hill Books.

George, F.H. (1968), 'The Use of Models in Science' in R.J. Chorley and P. Haggett (eds.), *Models in Geography*, Methuen, London, p. 43.

Grönroos, C. (1982), 'A Service Quality Model and its Marketing Implications', *European Journal of Marketing*, vol. 18, no. 4, pp. 36–44.

Grönroos, C. (1990a), *Service Management and Marketing. Managing Moments of Truth in Service Competition*, Lexington Books, Mass.

Grönroos, C. (1990b), 'Relationship Approach to Marketing in Service Contexts: The Marketing and Organisational Behaviour Interface', *Journal of Business Research*, vol. 20, pp. 3–11.

Hammons, C. and G.A. Maddux (1990), 'Total Quality

Management in the Public Sector', *Management Decision*, vol. 28, no. 4, pp. 15–19.

Juran, J.M. (1988), *Juran on Planning for Quality*, The Free Press, New York, NY.

Kuhn, A.H. (1962), 'Complex Interactive Models' in R.H. Frank, A.H. Kuhn and W.F. Massey (eds.), *Quantitative Techniques in Marketing Analysis*, Irwin, Homewood, Ill.

Morgan, N. and N. Piercy (1991), 'The Interface of Marketing and Quality: Research Propositions for Market-led Quality Strategy', *American Marketing Association Summer Educators Conference Proceedings*.

Parasuraman, A., V. Zeithaml and L. Berry (1985), 'A Conceptual Model of Service Quality and its Implications for Future Research', *Journal of Marketing*, vol. 49, Fall, pp. 41–50.

Phillips, L.W., D.R. Chang and R.D. Buzzell (1983), 'Product Quality, Cost Position and Business Performance: A Test of Some Key Hypotheses', *Journal of Marketing*, Spring, pp. 26–43.

Quimby, C., L. Parker and A.M. Weimerskirch (1991), 'How Exactly Do you Communicate Quality?', *Quality Progress*, June. pp. 52–4.

Revans, R. (1983), *The ABC of Action Learning*, Chartwell-Bratt, London.

Schmalensee, D.H. (1991), 'Marketers Must Lead Quality Improvement or Risk Becoming Irrelevant', *Services Marketing Newsletter*, vol. 7, no. 1, pp. 1–3.

Smith, S. (1987), 'How to Quantify Quality', *Management Today*, October, pp. 86–8.

Swan, J.E. and L.J. Combs (1976), 'Product Performance and Consumer Satisfaction', *Journal of Marketing*, vol. 40, April, pp. 25–33.

Witcher, B.J. (1990), 'Total Quality and the Marketing Concept', *The Quarterly Review of Marketing*, vol. 15, no. 2, Winter, pp. 1–6.

Customers' Perceptions of Service Quality in Financial Institutions

Gaston LeBlanc and Nha Nguyen

During the past decade, an increasing number of marketing scholars and practitioners have placed a considerable importance on the management of quality. Indeed several authors (Schoeffler, Buzzell and Heany, 1974; Buzzell and Wiersema, 1981; Garvin, 1983; Takeuchi and Quelch, 1983; Leonard and Sasser, 1982; Nollet, Kélada and Diorio, 1986) argue that quality has a direct bearing on a company's performance and future growth.

Schoeffler, Buzzell and Heany (1974) along with Buzzell and Wiersema (1981) establish a positive link between quality and return on investment, while Garvin (1983), in his study on the American air conditioning industry and its management philosophy towards quality, concludes that the mediocre quality of its products is a significant cause of the industry's decline in comparison to its Japanese counterpart. The same phenomenon is reported by Takeuchi and Quelch (1983) with respect to the automobile industry. As for services, quality control becomes even more important due in part to the costs associated with non-quality (Horovitz, 1986). According to Crosby (1984), the direct and indirect costs of mediocre quality in service industries can reach proportions of up to 40 per cent of revenues. Management must thus place considerable importance on achieving service quality. Consequently, efforts must be directed to the identification of evaluative criteria used by customers in their judgement process.

Berry (1980), along with Booms and Bitner (1981), argues that, due to the intangible nature of services, customers use elements associated with the physical environment when evaluating service quality. Managing the evidence and using environmental psychology are seen as important marketing tools. Levitt (1981) proposes that customers use appearances to make judgements about realities, and the less tangible a product the more powerful is the effect of packaging in judging that product. Hostage (1975), for his part, believes that a service firm's contact personnel comprise the major determinant of service quality, while Lewis and Booms (1983), Nightingale (1983), and Eiglier and Langeard (1987) propose that service quality resides in the ability of the service firm to satisfy its customer needs, i.e. customer satisfaction. Quality has thus become one of the main concerns of company officials (Leonard and Sasser, 1982), and is becoming a strategic variable which greatly affects marketing and production policies in many service firms.

Given the new strategic importance of quality, managerial practices towards it must therefore change. To assure higher quality products and services, the classical approach of recording and controlling quality as a purely technical act is no longer sufficient. A quality-conscious company must manage it (Leonard and Sasser, 1982). An overall approach aimed at planning, organising, administering, controlling and assuring quality must be adopted (Nollet, Kélada and Diorio, 1986).

A review of the marketing literature reveals that little attention has been given to the consumers' evaluative processes with regards to service quality and that most studies on the subject are rather descriptive and normative in nature. Two major reasons for this lack of empirical knowledge and explanatory analysis can be identified: first, quality has not often been regarded as a first order variable in the management process; second, since services are for the most part intangible, it is extremely difficult to conceptualise and measure quality. In this context, we examine the main aspects surrounding this elusive and indistinct construct and identify a set of factors that explain the perceived quality of the services of a financial institution.

WHAT WE KNOW ABOUT SERVICE QUALITY

THE CONCEPT OF QUALITY AS IT APPLIES TO SERVICES

The problem of evaluating service quality is more difficult and complex than product quality due to the intangible nature of services. Eiglier and Langeard (1987, p. 25), in their most recent work on the marketing of services, state that 'one cannot control the quality of services and reject those that do not reach a set standard before marketing them, as is the case for tangible products. The array of techniques and the finality of the quality controls at the end of the production line are thus useless.' This in fact means that service organisations must control quality before and during the service delivery process in order to prevent or redress any repercussions that poor quality service might have on the business.

To be able to grasp and better understand the concept of service quality, a knowledge of certain characteristics that distinguish services from goods must be understood. First, most services are intangible (Bateson, 1977; Shostack, 1977; Berry, 1980; Lovelock, 1981) because they consist of

acts and performances, not objects. A service may not be counted, stored or tested before being consumed. It is therefore difficult for the service provider not only to understand how its customers perceive the service offering, but to evaluate the quality of its service. Second, services are heterogeneous, in that their performance varies from one provider to another, from one customer to another and from day to day (Booms and Bitner, 1981). Third, services are perishable (Eiglier and Langeard, 1975). When a service is not consumed by the customer at the time and location specified, it is lost. Finally, with services there is an inability to separate production and consumption, which means that the customer usually participates in the production process. Due to their intangibility, heterogeneity, perishable nature and the inseparability of production and consumption, service quality becomes difficult to conceptualise and measure. Therefore, when marketing intangibles, the major concern of business managers becomes the provision and control of symbols and tangible clues used by the customer in evaluating the service. Quality is thus relative and subjective, and depends on the perceptions and expectations that the customer has with respect to the service offering.

SERVICE QUALITY IS DIFFICULT TO DEFINE AND OPERATIONALISE

A review of the literature reveals that few operational definitions of service quality have been offered. Crosby (1979) defines service quality as the compliance to specifications. Eiglier and Langeard (1987) argue that 'a good quality service is one that satisfies the customer'. They propose that quality should be evaluated according to three dimensions, namely a. the physical environment and contact personnel; b. the delivery process, these two elements being 'objective qualities'; and c. the results of customer satisfaction derived from the service encounter, referred to as 'subjective qualities'. Service quality is thus relative and depends directly on expectations and performances (Parasuraman, Zeithaml and Berry, 1984). Similarly, Lewis and Booms (1983) sug-

FIGURE 1:   A CONCEPTUAL MODEL OF SERVICE QUALITY

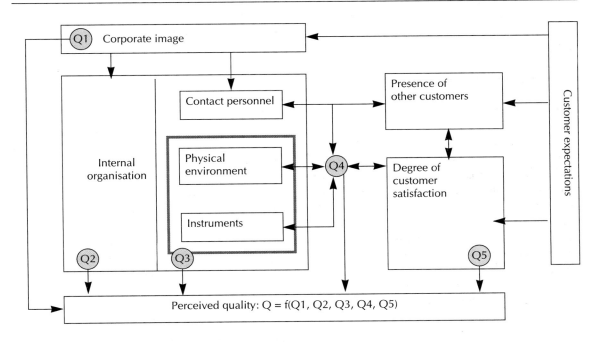

gest that service quality involves comparing customer expectations to the performances obtained from the service provided. Quality is thus perceived as the manner in which services, through their delivery system, satisfy customer needs.

Grönroos (1984) establishes a distinction between two forms of service quality: a. technical quality, what is received by the customer, the content of the service in itself; and b. functional quality, which involves the manner in which the service is provided. Functional quality is seen as being predominant in the customer's evaluative process. In a restaurant setting, for example, more emphasis would be given to a waiter's appearance and performance.

Lehtinen and Laitamaki (1984) propose three major determinants of service quality: a. institutional quality, i.e. corporate image; b. physical quality, which corresponds to the physical environment associated with the service-producing system; and c. interactive quality, which involves the interactions among the customers themselves.

CONCEPTUAL FRAMEWORK

While the literature on service quality is mostly normative and descriptive in nature it reveals three principal schools of thought with regards to how customers evaluate quality:

1. The first postulates that service quality resides in the physical environment associated with the service offering. These are the tangible elements of the service production system which act as indicators of perceived quality (Shostack, 1977; Berry, 1980; Levitt, 1981; Flipo, 1984; Lehtinen and Laitamaki, 1984).

2. The second proposes that service quality is achieved through the performance of contact personnel. Perceived quality thus lies in the staff's attitude and behaviour (Rathmell, 1974; Hostage, 1975; Solomon, Surprenant, Czepiel and Gutman, 1985).

3. The third seeks to describe perceived quality in terms of degree of customer satisfaction

derived from the service encounter (Lewis and Booms, 1983; Nightingale, 1983; Eiglier and Langeard, 1987).

Because of the difficulties associated with defining and operationalising this elusive concept, relatively few efforts have been made to explain service quality through models. In fact, only a limited number of major conceptual models have been developed (Lehtinen and Laitamaki, 1984; Grönroos, 1984; Parasuraman, Zeithaml and Berry, 1984). These proposed models hypothesise that service quality is mostly derived from a comparison of customer expectations and the service received. However, because of a lack of empirical testing, they do not show how the customer perceives quality, nor what determines or influences his/her perception of quality.

The three aforementioned schools of thought are not in the authors' opinion contradictory, but rather complementary in nature. Insights obtained from this existing knowledge form the basis of the service quality model presented in Figure 1. This model proposes that when asked to evaluate a service offering, the customer will view the concept of quality holistically. Nonetheless, his/her judgement, which is both overall and final, must be based on certain characteristics related either to the service provider, or to other elements associated with the service offering such as the appearance, reliability, competence, punctuality and discretion of staff, as well as other tangible clues like location, instruments used to provide service, size of institution, and décor and atmosphere.

These characteristics are combined into five quality components, namely corporate image, internal organisation, physical support of the service-producing system, customer/staff interaction and the degree of customer satisfaction.

Corporate image is defined by various attributes, including the name of the business, its reputation, prices, access to service, the distinctive character of the business, variety of services offered, promises of expected benefits, competitiveness and concern for customers' well-being.

Internal organisation refers to the instruments and staff that are not visible to customers, but which are necessary for operations to run smoothly. In general, the customer does not have any detailed or specific information on back office support systems, but still has the capacity to judge their effectiveness. Characteristics related to the internal organisation would include the skills of the back office personnel and their ability to offer support services in a timely manner, technology used by the institution, and communication with customers through promotional activities.

Physical environment and instruments include such tangible elements as décor and ambience associated with the service provider. These physical properties can encompass atmosphere, appearance of buildings and grounds, layout and furniture arrangement, business hours, parking facilities, location, and other instruments used to provide service.

The service encounter consists of customer/staff interactions. Dimensions associated with this encounter would include appearance of staff, friendliness, competence, punctuality and reliability, timeliness and confidentiality, attentiveness, staff attitude, behaviour of other customers, and the procedures used in service delivery.

Customer satisfaction is the outcome of the service encounter and reflects the comparison of customer expectations with the performances obtained from the service provided.

This conceptual framework sets the stage for an exploratory study on the determinants of service quality in financial institutions. It identifies the main components of service quality that quality-conscious managers should consider when deciding on the elements to include in the design and control of the institution's service offering.

METHODOLOGY

A number of credit unions serving mostly the French population in the province of New Brunswick were chosen for this study. This francophone population represents approximately 35 per cent of the total population. The credit unions for their part are major financial institutions located in the principal cities and rank amongst the top five in the chosen areas. The literature review and focus group interviews provided the basis for developing a questionnaire used to measure perceived quality. Focus group interviews were held with current users and the general prescribed guidelines recommended for these interviews were followed (Cox, Higginbotham and Burton, 1976; Calder, 1977; Fern, 1982). Combined with the literature review, the focus groups provided a broad spectrum of elements that were included in the questionnaire.

The questionnaire contained forty-five variables related to the financial institution's service offering. These variables were measured on a seven-point Likert-type scale where respondents indicated the extent to which each variable influenced their judgement of the institution's quality of service. The questionnaires were mailed to a systematic random sample of 2,500 people chosen from a list of 105,000 'user members' of the credit union. Personalised letters from the president of the credit union movement accompanied each questionnaire. Respondents were informed of the importance of the study and asked to complete the questionnaire within a three-week time frame. From the sample, a total of 1,224 completed usable questionnaires were returned within the specified three-week period, which constitutes a final sample that complies with a 3 per cent margin of error, nineteen out of twenty. This procedure represents a reasonable response rate of 49 per cent. The non-respondents are distributed as follows: 1,025 refused to answer, 175 had moved and 76 had only partially completed the questionnaire.

RESULTS

To provide a multivariate perspective on the forty-five variables related to perceived quality, a principal components factor analysis with varimax rotation was conducted. A seven-factor solution was obtained which accounted for 57.8 per cent of explained variance. A limit of our analytical procedure is that 42.2 per cent of variance is not accounted for and this information is thus

lost. The decision to include a variable in a factor was based on factor loadings greater than or equal to 0.50. The orthogonal factors (i.e. absence of correlation between factors) were then used as independent variables in a stepwise regression analysis (Green and Tull, 1974; Lion and Testu, 1978). In order to determine the number of factors to be retained in the factor solution, the rule that consists of choosing all factors whose eigenvalue is greater than one was followed (Lion and Testu, 1978; Lewis, 1984). Reliability of measures was assessed with the use of Cronbach's alpha (Churchill, 1979; Peter, 1979). Cronbach's alpha allows us to measure the reliability of the different factors. It consists of estimates of how much variation in scores of different variables is attributable to chance or random errors (Selltiz, Wrightsman and Cook, 1976). As a general rule a coefficient greater than or equal to 0.50 is considered acceptable and a good indication of construct reliability (Nunnally, 1967).

Table 1 provides the results of the factor analysis and Cronbach's reliability coefficient. It shows the variables loading on each factor, the factor name, the variance explained by each factor and the cumulative variance explained by the factor solution. Results of Cronbach's alpha reveal that measures are indeed reliable. The seven factors identified in Table 1 can be summarised as follows: Factor 1, 'Contact personnel', accounts for 30 per cent of explained variance and consists of variables related to the skills of the contact personnel. Variables such as friendly and courteous staff, competent staff, reliability and discretion of staff, appearance and punctuality are included in this factor. Factor 2, 'Internal organisation', accounts for 8 per cent of explained variance and is linked to characteristics pertaining to the perceived internal organisation of the business. Some of the variables that describe this factor are: information provided to customers, accuracy of transactions, operating procedures, hiring practices and use of customer feedback to improve services. Factor 3, 'Physical environment and instruments', accounts for 5.8 per cent of explained variance and includes variables which relate to the physical

TABLE 1:   RESULTS OF FACTOR ANALYSIS ON FORTY-FIVE VARIABLES MEASURING
            PERCEIVED QUALITY

Variables	Factor loadings	Factor name	% of variance explained	Cumulative variance explained %	Cronbach's reliability coefficient
Friendly and courteous staff	0.78				
Competent staff	0.78				
Customers are greeted on arrival	0.72				
Reliability and discretion of staff	0.72				
Transactions are confidential	0.71				
Appearance of staff	0.60	F1 Contact			
Punctuality of staff	0.60	personnel	30.0	30.0	0.90*
Customers are regularly informed of services offered	0.75				
Accuracy of transactions	0.67				
Operating procedures	0.65				
Hiring practices	0.65				
Customer feedback is used to improve services	0.65				
Competence of support staff	0.64				
Obtaining and making transactions by phone	0.61	F2 Internal			
Manager listens and responds to customer need	0.60	organisation	8.0	38.0	0.88
Décor and atmosphere	0.76				
Appearance of building and grounds	0.76				
Size of institution	0.75				
Layout and furniture arrangement	0.69				
Parking facilities are assured	0.62	F3 Physical			
Equipment and instruments used to provide service	0.61	environment			
Location	0.59	and instruments	5.8	43.9	0.86
Institution serves mostly francophone customers	0.72				
Institution's contribution to society	0.70				
Customers become part-owners	0.69				
Affiliation of institution with credit union movement	0.67				
Ease of membership	0.62	F4 Corporate			
Deposits are guaranteed secured	0.61	image	4.9	48.7	0.83
Number of customers waiting in line for service	0.75				
Behaviour of other customers waiting in line	0.66	F5 Customer			
Waiting time before being served	0.65	interaction	3.6	52.4	0.75*
Institution is capable of satisfying customer needs	0.88				
Degree to which needs are satisfied	0.86				
Degree to which past experiences were liked/disliked	0.81	F6 Satisfaction	3.0	55.4	0.87
Discussions with staff are assured confidential	0.63	F7 Customer/			
Business hours	0.51	personnel			
Service occurs in an incremental flow	0.51	interaction	2.4	57.8	0.71*

* Cronbach's alpha for Factors F1, F5 and F7, factors that represent the fourth component (Q4) of the model = 0.90.

Dependent variable: Respondents' overall evaluation of financial institutions' quality.

Independent variable: Seven orthogonal factors representing the components of perceived quality.

Variables	Beta	Significance
Satisfaction (F6)	0.74	••
Contact personnel (F1)	0.11	••
Internal organisation (F2)	0.09	••
Physical environment and instruments (F3)	0.09	••
Corporate image (F4)	0.09	••
Customer/personnel interaction (F7)	0.05	•

$R^2 = 59\%$; Durbin-Watson = 1.84; •• $p<0.01$; • $p< 0.05$

elements associated with the service-producing system. Examples include décor and atmosphere, appearance of building and grounds, equipment and instruments used to provide service, and size of institution.

Factor 4, 'Corporate image', accounts for 4.9 per cent of explained variance and includes variables that are closely tied to the credit union's image. Corporate image is described by the institution's contribution to society, the fact that members are part-owners, the ease of membership and the fact that deposits are guaranteed secured. Factor 5, 'Customer interaction', accounts for 3.6 per cent of explained variance and includes variables such as the number of customers waiting in line, their behaviour and the waiting time before being served. These variables relate to situations where several users are simultaneously requesting a given service.

Factor 6, 'Satisfaction', accounts for 3 per cent of explained variance and includes variables which are related to the output of the service-producing system, i.e. the institution's capacity to satisfy customer needs, the degree to which needs are satisfied and the degree to which past experiences were liked/disliked by the customer. Finally, Factor 7, 'Customer/personnel interaction', accounts for 2.4 per cent of explained variance and comprises variables that relate to interactions experienced during the service encounter. The variables describing this factor are confidentiality

of discussions with staff, business hours and the incremental flow in which service occurs.

Results indicate that these seven factors are closely related to the proposed conceptual model (Figure 1). Indeed, Factors 1, 5 and 7, i.e. contact personnel, customer interaction and customer/personnel interaction, are associated to Q4, interactive quality. Factor 2 is related to Q2, internal organisation quality, while Factor 3 represents Q3, physical environment and instruments quality. Factor 4 represents Q1, corporate quality, while Factor 6 represents Q5, customer satisfaction.

Table 2 presents the results of stepwise regression using respondents' overall judgement of the financial institutions' quality as the dependent variable, this variable being measured on a seven-point Likert-type scale, and the seven orthogonal factors presented in Table 1 as independent variables. The significant factors that remained in the equation and explain perceived service quality are shown in order of their importance based on beta coefficients. The higher the coefficient, the more the factor contributes to explaining service quality.

Results reveal that service quality is derived principally from customer satisfaction, i.e. the institution's capacity to meet customer expectations. Other factors that contribute to explaining service quality are: the contact personnel, through their behaviour; the internal organisation, through its back office support system; the tangible evidence associated with the physical environment and instruments used to provide service; the image, reflected by the corporate entity and the interactions that take place between contact personnel and customers during the service delivery process. Results also indicate that the customer interaction factor is not significant. This means that the interaction between customers when they are waiting for service has no bearing on their judgement of service quality. Although this factor is not significant, management must nonetheless assure that services are provided in a timely manner.

DISCUSSION

This article presents some insights on the concept of service quality and offers a conceptual model for evaluating quality in financial institutions. The empirical results support the model, and seem consistent with the literature. Certain authors (Lewis and Booms, 1983; Nightingale, 1983; Parasuraman, Zeithaml and Berry, 1984; Eiglier and Langeard, 1987) have proposed that service quality is related to the degree of customer satisfaction derived from the service offering. This study reveals that customer satisfaction is the most important factor in explaining service quality in financial institutions. This in itself is not a surprising revelation since a positive relation between degree of satisfaction and overall quality was expected. What is more interesting and complex about this relationship is the question of whether satisfaction and quality are two distinct concepts or whether satisfaction is a component of quality.

Also argued in the literature (Rathmell, 1974; Hostage, 1975; Shostack, 1977; Berry, 1980; Levitt, 1981; Flipo, 1984; Lehtinen and Laitamaki, 1984; Solomon, Surprenant, Czepiel and Gutman, 1985) is that service quality depends on the tangible characteristics associated with the service offering or on the performance of the service provider. These results, interestingly enough, indicate that dimensions related to the contact personnel and physical characteristics of the service-producing system are also determinants of perceived quality. Results in fact do not contradict existing knowledge but rather tend to support it. They in fact confirm the complementarity of the aforementioned schools of thought with regards to service quality.

As for the managerial implications of this study, it is apparent that management in financial institutions must act upon the tangible and intangible components associated with the service delivery process in order to meet customer expectations and achieve service quality. The tangible elements of the process are the contact personnel, the internal organisation and the physical environment. Since financial institutions offer services that require a high degree of contact between personnel and customers (Chase, 1978), special attention must be paid to the staff's behaviour. Managerial actions should be guided by certain characteristics such as the attitude of staff, their competence, appearance, and sense of professionalism. Quality standards must also be established based on the organisation's capacity to reduce the variability in performances. The internal organisation of the service firm must also be considered. Back office support staff must continuously provide pertinent information to customers on services offered and operating procedures must run smoothly while guaranteeing the accuracy of transactions. The physical environment and instruments used while providing service is another point to consider. Management must manage the evidence in such a way that the service experience is pleasant and the tangible elements such as furniture arrangement, décor, and the overall 'atmospherics' (Kotler, 1974) reinforce the institution's positioning statement. Corporate image is also an important dimension to consider when establishing quality standards. Image can vary on a tangible/intangible continuum where control can be exercised on its tangible dominant aspect such as guaranteed deposits and contribution to society by sponsoring charitable, cultural or sporting events, or on its intangible dominant aspect such as reputation or prestige.

Customer satisfaction being the most important dimension which explains service quality, management must therefore further investigate the process by which customer expectations are formed and compared to actual performances. Ensuring customer satisfaction all along the service delivery process is thus a key element of service quality. Control can be exercised before and during the process, by accentuating and controlling service delivery procedures (Shostack, 1977), or after the process through advertising that reinforces the guarantee of satisfaction.

It is apparent that financial institutions must strive to enhance the degree of customer satisfaction derived from the service encounter. Contact personnel, physical facilities and corporate image, having an impact on quality, must be continuously monitored, and enhanced when necessary. Involving contact personnel and back office personnel in quality improvement programmes should also be encouraged. Financial institutions wanting to maintain a competitive edge must now manage quality and encourage employee participation in the process of assuring it. Implied in the management and achievement of quality is a total organisational effort where marketers must work closely with all other departments such as personnel management, accounting, operations management, and facilities designers.

CONCLUSION

The phenomenal growth of service sectors around the world has led many marketing scholars as well as practitioners to question the applicability, in service firms, of concepts and theories developed mainly for goods marketers. This has increased the number of research papers related to services marketing, and brought about literature which is mostly descriptive and normative in nature. At this stage more empirical knowledge is needed concerning the customer's evaluative process with regards to service quality.

The objective of this study was to identify a set of factors capable of explaining perceived quality in financial institutions. The study has identified five groups of characteristics that explain the quality of the institution's offering, namely the degree of customer satisfaction, the contact personnel, the internal organisation, the physical environment and instruments, corporate image and the personnel/customer interaction during the service encounter. The results obtained for financial services, in this case credit unions, are encouraging and will lead to studies in other service businesses so that some kind of generalisation with regards to this elusive construct might be made.

REFERENCES

Bateson, J. (1977), 'Do We Need Service Marketing?' in Pierre Eiglier et al. *Marketing Consumer Services: New Insights*, Marketing Science Institute, Report No. 77-115, December, pp. 1–30.

Berry, L.L. (1980), 'Services Marketing Is Different', *Business*, May–June, pp. 24–8.

Booms, B.H. and Bitner, M.J. (1981), 'Marketing Strategies and Organization Structures for Services Firms' in J.H. Donnelly and W.R. George (eds.), *Marketing of Services*, American Marketing Association, Chicago, Ill., pp. 47–51.

Buzzell, R.D. and Wiersema, F.D. (1981), 'Successful Share-building Strategies', *Harvard Business Review*, January–February, p. 135.

Calder, B.J. (1977), 'Focus Groups and the Nature of Qualitative Marketing Research', *Journal of Marketing Research*, vol. XIV, August, pp. 536–64.

Chase, R. (1978), 'Where Does the Customer Fit in a Service Operation?', *Harvard Business Review*, November–December, pp. 137–42.

Churchill, G. (1979), 'A Paradigm for Developing Better Measures of Marketing Constructs', *Journal of Marketing Research*, February, pp. 64–73.

Cox, K., J. Higginbotham and J. Burton (1976), 'Applications of Focus Group Interviews in Marketing', *Journal of Marketing*, January, pp. 77–80.

Crosby, P.B. (1979), *Quality Is Free*, McGraw-Hill, NY.

Crosby, P.B. (1984), paper presented at the 'Bureau de

Commerce', Montreal, Canada (unpublished), November.

Eiglier, P. and Langeard, E. (1975), 'Une approche nouvelle du marketing des services', *Revue Française de Gestion*, November, pp. 97–110.

Eiglier, P. and Langeard, E. (1987), *Servuction, le marketing des services*, McGraw-Hill, Paris.

Fern, E.F. (1982), 'The Use of Focus Groups for Idea Generation: The Effects of Group Size, Acquaintanceship, and Moderator on Response Quantity and Quality', *Journal of Marketing Research*, vol. XIX, February, pp. 1–13.

Flipo, J.P. (1984), *Le management des entreprises de services*, Les editions d'organisation, Paris.

Garvin, D.A. (1983), 'Quality on the Line', *Harvard Business Review*, vol. 61, no. 5, September–October, pp. 65–73.

Green, P. and Tull, D. (1974), *Recherche et décisions en marketing*, Presses Universitaires de Grenoble.

Grönroos, C. (1983), *Strategic Management and Marketing in the Service Sector*, Marketing Science Institute, Cambridge, Mass.

Grönroos, C. (1984), 'A Service Quality Model and its Marketing Implications', *European Journal of Marketing*, vol. 18, no. 4, pp. 36–44.

Horovitz, J. (1986), 'La non-qualite tue', *Harvard – L'expansion*, Summer, pp. 53–61.

Hostage, G.M. (1975), 'Quality Control in a Service Business', *Harvard Business Review*, July–August, pp. 98–106.

Juran, J.M. (1981), 'La qualité des produits: un impératif pour l'Occident', *Revue Qualité*, December, pp. 2–5, 24–8.

Kotler, P. (1974), 'Atmospherics as a Marketing Tool', *Journal of Retailing*, vol. 49, no. 4, Winter, pp. 48–64.

Lehtinen, J. and Laitamaki, J. (1984), 'Applications of Service Quality and Services Marketing in Hospitals', Service Management Institute, Finland.

Leonard, F.S. and Sasser, E.W. (1982), 'The Incline of Quality', *Harvard Business Review*, vol. 60, no. 5, September–October, pp. 163–71.

Levitt, T. (1981), 'Marketing Intangible Products and Product Intangibles', *Harvard Business Review*, May–June, pp. 94–102.

Lewis, R. (1984), 'Isolating Differences in Hotel Attributes', *The Cornell Hotel Restaurant Administrative Quarterly*, November, pp. 64–77.

Lewis, R. and Booms, B. (1983), 'The Marketing Aspects of Service Quality' in L.L. Berry, G.L. Shostack and G. Upah (eds.), *Proceedings of American Marketing Association: Emerging Perspectives on Services Marketing*, pp. 99–104.

Lion, J. and Testu, F. (1978), *L'analyse factorielle*, Encyclopédie du Marketing II, Etude du marché, Editions techniques, Paris.

Lovelock, C. (1981), 'Why Marketing Management Needs to be Different for Services' in J.H. Donnelly and W.R. George (eds.), *Marketing of Services*, American Marketing Association, Chicago, Ill., pp. 5–9.

Nightingale, M. (1983), *Defining Quality for a Quality Assurance Programme ... A Study of Perceptions*, PQCS Management Consultants, London, England.

Nollet, J., J. Kélada and M. Diorio (1986), *La gestion des operations et de la production: une approche systémique*, Gaëtan Morin, Chicoutimi, Quebec.

Nunnally, J.C. (1967), *Psychometric Theory*, McGraw-Hill Book Company, NY.

Parasuraman, A., V. Zeithaml and L.L. Berry (1984), 'A Conceptual Model of Service Quality and its Implications for Future Research', Marketing Science Institute, Report no. 84-106, August, pp. 1–24.

Peter, P. (1979), 'Reliability: A Review of Psychometric Basics and Recent Marketing Practices', *Journal of Marketing Research*, February, pp. 6–17.

Rathmell, J. (1974), *Marketing in the Service Sector*, Winthrop Publishers Inc., Cambridge, Mass.

Schoeffler, S., R.D. Buzzell and D.E. Heany (1974), 'Impact of Strategic Planning on Profit Performance', *Harvard Business Review*, March–April, p. 137.

Selltiz, C., L.S. Wrightsman and W. Cook (1976), *Research Methods in Social Relations*, Holt, Rinehart and Winston, NY.

Shostack, G. Lynn (1977), 'Breaking Free from Product Marketing', *Journal of Marketing*, vol. 41, April, pp. 77–80.

Solomon, M.R., C. Surprenant, J.A. Czepiel and E. Gutman (1985), 'A Role Theory Perspective on Dyadic Interactions: The Service Encounter', *Journal of Marketing*, vol. 49, Winter, pp. 99–111.

Takeuchi, H. and J.A. Quelch (1983), 'Quality Is More than Making a Good Product', *Harvard Business Review*, July–August, pp. 139–45.

The Nature of Relationship Quality

V. Liljander and T. Strandvik

The concept perceived service quality is advanced by recognising the need for splitting it into two different concepts – (service) episode quality and (service) relationship quality. In the paper a conceptual framework is presented for relating the quality of each episode to the customer's perception of the overall relationship quality. This model represents a dynamic perspective on service quality.

BACKGROUND

It has been argued that long-lasting relations with customers would be beneficial for a service company. Relationship marketing has emerged as a new important approach by which marketing management can achieve customer retention. Customer retention is deemed to depend critically on the quality of and satisfaction with the service. The role of separate interactions, episodes in relation to the perception of overall quality, has, however, not been scrutinised. One reason for this is that the question arises only when a dynamic perspective is applied. Both service quality and satisfaction have traditionally been approached from a static perspective (Grönroos, 1993a). Empirical studies often use cross-sectional surveys to measure the service quality at a certain point of time, although initial attempts have been made to make static service quality models dynamic (Boulding et al., 1993). Customer retention indicates customer loyalty or some kind of relationship between the customer and the firm. The relation concept gives quite a different view of the exchange processes on the market compared to the static view. It is here proposed that *perceived relationship quality* is a core concept when analysing service quality from a dynamic perspective.

Rust and Oliver (1994) state that one of the most important issues facing service marketers today is the connection between quality, satisfaction and value. We agree with this and will, in this paper, present a relationship quality model that clarifies the relation between these concepts. In the model a distinction is made between episode quality and relationship quality. Satisfaction, service quality and value may all be experienced on both an episode and a relationship level. We will, however, extend the discussion on satisfaction, quality and value by including equity as an important part of relationship marketing. The question of relationship strength, which is closely connected to relationship quality, will also be discussed. The study draws on both traditional service quality literature and relationship studies in the industrial marketing literature. We are, however, solely focusing on the relation between private customers and service providers.

RELATIONS AND RELATIONSHIP MARKETING

Relationship marketing as a concept has been

Reprinted from Proceedings, Quality Management in Services IV, European Institute for Advanced Studies in Management (EIASM), Paris, May, 1994.

FIGURE 1:   THE RELATION BETWEEN THE CONCEPTS RELATION, EPISODES AND ACTS

RELATION: HOTEL GRAND

EPISODE 1	EPISODE 2	EPISODE 3
May 1992	August 1993	January 1994

Check-in Room   Breakfast Check-out   Check-in Room Dinner Breakfast Check-out   Check-in Room   Check-out

TIME

---

contrasted with transactional marketing. The traditional view of marketing, transaction marketing, is claimed to be focused on seeking new customers, while relationship marketing aims at long-term lasting relationships (Christopher et al., 1991; Grönroos, 1993b). Relationship marketing has been defined as establishing, maintaining, enhancing and terminating relations with customers and other partners. This focus is dominant in industrial marketing within the network paradigm, where marketing is defined as all activities that build, maintain and develop customer relations. Miettilä and Törnroos (1993) list three assumptions that are implicitly or explicitly present in the Interaction Approach of industrial marketing. First, interaction is mediated through human actors, which means that their perceptions, beliefs, attitudes and behaviour are central. Secondly, business interaction means mutual dependability, problem-solving and adaptation. Thirdly, relationships evolve over time and include the present situation, future goals and their own histories.

A comparison of these three statements to consumer service relationships reveals differences. The first statement is probably valid also for consumer services. The second might not be as important as in industrial relations. The third is, on the other hand, important. Increasingly, within the interaction-network paradigm, relations are thought to lead to *bonds* (Easton and

Araujo, 1989; Wilson and Mummalaneni, 1986). This implies that the partner is tied to the firm in different ways. In the industrial marketing literature it has been suggested that such bonds can be economic, legal, social, technological, etc. Such bonds may also be found in consumer markets.

DEFINITION OF AN EPISODE

Different terms are used in the literature to represent the division into a local and global view of performance, quality and satisfaction. We use the terms episode and relationship, as these are already used within the interaction research tradition in industrial marketing, and seem to reflect the current trend (Håkansson, 1982). An episode can be defined as an event of interaction which has a clear starting-point and an ending-point. Within the episode there can exist several interactions (acts). Figure 1 shows the relations between the concepts by illustrating a customer who has stayed several times at a given hotel.

The stay at a hotel represents an episode, consisting of a number of interactions or acts including check-in, breakfast, the room, bathroom, dinner, etc. When the guest stayed at the hotel for the first time (Episode 1) he used check-in services (Act 1), the room (Act 2), breakfast (Act 3), and check-out (Act 4). The second time he stayed at the hotel he used these same services, but in addition he ate dinner there, etc. It is thus possible to distinguish between different acts within an episode. The importance of the different acts which compose the episode may vary in explaining episode satisfaction (Danaber and Mattsson, 1994). An episode may also consist of only one act, depending on the service (e.g. drawing money from an ATM). The concepts are relative to the level of analysis. It is difficult in some cases to define exactly the limits of an episode. Such are continuous services like insurances, where the interaction might be very limited for years, including only one-way contact from the insurance company (bill, information) and the customer responding by paying the bill or requesting more information.

In earlier research a number of different concepts have been used which can be seen as synonyms or related to the concepts episode/relationship. These are 'transaction-specific/global', 'local/global', 'service encounter/overall' (Bitner and Hubbert, 1994), 'incident-specific/cumulative' (Rust and Oliver, 1994), 'transaction-specific/brand-specific' (Anderson and Fornell, 1994). Within industrial marketing episodes are often called transactions. Webster (1992) defines transaction at its purest level as 'a one-time exchange of value between two parties with no prior or subsequent interaction'. This is in line with other researchers' interpretation of a transaction in an industrial market (Dwyer et al., 1987; Heide, 1994).

The term episode is used within the interaction research tradition (Håkansson, 1982), where it is defined as having four elements: A. product or service exchange; B. information exchange; C. financial exchange; and D. social exchange. It is, in their view, important to distinguish between an individual episode and the longer-term aspects of a relationship that both affects and is affected by each episode. We feel that this definition could be used also in consumer markets.

Another concept, service encounter, which is often used within service quality research, intuitively refers only to the personal interaction between seller and buyer. Transactions and interactions (Storbacka, 1993) have also been used as synonyms for episodes. Both give, however, more

limited connotations compared to episodes as defined above. As interactions are often used to cover the interaction between people in a service situation, or can be interpreted as one act within an episode, we prefer the episode concept.

It is, however, important to distinguish our episode concept from how the same term is used in critical incident studies. There an incident is considered to be of an episodic nature contrasted to a multiattribute-approach (Stauss, 1993).

DIFFERENT TYPES OF RELATION

A relation consists of a number of episodes. There are, however, different situations for different types of service. If the service is of a continuous type, where the customer makes a contract about service delivery with the service provider, a relation is established when the contract is signed (e.g. Cable TV). If, on the other hand, the service is of a discrete type, i.e. the customer makes a separate decision each time which service provider to use, some type of relation is established when the second purchase is made (e.g. restaurant). One episode, i.e. the first purchase from a service provider, would not yet represent a relation. It is the necessary starting-point for a relation but it might be the first, and at the same time last, contact with the service provider. Often a relation is defined only as repurchase events. In other words, if the customer *buys* more than once it is considered to constitute a relation between the firm and the customer. In this very simple definition of a relation, no consideration is given to whether the customer has a choice or not.

A long-term relationship in industrial markets also exists when there is a contract between the parties (Dwyer et al., 1987; Heide, 1994; Webster, 1992), or when there simply is a repeat purchase situation (Dwyer et al., 1987; Heide, 1994). Thus, Dwyer et al. suggest that 'relational aspects start to appear when the buyer pays by check or the seller schedules delivery for next week' (p. 12), and Heide states that, 'Generally, when discrete exchange is abandoned, some form of relationship is crafted' (p. 74).

If we, however, adopt a more strict view on

FIGURE 2:   DIFFERENT TYPES OF RELATIONS

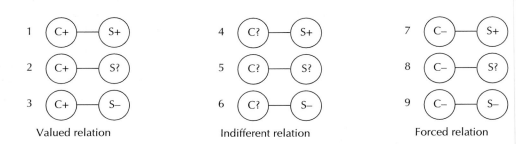

C = customer, S = service firm, + = commitment to establish and maintain relation, ? = indifference regarding relation, − = commitment to prevent or end relation

relations, as used within the interaction approach of industrial marketing, there will be a difference between loyalty based on repeat buying and a 'true' relation where both parties are *committed* to the relation. A relation is then characterised by some kind of economic, social, legal, or technological bonds between the customer and the firm. According to Martin and Goodell (1991), commitment for products can be described in a behavioural and an attitudinal dimension. It is of interest to look not only at the frequency of purchases and proportion of one service provider in total purchases, but at purchase preferences. Involvement with the service may affect which component of commitment describes loyalty best. For low-involvement services it may be the behavioural component and for high-involvement services the effect of attitudes may be greater. Random purchase behaviour is a sign of low service commitment. This type of behaviour may be found particularly for services with little differentiation. In our view a customer is positively committed only if the repeat purchase behaviour is based on a positive attitude. A negatively committed customer shows a negative attitude but might still buy repeatedly because of bonds.

When talking about consumer services we feel the focus has to be on the customers' side. In industrial markets mutual commitment is often

present (Håkansson and Snehota, 1993), which might not be the case in relations between private customers and service providers. Therefore, in consumer markets, it is more relevant to define a relation based on the customers' *attitudes and behaviour*. Another issue is the definition of when a relation is broken. In the continuous service case the discontinuation of the contract is the demarcation line. Discrete services represent again a less clear case. The customer might know that the relation is broken, but from the firm's point of view this is revealed only over time when the customer does not appear again.

Figure 2 lists all different combinations in a customer-service firm dyad regarding commitment in a relation between the two parties. The list is structured with priority given to the *customer's point of view* as this is considered to be the foundation of relationship quality. This is equivalent to the notion of customer-perceived service quality, where it is the customer's view of quality that is essential.

Three different types of relationship can be identified, a valued relation, an indifferent relation or a forced relation. The customer is respectively either positively committed, indifferent or negatively committed towards the service provider. In the same way that the customer can be committed to a service provider, the service provider can be committed to the customer, which shows as behaviour (actively contacting the consumer, giving individual information, extra benefits, etc.), and attitude (having a positive attitude towards the customer, preferring the customer to others, etc.).

Consequently we have nine different types of relation based on the minimum requirement that repeat purchasing can be observed or that a contract is made. More important is, however, to notice the situations where a relation is based on the customer's positive commitment. In these cases the customer has a positive attitude towards the company which is a future-oriented asset from the firm's point of view. Taking into consideration the other party in the relation brings in another dimension. Case 1 represents an ideal relation, following the definition within industrial marketing.

In a valued relation the customer is positively committed to the firm. The relationship is strong from the customer's viewpoint, i.e. he has a strong interest in keeping the relation alive. Case 1 is a relation characterised by *mutual commitment*. Both parties are interested in establishing, maintaining and enhancing the relation. This is the type of relation that has been dealt with in industrial marketing. Håkansson and Snehota (1993) have developed an analytical framework for business relationships between companies in the industrial markets. This framework is based on a definition of relationship as mutually oriented interaction over time between two parties, involving commitment and interdependence. They particularly stress the notion of mutual commitment as this represents a departure from the transaction-oriented view of exchange on the market. This definition and view of a relation (if defined at all) is typical within the interaction/network approach of industrial marketing. In the industrial context mutual commitment leads to multiple activity links, resource ties and actor bonds (Håkansson and Snehota, 1993, pp. 4–5). In the consumer market this type of intensive interaction might be more rare. In Case 2 the customer is very positive and loyal towards the company

but the company treats him like all other customers. There is no interest on the firm's part to distinguish between customers who have a relation with the company and those that have not. In Case 3 the customer wants to be a customer of the company but the service provider does not want to maintain the relationship. This could be the case in some bank relationships, e.g. where the customer is extremely unprofitable but, because of legal contracts, the bank cannot throw out the customer. The customer, on the other hand, may be interested in the relationship because he has financial difficulties and is unable to change bank.

In an indifferent relation the customer uses the company's services but he does so out of habit, and is neither positively nor negatively committed to the company. The customer is not in any way involved in the service, it has no particular importance to him. He might feel that there are small, if any, differences between different service providers, and his bonds to the service provider are probably weaker than in the cases where the customer is committed to the relationship. There may, however, also be strong economic, legal or technological bonds, but the customer still feels that all companies are the same. The idea of, for example, changing bank has never occurred to him. It is also possible that this is his second or third relationship in a portfolio of relations, and that he knows so little about the provider that this is the reason for indifference. Still he uses the company in a way that may be called a relation. In Case 4 the service company is interested in the customer and would like him to take a greater interest in the firm (e.g. deposit a greater proportion of his savings into the bank). In the fifth case both parties are indifferent, which could be the case for customers of, for example, a regular hamburger restaurant or pizzeria. The customer perceives no, or small, differences between the available service firms. In the sixth case the service company is negatively committed to the consumer, which could happen if a customer no longer fits into the firm's business

FIGURE 3:   DIFFERENT PATTERNS OF EPISODES IN A RELATION

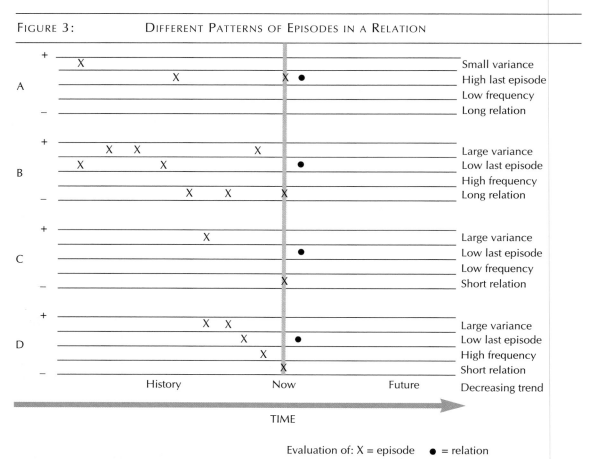

Evaluation of: X = episode   ● = relation

concept (size of savings in bank too small, does not dress 'correctly' for a fine restaurant, etc.).

Customers who have a forced relation with a service provider are negatively committed to the company. They would like to switch service provider if possible, but they are restricted by formal bonds, or the lack of alternatives. The latter can be seen as an exceptional case. A customer who is truly negative can still be an interesting customer for the service provider, who may thus be positive towards the relationship. Something may have occurred which turned a positive or indifferent customer into a negatively committed one. The bank may have made a mistake which the customer cannot accept, and he is prepared to switch banks as soon as it will be possible. The bank can either have an interest in

keeping the customer, no particular interest in the customer or be happy to get rid of him.

If a firm through direct marketing repeatedly approaches a customer, without this customer showing a preference for the firm, there is no relation. It might only be concluded that the firm is engaged in relationship marketing, with the aim of creating a relationship with the customer.

A problem becomes apparent when we wish to measure the customer's perception of a service episode versus his perceptions of a relationship. We will only point out some measurement problems here as it is beyond the scope of this paper. A discussion on the relative importance of the concepts can be found in Strandvik and Liljander (1994). When we measure only one particular episode, we make an assumption that this is a reli-

FIGURE 4: DIFFERENT RELATIONSHIP ASSORTMENTS (CUSTOMER'S POINT OF VIEW)

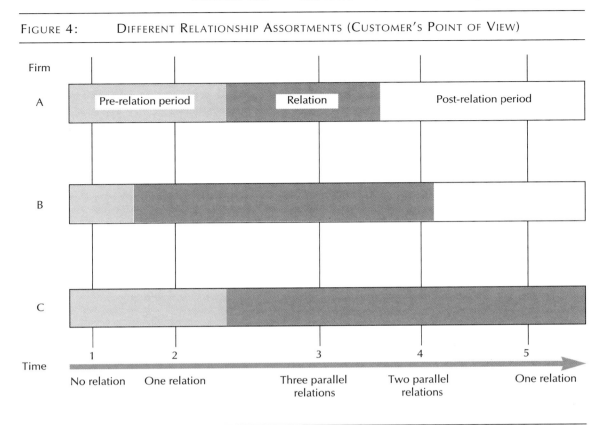

able sample of how the service provider is generally perceived. It does not take into account that the provider may have a particularly bad day, that the personnel may act differently because the customers are evaluating them, or that the customer may, or may not, have visited the company before. Figure 3 illustrates four fictive customers' perceptions of a company at different points in time.

The quality of service has clearly varied somewhat over time. When customers are asked to fill out a questionnaire, they all have different perceptions of the company for this episode (now). Thus the company will know that different customers perceive it differently but it does not know if this is how the customers normally perceive the company. The customers in Figure 3 have different histories with the service. Customer C has only one previous encounter with the company and customer A has only two previous encounters. For

customer A the variation in service between encounters is low, but for customer C it is very high. For customer D the trend is clearly downward and it is not likely that he will continue to frequent this company for long if the trend does not change. Customer B has all kinds of experiences with the company. What happens then when we ask the customers to give an evaluation of their relation over time with the company? In the example they have all marked the same spot on the scale. How is this possible? The problem with measuring a service relationship is that we do not know the importance that the customers give the different episodes. We may get an average of all episodes, as far as the customer can remember, we may get an average of some of the last episodes, or the value may be affected by one particular memorable episode. If the customer gives an average, we will not spot positive or negative trends in the service evaluation. Thus to under-

FIGURE 5:   SERVICE TYPES

	SELDOM USED	REGULARLY USED
DISCRETE	Hotel (holiday) Real estate services Holiday travel package Medical services Educational services Restaurant	Hotel (business) Restaurant Transportation Retailing Hairdresser
CONTINUOUS	Insurance Educational services Medical services	Banking services Cleaning services Telephone services Kindergarten Cable TV

stand the relation as it is perceived now, we need information about its history. It is possible to ask the customer also for the range of service performance that he has experienced with the company, but it should then be done in a way which gives us not only the highest and lowest performance, but what is 'normal' performance.

A customer can, of course, have simultaneous relations with several competing service providers. A hypothetical situation is depicted in Figure 4. When we look at a customer's history of relations with a service, we will probably find that the number of relations have changed over time. There is a pre-relation period when the potential customer is aware of alternatives, has some information, attitudes and beliefs, but has still not had the need for a relation.

This would be the case of, for example, children who do not yet have a bank account, or are not old enough to go to a discothèque. Then one relation begins, then perhaps after some time another, and later a third relation is established. Over time, some of these relations will be dropped (the customer moves, some force is applied on the relationship) and other relationships may be established. To get a better understanding of customers' relationships we need to study their histories, how they were started and why they were ended.

DIFFERENT TYPES OF SERVICES

One area that seems somewhat neglected in the service quality research is the question of differences in services. This is especially important when we look at the differences between studying service episodes and relationships. We look at the difference between services by emphasising both the contractual/discrete nature of services and their usage pattern, since these aspects have implications for whether it is practically possible to study episodes of, or/and relationships with, the service. A matrix which illustrates different types of services is depicted in Figure 5.

Analysed from the perspective of evaluating episodes vs. relations, some distinctions can be made between continuous services and discrete services. Discrete services consist of service episodes that are separate entities, e.g. restaurant services, repair services, hotel services, retailing services. Some are used regularly and often (transportation, retailing services), others are used only occasionally or just once (hotel services, real estate services, etc.). The customer makes each time a decision about which service provider to use.

Continuous services are often based on a contract and the customer uses the service on a regular basis, without making a choice each time, e.g. telephone, banking and insurance services. There are also services that fall in between discrete and continuous services. They have a long duration but are of a discrete type, e.g. holiday travel packages, educational services and medical services. It is also to be noted that although some consumers may use a certain type of service regularly, others may use the same service only seldom (e.g. medical services, educational services, hotel and restaurant services). Likewise, in some situations a service may be considered as discrete, and in another situation as continuous (one educational course/four-year education). This has implications for measuring episodes/relationships. Services that are of a discrete nature and are seldom used can be said to be episode-dominated. In the other cases relationship quality grows in importance.

RELATIONSHIP STRENGTH

Relationship strength is generally a question of how committed the customer is to the service provider and what drives that commitment. In the interaction approach and network approach within industrial marketing, bonds are considered to be present in relations. These have an influence on the relationship strength. Besides the bonds presented in this literature we propose that there might be strong psychological bonds, based on the customer's positive commitment.

Easton and Araujo (1989) give a conceptual overview of bond strength within the network approach. They stress that high bond strength is often taken for granted in industrial relationship studies, and mostly companies with high strength are chosen for research. Bond strength is also often inferred from the nature of the bond. Thus, if technological and social bonds are present, a strong relationship is assumed. Easton and Araujo suggest that the strength of a bond can be known only when it is put to the test, i.e. when one studies the force that it takes to break the bond. The authors suggest different strains which may appear

in the relationship. Because of environmental changes one of the partners may start to loosen the relationship with the aim of changing partner. Another external force could be alternative partners who try to disrupt the relationship. One partner can also start to move away from the other on some dimension within the relationship, or both partners may have been forced into a relation they prefer not to have. An interesting area of research would therefore be to study the processes which lead up to the breaking of bonds. When bonds are stretched to a breaking-point it would be possible to study their nature in more depth.

The issues mentioned by Easton and Araujo seem to be important also in consumer markets. It is of great interest to study the strength of bonds between a customer and service provider. How strong are the social bonds between a consumer and, for example, his bank, the restaurants he frequents, the stores where he shops, etc.? We could take any part of the sacrifices that a customer has to make to consume a service, and study how much more he would be prepared to sacrifice and still use the same service provider. How strong are, for example, the customer's economic and legal bonds with his bank? How much would they have to raise the interest rates or charges at the bank before he switches banks? Or will his social bonds with the bank manager keep him in his old bank, even if it became more expensive than to switch banks? We can also take the benefits that the consumer gets with the services, i.e. the quality dimensions of the service, and ask how much they could be lowered without him switching service provider. Will he stop to shop in a store if the personnel doesn't speak his language anymore (minority group)? Will he continue to use the same pub if his favourite bartender moves to another pub?

We can also look at actual incidents (positive and negative) that the consumer has experienced with the company. How did they affect the relationship? If a negative incident did not break the relationship, then why did it not? Were the bonds too strong, and in that case, what type of bonds were they?

Relationship length is usually considered as some kind of strength. It is, however, extremely difficult to determine what constitutes a long relationship (Easton and Araujo, 1989). This would have to be determined by the researchers separately for different services. Relationship strength has not been discussed in detail in the relationship marketing literature. Customer loyalty can implicitly be seen as a synonym of strength here. Christopher et al. (1991, p. 22), for example, mention this concept when discussing different levels in the customer relationship. They see increasing loyalty in 'the relationship marketing ladder of customer loyalty' where a customer can be a 'prospect', 'customer', 'client', 'supporter' or 'advocate'. The traditional 4Ps are thought to be effective in transforming a prospect to a customer, but to reach the higher levels other elements of marketing should be involved. It is considered to be a question of taking the customer beyond 'satisfaction' to 'delight' by delivering services that exceed expectations. The same idea is also present in much of the service quality literature (e.g. Rust and Oliver, 1994.)

Indications of different degrees of relationship strength could thus be, for example: A. if the customer talks positively/negatively about the company; B. the customer complains to the personnel/service provider; C. the customer simultaneously uses also competing service companies; D. the customer uses only company X; E. the customer would end his relations with the service company if there was an alternative; F. the degree to which the customer feels that his service company is better/worse than competing companies; G. his involvement in the company; H. degree to which customer tolerates mistakes without being upset with the company; and I. length of relationship.

RELATIONSHIP EQUITY

Within the marketing mix paradigm of consumer goods, brand equity has been introduced as an important factor (Aaker, 1991). Brand equity is defined as 'a set of brand assets and liabilities linked to a brand, its name and symbol, that add to or subtract from the value provided by the product or service to a firm and/or to that firm's customers' (Aaker, 1991, p. 15). Keller (1993) has defined customer-based brand equity as 'the differential effect of brand knowledge on consumer response to the marketing of the brand'. He further proposed that 'a brand is said to have positive (negative) customer-based brand equity if consumers react more (less) favourably to the product, price, promotion or distribution of the brand than they do to the same marketing mix element when it is attributed to a fictitiously named or unnamed version of the product or service'. Brand equity is seen as an intangible asset that is based on the consumer's response to a brand.

This view is heavily based on the marketing mix foundation, focusing on transactions with anonymous customers. The interesting thing is that the reason for introducing the concept is to point to *the value of the brand over time*. To relate brand equity to relations in this form, the definition has to be stretched, or given a wider interpretation, keeping the underlying, implicit meaning of the concept. A service firm can be considered to be a 'brand'. Brand equity should be conceived as relative value, as compared to some standard, for example, competitors, or not using the service at all.

We define relationship equity as the differential economic value of the customer's response to the service firm. Our suggestion is that it would theoretically be possible to consider a number of different reference points for calculating the difference in economic value, for example, a new unknown entrepreneur offering the same services, but the most realistic reference point would be the customer's current best alternative. This would mean that relationship equity is measured by comparing the focal relationship with the customer's best alternative and it would be determined in monetary terms: how much the customer is prepared to 'pay' to maintain the relation instead of switching to the alternative. Methods to measure brand equity have been proposed in Keller (1993) and Monroe (1990) but are not elaborated further in this paper.

FIGURE 6: A RELATIONSHIP QUALITY MODEL

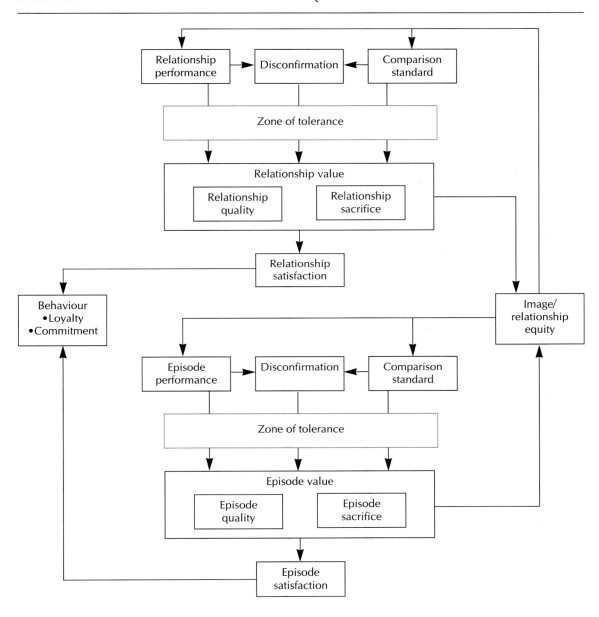

A PERCEIVED RELATIONSHIP QUALITY MODEL

In the service quality literature there is currently a discussion on the interrelationship between quality, satisfaction and value (see, for example, Oliver, 1993; Anderson and Fornell, 1994; Parasuraman et al., 1994; Rust and Oliver, 1994). In this section a dynamic customer-perceived service quality model is presented. The model integrates episodes with relations and the perceived measures with behaviour. All possible relations are not depicted in the model as these depend on situational characteristics and the type of service that is studied. Likewise, not all concepts are needed in all situations, or the importance of them in determining satisfaction or behaviour may vary.

One important aspect in the model is that service quality and satisfaction can be experienced both at an episode and a relationship level. There has been a lot of confusion regarding the differences between service quality and satisfaction. According to some service quality researchers satisfaction is connected to episodes, while service quality is connected to evaluations of a service over time (Parasuraman et al., 1988). It is only recently that the conceptual and empirical overlap between the two concepts has raised a debate among service quality researchers (Liljander and Strandvik, 1992, 1993b; Dabholkar, 1993; Oliver, 1993; Patterson and Johnson, 1993; Parasuraman et al., 1994; Rust and Oliver, 1994; Bitner and Hubbert, 1994; Bolton and Drew, 1994; Anderson and Fornell, 1994). The debate has been concerned with similarities and links between the concepts and the discussion has been kept on a conceptual level. In their latest article Parasuraman et al. (1994) take the view that quality precedes satisfaction, and that satisfaction can be measured for several transactions. The difference between satisfaction and service quality can, in our view, be explained by introducing value as a mediating variable (Strandvik and Liljander, 1994).

When we look at an episode in the model, perceived performance of the episode may affect episode quality either directly or indirectly through disconfirmation of a comparison standard. The comparison standard may be any of the standards mentioned in satisfaction and service quality literature (e.g. Woodruff et al., 1991; Zeithaml et al., 1993; Liljander and Strandvik, 1993b). Disconfirmation may be measured either directly or as an inferred measure. It can also be argued that performance already contains an implicit comparison with some comparison standard (performance is used as a synonym of perceived performance). Perceived performance is the consumer's cognitive evaluation of a service. The comparison standard may also influence the customer's performance evaluation directly, as has been shown in some studies (Liljander and Strandvik, 1994; Liljander, 1994a).

The core idea with tolerance zones is that customers may accept variations in service performance within a certain range. Earlier service quality models have postulated that customers react on all discrepancies between comparison standard and performance. If tolerance zones exist, this effect is moderated by them and less direct.

Earlier service quality models did not include the customer's sacrifices (money, effort in time spent, other sacrifices). Lately, however, some researches have suggested that at least price should be included (Koelemeijer et al., 1993; Parasuraman et al., 1994). In our model we consider sacrifice (Monroe, 1990; Liljander and Strandvik, 1993a) to be an important part of the satisfaction process. If the perceived quality and perceived sacrifices connected to one episode are in balance, or if quality exceeds the sacrifice, then the customer will perceive high value and will probably be satisfied. Liljander (1994b) found that episode value for a restaurant service had a strong effect on satisfaction, but also that the model which explained satisfaction best included also performance and direct disconfirmation. She also found that there were dissatisfied customers who nevertheless perceived positive episode value, and also satisfied customers who perceived negative episode value.

Different degrees of satisfaction will lead to different types of behaviour. The type of behaviour that usually has been studied is repurchase and recommendation behaviour. Still more important is, however, how these concepts are related to customers' actual behaviour, how committed they are to the service provider. Usually only intended behaviour is measured in both service quality and satisfaction studies.

The value perception will affect the general image (Grönroos, 1990) of the service provider. The image in turn affects the predictive expectations of the next service episode, and over time predictive expectations and performance will be equal.

Relationship performance consists of the experience of several episode performances. This is how performance is in fact measured by SERVQUAL (Parasuraman et al., 1988). In contrast to SERVQUAL we think that it would be possible to compare relationship performance to any of the standards proposed in the literature, with the exception of predictive expectations which are specifically connected to one service episode. Relationship performance can be seen as an average of all previous experiences or it may be measured as a range of performance levels (Poiesz and Bloemer, 1991). It is also possible that customers will be affected more by episodes that are near in time, and not consider the actual whole range of experience performances. Or they may be affected mainly by one or more critical episodes, positive or negative. This remains to be studied. What has been shown is that relationships are important and that relationship performance has a greater effect than episode performance on intended behaviour (Liljander, 1994a and b; Strandvik and Liljander, 1994).

Relationship sacrifice refers to all perceived sacrifices made over previous episodes, and is compared to a relationship quality measure. The customer thus evaluates what he gets (relationship benefits) with what he gives (relationship sacrifice). Relationship sacrifice includes also switching costs caused by possible exit barriers. This comparison leads to a perception of relationship value. Although the value of one episode may be perceived as low, the relationship value might still be high, due to all the benefits received on previous episodes. The same is true for relationship satisfaction, which is the overall satisfaction of several episodes. The relationship value affects behaviour through perceived relationship satisfaction. One dissatisfactory episode does not have to break the relationship if the previous episodes have been satisfactory.

In the model relationship quality is connected to relationship strength, i.e. behavioural aspects including loyalty and commitment, and to relationship equity. *Relationship strength* is defined as what it takes to break the relationship. Customers can get advantages by building a relation with a service provider. For example, customer loyalty programmes may give monetary advantages and the customer may get better service if he is known by the service personnel. Measured in economic terms the relationship strength is equal to *relationship equity*. Relationship equity is based on the customer's perceived *relationship value*. Relationship strength and equity drives future profitability of the company. A strong relationship equity indicates higher customer loyalty and reduced price sensitivity. Customers with high relationship equity are also less influenced by competitors' products.

DISCUSSION

What is the significance of relationship quality from the service firm's point of view? In a relationship a certain episode always has a history and a potential future. It is probable that the customer's evaluation of an episode is influenced by these factors. A customer interviewed at a certain point of time would likewise evaluate his relation with the service provider based on the history of the relation and on anticipation of the future. In traditional service quality measures there is no recognition of the dynamics within a relation. What the implications would be when measuring relationship quality is beyond the scope of this paper, but such aspects as the frequency of problems in the quality, resolution of problems, severity of problems, variation in performance, the trend in performance, rate of adaptation or learning – all dynamic aspects should be addressed.

The significance of episodes lies in the power of understanding which episodes represent relation-breaking incidents, or weaken the relationship, and, on the other hand, which kinds of episode result in a deeper, stronger relation between the customer and the firm. The evaluation of an episode has been the prevailing perspective in customer satisfaction studies. When focusing on service quality it has either explicitly (SERVQUAL) or implicitly been based on the accumulated, overall experience. When selecting only current customers of a service firm their answers will be heavily biased towards satisfaction with the relationship. This is, however, how most of the studies concerning service quality are done. Two other groups would probably give another answer when evaluating the service firm. These groups are A. customers that have ended their relationship with the firm and B. customers that never have bought from the service provider but are in the market.

As has been shown, a relation might emerge without relationship marketing. This is probably the most common case in the consumer markets. Actively focusing on and managing customer relationships has, however, been proposed within service marketing. What is important from the service firm's point of view is to study service quality as an indicator of the future potential and competitive advantage on the market. Applying a dynamic perspective on service quality would therefore be necessary. Return on quality has a time dimension. Further work along the lines proposed in this paper would represent one way forward.

REFERENCES

Aaker, David A. (1991), *Managing Brand Equity*, Free Press, NY.

Anderson, Eugene W. and Claes Fornell (1994), 'A Customer Satisfaction Process Research Prospectus' in Roland T. Rust and Richard L. Oliver (eds.), *Service Quality, New Directions in Theory and Practice*, Sage Publications, London, pp. 241–68.

Bitner, Mary Jo and Amy R. Hubbert (1994), 'Encounter Satisfaction Versus Overall Satisfaction Versus Quality: The Customer's Voice' in Roland T. Rust and Richard L. Oliver (eds.), *Service Quality, New Directions in Theory and Practice*, Sage Publications, London, pp. 79–94.

Bolton, Ruth N. and James H. Drew (1994), 'Linking Customer Satisfaction to Service Operations and Outcomes' in Roland T. Rust and Richard L. Oliver (eds.), *Service Quality, New Directions in Theory and Practice*, Sage Publications, London, pp. 173–200.

Boulding, William, Ajay Kalra, Richard Staelin and Valarie Zeithaml (1993), 'A Dynamic Process Model of Service Quality: From Expectations to Behavioural Intentions', *Journal of Marketing Research*, vol. XXX, February, pp. 7–27.

Christopher, Martin, Adrian Payne and David Ballantyne (1991), *Relationship Marketing: Bringing Quality, Customer Service and Marketing Together*, Butterworth-Heinemann Ltd, Oxford.

Danaber, Peter J. and Jan Mattsson (1994), 'Customer Satisfaction During the Service Delivery Process', presented at 3 Dienstleitungsmarketing-Workshop, 24–25.2.1994, Berlin, Germany.

Dabholkar, Prathiba A. (1993), 'Customer Satisfaction and Service Quality: Two Constructs or One', paper presented at 1993 Conference on Consumer Satisfaction, Dissatisfaction and Complaining Behaviour, 2–5 June, Knoxville, USA.

Dwyer, Robert F., Paul H. Schurr and Sejo Oh (1987), 'Developing Buyer–Seller Relationships', *Journal of Marketing*, vol. 51, April, pp. 11–27.

Easton, Geoffrey and Luis Araujo (1989), 'The Network Approach' in Lars Hallén and Jan Johansson (eds.), *Networks of Relationships in International Industrial Marketing, Advances in International Marketing*, vol. 3, JAI Press Inc., London, 97–119.

Grönroos, Christian (1990), *Service Management and Marketing: Managing Moments of Truth in Service Competition*, Lexington Books, Mass.

Grönroos, Christian (1993a), 'Toward a Third Phase in Service Quality Research: Challenges and Future Directions' in Teresa A. Swartz, David E. Bowen and Stephen W. Brown (eds.), *Advances in Services*

Marketing Management, vol. 2, JAI Press Inc., Greenwich, Connecticut, pp. 49–64.

Grönroos, Christian (1993b), 'From Marketing Mix to Relationship Marketing, Toward a Paradigm Shift in Marketing', working papers no. 263, Swedish School of Economics and Business Administration, Helsinki, Finland.

Håkansson, Håkan (1982), *International Marketing and Purchasing of Industrial Goods*, John Wiley & Sons, Chichester.

Håkansson, Håkan and Ivan Snehota (1993), 'The Content and Functions of Business Relationships', paper presented at 9th IMP Conference, 23–5 September 1993, Bath, UK.

Heide, Jan B. (1994), 'Interorganisational Governance in Marketing Channels', *Journal of Marketing*, vol. 58, January, pp. 71–85.

Keller, Kevin Lane (1993), 'Conceptualising, Measuring, and Managing Customer-based Brand Equity', *Journal of Marketing*, vol. 57, January, pp. 1–22.

Koelemeijer, Kitty, Henk Roest and Theo Verhallen (1993), 'An Integrative Framework of Perceived Service Quality and its Relations to Satisfaction/ Dissatisfaction, Attitude and Repurchase Intentions' in Josep Chias and Joan Sureda (eds.), *Marketing for the New Europe: Dealing with Complexity*, Proceedings, vol. 1, from European Marketing Academy Conference, Barcelona, 25–8 May, pp. 683–9.

Liljander, Veronica (1994a), 'Modeling Perceived Service Quality Using Different Comparison Standards', *Journal of Consumer Satisfaction, Dissatisfaction and Complaining Behavior*, vol. 7, forthcoming.

Liljander, Veronica (1994b), 'Introducing Deserved Service and Equity into Service Quality Models', paper presented at 3 Dienstleitungsmarketing-Workshop, 24–5.2.1994, Berlin, Germany.

Liljander, Veronica and Tore Strandvik (1992), 'The Relation between Service Quality, Satisfaction and Intentions', working papers no. 243, Swedish School of Economics and Business Administration, Helsinki, Finland.

Liljander, Veronica and Tore Strandvik (1993a), 'Estimating Zones of Tolerance in Perceived Service Quality', *International Journal of Service Industry Management*, vol. 4, no. 2, pp. 6–28.

Liljander, Veronica and Tore Strandvik (1993b), 'Different Comparison Standards as Determinants of Service Quality', *Journal of Consumer Satisfaction, Dissatisfaction and Complaining Behavior*, vol. 6, pp. 118–32.

Liljander, Veronica and Tore Strandvik (1994), 'The Relation between Service Quality, Satisfaction and Intentions' in Paul Kunst and Jos Lemmink (eds.), *Managing Service Quality, Volume II*, Paul Chapman Publishing Ltd, London.

Martin, Charles L. and Phillips W. Goodell (1991), 'Historical, Descriptive and Strategic Perspectives on the Construct of Product Commitment', *European Journal of Marketing*, vol. 25, no. 1, pp. 53–60.

Miettilä, Aino and Jan-Åke Törnroos (1993), 'The Meaning of Time in the Study of Industrial Buyer–Seller Relationships', series discussion and working papers 4, 1993, Turku School of Economics and Business Administration, Finland.

Monroe, Kent B. (1990), *Pricing – Making Profitable Decisions*, 2nd ed., McGraw-Hill, NY.

Oliver, Richard L. (1993), 'A Conceptual Model of Service Quality and Service Satisfaction: Compatible Goals, Different Concepts' in Teresa A. Swartz, David E. Bowen and Stephen W. Brown (eds.), *Advances in Services Marketing Management*, vol. 2, JAI Press Inc., Greenwich, Connecticut, pp. 65–85.

Parasuraman, A., Valarie A. Zeithaml and Leonard L. Berry (1988), 'SERVQUAL: A Multiple-item Scale for Measuring Consumer Perceptions of Service Quality, *Journal of Retailing*, vol. 64, no. 1, Spring, pp. 12–40.

Parasuraman, A., Valarie A. Zeithaml and Leonard L. Berry (1994), 'Reassessment of Expectations as a Comparison Standard in Measuring Service Quality: Implications for Future Research', *Journal of Marketing*, vol. 58, January, pp. 111–24.

Patterson, Paul G. and Lester W. Johnson (1993), 'Disconfirmation of Expectations and the Gap Model of Service Quality', *Journal of Consumer Satisfaction, Dissatisfaction and Complaining Behavior*, vol. 6, pp. 90–9.

Poiesz, Theo B.C. and José M.M. Bloemer (1991), 'Customer (Dis)satisfaction with the Performance of Complex Products and Services – The Applicability of the (Dis)confirmation Paradigm' in *Marketing Thought Around the World*, vol. 2, proceedings from European Marketing Academy Conference 1991, Dublin, pp. 446–62.

Rust, Roland T. and Richard L. Oliver (1994), 'Service Quality: Insights and Managerial Implications from the Frontier' in Roland T. Rust and Richard L. Oliver (eds.), *Service Quality, New Directions in Theory and Practice*, Sage Publications, London, pp. 1–20.

Stauss, Bernd (1993), 'Using Critical Incident Technique in Measuring and Managing Service Quality' in Eberhard E. Scheuing and William F. Christopher (eds.), *The Service Quality Handbook*, AMACOM,

American Marketing Association, NY, pp. 408–27.

Storbacka, Kaj (1993), 'Customer Relationship Profitability in Retail Banking', Research Reports no. 29, Swedish School of Economics and Business Administration, Helsinki, Finland.

Strandvik, Tore and Veronica Liljander (1994), 'A Comparison of Episode Performance and Relationship Performance for a Discrete Service', paper presented at Dienstleitungsmarketing-Workshop, 24–5.2.1994, Berlin, Germany.

Webster, Fredrick E., Jr (1992), 'The Changing Role of Marketing in the Corporation', *Journal of Marketing*, vol. 56, October, pp. 1–17.

Wilson, D.T. and V. Mummalaneni (1986), 'Bonding and Commitment in Buyer–Seller Relationships: A Preliminary Conceptualisation', *Industrial Marketing and Purchasing*, vol. 1, no. 3, pp. 44–58.

Woodruff, Robert B., D. Scott Clemons, David W. Schumann, Sarah F. Gardial and Mary Jane Burns (1991), 'The Standards Issue in SC/D Research: A Historical Perspective', *Journal of Consumer Satisfaction, Dissatisfaction and Complaining Behavior*, vol. 4, pp. 103–9.

Zeithaml. V., L. Berry and A. Parasuraman (1993), 'The Nature and Determinants of Customer Expectations of Service', *Journal of the Academy of Marketing Science*, vol. 21, no. 1, Winter, pp. 1–11.

Defining Marketing: A Market-oriented Approach

Christian Grönroos

Traditionally marketing in practice, marketing management, as it is perceived all over the Western world, is based on definitions agreed on in the US and presented in American textbooks. However, there are research traditions within at least two sub-areas of marketing emerging in Northern Europe, and gradually even spreading over larger parts of the world, which do not agree with the standard views of what marketing is.

The purpose of this article is to analyse the recently renewed American definition of marketing and its appropriateness in view of the modern marketing research in Finland and the Scandinavian countries. A definition of marketing which is more geared to the nature of modern marketing research and practice in Northern Europe is put forward. This definition is intended to be more market-oriented than the standard definitions of most textbooks on marketing and marketing management.

MARKETING AS A PHILOSOPHY: THE MARKETING CONCEPT

According to the marketing concept, which states what marketing as a philosophy is, the firm should base all its activities on the needs and wants of customers in selected target markets. At the same time, restrictions due to the surrounding society (laws, industry agreements, norms, etc.) have to be recognised. If this basic philosophy is taken into account by the firm, its operations should be successful and profitable.

This is also called a *market-oriented view* in contrast to *production orientation*, where the firm's activities are geared to existing technology, products or production processes.

THE MARKETING MIX MODEL

For a marketer it is easy to adopt the marketing concept as a basis for marketing planning. However, marketing as it is supposed to be implemented in practical business situations according to the standard marketing models of our textbooks may not always fit reality as perceived by top management.

As was indicated above, the marketing concept is transformed to marketing in practice in the standard literature on marketing management (for example, Kotler[1]). There are dozens of textbooks covering the topic in more or less exactly the same manner. This body of literature is reviewed by Gummesson.[2] The core of marketing is the marketing mix. The marketer, who in the organisational structure is placed in a marketing department, plans various means of competition, and blends them into a marketing mix, so that profit function is optimised. Pedagogically the marketing mix of different means of competition is labelled the 4Ps.[3]

Recently, the Ps of marketing mix have been

Reprinted with permission from *European Journal of Marketing*, vol. 23, no. 1, pp. 52–60.

found too limited, and, in the context of *mega-marketing*, Kotler,[4] adding *politics* and *public relations*, has expanded them to 6Ps, while there have been found to be as many as 7Ps in services marketing.[5] This is not a very valid way of redefining the core of marketing, when the old model is considered too limited, although it includes new perspectives and thus improves the older definition. However, it is equivalent to adding a few more items to a list, which is used as a definition of a phenomenon, in order to update the definition. Such a way of defining phenomena cannot be considered the best one. There are always items missing, whereas other items on the list become obsolete. No real change has occurred, so that the definition would better fit new conditions. (See also the criticism of this kind of expansion of the 4Ps in Gummesson.[2])

Marketing thought in the academic establishment, as well as among practitioners, is based on this marketing mix approach. The marketing mix model is widely considered the general marketing model over almost all the Western world. What is easily forgotten is the fact that this model was developed in North America, using empirical data concerned mainly with consumer packaged goods and durables. Moreover, the marketing environment is in many respects quite specific, e.g. a huge domestic market, a certain media structure, for instance, as far as TV and radio are concerned, and a non-oligopolistic, highly competitive distribution system.

This marketing model may cover many marketing situations in North America, but its general validity has more been taken for granted than formally proved.

In spite of all this, we have, for instance, no European marketing theory or model geared to European conditions. The marketing mix model has been used in our environment unchanged; moreover, it has also been applied to other types of product than the ones the empirical evidence behind the model covers. For example, in industrial marketing and in marketing of services, the marketing mix has already had a powerful impact, especially among American researchers. However,

within these areas, new approaches have emerged in Northern Europe.

The victorious crusade of the marketing mix approach is perhaps easy to understand, though. Marketing management was developed in a systematic way first in the US, and the new marketing thinking swept over Europe, where this pedagogically sound but in other respects in many situations less valid model was quickly accepted. Of course, nobody other than the European researchers are to blame for this. As one practitioner put it: ' we have been let down, but only by ourselves; we should be developing with greater purpose our own European management craft'[6] (p. 227).

AMERICAN MARKETING ASSOCIATION'S DEFINITION OF MARKETING

Traditionally, the American Marketing Association (AMA) seems to have been authorised to define what marketing is. In the renewed definition of 1985, marketing is described as follows: 'Marketing is the process of planning and executing the *conception, pricing, promotion* and *distribution* of ideas, goods and services to create exchange and satisfy individual and organisational objects' (author's italics).[7]

This definition is only a modernisation of the old one, which appears in standard marketing texts. No real shift in the views of what marketing is has occurred. It is only a new list of activities (in the old definition, the terms product, price, promotion and place were on the list). One major new aspect can be found, though: the fact that the *execution* of marketing plans has been upgraded and given the same priority as planning (interestingly enough, executing marketing decisions has been treated with the same importance as making marketing decisions, i.e. as planning, in Scandinavian literature on marketing for over a decade; see Gummesson[8]).

The definition inaugurated by the AMA states *what* marketing is, because of its nature as a list of items. The logical consequence is, of course, that anything other than 'conception, pricing, promotion and distribution' is by definition *not marketing*.

This definition is based on what is convenient for the firm to plan and execute as marketing. The activities of the AMA definition are easily defined and separated from other activities of the firm, and hence it is uncomplicated to organise for marketing. However, this definition does not take into consideration what the customer would want marketing to be. Of course, market research is conducted in order to find out what the market wants, but these pieces of research are more or less within the existing paradigm. Consequently, one may create new ways of doing old things, but in most cases the borderline of what a priori is considered marketing is not crossed.

As a marketing philosophy, the marketing concept is still valid. However, the standard way of transforming this concept to marketing in practice is *production-oriented* because it starts from the firm and not from the market. What is needed is a truly market-oriented definition of marketing.

NORDIC APPROACHES TO MARKETING RESEARCH

For more than ten years, researchers in Northern Europe have developed another approach to marketing within the areas of *industrial* and *services marketing*. This research is characterised by the fact that old walls dividing what marketing is from what it is not have been torn down. These walls, illustrated by the borderlines determined by the Ps of the marketing mix, have often become a burden for researchers, making innovative approaches seemingly wrong, outside the prevailing paradigm, and, therefore, impossible in the mind of the academic establishment.

This new research tradition can be described as hermeneutic and is aiming at developing a deeper understanding of the *marketing function* based on the customer relations and marketing situations that in fact exist. This research is highly empirical, although it is conceptual as well. It relies heavily on a close contact between researchers and the actors in the market-place and

on case studies as a research method, although more traditional, qualitative methods have also been used occasionally in situations where they fit in.

One may, in our opinion, talk about an emergent Nordic research tradition, although there have been few connections between research into industrial and services marketing, respectively. However, the research approaches and the methods used are very similar, and the results support each other, among other things, as far as the basic view of the marketing function is concerned. In industrial marketing, there is the *interaction/network approach*, which was born among researchers of the so-called IM Group in Sweden, and which has now spread outside Scandinavia to the Swedish-based IMP (International Marketing and Purchasing) Group (see, for example, Håkansson and Snehota;[9] Hammarkvist et al.;[10] Håkansson;[11] Håkansson and Johansson;[12] and Turnbull and Valla[13]).

In services marketing, the term *Nordic School of Services* has been adopted internationally by service researchers (see, for example, Gummesson;[8,14] Grönroos;[15,16,17] Lehtinen;[18,19] Grönroos and Gummesson;[20,21] and Gummesson and Grönroos[22]).

According to these approaches to industrial and services marketing respectively, the following is considered the core of marketing: the most important issue in marketing is to establish, strengthen and develop *customer relations* where they can be commercialised at a profit and where individual and organisational objectives are met.

MARKETING AND MARKET-ORIENTED MANAGEMENT

A key issue in modern Nordic research is the view of the marketing function. This function is not the same as the marketing department's. The latter's is an organisational solution only, whereas the size and diversity of the former depends on the nature of the customer relations. Hence, the marketing function is spread over a large part of the organisation outside the marketing department, and all of the activities which have an impact on the current and future buyer behaviour of the customers cannot be taken care of by marketing specialists only.

Many firms have responded to this fact and decreased the size and importance of their marketing departments to a considerable extent. In some cases, the marketing department has been closed down altogether. The responsibility for initiating and implementing marketing activities has been delegated to the line organisation. Thus, these firms have tried to achieve an integration between operations and marketing.[16]

Moreover, marketing is not only part of operations. Many staff and support functions include an element of marketing as well. In most firms, a large number of employees have something to do with marketing.[2] These employees may be in direct contact with some representatives of the customers (a household or an organisation) as, for example, over the counter in a bank, when rendering check-in and in-flight services in airline transportation, and in joint R&D projects, technical services, deliveries, customer training and telephone reception. In other cases, they may influence the customers indirectly. There are a lot of support functions which are required to enable other functions and persons to serve the consumer. Such persons will have to realise that other inter-firm functions, the operations of which depend on their service orientation, are, in fact, their *internal customers*.[2,23] Such internal customers have to be served as well as the ultimate, external customers are supposed to be.

As a matter of fact, there are frequently only a rather limited number of marketing specialists in a firm engaged in, for example, personal selling, mass communication, market research and marketing planning, whereas the employees involved in marketing-like contacts with the customers greatly outnumber the marketing specialists. The latter kind of employees are often called 'part-time marketers',[2] because their main job is something other than marketing, e.g. production, deliveries, technical service, invoicing, claims handling, telephone reception and R&D. Nevertheless, at the same time, they will have to

do their job in such a way, demonstrating such skills and service-mindedness, that the customers' trust in them is maintained and preferably strengthened. Simultaneously, the customers' trust in the firm itself will be maintained. If this is achieved, the employees are true 'part-time marketers' and fulfil their responsibilities as members of the total marketing function of the firm.

Far too often the 'part-time marketers' do not realise that they have this role as well, and if management fails to understand the dual responsibilities of many groups of employees, the situation becomes even more critical.

As marketing is spread all over the organisation, and the marketing specialists can take care of only a part of the total marketing function, the nature of marketing cannot be that of a specialist function only. Instead, marketing becomes an integral part of top management, where the marketing specialists may be needed to support management as far as, for instance, market research, personal selling and advertising are concerned. According to the Nordic research approach, it is more correct to view marketing as market-oriented management than as a separate function only (see, for example, Grönroos[17]).

THE CUSTOMER RELATION AS THE CORNERSTONE OF MARKETING

It is important to notice that marketing is not related to a predetermined set of means of competition in a marketing mix, and moreover, that the marketing function is not the same as the marketing department, which is supposed to be responsible for initiating, planning, executing and controlling the marketing activities of the firm, and that marketing is a management concern more than a specialist function only. Of course, one has to keep in mind that there are differences between industries, customers and even specific situations.

According to Nordic research, marketing revolves around customer relations, where the objectives of the parties involved are met through various kinds of exchanges. Customer relations is the key concept here. Exchanges take place in order to establish and maintain such relationships.

Long-term relationships with the customers especially are stressed in this research.[2] In contemporary American literature, such an approach to marketing is also emerging.[24,25] Establishing contact with a potential customer and achieving the first sales often cost so much that the return of that deal is minimal or even negative. Only when the relationship is continuing and leads to more business does the customer become more profitable to the seller. There are, of course, situations when this is not always or all true, but frequently enough it is much more profitable to try to develop enduring customer relations.

If such close and long-term customer relations can be achieved through, among other things, exchange of information, goods and services and social contacts, the possibility that this will lead to continued exchanges at a profit is high. The customer relation is commercialised. The same goes for consumer markets as well as industrial markets.

Furthermore, one should observe that in many situations there are several parties involved in a relation. The buyer and the seller act in a network consisting of, for example, suppliers, other customers, the customers' customers, financial organisations and political decision-makers. The whole network is part of the customer relation and has an impact on the development of the relation.[11]

THE ROLE OF PROMISES IN MARKETING

There is still another concept applied in modern Nordic marketing research which has to be included in a market-oriented framework of marketing. Calonius[26,27] has used the promise concept as an integral part of marketing. The background of this concept and its previous use in the marketing literature has been discussed by Calonius.[27]

In establishing and maintaining customer relations, the seller gives a set of promises which are connected with, for example, goods, services or systems of goods and services, financial solutions, materials administration, transfer of information, social contacts and a range of future commitments. On the other hand, the buyer gives another set of promises concerning his/her commitments in the relation. Then the promises have to be kept on both sides if the relation is expected to be maintained, developed and commercialised in the future for the mutual benefits of the seller and the buyer.

The promise concept is as important an element of the customer relation as the exchange concept. In fact, promises about the exchanges that are to take place are mutually given in the customer relations, and by the various exchanges that take place these promises are kept.

A NORDIC DEFINITION OF MARKETING

The marketing concept as a basic philosophy guiding marketing in practice still holds. There has been no debate over the concept itself. However, the definition of marketing in practice and the marketing management model have been criticised in much of the Nordic marketing research and in this article. A view of marketing, which is geared to the prevailing conditions in the market-place, the marketing situation, has been developed. The basic views of this approach are summarised in Figure 1.

In conclusion, we are going to suggest a Nordic definition of marketing which is developed according to the customers' views of the marketing function. This definition, based on the interaction/network approach to industrial marketing, the Nordic school of service approach to services marketing and the promise concept of buyer behaviour research by Calonius, can be stated as follows:

> Marketing is to establish, develop and commercialise long-term customer relationships, so that the objectives of the parties involved are met. This is done by a mutual exchange and keeping of promises.

This definition can, furthermore, be accompanied by the following supplement: the resources of the firm – personnel, technology and systems – have to be used in such a manner that the customer's trust in the various resources, respectively, and

---

FIGURE 1:   A NORDIC VIEW OF THE MARKETING FUNCTION – A SUMMARY

▷ The marketing models of the standard literature on marketing management of today are not always geared to the customer relationships of firms because they are based on North American marketing situations and empirical data from consumer packaged goods and durables.

▷ In today's competition, marketing is more a management issue than a specialist function only.

▷ The marketing function is spread all over the firm, far outside the realms of the marketing department. Because of this, there are a large number of 'part-time marketers' whose main duties are related to production, deliveries, invoicing, customer training, technical service, claims handling and telephone reception, and many other tasks and functions. In spite of these main duties, they have marketing responsibilities as well.

▷ Marketing is not only to plan and implement a given set of means of competition in a marketing mix, but to establish, develop and commercialise customer relations, so that individual and organisational objectives are met. The customer relation concept is the core of marketing thought.

▷ Promises of various kinds are mutually exchanged and kept in the relation between the buyer and seller, so that the customer relation may be established, strengthened and developed and commercialised.

---

thus in the firm itself is maintained and strengthened. The exchange of promises indicated in the definition may be of any kind, and concern any kind of thing or activity. The same goes for the various resources the representatives of the customer (a household or another organisation) meet in the relation. They cannot be predetermined and explicitly categorised.

Long-term customer relations mean that the objective of marketing is mainly to go for enduring relationships with the customers. Of course, sometimes and for some firms, perhaps even quite frequently, short-term sales may be profitable. However, generally speaking the long-term time span is vital to profitable marketing. Thus, commercialising the customer relations means that the cost–benefit ratio of transactions of goods, services or systems of goods and services is positive.

This definition does not say that the traditional elements of the marketing mix, such as advertising, personal selling, pricing and conceptualising the product, are less important than before. However, it demonstrates that so much else may be of importance to marketing, i.e. to establishing and developing long-term customer relations, than the means of competition of the traditional

marketing mix. In services marketing, the concept of interactive marketing has been introduced to demonstrate the importance of the marketing aspects of the everyday job of the 'part-time marketers'.[28,17] This concept has been found to be valid in industrial marketing as well.[21]

In many situations, perhaps most, the interactive marketing impact on the customer can be considered the most vital part of the total marketing function. Often, the competitive edge can be created by outstanding interactive marketing.

SUMMARY

The marketing definition put forward in this article is a truly market-oriented definition of marketing. It is based on conceptual, as well as empirical, research within the areas of industrial marketing, services marketing and the promise concept. Much of the empirical work has been done in Northern Europe, although the approach is spreading outside this part of the world. More research, especially concerning the application of this approach to the marketing function, from various types of product and customer as well as from different geographical areas, is now needed.

NOTES

1. P. Kotler (1984), *Marketing Management*, Prentice-Hall, Englewood Cliffs, NJ.

2. E. Gummesson (1987), *Marketing – Long Term Interactive Relationship*, research report, Stockholm University.

3. E.J. McCarthy (1964), *Basic Marketing, A Managerial Approach*, Homewood, Ill.

4. P. Kotler (1986), 'Megamarketing', *Harvard Business Review*, March–April.

5. B.H. Booms and M.J. Bitner (1982), 'Marketing Strategies and Organization Structures for Service Firms' in J.H. Donnelly and W.R. George (eds.), *Marketing of Services*, American Marketing Association, Chicago.

6. R.J. de Ferrer (1986), 'A Case of European Management', *International Management Development Review*, vol. 2.

7. 'AMA Board Approves New Marketing Definition', *Marketing News*, no. 5, 1 March, 1985.

8. E. Gummesson (1976), *Marknadsfunktionen i före-taget* (The Marketing Function in the Firm), Norstedts, Stockholm.

9. H. Håkansson and I. Snehota (1976), *Marknadsplanering = ett sätt att skapa nva problem?* (Marketing Planning – A Way of Creating New Problems?), Studentlitteratur, Lund.

10. K.-O. Hammarkvist et al. (1982), *Marknadsföring för konkurrenskfraft* (Marketing for Competitive Power), Stockholm.

11. H. Håkansson (1982), *International Marketing and Purchasing of Industrial Goods*, Wiley, NY.

12. H. Håkansson and J. Johansson (1982), *Analys av industriella affärsförbindelser* (Analysis of Industrial Business Relations), Marketing Technique Centre, Liber, Stockholm.

13. P.W. Turnbull and J.-P. Valla (eds.) (1986), *Strategies for International Marketing*, Croomhelm, London.

14. E. Gummesson (1987), 'The New Marketing – Developing Long-term Interactive Relationships', *Long Range Planning*, no. 4.

15. C. Grönroos (1979), *Marknadsföring av tjänster* (Marketing of Services), Marketing Technique Centre/Akademilitteratur/Swedish School of Economics, Stockholm.

16. C. Grönroos (1983), *Marknadsföring i tjänsteföretag* (Marketing in Service Firms), Liber, Stockholm.

17. C. Grönroos (1983), *Strategic Management and Marketing in the Service Sector*, Chartewell-Bratt, Bromley, and Studentlitteratur, Lund.

18. Lehtinen, J. (1982), *Asiakasohautuva palveluyritys* (Customer-oriented Service Firms), Weilin & Göös, Espoo, Finland.

19. J. Lehtinen (1982), *Plavelujen laatupainotteinen markkinointi* (Quality-oriented Marketing of Services), Weilin + Göös, Espoo, Finland.

20. C. Grönroos and E. Gummesson (1985), *Service Marketing: Nordic School Perspectives*, Stockholm University.

21. C. Grönroos and E. Gummesson (1985), 'Service Orientation in Industrial Marketing' in M. Venkatesan (ed.), *Creativity in Services Marketing: What's New, What Works, What's Developing*, American Marketing Association, Chicago.

22. E. Gummesson and C. Grönroos (1987), 'Service Quality – Lessons from the Product Sector', research report, American Marketing Association's Sixth Conference on Services Marketing, San Diego, Cal., September.

23. E. Gummesson (1987), *Quality – The Ericsson Approach*, Ericsson, Stockholm.

24. L.L. Berry (1983), 'Relationship Marketing' in L.L. Berry et al. (eds.), *Emerging Perspectives on Services Marketing*, American Marketing Association, Chicago.

25. B.B. Jackson (1985), 'Build Customer Relationships that Last', *Harvard Business Review*, November–December.

26. H. Calonius (1981), 'Behövs begreppet löfte' (Do we Need the Promise Concept?), *Marknadsvetande*, no. 1.

27. H. Calonius (1986), 'A Market Behaviour Framework' in K. Möllr and M. Paltschik (eds.), *Contemporary Research in Marketing*, proceedings from the 15th Annual Conference of the European Marketing Academy, Helsinki.

28. C. Grönroos (1982), 'An Applied Service Marketing Theory', *European Journal of Marketing*, vol. 16, no. 7.

SERVICES MARKETING
TEXT AND READINGS